International Investment Law and Globalization

In a context of neoliberal globalization, have the processes of elaboration and implementation of foreign investors' responsibilities by intergovernmental organizations reached the realm of legality? Using an analytical framework and a methodology that combine international law with international relations, this book provides a twofold answer to this question. First, it demonstrates that the normative integration of foreign investors' responsibilities in international investment law is fragmented and consistent with the interests of the most powerful actors. Second, while using the interactional theory of international law to assess the normative character of several international instruments elaborated and implemented by intergovernmental organizations, it highlights the sense of obligation that each instrument generates. The analysis demonstrates that such a codification process is marked by relations of power and has resulted in several social norms, with relatively few legal norms.

Jean-Michel Marcoux holds a PhD in Law (University of Victoria), an MA in International Studies (Institut québécois des hautes études internationales) and a BA in Public Affairs and International Relations (Université Laval). Interested in international economic law and international relations theory, he has published a dozen articles and chapters in peer-reviewed journals and collections of essays. He currently holds a position as a Postdoctoral Fellow at McGill University, Faculty of Law.

Routledge Research in International Law

For a full list of titles in this series, visit https://www.routledge.com/Routledge-Research-in-International-Law/book-series/INTNLLAW

Available:

International Criminal Law and Sexual Violence against Women
The Interpretation of Gender in the Contemporary International Criminal Trial
Daniela Nadj

Unilateral Acts
A History of a Legal Doctrine
Betina Appel Kuzmarov

Regional Developmentalism Through Law
The Use of Law to Support the Effective Establishment of an African Economic Community
Jonathan Bashi Rudahindwa

China's One Belt One Road Initiative and Private International Law
Poomintr Sooksripaisarnkit and Sai Ramani Garimella

Transnational Terrorist Groups and International Criminal Law
Anna Marie Brennan

The EU Social Market Economy and the Law
Theoretical Perspectives and Practical Challenges for the EU
Delia Ferri and Fulvio Cortese

Confronting Cyberespionage Under International Law
Oğuz Kaan Pehlivan

Russian Discourses on International Law
Sociological and Philosophical Phenomenon
P. Sean Morris

International Investment Law and Globalization

Foreign Investment, Responsibilities and Intergovernmental Organizations

Jean-Michel Marcoux

Routledge
Taylor & Francis Group
LONDON AND NEW YORK

First published 2019
by Routledge
2 Park Square, Milton Park, Abingdon, Oxon OX14 4RN

and by Routledge
52 Vanderbilt Avenue, New York, NY 10017, USA

First issued in paperback 2020

Routledge is an imprint of the Taylor & Francis Group, an informa business

British Library Cataloguing-in-Publication Data
A catalogue record for this book is available from the British Library

Library of Congress Cataloging-in-Publication Data
Names: Marcoux, Jean-Michel, author.
Title: International investment law and globalization : foreign investment, responsibilities and intergovernmental organizations / Jean-Michel Marcoux.
Description: New York : Routledge, 2018. | Series: Routledge research in international law | Includes bibliographical references and index.
Identifiers: LCCN 2018019306 | ISBN 9781138596221 (hbk)
Subjects: LCSH: Investments, Foreign (International law). | Investments, Foreign—Law and legislation. | Globalization.
Classification: LCC K3830 .M375 2018 | DDC 346/.092—dc23
LC record available at https://lccn.loc.gov/2018019306

ISBN 13: 978-0-367-58684-3 (pbk)
ISBN 13: 978-1-138-59622-1 (hbk)

Typeset in Galliard
by Swales & Willis Ltd, Exeter, Devon, UK

International Investment Law and Globalization

Foreign Investment, Responsibilities and Intergovernmental Organizations

Jean-Michel Marcoux

Routledge
Taylor & Francis Group
LONDON AND NEW YORK

First published 2019
by Routledge
2 Park Square, Milton Park, Abingdon, Oxon OX14 4RN

and by Routledge
52 Vanderbilt Avenue, New York, NY 10017, USA

First issued in paperback 2020

Routledge is an imprint of the Taylor & Francis Group, an informa business

British Library Cataloguing-in-Publication Data
A catalogue record for this book is available from the British Library

Library of Congress Cataloging-in-Publication Data
Names: Marcoux, Jean-Michel, author.
Title: International investment law and globalization : foreign investment, responsibilities and intergovernmental organizations / Jean-Michel Marcoux.
Description: New York : Routledge, 2018. | Series: Routledge research in international law | Includes bibliographical references and index.
Identifiers: LCCN 2018019306 | ISBN 9781138596221 (hbk)
Subjects: LCSH: Investments, Foreign (International law). | Investments, Foreign—Law and legislation. | Globalization.
Classification: LCC K3830 .M375 2018 | DDC 346/.092—dc23
LC record available at https://lccn.loc.gov/2018019306

ISBN 13: 978-0-367-58684-3 (pbk)
ISBN 13: 978-1-138-59622-1 (hbk)

Typeset in Galliard
by Swales & Willis Ltd, Exeter, Devon, UK

À mon Épouse
À mes parents

Contents

Acknowledgments

This book is the result of many discussions with inspiring people and several hours of research, which brought me to a point that I could never have imagined when I began my doctoral studies in September 2013. Research and writing of the dissertation that preceded this book occurred in Geneva, Montreal, New York, Paris, Quebec City, Victoria and Waterloo. I was also fortunate to present my work in various conferences and workshops that were held in Liverpool, Ottawa, Quebec City, Toronto and Waterloo. Now that the journey has come to an end, there are several people and institutions that I would like to thank for their contribution along the way.

This book would not have been possible without the expertise and engagement of the members of my supervisory committee. I wish to sincerely thank Professor Andrew Newcombe (University of Victoria), who provided comments of the utmost relevance on previous versions of the following chapters and supported my professional development in many ways. Having such a renowned expert in international investment law as the main supervisor of my doctoral research has generated invaluable opportunities in terms of academic publications and conferences. Moreover, I am indebted to Professor Theodore L. McDorman (University of Victoria) and Professor Michael C. Webb (University of Victoria) for their engagement and their thoughtful comments at various steps of the research. I would also like to emphasize the involvement of Professor A. Claire Cutler (University of Victoria) as the co-supervisor of my doctoral research from September 2013 to September 2016. Her work on private authority and her unique perspective on international investment law have extensively inspired this book. Professor Markus W. Gehring (University of Cambridge) acted as the external examiner of my dissertation and also provided highly relevant comments that were considered when preparing this book.

In addition to the members of my supervisory committee, I have met incredibly inspiring individuals who have contributed to this work in many ways. The foundations of the present analysis received substantive comments from Professor Michael M'Gonigle (University of Victoria) and Professor Hester A. Lessard (University of Victoria). I was also introduced to the interactional theory of international law by Professor Jeremy Webber (University of Victoria) and Professor Hoi Kong (McGill University). Aspects related to international investment law and foreign investors' responsibilities have been the subject of interesting conversations with experts whom I have met and who have agreed to discuss my project, such as Professor Charles-Emmanuel Côté (Université Laval), Professor Zachary Douglas QC (Graduate Institute of International and Development Studies) and Professor Patrick Dumberry (University of Ottawa). Friends and incredibly talented students from the graduate program in Law and Society at the University of Victoria have also been a significant source of inspiration over the past years.

I believe that a key contribution of this book relies on the inclusion of the perspective from individuals working for intergovernmental organizations involved in the codification of foreign investors' responsibilities. In this regard, I am indebted to the twenty individuals who graciously agreed to participate in the research project and shared their views with respect to the subject at hand. Their knowledge and their willingness to generously engage with the questions that were asked during semi-structured interviews provide a unique character to this work that could not have been possible without them.

The University of Victoria's Faculty of Law constitutes a vibrant intellectual environment that supports interdisciplinary research and critical thinking. I hope that the present book faithfully reflects the richness of this institution in this regard. Moreover, the Faculty of Law has generously provided financial support to conduct the aforementioned semi-structured interviews and to participate in academic conferences. This support is gratefully acknowledged.

The doctoral research that led to this book has also benefited from the financial support of the Fonds de recherche du Québec – Société et culture (from September 2013 to April 2014), the Joseph-Armand Bombardier Canada Graduate Scholarships Program of the Social Sciences and Humanities Research Council (from May 2014 to April 2017) and the International Law Research Program of the Centre for International Governance Innovation (from September 2015 to August 2016). I have completed the manuscript of this book while holding a position as a Postdoctoral Fellow at McGill University's Faculty of Law. This postdoctoral fellowship has been funded through the Fonds de recherche du Québec – Société et culture (from September 2017 to April 2018) and the Social Sciences and Humanities Research Council (since May 2018). Taken as a whole, these sources of funding have been instrumental in allowing me to complete my dissertation and to prepare this book.

Finally, I would like to express my greatest thanks to my family and my friends, whose support has been invaluable from the very beginning of this project. Most importantly, my deepest debt is to my wife. Her countless encouragements despite the distance between us have been of the utmost necessity to complete this journey.

Abbreviations

BIAC	Business and Industry Advisory Committee
BITs	Bilateral investment treaties
CAO	Compliance Advisor Ombudsman
CETA	*Comprehensive Economic and Trade Agreement*
COMESA	Common Market for Eastern and Southern Africa
EFTA	European Free Trade Association
EPA	Economic partnership agreement
EU	European Union
FCPA	*Foreign Corrupt Practice Act*
FDI	Foreign direct investment
FTAs	Free trade agreements
IBRD	International Bank for Reconstruction and Development
IDA	International Development Association
IFC	International Finance Corporation
IIAs	International investment agreements
ILO	International Labour Organization
MIGA	Multilateral Investment Guarantee Agency
NCPs	National Contact Points
NGOs	Nongovernmental organizations
OECD	Organisation for Economic Co-operation and Development
OHCHR	Office of the High Commissioner for Human Rights
OIC	Organisation of the Islamic Conference
PRAI	*Principles for Responsible Investment in Agriculture and Food Systems*
SADC	Southern African Development Community
TUAC	Trade Union Advisory Committee
UN	United Nations
UNCAC	*United Nations Convention Against Corruption*
UNCATOC	*United Nations Convention Against Transnational Organized Crime*
UNCTAD	United Nations Conference on Trade and Development
UNHCHR	United Nations High Commissioner on Human Rights

Introduction

In his seminal book *The Great Transformation: The Political and Economic Origins of Our Time*, Karl Polanyi aptly described how groups negatively impacted by self-regulating markets seek reform.[1] Relying on lessons drawn from the history of the nineteenth century, Polanyi argued that dynamics of modern societies are characterized by a double movement according to which efforts to establish a self-regulating market relying on *laissez-faire* and free trade conflict with a spontaneous movement of self-protection that emerges through various instruments of intervention. With growing international economic relations, the accuracy of the analysis offered by this author more than seventy years ago is striking. The need to incorporate social concerns often appears as a constant that must be addressed in parallel to any efforts to facilitate international economic relations.

International investment law evidences an attempt at completing such a double movement. The very inception of international investment agreements (IIAs) has been driven by a will to change relationships between states and foreign investors, with a view to increasing legal security for the latter and encouraging the flow of private capital to developing countries.[2] Alongside these efforts to provide legal security to investments in these states, there are long-standing concerns with respect to the negative impact that foreign investors can produce in local communities and the environment. Several decades after the preparation of a report on the impact of multinational corporations in world development by the Department of Economic and Social Affairs of the United Nations (UN),[3] this intergovernmental organization currently witnesses an attempt at elaborating a formal international agreement on transnational corporations and human rights.[4] The United Nations Conference on Trade and Development has also

1 Karl Polanyi, *The Great Transformation: The Political and Economic Origins of Our Time*, 2nd ed (Boston, MA: Beacon Press, 2001 [1944]) at 136–140.

2 See Hartley W Shawcross, "The Problems of Foreign Investment in International Law" (1961) 102 Rec des Cours 335 at 342–343. For the inception of IIAs, see e.g. Jeswald W Salacuse, "The Treatification of International Investment Law" (2007) 13 Law & Bus Rev Am 155 at 156–158.

3 Department of Economic and Social Affairs, *Multinational Corporations in World Development* (New York: United Nations, 1973).

4 See *Elaboration of an International Legally Binding Instrument on Transnational Corporations and other Business Enterprises with Respect to Human Rights*, HRC Res 26/9, 2014, UN Doc A/HRC/RES/26/9.

recently suggested the inclusion of provisions in IIAs to ensure responsible business conduct.[5] Intergovernmental organizations, multi-stakeholders initiatives and business enterprises have all adopted multiple instruments to influence the conduct of private firms when the latter are operating abroad.

While such initiatives demonstrate efforts to counterbalance the protections international investment law grants to foreign investors, it becomes of the utmost relevance to scrutinize the effect of this evolving codification of foreign investors' responsibilities. More precisely, considering the emergence of a double movement in international investment law, it is now opportune to take a closer look at this process to assess its normative character and to question whether these norm making processes have resulted in foreign investors having international legal obligations. Prior to delving into the bulk of the analysis, this introductory chapter describes the scope of the present book (1), provides some clarifications regarding corporate social responsibility initiatives (2), addresses the specific contribution that the book brings (3) and provides a brief overview of the upcoming chapters (4).

1. Framing the Analysis

With a view to analyzing the normative character of international initiatives that are emerging in parallel to international investment law to address the general lack of accountability of foreign investors, the question that animates this book is posited as follows: In a context of neoliberal globalization, have the processes of elaboration and implementation of foreign investors' responsibilities by intergovernmental organizations reached the realm of legality? Such a question encompasses several aspects that must be unpacked to properly delimit its scope.

Any analysis of the codification of foreign investors' responsibilities that does not acknowledge the broader context in which this process occurs risks obfuscating crucial variables. It is by bearing this aspect in mind that the question underlying this book explicitly refers to the overarching context of *globalization* that can affect the various initiatives elaborated and implemented by intergovernmental organizations. In fact, anchoring the analysis in this context provides a basis for considering relations of power between state and non-state actors that are often avoided in traditional legal studies. Following Held and his collaborators, globalization can be defined as "a process (or set of processes) which embodies a transformation in the spatial organization of social relations and transactions . . . generating transcontinental and interregional flows and networks of activity, interaction, and the exercise of power."[6] Applied to international investment law and the codification of foreign investors' responsibilities,

5 UNCTAD, *World Investment Report 2015: Reforming International Investment Governance* (New York and Geneva: United Nations, 2015) at 128.

6 David Held et al, *Global Transformations: Politics, Economics and Culture* (Cambridge: Polity Press, 1999) at 16.

this definition suggests that the design and the implementation of international norms are deeply integrated into processes pertaining to the transformation of social relations and the exercise of power.

More precisely, without dismissing the role of state actors, participation of non-state actors regarding the elaboration and the implementation of norms in an era of globalization must be acknowledged. With respect to international investment law, several authors identify capital-exporting states, capital-importing states, intergovernmental organizations, foreign investors and nongovernmental organizations (NGOs) as playing a crucial role.[7] International investment law-making occurring in a context of globalization is thus characterized by social interactions and relations of power between state and non-state actors that must be openly integrated into the analysis of the evolving codification process at hand.

Another aspect of the analysis that is highlighted by explicitly referring to the context of *neoliberal* globalization relates to the uneasy relationship between neoliberalism and the codification process at hand. While an exploration of neoliberalism's core principles is beyond the ambit of this book, it is worth emphasizing that its advocates portray globalized free markets and minimal state intervention as indispensable tools for the realization of a better functioning economy, in addition to the protection of private property that characterizes classical liberalism.[8] It is plain that the adoption of IIAs that grant substantive protections and procedural rights to foreign investors fits such policies, forming an integral part of the broader neoliberal trend in which the codification of foreign investors' responsibilities is evolving.[9] By contrast, international initiatives elaborated and implemented by intergovernmental organizations to hold private investors accountable for harm caused abroad do not sit well with policies that reflect the neoliberal ideal of self-regulation and can even be considered as a departure from them. Hence the relevance of assessing the normative integration of foreign investors' responsibilities in international investment law.

Despite the existence of multi-stakeholders and private initiatives with respect to corporate social responsibility, the research question is also deliberately limited

7 See e.g. Peter T Muchlinski, *Multinational Enterprises and the Law*, 2nd ed (Oxford: Oxford University Press, 2007) at 82–85 [Muchlinski, *Multinational Enterprises*]; Muthucumaraswamy Sornarajah, *The International Law on Foreign Investment*, 3rd ed (Cambridge: Cambridge University Press, 2010) at 6.

8 See Simon Lee & Stephen McBride, "Introduction: Neo-Liberalism, State Power and Global Governance in the Twenty-First Century" in Simon Lee & Stephen McBride, eds, *Neo-Liberalism, State Power and Global Governance* (Dordrecht: Springer, 2007) 1 at 5–6; Rachel S Turner, *Neo-liberal Ideology: History, Concepts and Policies* (Edinburgh: Edinburgh University Press, 2008) at 115 and 132–136; Manfred B Steger & Ravi K Roy, *Neoliberalism: A Very Short Introduction* (Oxford: Oxford University Press, 2010) at 3, 5 and 11.

9 See Peter Muchlinski, "The Changing Face of Transnational Business Governance: Private Corporate Law Liability and Accountability of Transnational Groups in a Post-Financial Crisis World" (2011) 18 Ind J Global Legal Stud 665 at 666–667; Muthucumaraswamy Sornarajah, *Resistance and Change in the International Law on Foreign Investment* (Cambridge: Cambridge University Press, 2015) at 13.

to the consideration of normative developments occurring under the auspices of ***intergovernmental organizations.*** Far from pretending to account for all possible avenues for imposing responsibilities on private investors operating abroad, the focus of this book is to critically assess what intergovernmental organizations have accomplished so far. Since the aforementioned report from the UN Department of Economic and Social Affairs, international instruments codifying foreign investors' responsibilities have been elaborated and implemented under the auspices of organizations such as the Organisation for Economic Co-operation and Development (OECD), the International Labour Organization (ILO), the UN and the World Bank Group.

Scholars in international law and international relations theory shed light on the general role of intergovernmental organizations with respect to the elaboration and the implementation of international norms. Some international law scholars stress that these organizations are authorized by states to accomplish a specific set of actions, ranging from the elaboration of international treaties to the adoption of hortatory initiatives.[10] The scope of the authority granted by member states to intergovernmental organizations nevertheless evolves through time and according to changing circumstances. Moreover, drawing on international relations theory, several authors emphasize the ability of intergovernmental organizations to socialize states according to the norms prevailing in these organizations.[11] In the specific case of the regulation of foreign investors, Muchlinski emphasizes that intergovernmental organizations have received an "agency" by their member states to address the question of responsibilities[12] and that the quasi-legislative power of these organizations exists "over and outside" the states.[13] While state representatives are undoubtedly involved in the elaboration of international initiatives that address the lack of accountability of foreign investors, experts and civil society organizations also play a substantial role in this task.

In addition to focusing on initiatives adopted by intergovernmental organizations, four other criteria have been considered to select international instruments. First, this analysis is limited to instruments ***adopted*** by intergovernmental

10 See José E Alvarez, *International Organizations as Law-Makers* (Oxford: Oxford University Press, 2005) at 8 and 15; Ian Johnstone, "Law-Making in International Organizations: Perspectives from IL/IR Theory" in Jeffrey L Dunoff & Mark A Pollack, eds, *Interdisciplinary Perspectives on International Law and International Relations: The State of the Art* (Cambridge: Cambridge University Press, 2013) 266 at 269–276; Jan Klabbers, *An Introduction to International Organizations Law*, 3rd ed (Cambridge: Cambridge University Press, 2015) at 154–188.

11 See e.g. Martha Finnemore, *National Interests in International Society* (Ithaca, NY: Cornell University Press, 1996) [Finnemore, *National Interests*]; Michael N Barnett & Martha Finnemore, "The Politics, Power, and Pathologies of International Organizations" (1999) 53 Int'l Organization 699 at 700.

12 Peter Muchlinski, "Human Rights, Social Responsibility and the Regulation of International Business: The Development of International Standards by Intergovernmental Organisations" (2003) 3 Non-St Actors & Int'l L 123 at 145.

13 Muchlinski, *Multinational Enterprises*, *supra* note 7 at 84.

organizations. Even if they might be considered to explain the normative development that led to other initiatives, any instruments whose negotiations have not been finalized (*e.g.* the UN *Code of Conduct on Transnational Corporations*)[14] are not included in the present analysis. Second, in order to limit the scope of instruments considered, this examination focuses on *multilateral* intergovernmental organizations in contrast to regional organizations. Third, the instruments must provide specific *standards of conduct* that are expected from foreign investors. A declaration of the necessity of addressing the lack of accountability of private firms,[15] a framework generally seeking to improve the consideration of sustainable development in international investment policy[16] or a guide to assess human rights impact[17] thus do not provide sufficiently precise standards of conduct to be included in the present analysis. Although these instruments can contribute to the emergence of an investment climate that is more responsive to issues of human rights and sustainable development, the absence of specific indications regarding the conduct of private actors implies that they do not directly contribute to the codification of foreign investors' responsibilities. Fourth, an *extraterritorial dimension* must also underlie the scope of the instruments. While there are other examples of international initiatives that require action by states against legal persons,[18] this book focuses on norms that are specifically applicable to investors when they are operating in a host state that differs from their state of origin. Amidst the initiatives that meet these criteria, a total of nine distinct instruments are considered for present purposes (see Table 1).

The OECD has been particularly active in elaborating international initiatives that concern foreign investors' responsibilities. After their first adoption in 1976, the *OECD Guidelines for Multinational Enterprises* (*OECD Guidelines*)[19] went through several revisions. While the most recent version of these guidelines was adopted in 2011,[20] considerable changes were made to this instrument in 2000.[21] An international agreement pertaining to the fight against corruption was also

14 *Code of Conduct on Transnational Corporations (Draft)*, 1990, UN Doc E/1990/94 [UN Draft Code of Conduct].

15 See e.g. EC, Commission, *A Renewed EU Strategy 2011–14 for Corporate Social Responsibility* (Brussels: EC, 2011).

16 UNCTAD, *Investment Policy Framework for Sustainable Development* (New York and Geneva: United Nations, 2015).

17 International Business Leaders Forum et al, *Guide to Human Rights Impact Assessment and Management* (2010), online: Global Compact www.unglobalcompact.org/docs/issues_doc/human_rights/GuidetoHRIAM.pdf (accessed on 26 March 2018).

18 For an analysis of these instruments, see Andrew Clapham, *Human Rights Obligations of Non-state Actors* (Oxford: Oxford University Press, 2006) at 247–252.

19 *Declaration on International Investment and Multinational Enterprises*, 21 June 1976, Doc No C(76)99/FINAL (1976), Annex 1.

20 *Declaration on International Investment and Multinational Enterprises*, 25 May 2011, Doc No C/MIN(2011)11/FINAL (2011), Annex 1.

21 *Declaration on International Investment and Multinational Enterprises*, 27 June 2000, Doc No C(2000)96/REV1 (2000), Annex 1.

Table 1 Instruments Analyzed in the Book

Intergovernmental organization	*Name of the instrument*	*First version*	*Latest version*
OECD	*Guidelines for Multinational Enterprises*	1976	2011
	Convention on Combating Bribery of Foreign Public Officials in International Business Transactions	1997	N/A
	Recommendation of the Council for Further Combating Bribery of Foreign Public Officials in International Business Transactions	2009	2010
ILO	*Tripartite Declaration of Principles concerning Multinational Enterprises and Social Policy*	1977	2017
UN	Global Compact	2000	2004
	Norms on the Responsibilities of Transnational Corporations and other Business Enterprises with Regard to Human Rights	2003	N/A
	United Nations Convention Against Corruption	2003	N/A
	Guiding Principles on Business and Human Rights	2011	N/A
World Bank Group	*International Finance Corporation's Performance Standards on Environmental and Social Sustainability*	2006	2012

adopted under the auspices of the OECD. While being addressed to states, the *Convention on Combating Bribery of Foreign Public Officials in International Business Transactions* (*OECD Anti-Bribery Convention*)[22] requires the establishment of the liability for legal persons involved in corrupt practices. More recently, these efforts to curb corruption led to the adoption of another instrument that also meets the criteria elaborated above, namely the *Recommendation of the Council for Further Combating Bribery of Foreign Public Officials in International Business Transactions* (*OECD 2009 Recommendation*).[23]

The ILO has also elaborated and implemented international instruments that meet the criteria mentioned above. Shortly after the adoption of the first version of the *OECD Guidelines*, the ILO adopted the *Tripartite Declaration of Principles concerning Multinational Enterprises and Social Policy* (*ILO Tripartite Declaration*)[24] in 1977. Substantial modifications were subsequently made to this

22 *Convention on Combating Bribery of Foreign Public Officials in International Business Transactions*, 17 December 1997, 37 ILM 1 (entered into force 15 February 1999).

23 *Recommendation of the Council for Further Combating Bribery of Foreign Public Officials in International Business Transactions*, 26 November 2009, Doc No C(2009)159/REV1/FINAL (amended on 18 February 2010, Doc No C(2010)19).

24 *Tripartite Declaration of Principles concerning Multinational Enterprises and Social Policy*, November 1977, 17 ILM 422.

declaration in 2000, in 2006 and in 2017.[25] While the small number of initiatives arising from this intergovernmental organization contrasts with what can be observed in other forums, it must be stressed that the ILO focuses primarily on the area of labour rights and thus covers only a limited range of foreign investors' responsibilities.

Other UN agencies have been involved in the codification process beside the ILO. Nine years after the failed attempt at adopting a code of conduct,[26] the UN Secretary-General announced the elaboration of the UN Global Compact.[27] The UN Sub-Commission on the Promotion and the Protection of Human Rights (Sub-Commission) also deployed several efforts to adopt the *Norms on the Responsibilities of Transnational Corporations and other Business Enterprises with Regard to Human Rights* (*UN Norms*)[28] in 2003. While the UN Human Rights Commission has later considered this instrument as having "no legal standing,"[29] its adoption by the Sub-Commission suggests that the *UN Norms* remain an integral part of the codification process occurring at the UN. Another initiative that meets the selection criteria can be found in the *United Nations Convention Against Corruption* (*UNCAC*),[30] which requires the establishment of the liability of legal persons for participation in corruption. Finally, as this instrument is currently drawing considerable attention from various international actors and experts, the *Guiding Principles on Business and Human Rights* (*UN Guiding Principles*)[31] developed by the Special Representative of the Secretary-General on the issue of human rights and transnational corporations and other business enterprises (Special Representative) are also included in this book.

Another intergovernmental organization that has adopted instruments to codify foreign investors' responsibilities is the World Bank Group. While other

25 *Tripartite Declaration of Principles concerning Multinational Enterprises and Social Policy*, November 2000, 41 ILM 186; *Tripartite Declaration of Principles concerning Multinational Enterprises and Social Policy*, March 2006, online: ILO www.ilo.org/empent/Publications/WCMS_211136/lang--en/index.htm (accessed 26 March 2018); *Tripartite Declaration of Principles concerning Multinational Enterprises and Social Policy*, March 2017, online: ILO www.ilo.org/empent/Publications/WCMS_094386/lang--en/index.htm (accessed 26 March 2018).

26 See *UN Draft Code of Conduct*, *supra* note 14.

27 United Nations Global Compact, online: United Nations Global Compact www.unglobalcompact.org/AboutTheGC/TheTenPrinciples/index.html (accessed 26 March 2018).

28 *Norms on the Responsibilities of Transnational Corporations and other Business Enterprises with Regard to Human Rights*, 2003, UN Doc E/CN.4/Sub.2/2003/12/Rev.2.

29 *Responsibilities of Transnational Corporations and related Business Enterprises with regard to Human Rights*, ESC Dec 2004/116, UNESCOR, 2004, Supp No 3, UN Doc E/CN.4/2004/127, 332 at 333.

30 *United Nations Convention Against Corruption*, 31 October 2003, 2349 UNTS 41 (entered into force 14 December 2005).

31 Special Representative of the Secretary-General on the issue of human rights and transnational corporations and other business enterprises, *Guiding Principles on Business and Human Rights: Implementing the United Nations 'Protect, Respect and Remedy' Framework*, 2011, UN Doc A/HRC/17/31.

agencies of this intergovernmental organization have adopted similar initiatives, the International Finance Corporation (IFC) established standards that must be met by foreign investors when they are responsible for the implementation and the operation of a project financed by this agency. It is in this regard that the *International Finance Corporation's Performance Standards on Social & Environmental Sustainability* (*IFC Performance Standards*)[32] were adopted in 2006 and a revised version entered into application in 2012.[33]

When considering this pool of instruments, it clearly appears that the bulk of the international initiatives that have been adopted by intergovernmental organizations to codify foreign investors' responsibilities are informal to the extent that they fall beyond the traditional sources of international law. More precisely, these instruments do not fit within the sources that are enumerated in Article 38(1) of the *Statute of the International Court of Justice* (*i.e.* treaties, international customary law and general principles of international law).[34] Regardless of their status under international law, it is here submitted that a detailed examination of these instruments is essential to understand the direction toward which the codification process that is occurring within intergovernmental organizations is pointing.

Considering the informal character of several instruments analyzed in this book, identifying a generic concept that applies to the entire pool of initiatives is necessary. It is in this regard that the concept of *norm* – which is defined as "a standard of appropriate behavior for actors with a given identity"[35] – stems at the core of this analysis. Although some international relations authors contend that the distinction between social norms and legal norms remains unclear,[36] the distinctive character of legal norms as "binding" is extensively discussed by international legal scholars. For example, Malanczuk maintains that "what distinguishes the rules and principles of international law from 'mere morality' is that they are accepted in practice as legally binding by states in their intercourse because they are useful to reduce complexity and uncertainty in international relations."[37] Similarly, d'Aspremont maintains that "bindingness" constitutes the

32 *International Finance Corporation's Performance Standards on Social & Environmental Sustainability*, 30 April 2006, online: IFCwww.ifc.org/wps/wcm/connect/Topics_Ext_Content/IFC_External_Corporate_Site/IFC+Sustainability/Our+Approach/Risk+Management/Performance+Standards/ (accessed 26 March 2018).

33 *International Finance Corporation's Performance Standards on Environmental and Social Sustainability*, 1 January 2012, online: IFC www.ifc.org/wps/wcm/connect/Topics_Ext_Content/IFC_External_Corporate_Site/IFC+Sustainability/Our+Approach/Risk+Management/Performance+Standards/ (accessed 26 March 2018).

34 See *Statute of the International Court of Justice*, 26 June 1945, 59 US Stat 1031 (entered into force 24 October 1945), art 38(1).

35 Martha Finnemore & Kathryn Sikkink, "International Norm Dynamics and Political Change" (1998) 52 Int'l Organization 887 at 891.

36 See e.g. Martha Finnemore, "Are Legal Norms Distinctive?" (2000) 32 NYU J Int'l L & Pol 699 at 703.

37 Peter Malanczuk, *Akehurst's Modern Introduction to International Law*, 7th rev ed (London: Routledge, 1997) at 6–7.

very DNA of the discipline of international law.[38] Despite important variations within the discipline of international law regarding the source of this binding character, legal norms are characterized by an uneasiness to circumvent compliance with the standards of behavior that they articulate.

This important distinction between social norms and legal norms becomes essential when assessing the normative character of international instruments codifying foreign investors' responsibilities. Analyzing whether such instruments belong to the realm of legality and can more effectively order the conduct of international actors can be accomplished by scrutinizing the sense of obligation emanating from the elaboration and the implementation of these initiatives, regardless of their formal or informal character under international law. To put it differently, the concept of legality that lies at the heart of the question underlying this book invites a nuanced analysis of the sense of obligation that results from international instruments rather than a strict focus on the form in which these norms are embedded.

Using such a nuanced understanding of the sense of obligation emanating from international norms to determine their legal character suggests that informal international instruments can be considered as legal norms. By the same token, relying on a sense of obligation that does not strictly depend upon the form of a norm under international law ultimately implies that formal international agreements do not automatically belong to the realm of legality. Although such a statement can appear as relatively contentious, the key element to avoid confusion is that the concept of legal norm used for present purposes is not conflated to the law formally applied by an international tribunal.[39] For present purposes, even if it cannot expressly be applied by an international tribunal, an international norm can be considered as an international legal norm if it creates a sense of obligation amidst international actors.

In sum, by explicitly referring to the context of neoliberal globalization, the book aims to stress that the codification of foreign investors' responsibilities is anchored in a social process marked by relations of power and does not sit well with policies that are characterized by the liberalization of international investment. Furthermore, instead of solely accounting for the relationship between international instruments elaborated under the auspices of intergovernmental organizations and the formal sources of international law, the present analysis of their normative character illuminates a more complete sense of obligation that emanates from these initiatives. By considering the active role of state and non-state actors in developing norms that transcend formal sources of international law in parallel to the international investment regime, such an analysis points toward concepts and tools reaching beyond the sole discipline of international law.

38 Jean d'Aspremont, *Bindingness*, ACIL Research Paper 19 (Amsterdam, 2015).

39 See e.g. Thomas Schultz, *Transnational Legality: Stateless Law and International Arbitration* (Oxford: Oxford University Press, 2014) at 11.

2. A Word on Corporate Social Responsibility

As far as the codification of foreign investors' responsibilities is concerned, this book focuses on initiatives elaborated and implemented under the auspices of intergovernmental organizations. This focus inevitably leaves aside corporate social responsibility initiatives that are deemed to influence business cultures and decision-making procedures in a way that ultimately contributes to improve the impact that private actors can have in local communities and the environment. In fact, one can identify several initiatives led by a broad set of stakeholders with a view to addressing the lacunas that result from the absence of a clear regulatory framework at the international level and that operate in addition to intergovernmental organizations' initiatives.[40] Beyond several corporate codes of conduct, these initiatives include the Voluntary Principles on Security and Human Rights[41] and the Extractive Industry Transparency Initiative,[42] among others.

Interestingly, the concept of corporate social responsibility appears as being distinct from the realm of legality. For example, there are significant differences at the normative level between the idea of corporate social responsibility and the field of business and human rights.[43] Corporate social responsibility is often conceived as fundamentally voluntary and operating beyond the requirements of the law. According to Wettstein, "[t]he law does not actively intervene and enforce [corporate social responsibility], but rather provides a passive frame that shapes the context for the respective initiatives."[44]

This voluntarism does not sit well with an analysis that seeks to assess whether international instruments have reached the realm of legality. In addition to a pragmatic choice to reduce the number of instruments considered for present purposes, the inherent voluntary character of corporate social responsibility initiatives thus partly justifies their exclusion from the scope of the analysis. However, some references to corporate social responsibility are included when addressing the normative integration of foreign investors' responsibilities in international investment law. Several corporate social responsibility initiatives can also be potentially relevant with respect to the practice of intergovernmental organizations' norms that are analyzed in this book. In fact, when assessing the practice surrounding the initiatives emanating from intergovernmental organizations, some references to multi-stakeholder initiatives are expressly made in the upcoming chapters.

40 See e.g. Justine Nolan, "Mapping the Movement: The Business and Human Rights Regulatory Framework" in Dorothée Baumann-Pauly & Justine Nolan, eds, *Business and Human Rights: From Principles to Practice* (London: Routledge, 2016) 32 at 44–46.

41 Voluntary Principles on Security and Human Rights, online: Voluntary Principles www.voluntary-principles.org (accessed 26 March 2018).

42 Extractive Industry Transparency Initiative, online: EITI https://eiti.org (accessed 26 March 2018).

43 For this distinction, see Florian Wettstein, "From Side Show to Main Act: Can Business and Human Rights save Corporate Responsibility?" in Dorothée Baumann-Pauly & Justine Nolan, eds, *Business and Human Rights: From Principles to Practice* (London: Routledge, 2016) 78 at 79–82.

44 *Ibid* at 81.

3. An Interdisciplinary Contribution

This book addresses a topic that has already been extensively discussed in the literature and approached from several angles. As far as international investment law is concerned, some authors address innovations in IIAs pertaining to foreign investors' responsibilities,[45] account for instances in which investor misconduct has been taken into consideration by international investment arbitration tribunals[46] or generally examine functionally differentiated normative orders that evolve in parallel to international investment law.[47] Other authors focus on relations of power underlying the international investment lawmaking process, suggesting that the general absence of binding norms pertaining to foreign investors' responsibilities in international investment law results from the ability of powerful actors to interfere with attempts at elaborating these responsibilities.[48]

With respect to the codification process that takes place within intergovernmental organizations, some authors provide extensive descriptions of international

45 See e.g. Jarrod Hepburn & Vuyelwa Kuuya, "Corporate Social Responsibility and Investment Treaties" in Marie-Claire Cordonier Segger, Markus W Gehring & Andrew Newcombe, eds, *Sustainable Development in World Investment Law* (Alphen aan den Rijn: Kluwer Law International, 2011) 589; Patrick Dumberry & Gabrielle Dumas-Aubin, "How to Impose Human Rights Obligations on Corporations under Investment Treaties? Pragmatic Guidelines for the Amendment of BITs" in Karl P. Sauvant, ed, *Yearbook on International Investment Law & Policy 2011–2012* (Oxford: Oxford University Press, 2013) 569; Karsten Nowrot, "How to Include Environmental Protection, Human Rights and Sustainability in International Investment Law?" (2014) 15 J World Invest & Trade 612.

46 See e.g. Clara Reiner & Christoph Schreuer, "Human Rights and International Investment Arbitration" in Pierre-Marie Dupuy, Francesco Francioni & Ernst-Ulrich Petersmann, eds, *Human Rights in International Investment Law and Arbitration* (Oxford: Oxford University Press, 2009) 82; Peter Muchlinski, "'Caveat Investor'? The Relevance of the Conduct of the Investor under the Fair and Equitable Treatment Standard" (2006) 55:3 ICQL 527; Andrew Newcombe, "Investor Misconduct: Jurisdiction, Admissibility or Merits?" in Chester Brown & Kate Miles, eds, *Evolution in Investment Treaty Law and Arbitration* (Cambridge: Cambridge University Press, 2011) 187; Jason Webb Yackee, "Investment Treaties and Investor Corruption: An Emerging Defense for Host States" (2012) 52 Va J Int'l L 723.

47 See e.g. Peter Muchlinski, "Corporate Social Responsibility" in Peter Muchlinski, Frederico Ortino & Christoph Schreuer, eds, *The Oxford Handbook of International Investment Law* (Oxford: Oxford University Press, 2008) 637; Pierre-Marie Dupuy, "Unification Rather than Fragmentation of International Law? The Case of International Investment Law and Human Rights Law" in Pierre-Marie Dupuy, Francesco Francioni & Ernst-Ulrich Petersmann, eds, *Human Rights in International Investment Law and Arbitration* (Oxford: Oxford University Press, 2009) 45; Jorge E Viñuales, "Foreign Investment and the Environment in International Law: An Ambiguous Relationship" (2010) 80:1 BYIL 244.

48 See e.g. A Claire Cutler, "Constituting Capitalism: Corporations, Law, and Private Transnational Governance" (2009) 5 STAIR 99; Peter Muchlinski, "Multinational Enterprises as Actors in International Law: Creating 'Soft Law' Obligations and 'Hard Law' Rights" in Math Noortmann & Cedric Ryngaert, eds, *Non-State Actors Dynamics in International Law: From Law-Takers to Law-Makers* (Farnham: Ashgate Publishing, 2010) 9; David Schneiderman, *Resisting Economic Globalization: Critical Theory and International Investment Law* (New York: Palgrave Macmillan, 2013); Kate Miles, *The Origins of International Investment Law: Empire, Environment and the Safeguarding of Capital* (Cambridge: Cambridge University Press, 2013).

instruments, while suggesting that the lack of a formal character for the majority of initiatives elaborated and implemented by these organizations necessarily entails a "non-binding" nature.[49] Others emphasize the normative value of informal instruments, while sometimes assuming that the mere accumulation of informal instruments may lead to the elaboration of binding standards under international law.[50] Finally, scholars have addressed this topic through critical perspectives, emphasizing the inadequacy of existing instruments[51] or the extent to which powerful actors have prevented such developments under the auspices of intergovernmental organizations.[52]

The consideration of previous studies allows emphasizing that the analysis of the codification of foreign investors' responsibilities involves at least two factors that reach beyond the boundaries of a single discipline. In fact, this codification process encompasses ***normative developments***, both with respect to international investment law and efforts deployed within intergovernmental organizations. These developments must be considered, even if they emerge beyond the domain of states and are not included in formal international treaties. However, one must be careful not to adopt an overly optimist approach and suggest that the accumulation of these initiatives necessarily contributes to impose effective requirements on private actors operating abroad. Hence the importance of considering ***relations of power between international actors*** that participate in the international lawmaking process. The fact that state and non-state actors are involved calls

49 See e.g. Sarah Joseph, "Taming the Leviathans: Multinational Enterprises and Human Rights" (1999) 46:02 Nethl Int'l L Rev 171; Olivier De Schutter, "The Challenge of Imposing Human Rights Norms on Corporate Actors" in Olivier De Schutter, ed, *Transnational Corporations and Human Rights* (Portland, OR: Hart Publishing, 2006) 1; Clapham, *supra* note 18; Markos Karavias, *Corporate Obligations under International Law* (Oxford: Oxford University Press, 2013).

50 See e.g. Jennifer A Zerk, *Multinationals and Corporate Social Responsibility: Limitations and Opportunities in International Law* (Cambridge: Cambridge University Press, 2006); Larry Catá Backer, "Multinational Corporations, Transnational Law: The United Nations' Norms on the Responsibilities of Transnational Corporations as a Harbinger of Corporate Social Responsibility in International Law" (2006) 37 Colum Hum Rts L Rev 287; Elisa Morgera, "From Corporate Social Responsibility to Accountability Mechanisms" in Pierre-Marie Dupuy & Jorge E Viñuales, eds, *Harnessing Foreign Investment to Promote Environmental Protection: Incentives and Safeguards* (Cambridge: Cambridge University Press, 2013) 321.

51 See e.g. Robert McCorquodale, "Corporate Social Responsibility and International Human Rights Law" (2009) 87 J Bus Ethics 385; Surya Deva, *Regulating Corporate Human Rights Violations: Humanizing Business* (London: Routledge, 2012); David Bilchitz, "A Chasm Between 'Is' and 'Ought'? A Critique of the Normative Foundations of the SRGS's Framework and the Guiding Principles" in Surya Deva & David Bilchitz, eds, *Human Rights Obligations of Business: Beyond the Corporate Responsibility to Protect?* (Cambridge: Cambridge University Press, 2013) 107.

52 See e.g. Penelope Simons, "International Law's Invisible Hand and the Future of Corporate Accountability for Violations of Human Rights" (2012) 3:1 J Hum R and Env't 5; David Bilchitz & Surya Deva, "The Human Rights Obligations of Business: A Critical Framework for the Future" in Surya Deva & David Bilchitz, eds, *Human Rights Obligations of Business: Beyond the Corporate Responsibility to Protect?* (Cambridge: Cambridge University Press, 2013) 1; Penelope Simons & Audrey Macklin, *The Governance Gap: Extractive Industries, Human Rights, and the Home State Advantage* (New York: Routledge, 2014).

upon an analysis of the ability of powerful actors to orient this process according to their own interests. Given the necessity of addressing these two factors, this book adopts an interdisciplinary perspective that combines international law and international relations.

The articulation of these two disciplines has drawn several scholars' attention for almost thirty years.[53] Of course, one can perceive a fundamental difference between international law and international relations with respect to the objects of inquiry that these disciplines examine. While the former primarily focuses on the content of international norms and their implementation in specific circumstances, the latter mainly explains the behavior of international actors and decision-making processes surrounding these norms.[54] Despite this important distinction, a complete analysis of one of these two objects cannot be conducted in isolation of the other. Along these lines, the present book is premised on the assumption that an avowed consideration of normative developments and relations of power underlying the codification of foreign investors' responsibilities requires a genuine combination of analytical tools from international law and international relations.

With respect to the analytical framework underlying the analysis presented in the upcoming chapters, this book combines *legal pluralism* and *critical constructivism*. The reliance on a legal pluralist approach to analyze international law is grounded in the study of international norms emerging beyond states. It thus implies a significant departure from a conception that is limited to norms that are embedded in traditional sources of international law.[55] Given the active participation of state and non-state actors in the international lawmaking process, legal pluralism emphasizes the emergence of various bodies of norms that are tied to specific areas of regulation, without being fully coordinated one with another.[56] While providing a rationale to explain the weak normative compatibility between different normative orders that focuses

53 See e.g. Kenneth W Abbott, "Modern International Relations Theory: A Prospectus for International Lawyers" (1989) 14 Yale J Int'l L 335; Judith Goldstein et al, "Introduction: Legalization and World Politics" (2000) 54 Int'l Organization 385; Jeffrey L Dunoff & Mark A Pollack, "International Law and International Relations: Introducing an Interdisciplinary Dialogue" in Jeffrey L Dunoff & Mark A Pollack, eds, *Interdisciplinary Perspectives on International Law and International Relations: The State of the Art* (Cambridge: Cambridge University Press, 2013) 3.

54 See e.g. Friedrich V Kratochwil, *Rules, Norms, and Decisions: On the Conditions of Practical and Legal Reasoning in International Relations and Domestic Affairs* (Cambridge: Cambridge University Press, 1991) at 1; Oona Anne Hathaway & Harold Hongju Koh, *Foundations of International Law and Politics* (New York: Foundation Press, 2005) at 1.

55 See e.g. Jean-Philippe Robé, "Multinational Enterprises: The Constitution of a Pluralistic Legal Order" in Gunther Teubner, ed, *Global Law Without a State* (Aldershot: Dartmouth, 1997) 45 at 49 and 54–56; Paul Schiff Berman, "Global Legal Pluralism" (2007) 80 S Cal L Rev 1155 at 1169–1170; Brian Z Tamanaha, "Understanding Legal Pluralism: Past to Present, Local to Global" (2008) 30 Sydney L Rev 375 at 387–390; Michael A Helfand, "Introduction" in Michael A Helfand, ed, *Negotiating State and Non-State Law: The Challenge of Global and Local Legal Pluralism* (Cambridge: Cambridge University Press, 2015) 1 at 2.

56 See e.g. Andreas Fischer-Lescano & Gunther Teubner, "Regime-Collisions: The Vain Search for Legal Unity in the Fragmentation of Global Law" (2004) 25 Mich J Int'l L 999 at 1009.

on diverse rationalities within global society,[57] an international legal pluralist approach only weakly accounts for the profound roots of this phenomenon. In fact, legal pluralism generally avoids explaining which interests are ultimately served by this weak normative compatibility.

Normative transformations occurring in international economic law nevertheless result from contests of power between actors seeking to ensure that regulatory changes remain consistent with their own goals.[58] Recalling that relations of power and the behavior of international actors is the object of inquiry of international relations, a critical constructivist approach becomes particularly relevant. In its mainstream form, constructivism is a theory that focuses on the importance of ideas and norms in shaping international relations, as well as the mutual constitution between agents and social structures.[59] While such a conception tends to put forward a perspective of social constructions that is consensual and that obscures the extent to which actors' interests are not equally represented, critical constructivism grants a less autonomous role to ideas and norms in shaping international relations and emphasizes that constructions of reality "reflect, enact and reify relations of power."[60]

Brunnée and Toope have elaborated an interactional theory of international law that combines legal pluralism and (critical) constructivism.[61] According to the interactional theory, the singularity of legality lies on the sense of obligation that legal norms generate, regardless of their relationship with formal sources of international law. Legal norms thus emerge when international norms are embedded in shared understandings, meet a set of criteria of legality and are implemented according to a practice of legality. More specifically, by relying on concepts from the constructivist approach in international relations (*i.e.* norm entrepreneurs, epistemic communities and communities of practice), the interactional theory sheds light on the interactions through which international actors reach shared understandings with respect to the legal nature of an international norm and implement it according to a practice that reinforces its legal character. Despite the

57 See e.g. *ibid* at 1017.

58 See e.g. John Braithwaite & Peter Drahos, *Global Business Regulation* (Cambridge: Cambridge University Press, 2000) at 19; David Schneiderman, "Power and Production in Global Legal Pluralism: An International Political Economy Approach" in Amanda Perry-Kessaris, ed, *Socio-Legal Approaches to International Economic Law: Text, Context, Subtext* (New York: Routledge, 2013) 98 at 99.

59 See e.g. Finnemore, *National Interests*, *supra* note 11; Alexander Wendt, *Social Theory of International Politics* (Cambridge: Cambridge University Press, 1999); Emanuel Adler, "Constructivism in International Relations: Sources, Contributions and Debates" in Walter Carlsnaes, Thomas Risse & Beth A Simmons, eds, *Handbook of International Relations*, 2nd ed (London: Sage Publications, 2013) 112.

60 See Martha Finnemore & Kathryn Sikkink, "Taking Stock: The Constructivist Research Program in International Relations and Comparative Politics" (2001) 4:1 Ann Rev Pol Science 391 at 398. See also Adriana Sinclair, *International Relations Theory and International Law: A Critical Approach* (Cambridge: Cambridge University Press, 2010).

61 See Jutta Brunnée & Stephen J Toope, *Legitimacy and Legality in International Law: An Interactional Account* (Cambridge: Cambridge University Press, 2010) at 1–87.

reliance of the interactional theory on a more traditional version of the constructivist approach in international relations, there are no insurmountable obstacles that would prevent the amendment of this framework with a view to emphasizing how powerful actors seek to influence the outcome of this process.[62] The interactional theory also posits that adherence to eight criteria of legality – *i.e.* promulgation, generality, non-retroactivity, clarity, non-contradiction, not asking the impossible, constancy and congruence between rules and official action – ensures that international norms are perceived as legitimate and that they tend to generate a sense of obligation to act accordingly.

To be clear, two analytical approaches are used in the present book, namely legal pluralism (from international law) and critical constructivism (from international relations theory). It is here submitted that the combination of these approaches is relevant to analyze the codification of foreign investors' responsibilities in a context of neoliberal globalization. As far as the normative integration of these responsibilities in international investment law is concerned, legal pluralism suggests that the emergence of functionally differentiated normative orders pertaining to areas of foreign investors' responsibilities can only be weakly compatible with international investment law. When considering the postulates of critical constructivism, this weak normative integration can be further explained by exploring relations of power and the interests of powerful actors involved in the international investment lawmaking process. With respect to instruments elaborated and implemented by intergovernmental organizations, the application of the interactional theory of international law – itself based on legal pluralism and (critical) constructivism – allows assessing the sense of obligation that emanates from each instrument by considering the existence of shared understandings, their consistency with criteria of legality and the emergence of a practice of legality. Such an analysis provides evidence to position these instruments on a continuum that varies from social norms to legal norms.

As far as methods are concerned, this book supplements the interpretation of primary sources in international law (*e.g.* international agreements and resolutions) with a critical discourse analysis of statements and reports submitted to intergovernmental organizations. Combining the relevance of discourses in shaping reality with the critical theory paradigm in qualitative research, critical discourse analysis aims to illuminate ideologies and relations of power that underpin various forms of statements and practices.[63] Assuming that discourses

62 See Hélène Mayrand, "L'apport mutuel entre constructivism et théories critiques" in Rémi Bachand, ed, *Théories critiques et droit international* (Brussels: Bruylant, 2013) 147 at 170–171.

63 See e.g. Teun A Van Dijk, "Critical Discourse Analysis" in Deborah Schiffrin, Deborah Tannen & Heidi H Hamilton, eds, *The Handbook of Discourse Analysis* (Malden, MA: Blackwell Publishing, 2001) 352 at 354–355, Lilie Chouliaraki & Norman Fairclough, "The Critical Analysis of Discourse" in William K Carroll, ed, *Critical Strategies for Social Research* (Toronto: Canadian Scholars' Press, 2004) 262 at 267; Gilbert Weiss & Ruth Wodak, "Theory, Interdisciplinarity and Critical Discourse Analysis" in Gilbert Weiss & Ruth Wodak, eds, *Critical Discourse Analysis: Theory and Interdisciplinarity* (New York: Palgrave Macmillan, 2003) 1 at 12.

articulate differences in power regarding hierarchical social structures, this method acknowledges that such discourses inevitably become instruments of power as well as a starting point for resistance.[64]

Despite the presence of a vast variety of reports and statements that can be found on intergovernmental organizations' websites, discursive materials are not necessarily available for all the international instruments considered for present purposes. In this regard, conversations with insiders generally reveal a more complete and diversified perspective than what can be found in publicly available documents or through mere observation of people.[65] Considering these elements, this book applies a critical discourse analysis to transcripts of semi-structured interviews. This additional source of discourse thus provides key unpublished information to assess the normative character of international instruments and sheds light on whether discourses of individuals from intergovernmental organizations reflect relations of power that are at play.

More precisely, this book benefits from a total of twenty semi-structured interviews that were conducted with individuals from four intergovernmental organizations (*i.e.* the OECD, the UN, the ILO and the World Bank Group). In order to recruit participants, emails were sent to potential interviewees and a snowball sampling was used as the participation of the first participants were confirmed. Discussions with the interviewees focused on the existence of shared understandings between the various actors involved in the elaboration of the instruments, as well as the practice characterizing the actions of actors since their adoption. Attention was paid when elaborating the interview guide to orient the discussions toward the relative influence of different actors involved in the elaboration and the implementation of the instruments within intergovernmental organizations. Interviews were recorded and transcribed with a view to increasing the reliability of the data, and transcripts were made available for comments from participants.

Overall, the contribution that the present book brings to the study of the codification of foreign investors' responsibilities relies on its interdisciplinary character, which provides a contextualized analysis of the normative integration of these responsibilities in international investment law and a nuanced understanding of the normative character of existing initiatives elaborated under the auspices of intergovernmental organizations. Thanks to a combination of concepts from the disciplines of international law and international relations, the contribution of this book is twofold. In contrast to the idea that international investment law inevitably fails to impose any forms of obligations on foreign investors, it demonstrates that the normative integration of foreign investors' responsibilities in this regime is fragmented and consistent with the interests of

64 See Ruth Wodak & Michael Meyer, "Critical Discourse Analysis: History, Agenda, Theory, and Methodology" in Ruth Wodak & Michael Meyer, eds, *Methods in Critical Discourse Analysis* (Thousand Oaks, CA: Sage Publications, 2009) 1 at 10.

65 See Alan Bryman, *Social Research Methods* (Oxford: Oxford University Press, 2001) at 329.

the most powerful actors involved in the lawmaking process. It also shows that the evolving codification process by intergovernmental organizations is characterized by a majority of social norms, with relatively few legal norms.

4. The Book in a Nutshell

With a view to offering a comprehensive understanding of the evolving codification of foreign investors' responsibilities that is taking place under the auspices of intergovernmental organizations and within the broader context of international investment law, the upcoming chapters are structured according to two parts, namely a macro-level analysis focusing on the international investment regime (Part I) and a micro-level analysis addressing instruments elaborated by intergovernmental organizations (Part II). These two levels of analysis remain strongly interrelated, as the examination of the normative integration of foreign investors' responsibilities in international investment law provides an important context in which intergovernmental organizations' norms emerge. This section of the introduction thus provides a brief overview of each part and highlights key results that are found in each chapter.

Part I delves into the examination of the subject at hand by addressing the codification process at a macro-level. Inspired by the emergence of functionally differentiated normative orders that are posited in legal pluralism, it begins by assessing the degree of normative integration of foreign investors' responsibilities in international investment law. Chapter 1 proceeds by determining whether various areas of responsibilities (*i.e.* human rights, environmental protection, labour rights and corruption) are included in IIAs provisions. It focuses on provisions emphasizing the observance of international initiatives pertaining to foreign investors' responsibilities and states' obligation to fight corruption. Ultimately, Chapter 1 demonstrates that the normative integration of foreign investors' responsibilities in IIAs is fragmented. While this integration is weak for most of these areas (*i.e.* human rights, environmental protection and labour rights), some provisions pertaining to the prohibition of corruption require concrete actions by states and strong consequences for investors.

Exploring the normative integration of foreign investors' responsibilities in international investment law would be incomplete without addressing decisions from international investment arbitration tribunals. Chapter 2 thus focuses on the consideration of the negative impact related to foreign investors' activities in societies and the environment when these tribunals assess the legality of a measure adopted by the respondent state. With respect to the areas of human rights and environmental protection, this chapter sheds light on an inconsistent approach. While some tribunals have demonstrated a considerable level of responsiveness to the negative impact of these activities, others have expressly refused to address issues pertaining to human rights and environmental protection. By contrast, international investment arbitration tribunals having to decide a claim in which there is clear evidence of corruption on the side of the claimant have consistently concluded that the investor loses its right to seek redress through international arbitration. Echoing finding pertaining to IIAs, this chapter demonstrates a fragmented normative integration of foreign investors' responsibilities in international investment arbitration.

In order to include in this macro-level analysis an explicit consideration of relations of power that characterize the international investment lawmaking process, Chapter 3 draws from a critical constructivist approach and a critical discourse analysis to assess the consistency of this fragmented normative integration with the most powerful actors' interests. Relying on publicly available statements from state and non-state actors pertaining to the codification of these responsibilities in various areas, this analysis shows that consultations conducted under the auspices of intergovernmental organizations inevitably reproduce relations of power. While many capital-exporting states and foreign investors are strongly opposed to the imposition of responsibilities in the areas of human rights, environmental protection and labour rights, these powerful actors are more willing to support the adoption of binding norms in the area of corruption. In light of these findings, this chapter concludes that the fragmented normative integration of foreign investors' responsibilities in international investment law generally reflects the interests of the most powerful actors that are involved in the international investment lawmaking process.

Part II adopts a micro-level of analysis and positions each international instrument elaborated and implemented under the auspices of intergovernmental organizations on a continuum varying from social norms to legal norms. Each chapter of this part draws from the interactional theory of international law and partly relies on a critical discourse analysis. More specifically, after emphasizing OECD's efforts to promote free market and neoliberal policies, Chapter 4 focuses on international instruments arising from this intergovernmental organization. Since the adoption of their first version, the *OECD Guidelines* have become a widely disseminated social norm and have evolved closer to the realm of legality. However, the persistent opposition from powerful actors to depart from an instrument whose observance is voluntary and the absence of recognition of any binding character to the *OECD Guidelines* impede their consideration as an international legal norm. By contrast, efforts devoted by the OECD to prohibit corruption have led to the development of instruments that generate a sense of obligation. The *OECD Anti-Bribery Convention* and the *OECD 2009 Recommendation* both rely on the support from powerful actors with respect to the elaboration and the implementation of international instruments that address the liability of legal persons for the bribery of foreign public officials in international business transactions. Regardless of their different form under international law, Chapter 4 argues that the *OECD Anti-Bribery Convention* and the *OECD 2009 Recommendation* are international legal norms.

Chapter 5 continues the micro-level analysis of the codification of foreign investors' responsibilities by considering the work accomplished by the ILO. Although the tripartite structure of this intergovernmental organization provides a unique institutional context to elaborate such norms, the ILO is often considered as struggling to implement standards that effectively influence the conduct of international actors in a context of neoliberal globalization. In this regard, the analysis of the *ILO Tripartite Declaration* demonstrates that the elaboration and the implementation of this informal international instrument has led to a social norm that hardly manages to influence the behavior of international actors. In addition to efforts from powerful actors to preserve its voluntary character and various issues with respect to its provisions, the *ILO Tripartite Declaration* now appears to be in the shadow of other international instruments codifying foreign investors' responsibilities.

After contextualizing these instruments amidst the historical efforts to establish a New International Economic Order, Chapter 6 examines four different international instruments elaborated and implemented under the auspices of various UN agencies. First, while this initiative has always been intended as a learning platform to encourage responsible business conduct, an interactional account of the UN Global Compact unsurprisingly sheds light on a widely disseminated social norm that nevertheless remains far from being a legal norm. Second, even if the members of the UN Sub-Commission proposed to elaborate an international binding instrument, the stark opposition from powerful actors and various issues with respect to their provisions have prevented the *UN Norms* from reaching the threshold of legality. The current absence of a sustained practice even sheds doubts over the status of this instrument as an international social norm nowadays. Third, the analysis of the *UN Guiding Principles* suggests that the support from powerful actors involved in their elaboration and their implementation is strongly related to the avowed intent of the Special Representative not to impose additional legal obligations to states and business enterprises. However, the absence of an express voluntary character to the corporate responsibility to respect human rights and some aspects of the current practice underlying this instrument could eventually bring this social norm closer to the realm of legality. Fourth, the flexibility characterizing its provisions and the elaboration of an implementation mechanism focusing primarily on dialogue for best practices render the *UNCAC* as a strong social norm that generally fails to meet the threshold of legality. Despite its formal character under international law, the *UNCAC* cannot be considered as a genuine legal norm according to an interactional account.

Finally, Chapter 7 addresses the specific case of performance standards adopted by an institution of the World Bank Group, namely the IFC. The support of the various agencies of the World Bank Group for the protection of international investment is undeniable. Yet, an interesting identity shift toward an increasing consideration of environmental and social sustainability has paved the way to the elaboration of instruments such as the *IFC Performance Standards*. While these standards articulating responsibilities for private enterprises that operationalize a project funded by the IFC are not enshrined in a formal international agreement, they unambiguously constitute an international legal norm for the IFC and its clients. In addition to the initial will to elaborate an international instrument whose observance is mandatory to obtain funding from the IFC, Chapter 7 highlights the legitimacy of these standards and the emergence of a practice that is geared toward compliance.

Part I

Foreign Investors' Responsibilities and International Investment Law

A Macro-Level Analysis

Analyzing the processes of elaboration and implementation of foreign investors' responsibilities by intergovernmental organizations calls upon a consideration of these responsibilities in international investment law. Efforts to codify standards of appropriate conduct for private actors operating abroad have emerged in a context where states ratify international agreements to provide protections to foreign investors. Part I of this book thus examines the normative integration of foreign investors' responsibilities in international investment law. Instead of suggesting that this regime fails to impose any obligations on foreign investors, it is here demonstrated that the normative integration of foreign investors' responsibilities is fragmented and consistent with the interests of the most powerful actors involved in the international investment lawmaking process. When considering various areas of responsibilities (*i.e.* human rights, environmental protection, labour rights and corruption), one can identify important distinctions regarding the extent to which they are taken into consideration in international investment agreements (Chapter 1) and decisions from arbitration tribunals (Chapter 2). This examination is supplemented with a critical discourse analysis of statements submitted by international actors to demonstrate that this fragmented normative integration is consistent with the interests of actors that can more directly influence the outcome of the normative process (Chapter 3).

1 Addressing the Lack of Accountability in International Investment Agreements

Introduction

Concerns regarding the lack of accountability of foreign investors remain of the utmost relevance when one looks at current discussions in international investment law. Among the several aspects that have been addressed with respect to this branch of international law, the asymmetry of obligations in international investment agreements (IIAs) is a recurring theme.[1] While these agreements subject host states to specific rules pertaining to the protection of foreign investors and investments, IIAs are often considered as being silent as far as the responsibilities of foreign investors and home states are concerned.

As a first step to analyze the normative integration of foreign investors' responsibilities in international investment law, Chapter 1 focuses on the provisions of IIAs to examine whether these agreements adequately take into consideration the negative impact that foreign investors' activities can have in local communities and the environment. In line with the assumptions of the legal pluralist approach,[2] this chapter considers functionally differentiated normative orders pertaining to areas of foreign investors' responsibilities that have emerged in parallel to the elaboration of rules pertaining to the protection of international investment. In addition to the codification of standards regarding human rights,

1 See e.g. Peter T Muchlinski, "Regulating Multinationals: Foreign Investment, Development, and the Balance of Corporate and Home Country Rights and Responsibilities in a Globalizing World" in José E Alvarez et al, eds, *The Evolving International Investment Regime: Expectations, Realities, Options* (Oxford: Oxford University Press, 2011) 30 at 31 [Muchlinski, "Regulating Multinationals"]; Patrick Dumberry & Gabrielle Dumas-Aubin, "How to Impose Human Rights Obligations on Corporations under Investment Treaties? Pragmatic Guidelines for the Amendment of BITs" in Karl P. Sauvant, ed, *Yearbook on International Investment Law & Policy 2011–2012* (Oxford: Oxford University Press, 2013) 569 at 569 and 573; Patrick Dumberry, "Corporate Investors' International Legal Personality and their Accountability for Human Rights Violations under IIAs" in Armand de Mestral & Céline Lévesque, eds, *Improving International Investment Agreements* (New York: Routledge, 2013) 179 at 179; Kate Miles, *The Origins of International Investment Law: Empire, Environment and the Safeguarding of Capital* (Cambridge: Cambridge University Press, 2013) at 125–154; Karsten Nowrot, "How to Include Environmental Protection, Human Rights and Sustainability in International Investment Law?" (2014) 15 J World Invest & Trade 612 at 619.

2 See section 3 of the introduction.

several intergovernmental organizations have adopted initiatives with respect to environmental protection and labour rights. What is more, informal international instruments and international treaties have been negotiated under the auspices of intergovernmental organizations regarding corruption. Having acknowledged the existence of these normative orders, it becomes possible to assess the extent to which these four areas of foreign investors' responsibilities (*i.e.* human rights, environmental protection, labour rights and corruption) are normatively integrated in IIAs.

This chapter focuses on the current practice of states when drafting IIAs. Although a survey completed by the Organisation for Economic Co-operation and Development (OECD) in 2014 suggests that provisions generally relating to the advancement of sustainable development or to the promotion of responsible business conduct have become a dominant treaty practice in recent years, the same survey concludes that only 12% of IIAs include such provisions.[3] An exhaustive presentation of formulations that are included in IIAs to account for any issues that transcend investment protection is beyond the scope of this research. Rather, the analysis focuses on provisions that can be used to address harms related to foreign investors' activities. A consideration of functionally differentiated normative orders that relate to areas of foreign investors' responsibilities and that evolve in parallel to international investment rules allows concluding that the normative integration of foreign investors' responsibilities in IIAs is *fragmented*. In fact, most provisions found in these agreements emphasize the voluntary character of corporate social responsibility and rely on hortatory language when it comes to the areas of human rights, environmental protection and labour rights. These provisions generally point toward a relatively weak normative integration of these concerns in IIAs (1). By contrast, the provisions that are likely to bear the most concrete consequences for foreign investors are those in which states recall their obligations to prosecute corrupt practices or prevent an investor from submitting a claim to arbitration if the investment has been made through corruption (2).

Before developing the argument any further, it is important to emphasize that the analysis provided in Chapter 1 and Chapter 2 differs from studies that address the conflict of norms.[4] While the theory of norm conflict presents incompatibility as a situation in which applying one legal norm necessarily implies the violation of another, such incompatibility is limited to instances in which a simultaneous observation of two legal norms by the same actor is impossible. The analysis of the normative integration of foreign investors' responsibilities in international investment law requires a more flexible conception of compatibility. The present

3 See Kathryn Gordon, Joachim Pohl & Marie Bouchard, *Investment Treaty Law, Sustainable Development and Responsible Business Conduct: A Fact Finding Survey*, OECD Working Paper on International Investment No 2014/1 (Paris, 2014) at 5.

4 See generally Jörg Kammerhofer, "The Theory of Norm Conflict Solutions in International Investment Law" in Marie-Claire Cordonier Segger, Markus W Gehring & Andrew Newcombe, eds, *Sustainable Development in World Investment Law* (Alphen aan den Rijn: Kluwer Law International, 2011) 83.

analysis thus focuses on the interaction between international obligations of *states* under international investment law and other norms that relate to the conduct of *foreign investors*. Instead of assessing whether emerging norms seeking to hold foreign investors accountable under international law conflict with international investment law, the aim of this chapter is to account for the extent to which these different responsibilities coexist under international investment law. Restated, the idea is to assess the extent to which states' obligations under international investment law can be interpreted in light of foreign investors' responsibilities in various areas that form functionally differentiated normative orders. Instead of scrutinizing potential conflicts of norms, one can thus consider various degrees of normative integration between these normative orders and international investment law.

1. Provisions on Foreign Investors' Responsibilities

With a view to addressing harms related to foreign investors' activities, states can choose among various possibilities to explicitly account for the responsibilities of these private actors within IIAs. More specifically, three different avenues are discernable from the practice of states: addressing the matter in the preamble of IIAs (1.1), including a general reference to foreign investors' responsibilities in a separate provision of the agreement (1.2) and referring to specific instruments adopted by intergovernmental organizations (1.3).

1.1 Preambles

As far as the first option is concerned, the signatory states of an IIA can choose to acknowledge the relevance of foreign investors' responsibilities in the preamble of the agreement. While there are several instances where states have used the language of preambles to emphasize their capacity to regulate,[5] a clear reference to foreign investors' responsibilities is far less frequent. Some IIAs that include a reference to "corporate social responsibility" are nevertheless worth mentioning. The relevance of this concept and encouragements for enterprises to respect corporate social responsibility norms are provided in the preamble of several IIAs signed by the European Free Trade Association (EFTA)[6] and Canada.[7]

5 See Kathryn Gordon & Joachim Pohl, *Environmental Concerns in International Investment Agreements: A Survey*, OECD Working Paper on International Investment No 2011/1 (Paris, 2011).

6 See e.g. *Free Trade Agreement between the Republic of Colombia and the EFTA States*, 25 November 2008, online: EFTA www.efta.int/media/documents/legal-texts/free-trade-relations/colombia/EFTA-Colombia%20Free%20Trade%20Agreement%20EN.pdf (accessed 26 March 2018) (entered into force 1 July 2011), Preamble [*EFTA–Colombia FTA*]; *Free Trade Agreement between the EFTA States and Georgia*, 27 June 2016, online: EFTAwww.efta.int/sites/default/files/documents/legal-texts/free-trade-relations/georgia/EFTA-Georgia-FTA-Main-Agreement.PDF (accessed 26 March 2018) (entered into force 1 September 2017), Preamble [*EFTA–Georgia FTA*].

7 See e.g. *Free Trade Agreement between Canada and the Republic of Peru*, 29 May 2008, Can TS 2009 No 15 (entered into force 1 August 2009), Preamble [*Canada–Peru FTA*]; *Free Trade Agreement between Canada and the Republic of Colombia*, 21 November 2008, Can TS 2011

The preamble of a bilateral investment treaty (BIT) signed between Switzerland and Kosovo also refers to the aim of encouraging investors to respect corporate social responsibility norms and principles that are internationally recognized.[8] More recently, the draft model BIT adopted by Norway in 2015 unambiguously emphasizes the importance of this concept in its preamble[9] and a call to encourage enterprises "to respect internationally recognized guidelines and principles of corporate social responsibility" can be found in the preamble of the *Comprehensive Economic and Trade Agreement* (*CETA*) between Canada and the European Union (EU).[10]

Beyond the reliance on corporate social responsibility, some states have chosen to expressly refer to "obligations" of foreign investors in the preamble of an agreement. For example, the preamble of the Southern African Development Community (SADC) model BIT emphasizes that the parties are "[s]eeking an overall balance of the rights and obligations among the State Parties, the investors and the investments."[11] While investment arbitration tribunals can rely on the language included in preamble to illuminate the object and the purpose of IIAs, it must be noted that current examples are particularly broad and do not offer any specific guidance with respect to the content of foreign investors' responsibilities.

1.2 Separate Provisions

A second option considered by states is the inclusion of separate provisions within IIAs that detail more precisely how various actors should approach these

No 11 (entered into force 15 August 2011), Preamble [*Canada–Colombia FTA*]. See also *Agreement between the Government of Canada and the Government of Burkina Faso for the Promotion and Protection of Investments*, 20 April 2015, online: Global Affairs Canada http://international.gc.ca/trade-commerce/trade-agreements-accords-commerciaux/agr-acc/burkina_faso/fipa-apie/index.aspx?lang=eng (accessed 26 March 2018) (entered into force 11 October 2017), Preamble [*Canada–Burkina Faso BIT*].

8 *Accord entre la Confédération suisse et la République du Kosovo concernant la promotion et la protection réciproque des investissements*, 27 October 2011, online: Confédération suisse www.admin.ch/opc/fr/official-compilation/2012/3733.pdf (accessed 26 March 2018) (entered into force 13 June 2012), Preamble.

9 Norway, *Agreement between the Kingdom of Norway and ____ for the Promotion and the Protection of Investment* (13 May 2015), online: Government of Norway www.regjeringen.no/contentassets/e47326b61f424d4c9c3d470896492623/draft-model-agreement-english.pdf (accessed 26 March 2018) [*Norway Model BIT*].

10 *Comprehensive Economic and Trade Agreement (CETA) between Canada, of the one Part, and the European Union, of the other Part*, 29 February 2016, online: European Commission's Directorate General for Trade http://trade.ec.europa.eu/doclib/docs/2016/february/tradoc_154329.pdf (accessed 26 March 2018) (entered into force 21 September 2017), Preamble [*CETA*].

11 Southern African Development Community, *SADC Model Bilateral Investment Treaty Template* (July 2012), online: International Institute for Sustainable Development www.iisd.org/itn/wp-content/uploads/2012/10/sadc-model-bit-template-final.pdf (accessed 26 March 2018), art 22(2) [*SADC Model BIT*].

responsibilities. One of the earliest examples of the inclusion of such a provision can be found in the *Agreement on Promotion, Protection and Guarantee of Investments Among Member States of the Organisation of the Islamic Conference* (*OIC IIA*) that was signed in 1981.[12] Without specifically referring to an area of responsibilities, Article 9 of this agreement thus provides the following:

> The *investor shall be bound* by the laws and regulations in force in the host state and shall refrain from all acts that may disturb public order and morals or that may be prejudicial to the public interest. He is also to refrain from exercising restrictive practices and from trying to achieve gains through unlawful means.[13]

Of course, the possibility of imposing direct obligations on foreign investors to that extent is highly contentious in international investment law and falls beyond the scope of this chapter. For the purposes of the present argument, suffice it to say that such a provision demonstrates an attempt at further integrating foreign investors' responsibilities within IIAs.

The majority of IIAs address foreign investors' responsibilities in a less concrete way. Several free trade agreements (FTAs) concluded by Canada include a separate article on corporate social responsibility amidst the standards pertaining to the protection accorded to foreign investment:

> Each Party *should encourage* enterprises operating within its territory or subject to its jurisdiction to *voluntarily incorporate* internationally recognized standards of corporate social responsibility in their internal policies, such as statements of principle that have been endorsed or are supported by the Parties. These principles address issues such as labour, the environment, human rights, community relations and anti-corruption. *The Parties remind those enterprises of the importance of incorporating such corporate social responsibility standards in their internal policies.*[14]

A shorter provision regarding corporate social responsibility can also be found in the initial text of the *Trans-Pacific Partnership*,[15] as well as in the more recent

12 *Agreement on Promotion, Protection and Guarantee of Investments Among Member States of the Organisation of the Islamic Conference*, 5 June 1981, online: Investment Policy Hub: http://investmentpolicyhub.unctad.org/Download/TreatyFile/2399 (accessed 26 March 2018) (entered into force 23 September 1986).

13 *Ibid*, art 9 [emphasis added].

14 *Canada–Peru FTA*, *supra* note 7, art 810 [emphasis added]. See e.g. *Canada–Colombia FTA*, *supra* note 7, art 816; *Free Trade Agreement between Canada and the Republic of Korea*, 11 March 2014, Can TS 2015 No 3 (entered into force 1 January 2015), art 8.16 [*Canada–Korea FTA*].

15 *Trans-Pacific Partnership*, 4 February 2016, online: New Zealand Foreign Affairs and Trade www.mfat.govt.nz/en/about-us/who-we-are/treaty-making-process/trans-pacific-partnership-tpp/text-of-the-trans-pacific-partnership/ (accessed 26 March 2018), art 9.17.

Comprehensive and Progressive Agreement for Trans-Pacific Partnership.[16] While this practice was initially limited to the investment chapter of some FTAs, recent Canadian BITs also include a similar provision on corporate social responsibility.[17]

However, other provisions of these FTAs and BITs limit the potential effect of a corporate social responsibility clause. In fact, the investor–state dispute settlement mechanism established in the overwhelming majority of these agreements specifically mentions that an investor cannot submit a claim pertaining to the obligation of the state with respect to the promotion of corporate social responsibility.[18] In some instances (*e.g.* the *Canada–Peru FTA* and the *Canada–Colombia FTA*), these agreements provide that such concerns may be addressed by a Committee on Investment that acts as a forum for the states to consult on various investment-related issues.[19]

The practice chosen by the United States slightly differs from the Canadian one. Instead of including a separate provision in the investment chapter of FTAs, this country has sporadically opted for an even broader reference to principles of corporate social responsibility in a different chapter that focuses on the environment. Therefore, some agreements include the following text: "[E]ach Party *should encourage* enterprises operating within its territory or jurisdiction to *voluntarily incorporate* sound principles of corporate stewardship in their internal policies, such as those principles or agreements that have been endorsed by both Parties."[20]

The EU has also adopted some IIAs that fit this development. In an economic partnership agreement (EPA) signed with the CARIFORUM states, the parties agree to take measures that are necessary to frame the conduct of the investors.[21]

16 *Comprehensive and Progressive Agreement for the Trans-Pacific Partnership*, 8 March 2018, online: New Zealand Foreign Affairs and Trade www.mfat.govt.nz/en/trade/free-trade-agreements/free-trade-agreements-concluded-but-not-in-force/cptpp/comprehensive-and-progressive-agreement-for-trans-pacific-partnership-text/#chapters (accessed 26 March 2018), art 9.17.

17 See e.g. *Agreement between the Government of Canada and the Government of the Republic of Benin on the Promotion and Reciprocal Protection of Investments*, 8 January 2013, Can TS 2014 No 13 (entered into force 12 May 2014), art 16 [*Canada–Benin BIT*]; *Agreement between Canada and the Republic of Serbia for the Promotion and Protection of Investments*, 1 September 2014, Can TS 2015 No 6 (entered into force 7 April 2015), art 16 [*Canada–Serbia BIT*]; *Canada–Burkina Faso BIT*, *supra* note 7, art 16; Canada, *Agreement between Canada and ____ for the Promotion and Protection of Investments* (25 August 2014) (on file with the author), art 16 [*Canada Model BIT*].

18 *Canada–Peru FTA*, *supra* note 7, arts 819(1) and 820(1); *Canada–Colombia FTA*, *supra* note 7, arts 819 and 820; *Canada–Korea FTA*, *supra* note 14, arts 8.18 and 8.19(1); *Canada–Benin BIT*, *ibid*, arts 23(1)(a) and 23(2)(a); *Canada–Serbia BIT*, *ibid*, arts 21(1)(a) and 21(2)(a); *Canada Model BIT*, *ibid*, arts 21(1)(a) and 21(2)(a).

19 *Canada–Peru FTA*, *ibid* art 817(2); *Canada–Colombia FTA*, *ibid*, art 817(3).

20 See e.g. *United States–Singapore Free Trade Agreement*, 6 May 2003, 42 ILM 1026 (entered into force 1 January 2004), art 18.9 [*USA–Singapore FTA*] [emphasis added]; *United States–Chile Free Trade Agreement*, 6 June 2003, 42 ILM 1026 (entered into force 1 January 2004), art 19.10.

21 *Economic Partnership Agreement between the CARIFORUM States, of the one part, and the European Community and its Members, of the other part*, 15 October 2008, 289 OJ 3, art 72 [*EC–CARIFORUM EPA*].

Such measures must ensure that investors' activities remain in accordance with labour standards and that they do not circumvent international environmental obligations arising from agreements to which the states are parties.[22] What is more, while articulating the European international investment policy in 2011, the European Parliament reiterated "its call for a corporate social responsibility clause and effective social and environmental clauses to be included in every FTA the EU signs."[23] In 2013, the European Parliament recalled this statement in the context of the negotiations for a BIT between the EU and China.[24] It will thus be interesting to observe whether future IIAs adopted by the EU will go beyond the language found in *CETA*'s preamble and refer to foreign investors' responsibilities in a separate provision.

African states have opted for instruments that integrate such responsibilities more deeply. The *Common Market for Eastern and Southern Africa (COMESA) Agreement on a Common Investment Area*, for example, includes a provision related to recommendations made by a committee in regard to the development of minimum standards with respect to several investment-related issues.[25] The list of these issues includes environmental and social impact assessments, labour standards, respect for human rights, conduct in conflict zones and corruption. To a certain extent, this investment agreement also reflects the approach in the Organisation of the Islamic Conference IIA by the inclusion of a provision stating that "COMESA investors and their investments shall comply with all applicable domestic measures of the Member State in which their investment is made."[26]

In addition to agreements adopted by states, some model BITs address more specifically foreign investors' responsibilities in the areas of human rights, environmental protection and labour rights. The SADC model BIT thus echoes the COMESA's attempt at imposing direct obligations on foreign investors by elaborating several provisions that address the responsibilities of private actors. For example, the effects of investment on third persons, the local community and the environment are explicitly taken into account in the non-discrimination standard.[27] Furthermore, this model includes obligations for the investors in regard to compliance with domestic law, provision of information to the host

22 *Ibid*, art 72(2)–72(3).

23 European Parliament, *Resolution of 6 April 2011 on the Future European International Investment Policy*, online: European Parliament www.europarl.europa.eu/sides/getDoc.do?pubRef=-//EP//TEXT+TA+P7-TA-2011-0141+0+DOC+XML+V0//EN (accessed 26 March 2018) at para 27.

24 European Parliament, *Resolution of 9 October 2013 on the EU–China Negotiations for a Bilateral Investment Agreement*, online: European Parliament www.europarl.europa.eu/sides/getDoc.do?type=TA&language=EN&reference=P7-TA-2013-411 (accessed 26 March 2018) at paras K and 33 [European Parliament, *Resolution of 9 October 2013*].

25 *Investment Agreement for the COMESA Common Investment Area*, 2007, online: Investment Policy Hub http://investmentpolicyhub.unctad.org/Download/TreatyFile/3092 (accessed 26 March 2018), art 7.2 [*COMESA Investment Agreement*].

26 *Ibid*, art 13.

27 *SADC Model BIT*, *supra* note 11, art 4(1) and 4(2).

state, environmental and social impact assessments, environmental management, corporate governance standards, investor liability, transparency, as well as human rights, environmental protection and labour rights.[28] It is also recognized that the determination of a breach of these obligations by an investor shall be taken into account by the tribunal in an investment dispute.[29] Another model BIT that includes a similar chapter on foreign investors' obligations was adopted by India in 2015, with provisions pertaining to compliance with domestic laws and corporate social responsibility.[30] Despite these model BIT provisions, it must nevertheless be recalled that the overwhelming majority of formal IIAs refer to foreign investors' responsibilities through language that recalls the voluntary nature of corporate social responsibility initiatives.

1.3 References to International Instruments

Drafters of IIAs have considered a third option to address foreign investors' responsibilities, namely through a direct reference to instruments adopted by intergovernmental organizations. Some documents providing a basis for the negotiations of IIAs are thus worth considering. For example, the European Parliament refers to these types of international instruments in the resolution adopted to steer the negotiations of a BIT between the EU and China. In addition to reiterating its call for a corporate social responsibility clause discussed above, the European Parliament has mentioned that such a clause had to be in line with the *Guiding Principles on Business and Human Rights* elaborated under the auspices of the United Nations (UN).[31] It has also affirmed "that investors should, respectively, apply the *[International Labour Organization] Tripartite Declaration on Multinational Enterprises and Social Policy* and the *OECD Guidelines for Multinational Enterprises*."[32] Along the same lines, in its recommendations to the European Commission on the negotiations for the *Transatlantic Trade and Investment Partnership*, the European Parliament recommended to "address investors' obligations and responsibilities by referring, inter alia, to the OECD principles for multinational enterprises and to the UN principles on [b]usiness and human rights as benchmarks."[33] More recently, in the model BIT developed by Norway, Article 31 establishes an

28 *Ibid*, arts 11–18.

29 *Ibid*, art 19(1).

30 India, *Bilateral Investment Treaty between the Government of the Republic of India and* _____ (28 December 2015), online: Investment Policy Hub http://investmentpolicyhub.unctad.org/Download/TreatyFile/3560 (accessed 26 March 2018), arts 11–12.

31 European Parliament, *Resolution of 9 October 2013*, *supra* note 24 at para 33.

32 *Ibid* at para 33.

33 European Parliament, *Report Containing the European Parliament's Recommendations to the European Commission on the Negotiations for the Transatlantic Trade and Investment Partnership* (1 June 2015), online: European Parliament www.europarl.europa.eu/sides/getDoc.do?pubRef=-//EP//NONSGML+REPORT+A8-2015-0175+0+DOC+PDF+V0//EN (accessed 26 March 2018) at para 1(d)(xiii).

obligation on states "to *encourage* investors to conduct their investment activities in compliance with the OECD Guidelines for Multinational Enterprises, the UN Guiding Principles on Business and Human Rights and to participate in the United Nations Global Compact."[34]

In addition to references included in instruments intended to guide the negotiations of IIAs, some formal international treaties explicitly mention international instruments adopted by intergovernmental organizations regarding foreign investors' responsibilities. Some countries have chosen to mention these international instruments in the preamble of IIAs. For example, some BITs signed by Austria include an explicit reference to the *OECD Guidelines for Multinational Enterprises* and to the UN Global Compact.[35] Several IIAs adopted by the EFTA also refer to these instruments in their preamble,[36] while the preamble of *CETA* includes a reference to the *OECD Guidelines for Multinational Enterprise*.[37]

Other IIAs refer to international instruments codifying foreign investors' responsibilities in a separate provision of the agreement. Thus, among the numerous annexes and joint declarations adopted with the agreement establishing an association between the European Community and the Republic of Chile, the parties agreed to "remind their multinational enterprises of their recommendation to observe the *OECD Guidelines for Multinational Enterprises*, wherever they operate."[38] Entitled "Promotion of Investments," Article 2 of the BIT between the Netherlands and the United Arab Emirates also mentions that "[e]ach Contracting Party shall promote as far as possible and in accordance with their domestic laws the application of the *OECD Guidelines for Multinational Enterprises* to the extent that this is not contrary to their domestic laws."[39]

Although the negotiation of treaties that expressly incorporate foreign investors' responsibilities appears as a relevant way to counter the unbalanced character of international investment law, most of the current provisions demonstrate

34 *Norway Model BIT*, *supra* note 9, art 31 [emphasis added].

35 See e.g. *Agreement between the Government of the Republic of Kosovo and the Government of the Republic of Austria on Promotion and Protection of Investments*, 22 January 2010, online: Ministry of Foreign Affairs www.mfa-ks.net/repository/docs/Marrveshja_Ks-Aus_(anglisht).pdf (accessed 26 March 2018), Preamble; *Agreement for the Promotion and Protection of Investment between the Republic of Austria and the Republic of Tajikistan*, 15 December 2010, online: Investment Policy Hub http://investmentpolicyhub.unctad.org/Download/TreatyFile/3308 (accessed 26 March 2018) (entered into force 21 December 2012), Preamble.

36 See e.g. *EFTA–Colombia FTA*, *supra* note 6, Preamble; *EFTA–Georgia FTA*, *supra* note 6, Preamble.

37 *CETA*, *supra* note 10, Preamble.

38 *Agreement Establishing an Association between the European Community and its Member States, of the one Part, and the Republic of Chile, of the other Part*, 30 December 2002, OJ, L/352 (entered into force 1 February 2003) at 1444.

39 *Agreement on Encouragement and Reciprocal Protection of Investments between the Kingdom of the Netherlands and the United Arab Emirates*, 26 November 2013, online: Investment Policy Hub http://investmentpolicyhub.unctad.org/Download/TreatyFile/4774 (accessed 26 March 2018), art 2(3).

the difficulty in addressing this issue. In fact, several authors argue that these provisions are likely to complicate the adoption of IIAs.[40] With relatively few exceptions,[41] one must thus not be surprised to see that the issue of foreign investors' responsibility is often addressed through hortatory language that merely exposes general commitments from the signatory states with respect to human rights, environmental protection and labour rights. Moreover, the inclusion of such provisions does not impose concrete obligations on states to develop laws on foreign investors' responsibilities and does not generally require investors to adopt a specific conduct that is in line with these standards. Taken together, such limitations support the argument that the normative integration of foreign investors' responsibilities in IIAs remains relatively weak in the areas of human rights, environmental protection and labour rights.

2. A Stronger Integration of Corruption

In contrast to the other areas in which foreign investors' activities can generate negative effects, the responsibilities of these private actors regarding corruption are more firmly taken into account in some IIAs. Although relatively few examples currently exist, a limited number of states have chosen to stress the actions that are required to prosecute bribery and corruption within IIAs. Beyond the inclusion of corruption in provisions that broadly pertain to corporate social responsibility[42] and other references to the obligations of the state parties to combat corruption within IIAs,[43] some provisions thus specifically address the punishment of this conduct and suggest a stronger normative integration of foreign investors' responsibilities in this regard.

For example, the SADC model BIT posits that investors have an obligation not to engage in corrupt practices, both with respect to the pre-establishment

40 See e.g. Muchlinski, "Regulating Multinationals", *supra* note 1 at 46–47; Andrea K Bjorklund, "Improving the International Investment Law and Policy System, Report of the Rapporteur – Second Columbia International Investment Conference: What's Next in International Investment Law and Policy?" in José E Alvarez et al, eds, *The Evolving International Investment Regime: Expectations, Realities, Options* (Oxford: Oxford University Press, 2011) 213 at 230.

41 See the discussions pertaining to the *OIC IIA*, the *EC–CARIFORUM EPA*, the *COMESA Investment Agreement*, the *SADC Model BIT* and the India Model BIT above.

42 See the provisions from the agreements signed by Canada in the previous section.

43 One example can be found in the *EU–South Korea FTA*, in which "[t]he Parties recall their obligations under the OECD Convention on Combatting Bribery of Foreign Public Officials in International Business Transactions." See *Free Trade Agreement between the European Union and its Members, of the one Part, and the Republic of Korea, of the other Part*, 6 October 2010, 127 OJ 6 (entered into force July 2011), Annex 2-D, art 4. See also BITs concluded by Japan. See e.g. *Agreement between Japan and the Sultanate of Oman for the Reciprocal Promotion and Protection of Investment*, 19 June 2015, online: Investment Policy Hub http://investmentpolicyhub.unctad.org/Download/TreatyFile/3481 (accessed 26 March 2018) (entered into force 21 July 2017), art 8.

and the post-establishment phases of the investment.[44] More specifically, Article 10(1) of this model BIT provides that

> [i]nvestors and their [i]nvestments shall not, prior to the establishment of an investment or afterwards, offer, promise of give any undue pecuniary or other advantage whether directly or through intermediairies, to a public official of the Host State, or a member of an official's family or business associate or other person in close proximity to an official, for that official or for a third party, in order that the official or third party act or refrain from acting in relation to the performance of official duties, in order to achieve any favour in relation to a proposed investment or any licences, permits, contracts or other rights in relation to an Investment.[45]

In addition to this model BIT, a strong normative integration of foreign investors' responsibilities with respect to the area of corruption is also found in formal international instruments. For example, in a separate chapter from the provisions pertaining to investment, Article 21.5 of the *United States–Singapore FTA* states that "[e]ach party reaffirms its firm existing commitment to the adoption, maintenance, and enforcement of effective measures, ***including deterrent penalties***, against bribery and corruption in international business transactions."[46] In the same vein, the EPA between the European Community and CARIFORUM states obliges the parties to adopt measures that prohibit corruption and hold investors liable for any corrupt practices in regard to their investment.[47] More recent association agreements signed by the EU also include similar provisions. For example, the association agreement between the EU and Georgia includes an article entitled "Legal proceedings, investigation and prosecution."[48] This article requires that authorities "bring legal proceedings, including, if appropriate, ***investigation and prosecution*** of suspected and actual cases of fraud, corruption or any other irregularity, including conflict of interests."[49]

One of the most vivid example of a strong normative integration of foreign investors' responsibilities pertaining to the area of corruption can be found in *CETA*.[50] Rather than emphasizing an obligation for states to prosecute this crime, this agreement specifically addresses the issue of corruption within the provisions that relate to the scope of the resolution of investment disputes between investors and states. More specifically, paragraph 8.18(3) provides that "an investor may

44 *SADC Model BIT*, *supra* note 11, art 10.

45 *Ibid*, art 10(1).

46 *USA–Singapore FTA*, *supra* note 20, art 21.5 [emphasis added].

47 *EC–CARIFORUM EPA*, *supra* note 21, art 72.

48 *Association Agreement between the European Union and the European Atomic Energy Community and that Member States, of the one part, and Georgia, of the other part*, 27 June 2014, OJ, L/261 (entered into force 1 July 2016) at 4, art 395.

49 *Ibid*, art 395.

50 *CETA*, *supra* note 10.

not submit a claim under this [s]ection if the investment has been made through fraudulent misrepresentation, concealment, corruption, or conduct amounting to an abuse of process."[51] Although perhaps limited to the pre-establishment phase of the investment, this provision unambiguously imposes an obligation for investors not to rely on corruption in order to seek redress under the investor-state arbitration mechanism established by *CETA*.

Similarly, in a BIT recently signed between the Slovak Republic and the Islamic Republic of Iran, the state parties have agreed that an investor may not submit a claim to international investment arbitration "where the investor or the investment has violated the [h]ost state law."[52] More interestingly, Article 14(2) of this agreement expressly provides that bribery and corruption constitute "violations [that] shall always be considered sufficiently serious or material to require dismissal of the claim."[53]

In sum, in contrast to provisions that merely encourage foreign investors to observe voluntary initiatives, there are some examples of IIAs that emphasize the obligation for states to prosecute corruption and that provide concrete consequences for foreign investors whose activities are tainted with illegality. Considering the impact that such provisions can have on foreign investors, these examples suggest a stronger normative integration of foreign investors' responsibilities regarding corruption in IIAs than the areas of human rights, environmental protection and labour rights.

Conclusion

An assessment of the normative integration of foreign investors' responsibilities within IIAs is a key step in understanding the quest for the redress of imbalances between foreign investors' protections and obligations. Considering that the primary goal of IIAs is to protect foreign investors and their investments rather than imposing standards to these private actors, the fact these international agreements appear as unbalanced is hardly surprising. Several normative developments nevertheless evidence various degrees of integration of foreign investors' responsibilities in IIAs. By focusing on functionally differentiated normative orders that pertain to areas of foreign investors' responsibilities (*i.e.* human rights, environmental protection, labour rights and corruption), this chapter has demonstrated that the normative integration of these normative orders varies considerably.

With respect to provisions that address the issue of foreign investors' responsibilities, the overwhelming majority of provisions are limited to the concept of corporate social responsibility and address several areas in hortatory terms. This trend is nevertheless different in the area of corruption, for which a limited

51 *Ibid*, art 18.8(3).

52 *Agreement between the Slovak Republic and the Islamic Republic of Iran*, 19 January 2016, online: Investment Policy Hub http://investmentpolicyhub.unctad.org/Download/TreatyFile/3601 (accessed 26 March 2018) (entered into force 30 August 2017), art 14(2).

53 *Ibid*, art 14(2).

number of states recall their engagements to prosecute corrupt practices and emphasize that investments made through corruption cannot be the object of an international arbitration claim. While the normative integration of foreign investors' responsibilities appears to be fairly strong in the area of corruption, it thus remains relatively weak in the areas of human rights, environmental protection and labour rights. Rather than suggesting that IIAs fail to impose any form of obligations on foreign investors, a consideration of these areas of responsibilities that evolve in parallel to international investment law allows concluding that the normative integration of foreign investors' responsibilities in IIAs is fragmented.

2 Foreign Investors' Responsibilities in International Investment Arbitration

Introduction

In addition to the examination of provisions within international investment agreements (IIAs), an analysis of the normative integration of foreign investors' responsibilities in international investment law must consider developments occurring in international investment arbitration. The jurisdiction of an international investment arbitration tribunal is often limited to analyzing a potential violation of provisions that are found in an IIA. Consequently, given that IIAs often weakly address foreign investors' responsibilities, the conduct of an investor would not normally constitute the basis of an international investment dispute. Yet, given that the conduct of investors can arise as a defense of respondent states,[1] it becomes paramount to scrutinize how tribunals deal with the negative impact that foreign investors' activities can have in local communities and the environment. To be clear, this chapter does not address every instance in which a state adopted a measure that could be defended on human rights or environmental protection grounds.[2] Rather, the decisions that are analyzed below are limited to examples in which the negative impact of the claimant's activities and conduct were expressly raised in the defense of the respondent state.

1 See e.g. Peter Muchlinski, "'Caveat Investor'? The Relevance of the Conduct of the Investor under the Fair and Equitable Treatment Standard" (2006) 55:3 ICQL 527; Andrew Newcombe, "Investor Misconduct" in Armand de Mestral & Céline Lévesque, eds, *Improving International Investment Agreements* (New York: Routledge, 2013) 195 [Newcombe, "Investor Misconduct"]; Muthucumaraswamy Sornarajah, *Resistance and Change in the International Law on Foreign Investment* (Cambridge: Cambridge University Press, 2015) at 300–346.

2 See e.g. Clara Reiner & Christoph Schreuer, "Human Rights and International Investment Arbitration" in Pierre-Marie Dupuy, Francesco Francioni & Ernst-Ulrich Petersmann, eds, *Human Rights in International Investment Law and Arbitration* (Oxford: Oxford University Press, 2009) 82 at 89–90; Moshe Hirsch, "Investment Tribunals and Human Rights: Divergent Paths" in Pierre-Marie Dupuy, Francesco Francioni & Ernst-Ulrich Petersmann, eds, *Human Rights in International Investment Law and Arbitration* (Oxford: Oxford University Press, 2009) 97 at 89–105; Riccardo Pavoni, "Environmental Rights, Sustainable Development, and Investor-State Case Law: A Critical Appraisal" in Pierre-Marie Dupuy, Francesco Francioni & Ernst-Ulrich Petersmann, eds, *Human Rights in International Investment Law and Arbitration* (Oxford: Oxford University Press, 2009) 525; Tamar Meshel, "Human Rights in Investor–State Arbitration: The Human Right to Water and Beyond" (2015) 6 J Int Disp Settlement 277.

More specifically, the idea animating this chapter is to analyze the content of decisions from international investment arbitration tribunals to assess whether arbitrators have demonstrated responsiveness to the negative impact of foreign investors' activities. Echoing the legal pluralist approach that underlies the previous chapter,[3] Chapter 2 considers areas of foreign investors' responsibilities as functionally differentiated normative orders that have emerged in parallel with international investment rules and principles. For present purposes, the examination of the normative integration of foreign investors' responsibilities in international investment arbitration thus focuses on the areas of human rights, environmental protection and corruption.

This analysis shows differences in the way tribunals have considered these areas of responsibilities, pointing once again towards *fragmentation*. In some instances, the reasoning of these tribunals has taken into account the ability of the respondent state to limit the negative impact of foreign investors' activities in the areas of human rights and environmental protection (1). However, several tribunals have avoided engaging with these adverse effects (2). It is here submitted that the lack of a consistent approach demonstrates a fairly weak normative integration of foreign investors' responsibilities with respect to these two areas in international investment arbitration. By contrast, the prohibition of corruption has played a more significant role in influencing the outcome of international investment disputes when there is clear evidence that the claimant was involved in corrupt practices (3). This consistent approach indicates a stronger normative integration regarding this area of foreign investors' responsibilities.

1. Some Considerations of Human Rights and Environmental Issues

Before delving into the analysis of instances in which international investment arbitration tribunals have not fully considered the negative impact related to foreign investors' activities, it must be emphasized that other tribunals have left more room to such a consideration. On several occasions, tribunals have had to decide on the legality of measures adopted by a respondent state in response to harms related to foreign investors' activities in the areas of human rights and environmental protection. While the complexity of these cases cannot be fully captured in the limited number of pages devoted to this analysis, this section seeks to identify the adverse effects that were addressed by the contested measure and the extent to which each tribunal considered these effects in its decision. As suggested by the decisions below, some tribunals have openly taken into account the host state's ability to regulate foreign investors' activities in order to limit their negative impact on human rights and the environment.

One of the earliest instances where such a negative impact has been taken into account can be found in *Southern Pacific Properties (Middle East) Limited v Arab*

3 For a brief summary of legal pluralism in international law, see section 3 of the introduction.

Republic of Egypt (*Southern Pacific Properties*).[4] In this dispute, an agreement between the investor and the Egyptian General Organization for Tourism and Hotels provided the incorporation of a joint venture company to develop tourist complexes near pyramids in Egypt.[5] When a project related to this joint venture was considered as posing a threat to undiscovered antiquities,[6] a public agency withdrew its former approval of the project and a presidential decree cancelled a previous authorization to use part of the lands for tourist activities.[7] Although the tribunal found that "[t]he obligation to pay fair compensation in the event of expropriation applies equally where antiquities are involved,"[8] the tribunal explicitly considered the negative impact of the investment when valuing the claimant's loss. The tribunal thus agreed with the respondent state's contention that "the project was located in an area where the [c]laimants should have known there was a risk that antiquities would be discovered."[9]

In *Emilio Agustín Maffezini v Kingdom of Spain*, the claimant challenged an environmental impact assessment required by a Spanish agency for an investment related to the production and distribution of chemical products.[10] According to the foreign investor, there had been pressures to make the investment before the assessment was completed and additional costs were related to this process.[11] After reviewing the applicable legislation, the tribunal concluded that an environmental impact assessment procedure was "basic for the adequate protection of the environment and the application of appropriate preventive measures,"[12] and that the host state could not be held responsible for decisions taken by the investor regarding this procedure.[13]

Environmental concerns were also at stake in *Parkerings-Companiet AS v Republic of Lithuania*.[14] In that case, a municipality rejected a multi-storey car parks project and refused to conclude specific agreements with the foreign investor's subsidiary.[15] When the municipality authorized another company to build a car park on the same site, the claimant alleged that the host state had violated its most-favored-nation treatment obligation.[16] While the claimant argued that both projects were facing similar circumstances,[17] the tribunal stressed that the

4 *Southern Pacific Properties (Middle East) Limited v Arab Republic of Egypt* (1992), Award, 8 ICSID Review 328 (ICSID) [*Southern Pacific Properties*].
5 *Ibid* at para 43.
6 *Ibid* at para 62.
7 *Ibid* at paras 64–65.
8 *Ibid* at para 159.
9 *Ibid* at para 251.
10 *Emilio Agustin Maffezini v Kingdom of Spain* (2000), Award, 5 ICSID Rep 419 (ICSID).
11 *Ibid* at para 65.
12 *Ibid* at para 67.
13 *Ibid* at para 71.
14 *Parkerings-Companiet AS v Republic of Lithuania* (2007), Award, online: italaw www.italaw.com/sites/default/files/case-documents/ita0619.pdf (accessed 26 March 2018) (ICSID).
15 *Ibid* at para 363.
16 *Ibid* at paras 363 and 374.
17 *Ibid* at para 364.

host state's departments and commissions had already raised environmental concerns pertaining to the initial project.[18] Ultimately, the tribunal concluded that a differentiated treatment between two foreign investors was not in breach of the most-favored-nation treatment clause of the IIA given the large opposition and adverse effects related to the claimant's project.[19]

Suez, Sociedad General de Aguas de Barcelona S.A. and Vivendi Universal S.A. v Argentine Republic and *AWG Group v Argentine Republic* (*Suez et al.*) relate to a concession for water distribution and waste water treatment services.[20] Among the various aspects that were raised by the respondent state to justify the termination of the concession, concerns regarding the level of nitrates in the water were advanced.[21] When assessing whether the termination of the concession violated Argentina's obligation to guarantee fair and equitable treatment to the claimants, the tribunal mentioned the following:

> The alleged high nitrate levels in the water may indeed have been an unjustified pretext. Nonetheless, *there is evidence in the record that such high levels may have existed.* Whether Argentina breached the Concession Contract by terminating it is a matter for the dispute resolution procedures provided in that contract. *In viewing the circumstances as a whole and the situation that existed at the time of the termination*, the tribunal finds that the record is insufficient to establish that Argentina's treatment of the Claimant's investment in terminating the Concession attained the level of violating the fair and equitable standards required by the three applicable [bilateral investment treaties].[22]

Although other measures adopted by Argentina were found to be in violation of its obligations under international investment law,[23] the tribunal considered the foreign investors' responsibility to provide water meeting acceptable levels of nitrate among the circumstances surrounding the measure that was challenged by the claimants.

Similarly, in *Impregilo S.p.A v Argentine Republic* (*Impregilo*), the tribunal relied on a provision from a concession contract for water distribution according to which the concessionaire had to "perform all tasks related to service provision required under the applicable laws to guarantee effective supply to [u]sers, the *protection of public health* and the *rational use of resources.*"[24] When addressing the reasons that led to the termination of the concession, the tribunal also referred to

18 *Ibid* at para 385.

19 *Ibid* at paras 392, 395 and 396.

20 *Suez, Sociedad General de Aguas de Barcelona S.A. and Vivendi Universal S.A. v Argentine Republic* and *AWG Group v Argentine Republic* (2010), Decision on Liability, online: italaw www.italaw.com/sites/default/files/case-documents/ita0826.pdf (accessed 26 March 2018) (ICSID).

21 *Ibid* at paras 36 and 52.

22 *Ibid* at para 246.

23 *Ibid* at para 247.

24 *Impregilo S.p.A. v Argentine Republic* (2011), Award, online: italaw www.italaw.com/sites/default/files/case-documents/ita0418.pdf (accessed 26 March 2018) (ICSID) at para 232 [emphasis added].

several elements recalling that the concessionaire had failed to comply with drinking water and sewerage services quality levels.[25] In light of the reasons provided by the respondent state to support the termination of the concession contract, the tribunal concluded that such termination did not constitute an expropriation.[26] Furthermore, after finding acts of the host states that violated the standard of fair and equitable treatment, the tribunal was unable to conclude that the concession would have been profitable for the foreign investor.[27] Thus, when calculating damages applicable to the case at hand, the tribunal partly relied on the responsibility of the foreign investor in the failure of the concession.[28]

Another decision pertaining to a concession for water and sewage services involving Argentina probably renders the highest level of responsiveness from an international investment tribunal with respect to the area of human rights so far. In *Urbaser S.A. and Consorcio de Aguas Bilbao Bizkaia Ur Partzuergoa v Argentine Republic*, the respondent state advanced several aspects related to water quality to justify the termination of a contract.[29] Amidst these aspects, the tribunal held that the failure to provide funding by the investors could have led to an increased exposure to health diseases caused by excessive nitrate concentrations and was therefore considered as an adequate ground to terminate the contract.[30] The tribunal added that "the failure to ensure compliance with the required [n]itrate levels appears of some gravity, in light of the *threat to the population's health* and in particular small children and other vulnerable people."[31]

Furthermore, when assessing a counterclaim from the respondent state, the tribunal rejected the claimants' principled objection according to which "the asymmetric nature of the [bilateral investment treaty] means that this [t]reaty does not provide for any right of the host [s]tate and, correspondingly, does not impose *any obligation upon the investor*."[32] While referring to the *United Nations Guiding Principles on Business and Human Rights*, the tribunal then addressed the issue of human rights responsibilities for private actors in the following terms:

> The [t]ribunal may mention in this respect that international law accepts corporate social responsibility as a standard of crucial importance for companies operating in the field of international commerce. This standard includes *commitment to comply with human rights in the framework of those entities' operations* conducted in countries other than the country of their seat or incorporation.

25 *Ibid* at paras 263 and 265.
26 *Ibid* at para 283.
27 *Ibid* at para 375.
28 *Ibid* at para 378.
29 *Urbaser S.A. and Consorcio de Aguas Bilbao Bizkaia Ur Partzuergoa v Argentine Republic* (2016), Award, online: italaw www.italaw.com/sites/default/files/case-documents/italaw8136_1.pdf (accessed 26 March 2018) (ICSID) at paras 910–917 and 927–930.
30 *Ibid* at para 912.
31 *Ibid* at para 944 [emphasis added].
32 *Ibid* at para 1182.

> In light of this more recent development, it can no longer be admitted that companies operating internationally are immune from becoming subjects of international law. . . . At this juncture, it is therefore to be admitted that the human right for everyone's dignity and its right for adequate housing and living conditions are complemented by an *obligation* on all parts, public and private parties, ***not to engage in activity aimed at destroying such rights.***[33]

These excerpts show a clear consideration by the tribunal of the negative impact that the claimants' conduct has had on the population's health, as well as a notable openness to impose human rights obligations on foreign investors under international law.

Three additional cases related to the safety of products manufactured by foreign investors suggest that some tribunals took into account the impact of foreign investors' activities when assessing a measure challenged by a claimant. In *Chemtura Corporation v Canada*, the foreign investor challenged measures related to the registration of lindane, a pesticide produced by the claimant and whose use was found to entail risks for the environment and for human health.[34] After stressing that its role was not to determine whether the use of lindane was dangerous or not,[35] the tribunal maintained that these registration measures were in line with legitimate regulatory concerns and the host state's international commitments.[36] After balancing the evidence presented by both parties, the tribunal thus acknowledged that a measure adopted to regulate negative effects resulting from the claimant's activities was consistent with the host state's obligations under international investment law.

The legality under international investment law of the host state's measures intended to ensure the safety of products provided by a foreign investor is also evidenced by *Spyridon Roussalis v Romania*.[37] Among the measures that were challenged by the claimant in that case, Spyridon Roussalis alleged that various orders from the host state's agencies pertaining to its food outlet and refrigerated food warehouse constituted a violation of standards included in an IIA.[38] To justify the measures that it adopted, the respondent state stressed that the investor's facilities did not comply with the food safety regulations and that the measures were taken due to serious public health considerations.[39] The tribunal concluded that "suspending or revoking operating permits may be regarded as a reasonable and appropriate measure to penalize serious irregularities to the

33 *Ibid* at paras 1195 and 1199 [emphasis added].
34 *Chemtura Corporation v Canada* (2010), Award, online: italaw www.italaw.com/sites/default/files/case-documents/ita0149_0.pdf (accessed 26 March 2018) (UNCITRAL) at paras 32 and 44.
35 *Ibid* at para 134.
36 *Ibid* at paras 147, 216 and 266.
37 *Spyridon Roussalis v Romania* (2011), Award, online: italaw www.italaw.com/sites/default/files/case-documents/ita0723.pdf (accessed 26 March 2018) (ICSID).
38 *Ibid* at paras 631–632.
39 *Ibid* at paras 642 and 664.

food and safety regulations."[40] As a result, the claimant failed to prove that the measures at hand were unjustifiable, disproportionate or discriminatory.[41]

In *Apotex Holdings Inc. and Apotex Inc. v United States of America*, agencies of the respondent states found that drugs produced in facilities operated by Apotex Inc. did not meet good manufacturing practices and thus prevented the branch indirectly owned by Apotex Holdings Inc. from receiving these drugs for sale in the United States.[42] Even after emphasizing that it did not receive any evidence that these drugs had caused actual harm to any patient,[43] the tribunal considered the failure of the claimants to address problems related to their manufacturing practices when analyzing the circumstances of the treatment granted to the investors.[44] The tribunal also took into account the claimants' own recognition of material deficiencies occurring in Apotex Inc.'s facilities when assessing whether measures adopted by the host state were consistent with the fair and equitable treatment treaty provision.[45]

The recognition of the host state capacity to adopt measures aimed at limiting negative effects of foreign investors' activities can also be found in international investment disputes involving extractive firms, sometimes in a subtler way. In *Burlington Resources Inc. v Republic of Ecuador* (*Burlington*), the respondent state sought to justify the physical occupation of two exploration and exploitation areas in which the claimant had acquired interests by relying on environmental harms that could have resulted from the shutdown of oil wells.[46] Even if the tribunal was not convinced that such abandonment would have entailed environmental damages and decided that the physical occupation ultimately amounted to an expropriation,[47] it is worth noting that it nevertheless included potential negative effects on the environment in its analysis. In fact, rather than disregarding the relevance of these potential harms, the tribunal concluded that there was a lack of evidence pertaining to any significant risk of environmental damages.[48] Further to counterclaims filed by Ecuador, the tribunal ultimately found that the claimant was liable for the costs of restoring the environment in areas where it operated and ordered the payment of damages amounting to nearly USD 40 million.[49]

40 *Ibid* at para 687.
41 *Ibid* at para 680.
42 *Apotex Holdings Inc. and Apotex Inc. v United States of America* (2014), Award, online: italaw www.italaw.com/sites/default/files/case-documents/italaw3324.pdf (accessed 26 March 2018) (ICSID) at paras 2.18, 2.21, 2.24.
43 *Ibid* at para 3.62.
44 *Ibid* at para 8.76.
45 *Ibid* at para 9.60.
46 *Burlington Resources Inc. v Republic of Ecuador* (2012), Decision on Liability, online: italaw www.italaw.com/sites/default/files/case-documents/italaw1094_0.pdf (accessed 26 March 2018) (ICSID) at paras 169 and 501–502.
47 *Ibid* at para 537.
48 *Ibid* at para 526.
49 *Burlington Resources Inc. v Republic of Ecuador* (2017), Decision on Counterclaims, online: italaw www.italaw.com/sites/default/files/case-documents/italaw8206.pdf (accessed 26 March 2018) (ICSID) at para 1099.

The consideration of environmental harms resulting from the activities of an extractive firm in Ecuador is even more vivid in the interim decision on an environmental counterclaim in *Perenco Ecuador Limited v Republic of Ecuador* (*Perenco*).[50] Amidst a dispute related to breaches by Ecuador of its obligations under an IIA and participation contracts signed by the claimant,[51] the respondent state alleged the existence of an "environmental catastrophe" in the area operated by the investor.[52] Even if this dispute is still pending, several excerpts from the interim decision demonstrate an unambiguous responsiveness from the tribunal to address the negative impact related to extractive activities. In the introduction of its interim decision, the tribunal mentioned that it

> agrees that if a legal relationship between an investor and the [s]tate permits the filing of a claim by the [s]tate for environmental damage caused by the investor's activities and such a claim is substantiated, the [s]tate is entitled to full reparation in accordance with the requirements of the applicable law.[53]

Most importantly, while highlighting several flaws in the investor's environmental practices (*e.g.* failure to conduct biennial environmental audits, irregularities in management of drill cuttings and mud pits, irregularities in wastewater treatment, contaminated soils and irregular waste and chemical management),[54] the tribunal held that it will not dispose of this claim on a simple burden of proof approach.[55]

In *Gold Reserve Inc. v Bolivarian Republic of Venezuela* (*Gold Reserve*), the respondent state sought to justify the revocation of a construction permit by raising the negative effects of mining activities on the environment and the populations located near a mining project.[56] In this regard, the tribunal provided the following statement:

> *The Tribunal acknowledges that a State has a responsibility to preserve the environment and protect local populations living in the area where mining activities are conducted.* However, this responsibility does not exempt a State from complying with its commitments to international investors by searching ways and means to satisfy *in a balanced way* both conditions.[57]

50 *Perenco Ecuador Limited v Republic of Ecuador* (2015), Interim Decision on the Environmental Counterclaim, online: italaw www.italaw.com/sites/default/files/case-documents/italaw6315.pdf (accessed 26 March 2018) (ICSID).

51 *Ibid* at para 4.

52 *Ibid* at para 34.

53 *Ibid* at para 34.

54 *Ibid* at paras 406–446.

55 *Ibid* at para 407.

56 *Gold Reserve Inc. v Bolivarian Republic of Venezuela* (2014), Award, online: italaw www.italaw.com/sites/default/files/case-documents/italaw4009.pdf (accessed 26 March 2018) (ICSID Additional Facility) at paras 593–594.

57 *Ibid* at para 595 [emphasis added].

By insisting on the importance of balancing such concerns with the host state's obligations under the IIA, the tribunal avoided suggesting that such obligations prevent the consideration of adverse effects related to foreign investors' activities. The tribunal also mentioned that the respondent state had the opportunity to assess the environmental impact of the project prior to delivering the construction permit.[58] At the end of the day, the tribunal's finding that the revocation violated the fair and equitable treatment is thus more related to the host state's failure to assess this impact appropriately than to a lack of consideration of foreign investors' responsibilities.[59]

A similar conclusion can be found in another investment dispute between a Canadian mining company and Venezuela. In *Crystallex International Corporation v Bolivarian Republic of Venezuela* (*Crystallex*), the foreign investor challenged the denial of an environmental permit to mining exploitation, among others.[60] According to the respondent state, the reasons justifying such a denial included concerns for the environment and Indigenous communities surrounding the area.[61] Even if the tribunal found that the denial of the environmental permit amounted to a breach of the respondent state's obligations pertaining fair and equitable treatment[62] and expropriation,[63] it nevertheless emphasized the right of the state to address the negative environmental impact of the foreign investor's activities:

> There is no question that Venezuela had the right (and the responsibility) to raise concerns relating to global warming, environmental issues in respect of the Imataca Reserve, biodiversity, and other related issues. The [t]ribunal, however, believes that the way they were put forward by Venezuela in the [p]ermit denial letter present significant elements of arbitrariness and evidences of lack of transparency and consistency.[64]

More recently, a tribunal demonstrated a particularly striking level of responsiveness regarding harms related to a foreign investor's activities in *Copper Mesa Mining Corporation v Republic of Ecuador* (*Copper Mesa Mining*).[65] In this dispute, a mining company submitted a claim pertaining to the alleged illegal revocation and termination of three mining concessions in Ecuador.[66] Even if

58 *Ibid* at para 596
59 *Ibid* at para 600.
60 *Crystallex International Corporation v Bolivarian Republic of Venezuela* (2016), Award, online: italaw www.italaw.com/sites/default/files/case-documents/italaw7194.pdf (accessed 26 March 2018) (ICSID Additional Facility) at para 7.
61 *Ibid* at paras 44 and 324.
62 *Ibid* at para 623.
63 *Ibid* at para 718.
64 *Ibid* at para 591.
65 *Copper Mesa Mining Corporation v Republic of Ecuador* (2015), Award, online: italaw www.italaw.com/sites/default/files/case-documents/italaw7443.pdf (accessed 26 March 2018) (UNCITRAL).
66 *Ibid* at para 1.9.

the tribunal found that the respondent state violated its obligations with respect to expropriation and fair and equitable treatment,[67] it explicitly decided that the claimant's injury regarding one concession was partly caused by its "own contributory negligent acts and omissions and unclean hands."[68] According to the tribunal,

> a foreign investor, by its local agents, whatever the illegal provocation by local residents in the form of road-blocks, violence arson and other impediments, should not resort to recruiting and using armed men, firing guns and spraying mace at civilians, not as an accidental or isolated incident but as part of premeditated, disguised and well-funded plans to take the law into its own hands.[69]

Concretely, the tribunal considered that the claimant's contribution to its own injury amounted to 30 per cent of the compensation owed to the foreign investor.[70]

In *William Ralph Clayton, William Richard Clayton, Douglas Clayton, Daniel Clayton and Bilcon of Delaware v Government of Canada* (*Bilcon*), the majority of the tribunal concluded that the treatment by Canada of the investors' proposal to operate a quarry and a marine terminal constituted breaches of provisions pertaining to the minimum standard of treatment and the national treatment.[71] Among others, the tribunal found that the reliance on the concept of "community core values" in the environmental assessment of the project was unprecedented and constituted a violation of the fair and equitable treatment.[72] Even if one arbitrator considered these efforts to be largely insufficient,[73] it must nevertheless be noted that the majority of the tribunal emphasized the right of the respondent state to limit the negative environmental and social impact of the investment. As mentioned by the majority of the tribunal:

> To avoid any possible misunderstanding, the [t]ribunal has absolutely no doubt that the extent to which community members value various assessable components can be an entirely legitimate part of an environmental assessment. . . . The [t]ribunal takes issue with the 'community core values' approach as

67 *Ibid* at paras 6.67, 6.123,
68 *Ibid* at para 6.97.
69 *Ibid* at para 6.99.
70 *Ibid* at para 6.102.
71 *William Ralph Clayton, William Richard Clayton, Douglas Clayton, Daniel Clayton and Bilcon of Delaware v Government of Canada* (2015), Award on Jurisdiction and Liability, online: italaw www.italaw.com/sites/default/files/case-documents/italaw4212.pdf (accessed 26 March 2018) (UNCITRAL) [*Bilcon*, Award on Jurisdiction and Liability].
72 *Ibid* at paras 450–452 and 503–543.
73 *William Ralph Clayton, William Richard Clayton, Douglas Clayton, Daniel Clayton and Bilcon of Delaware v Government of Canada* (2015), Dissenting Opinion of Professor Donald McRae, online: italaw www.italaw.com/sites/default/files/case-documents/italaw4213.pdf (accessed 26 March 2018) (UNCITRAL) at paras 44–51.

> presented and applied by the [Joint Review Panel], not with the notion that the valuation placed on assessable components can be an integral part of conducting a proper assessment, including the assessment of social effects.[74]

To a certain extent, despite its findings of a violation of treaty provisions, such an award can thus be considered as an example of a normative integration of foreign investors' responsibilities.

A highly anticipated decision involving a tobacco company can also be considered as an instance in which an international investment arbitration tribunal has demonstrated significant responsiveness to the negative impact of the claimants' activities. In *Philip Morris Brands SÀRL, Philip Morris Products S.A. and Abal Hermanos S.A. v Oriental Republic of Uruguay*, the tribunal had to decide whether various tobacco-control measures adopted by the respondent state constituted violations of an IIA signed between Uruguay and Switzerland.[75] After emphasizing the highly addictive and lethal impact of cigarettes,[76] the tribunal often stressed the ability of the respondent state to adopt public health measures. For example, when assessing whether the measures adopted by Uruguay amounted to an expropriation, the tribunal concluded that they were "a valid exercise by Uruguay of its police powers for the protection of public health [and that] they cannot constitute an expropriation of the [c]laimants' investment."[77] Similarly, with respect to the fair and equitable treatment of the investment, the tribunal maintained that "the present case concerns a legislative policy decision taken against the background of a strong scientific consensus as to the lethal effects of tobacco."[78] It then concluded that "[s]ubstantial deference is due in that regard to national authorities' decisions as to the measures which should be taken to address an acknowledged and major public health problem."[79]

At this point, it must be emphasized that the consideration of the adverse impact of foreign investors' activities in international investment arbitration does not guarantee that the tribunal decides the claim in favor of the respondent state. As mentioned above, the tribunals in *Southern Pacific Properties*, *Suez et al.*, *Impregilo*, *Burlington*, *Gold Reserve*, *Crystallex*, *Copper Mesa Mining* and *Bilcon* all concluded that the respondent state had breached its obligations under international investment law. Nevertheless, these cases include some passages where tribunals took into account certain forms of foreign investors' responsibilities. These tribunals demonstrated responsiveness regarding the possibility for respondent states to adopt measures that seek to limit the negative impact of foreign investors' activities even when claims

74 *Bilcon*, Award on Jurisdiction and Liability, *supra* note 71 at para 531.

75 *Philip Morris Brands SÀRL, Philip Morris Products S.A. and Abal Hermanos S.A. v Oriental Republic of Uruguay* (2016), Award, online: italaw www.italaw.com/sites/default/files/case-documents/italaw7417.pdf (accessed 26 March 2018) (ICSID) at para 9.

76 *Ibid* at paras 74 and 133.

77 *Ibid* at para 307.

78 *Ibid* at para 418.

79 *Ibid* at para 418.

primarily focus on issues that reach beyond the environmental or human rights nature of the measures at hand (*e.g.* due process). A strong normative integration of foreign investors' responsibilities in international investment arbitration depends upon the extent to which tribunals acknowledge such a possibility in their reasoning.

Clearly, it would be inaccurate to conclude that all international investment arbitration tribunals have neglected negative effects related to foreign investors' activities when assessing whether a measure had breached a host state's obligations under an IIA. Some tribunals have explicitly acknowledged that the regulation of adverse effects related to foreign investors' activities could remain consistent with IIA provisions or could be considered to prevent the payment of damages. Although such decisions point toward a strong normative integration of foreign investors' responsibilities when considering whether a respondent state has breached its obligations under international investment law, this integration is seriously put into question when one considers decisions reached by other tribunals.

2. The Avoidance of Human Rights and Environmental Issues

By contrast to the aforementioned decisions, several tribunals have given priority to the protections accorded in IIAs and refrained from explicitly taking into account foreign investors' responsibilities in their reasoning. Despite the existence of decisions in which international investment arbitration tribunals have demonstrated some responsiveness in this regard, the lack of consideration for harms related to foreign investors' conduct in several cases shows that such responsibilities in the areas of human rights and environmental protection are still far from being fully integrated in international investment arbitration.

For example, in *Compañía del Desarrollo de Santa Elena, S.A. v Republic of Costa Rica* (*Santa Elena*),[80] a dispute resulted from the compensation to be paid for the expropriation of a property that was supposed to be developed as a touristic resort and a residential community by the investor.[81] The decree adopted by the respondent state expressly mentioned that the purpose of the expropriation was to protect the flora and fauna in the region.[82] The tribunal unequivocally disregarded the environmental justifications underlying the direct expropriation. Prior to determining the amount of the compensation to be paid by the respondent state, the tribunal mentioned the following consideration:

> While an expropriation or taking for environmental reasons may be classified as a taking for a public purpose, and thus may be legitimate, the fact that the property was taken for this reason does not affect either the nature or the

80 *Compañía del Desarrollo de Santa Elena, S.A. v Republic of Costa Rica* (2000), Award, 39 ILM 1317 (ICSID) at para 50.

81 *Ibid* at paras 16 and 54.

82 *Ibid* at para 18.

> measure of compensation to be paid for the taking. *That is, the purpose of protecting the environment for which the property was taken does not alter the legal character of the taking for which adequate compensation must be paid.*[83]

Twelve years after *Santa Elena*, another investment dispute involving Costa Rica was decided without fully taking into account the negative environmental effects of a foreign investment. In *Marion Unglaube and Reinhard Unglaube v Republic of Costa Rica*, the claimants challenged measures adopted by the host state with respect to properties that they owned in the vicinity of the nesting habitat of an endangered turtle species.[84] The respondent state alleged that the protection of nesting sites from human activity and beachside development was essential to protect the leatherback turtle.[85] The tribunal began its analysis by noting that

> [w]hile the subject of the protection of endangered species is an important one, the [t]ribunal finds that the crucial elements of this dispute involve more mundane issues of fact and law as they relate to the legality of the actions in dispute between the [p]arties.[86]

Despite a brief consideration of the environmentally-sensitive surroundings in determining the fair-market value of the investment,[87] the tribunal chose to rely on the *Santa Elena* award to recall that the intent of the host state when adopting an expropriatory measure was less important than the impact of the measure on the investment.[88]

Specific measures adopted by Mexico in regard to the treatment and management of hazardous waste were also challenged by foreign investors in several cases. In *Metalclad Corporation v Mexico*, public authorities partly relied on environmental justifications to deny a municipal construction permit to the foreign investor.[89] According to the tribunal, the decision of public authorities was influenced by the "ecological concerns regarding the environmental effect and impact on the site and surrounding communities."[90] Although the tribunal avowedly recognized the existence of such issues, it ruled that the denial of permit by the host state breached treaty provisions pertaining to fair and equitable treatment and expropriation.[91] More specifically, according to the tribunal:

83 *Ibid* at para 71 [emphasis added].

84 *Marion Unglaube and Reinhard v Republic of Costa Rica* (2012), Award, online: italaw www.italaw.com/sites/default/files/case-documents/ita1052.pdf (accessed 26 March 2018) (ICSID) at para 37.

85 *Ibid* at para 102.

86 *Ibid* at para 167.

87 *Ibid* at para 309.

88 *Ibid* at paras 217–218.

89 *Metalclad Corporation v Mexico* (2001), Award, 40 ILM 36 (ICSID Additional Facility) at para 50.

90 *Ibid* at para 92.

91 *Ibid* at paras 101 and 104–107.

> Even if Mexico is correct that a municipal construction permit was required, the evidence also shows that, as to hazardous waste evaluations and assessments, the federal authority's jurisdiction was controlling and the authority of the municipality only extended to appropriate construction considerations. Consequently, *the denial of the permit by the [m]unicipality by reference to environmental impact considerations in the case of what was basically a hazardous waste disposal landfill, was improper, as was the municipality's denial of the permit for any reason other than those related to the physical construction or defects in the site.*[92]

Furthermore, in *Técnicas Medioambientales Tecmed S.A. v Mexico*, the tribunal assessed the legality of the refusal to renew an existing federal operating license to an investor operating a hazardous waste facility.[93] One of the arguments raised by the respondent state to justify its measure was the negative attitude of the community with respect to the investor's operations.[94] However, echoing the *Santa Elena* award, the arbitration tribunal concluded that measures that seek to prevent harms related to a foreign investor's activities must nonetheless meet the requirements of the IIA:

> [W]e find no principle stating that regulatory administrative actions are *per se* excluded from the scope of the [a]greement, *even if they are beneficial to society as a whole – such as environmental protection* – particularly if the negative or economic impact of such actions on the financial position of the investor is sufficient to neutralize the value, or economic or commercial use of its investment without receiving any compensation whatsoever.[95]

Other environmental issues regarding a foreign investment were at stake in *Empresas Lucchetti, S.A. and Lucchetti Peru S.A. v Republic of Peru*.[96] In that case, the respondent state annulled permits granted for the construction of an industrial pasta plant located near a protected wetland, arguing that such activities could pose environmental problems.[97] Although the tribunal decided that it lacked jurisdiction because the dispute had crystallized before the entry into force of the applicable IIA,[98] it nevertheless clearly disregarded the relevance of environmental harms related to the claimants' activities in reaching this decision:

92 *Ibid* at para 86. See also para 106.
93 *Técnicas Medioambientales Tecmed S.A. v Mexico* (2004), Award, 43 ILM 133 (ICSID Additional Facility) at para 39.
94 *Ibid* at para 49.
95 *Ibid* at para 121 [emphasis added].
96 *Empresas Lucchetti, S.A. and Lucchetti Peru S.A. v Republic of Peru* (2005), Award, online: italaw www.italaw.com/sites/default/files/case-documents/ita0275.pdf (accessed 26 March 2018) (ICSID).
97 *Ibid* at paras 18–19.
98 *Ibid* at para 53 and 58.

"The [t]ribunal does not need to examine the possible motives for the administrative measures in relation to the plant. . . . It is sufficient to note that there were a series of administrative measures that negatively affected the progress of construction."[99]

In contrast to the aforementioned claims that were filed against Argentina with respect to water concessions, the case of *Azurix Corp v Republic of Argentina* is one in which the foreign investor's responsibility was not fully taken into account by the tribunal.[100] Among the various measures that were challenged by the claimant, one was related to the quality of water that was supplied by the investor. Following an algae bloom in a water reservoir, public authorities issued regulations to order a 100% discount on invoices for services provided by the investor during the contamination period.[101] According to the respondent state, the investor was responsible for guaranteeing an efficient provision of water to users, the protection of public health and the rational use of resources.[102] When analyzing the legality of the measure adopted by the host state, the tribunal highlighted the disregard of the public authorities' contribution with respect to the algae incident.[103] In fact, the tribunal ruled that "governments have to be vigilant and protect public health of citizens but the statements and actions of the provincial authorities contributed to the crisis rather than assisting in solving it."[104] Therefore, when discussing whether the series of measures adopted by the respondent state was tantamount to expropriation, the tribunal argued that "the issue is not so much whether the measure concerned is legitimate and serves a public purpose, but *whether it is a measure that, being legitimate and serving a public purpose, should give rise to a compensation claim*."[105] Although the state retains the ability to limit harms related to the activities of a foreign investor, such a conclusion suggests that the measure must not frustrate the interests of the private actor.

The primary focus of some investment arbitration tribunals on the protection accorded to foreign investors is also exemplified by *Glamis Gold, Ltd v United States of America*.[106] In this case, the claimant challenged delays by federal agencies in analyzing a mining project and environmental regulations requiring the complete backfilling of open-pit mines located near a Native American sacred site.[107] Interestingly, several third parties used *amicus curiae* submissions to address issues

99 *Ibid* at para 29.

100 *Azurix Corp v Republic of Argentina* (2006), Award, online: italaw www.italaw.com/sites/default/files/case-documents/ita0061.pdf (accessed 26 March 2018) (ICSID).

101 *Ibid* at paras 124–126.

102 *Ibid* at para 129.

103 *Ibid* at para 144.

104 *Ibid* at para 144.

105 *Ibid* at para 310 [emphasis added].

106 *Glamis Gold, Ltd v United States of America* (2009), Award, 48 ILM 1039 (UNCITRAL) [*Glamis*].

107 *Ibid*, at para 11.

pertaining to the responsibilities of the investor in that case.[108] For example, the submission from the Quechan Indian Nation argued that the tribunal should interpret the provisions of the IIA in light of Indigenous peoples' rights[109] and emphasized the emergence of corporate social responsibility norms at the international level.[110] Environmental organizations also pointed out negative effects related to hard rock mining in another *amicus curiae* submission.[111] Ultimately, the tribunal dismissed the claim.[112] Despite a brief consideration of harms related to the proposed mining project to conclude that the measures adopted by the host states were not arbitrary,[113] it nonetheless clearly appears that the human rights and environmental aspects related to the activities of the private actor were not taken into account in the final award. In referring to these issues, the tribunal stated:

> The [t]ribunal is aware that the decision in this proceeding has been awaited by private and public entities concerned with environmental regulation, the interests of indigenous peoples, and the tension sometimes seen between private rights in property and the need of the State to regulate the use of the property. However, given the Tribunal's holdings, *the Tribunal is not required to decide many of the most controversial issues raised in this proceeding*. The Tribunal observes that a few awards have made statements not required by the case before it. *The Tribunal does not agree with this tendency; it believes that its case specific mandate and the respect demanded for the difficult task faced squarely by some future tribunal instead argues for it to confine its decision to the issues presented.*[114]

Another example of the weak normative integration of foreign investors' responsibilities in the area of human rights can be found in a procedural order regarding the arbitration proceedings in *Bernhard Von Pezold and others v Republic of Zimbabwe* (*Von Pezold*) and *Border Timbers Limited, Border Timbers International (Private) Limited, and Hangani Development Co. (Private) Limited v Republic of Zimbabwe* (*Border Timbers*).[115] Through this order, an application by a human rights non-governmental organization and Indigenous communities was

108 *Ibid* at paras 267–286.

109 *Glamis Gold, Ltd v United States of America* (2006), Quechan Indian Nation Supplemental Non-Disputing Party Submission, online: USTR www.state.gov/documents/organization/75016.pdf (accessed 26 March 2018) (UNCITRAL) at 1.

110 *Ibid* at 12–13.

111 *Glamis Gold, Ltd v United States of America* (2006), Sierra Club and Earthworks Non-Disputing Party Submission, online: USTR www.state.gov/documents/organization/74832.pdf (accessed 26 March 2018) (UNCITRAL) at paras 3–4.

112 *Glamis, supra* note 106 at paras 14, 18, 26, 534–536 and 830.

113 *Ibid* at para 805.

114 *Ibid* at para 8 [emphasis added].

115 *Bernhard Von Pezold and others v Republic of Zimbabwe and Border Timbers Limited, Border Timbers International (Private) Limited, and Hangani Development Co. (Private) Limited v Republic of Zimbabwe* (2012), Procedural Order No 2, online: italaw www.italaw.com/sites/default/files/case-documents/ita1043.pdf (accessed 26 March 2018) (ICSID).

denied by the tribunal in a case involving questions of access to land in Zimbabwe. In addition to noting that the circumstances of the application gave rise to "legitimate doubts as to the independence or neutrality of the [p]etitioners,"[116] the tribunal unambiguously stressed that it was not persuaded that the consideration of international human rights law was part of its mandate.[117] More specifically, the tribunal did not consider that the proposed submission would address "a matter within the scope of the dispute," recalling that "[t]he disputes in these conjoined arbitrations arise out of the allegedly unlawful measures taken by the [r]espondent against the [c]laimants and their investments."

Such a narrow perspective as to what should be taken into account by an international investment arbitration tribunal was echoed in a final award related to this dispute.[118] The latter involved land policies adopted by Zimbabwe with a view to favoring Black Indigenous peoples.[119] Despite acknowledging that the case at hand was rooted in deep context and history,[120] the tribunal sought to frame the dispute as being solely limited to international investment law. As mentioned by the tribunal in the introduction of the award:

> Oftentimes during these proceedings, members of the [t]ribunal had to remind themselves that their remit was not one of a commission of inquiry into what has been described as the 'March of History', but rather *strictly that of an [a]rbitral [t]ribunal mandated to adjudicate a dispute or disputes in accordance with the Convention of the International Centre for Settlement of Investment Disputes . . . and applicable law.*[121]

More recently, the tribunal in *Bear Creek Mining Corporation v Republic of Peru* demonstrated a weak level of responsiveness pertaining to the negative impact of a Canadian mining company with respect to several social and environmental matters.[122] This dispute revolved around decrees that ended the claimant's rights to operate a mining concession located close to Indigenous communities.[123] Interestingly, the tribunal summarized *amicus curiae* submissions that emphasized the risks posed by the operations for the population and the environment, as well as the lack of a social license to develop the mining project.[124] However,

116 *Ibid* at para 56.

117 *Ibid* at para 59.

118 *Bernhard Friedrich Arnd Rüdiger Von Pezold and others v Republic of Zimbabwe* (2015), Award, online: italaw www.italaw.com/sites/default/files/case-documents/italaw7095_0.pdf (accessed 26 March 2018) (ICSID).

119 *Ibid* at para 3.

120 *Ibid* at para 2.

121 *Ibid* at para 4 [emphasis added].

122 *Bear Creek Mining Corporation v Republic of Peru* (2017), Award, online: italaw www.italaw.com/sites/default/files/case-documents/italaw9381.pdf (accessed 26 March 2018) (ICSID).

123 *Ibid* at paras 202–203.

124 *Ibid* at paras 218–230.

after finding that one of the decrees adopted by the respondent state effected an indirect expropriation,[125] the majority of the tribunal refused to acknowledge that the claimant contributed to the social unrest that led to the adoption of this decree. The tribunal thus decided that

> [w]hile . . . further actions by [c]laimant would have been feasible, on the basis of the continued coordination with and support by [r]espondent's authorities, the [t]ribunal concludes that [c]laimant could take it for granted to have complied with all legal requirements with regard to its outreach to the local communities and that [r]espondent, after its continuous approval and support with [c]laimant's conduct, cannot in hindsight claim that this conduct was contrary to the [International Labour Organization] Convention or was insufficient, and caused and contributed to the social unrest in the region.[126]

Most importantly, when assessing the value of the investment, the majority of the tribunal explicitly maintained that Indigenous communities were not a respondent party in this dispute and that their opposition to the mining project did not relieve the respondent state from paying damages for its breach of the IIA.[127]

Relying on the above-mentioned cases, two conclusions can be drawn. First, *amicus curiae* submissions present a procedural means through which third parties can address human rights and environmental protection issues within international investment arbitration. However, as demonstrated by the procedural order in *Von Pezold* and *Border Timber*, the authorization to submit an *amicus curiae* brief remains far from automatic. Furthermore, the approval to submit these briefs appears to be primarily driven by efforts to increase transparency rather than to include foreign investors' responsibilities in the reasoning of the arbitrators.[128] Even when submissions are authorized, tribunals are thus not obliged to consider, either explicitly or implicitly, arguments that are provided by *amicus curiae.*[129] Given that these briefs generally appear to have little effects, if any, on the outcome of a particular case, addressing foreign investors' responsibilities through these submissions falls short of ensuring a strong normative integration of these responsibilities in international investment arbitration.

125 *Ibid* at paras 415–416.

126 *Ibid* at para 567.

127 *Ibid* at paras 657 and 666.

128 See Reiner & Schreuer, *supra* note 2 at 93.

129 See *Glamis*, *supra* note 106 at paras 8 and 274. See also James Harrison, "Human Rights Arguments in Amicus Curiae Submissions: Promoting Social Justice?" in Pierre-Marie Dupuy, Francesco Francioni & Ernst-Ulrich Petersmann, eds, *Human Rights in International Investment Law and Arbitration* (Oxford: Oxford University Press, 2009) 396 at 415; Patrick Dumberry & Gabrielle Dumas-Aubin, "When and How Allegations of Human Rights Violations can be Raised in Investor–State Arbitration" (2012) 13:3 J World Invest & Trade 349 at 371.

Second, several tribunals have ignored adverse effects related to private actors' activities when addressing an investor claim. There has been a reluctance and non-engagement by some investment arbitration tribunals with issues pertaining to human rights and environmental protection in several instances.[130] When a measure had been adopted by a host state to limit harms related to foreign investors' activities in these areas, several arbitration tribunals have decided that the protection accorded to foreign investment should prevail. Despite a more nuanced approach adopted by other tribunals, the lack of consideration of the negative impact of foreign investors' activities in several instances suggests an overall weak normative integration of human rights and environmental issues in international investment arbitration.

3. A More Consistent Consideration of Corruption

In a way that sharply contrasts with the lack of consistency of investment arbitration tribunals to account for harmful foreign investors' activities in the areas of human rights and environmental protection, evidence of corrupt practices by foreign investors has had a more significant influence on the outcome of international investment disputes. Such practices often fall under the broader categories of "investor misconduct," which can be understood as including fraud and illegality.[131] Recalling that the present research focuses on foreign investors' responsibilities for harms caused in the communities in which they operate, this section is limited to cases where investment arbitration tribunals have had to deal with allegations of corruption on the claimant's part.[132]

The importance of considering foreign investors' responsibilities with respect to the area of corruption has not always been strongly integrated in international investment arbitration. In this regard, it is worth noting that the majority of the tribunal in *Southern Pacific Properties (Middle East) Limited v Arab Republic of Egypt* only tangentially addressed allegations of corruption in 1992.[133] By contrast, a dissenting arbitrator in that case emphasized that overlooking the significance of such allegations seemed "not to be in consistence with the due legal

130 See Reiner & Schreuer, *supra* note 2 at 90; Hirsch, *supra* note 2 at 106–107; Sornarajah, *supra* note 1 at 472; Jorge Daniel Taillant & Jonathan Bonnitcha, "International Investment Law and Human Rights" in Marie-Claire Cordonier Segger, Markus W Gehring & Andrew Newcombe, eds, *Sustainable Development in World Investment Law* (Alphen aan den Rijn: Kluwer Law International, 2011) 59 at 78; Andreas Kulick, *Global Public Interest in International Investment Law* (Cambridge: Cambridge University Press, 2012) at 258 and 300; Kate Miles, *The Origins of International Investment Law: Empire, Environment and the Safeguarding of Capital* (Cambridge: Cambridge University Press, 2013) at 210.

131 See Newcombe, "Investor Misconduct", *supra* note 1 at 196; Andrew Newcombe, "Investor Misconduct: Jurisdiction, Admissibility or Merits?" in Chester Brown & Kate Miles, eds, *Evolution in Investment Treaty Law and Arbitration* (Cambridge: Cambridge University Press, 2011) 187 at 188 [Newcombe, "Investor Misconduct: Jurisdiction"].

132 For an analysis of cases that imply fraudulent and illegal acts from the investor, see generally Newcombe, "Investor Misconduct", *ibid*; Jarrod Hepburn, "In Accordance with Which Host State Laws? Restoring the 'Defence' of Investor Illegality in Investment Arbitration" (2014) 5 J Int'l Disp Settlement 531.

133 *Southern Pacific Properties*, *supra* note 4 at para 204.

protection of the [r]espondent's inherent right of defense."[134] After explicitly referring to the provision of the *Guidelines for Multinational Enterprises* regarding the prohibition of corruption and considering efforts made by the respondent state to provide evidence of corrupt practices adopted by the claimant, the dissenting arbitrator maintained that a closer scrutiny of these allegations was necessary.[135] Subsequently, several tribunals have referred to the importance of addressing allegations of corrupt practices and the impact of these practices if the respondent state could provide evidence that they were related to the investment.[136]

This impact appears to be even more concrete when considering cases in which tribunals have found such evidence. In *World Duty Free Company Limited v Republic of Kenya* (*World Duty Free*),[137] the investment arbitration tribunal's jurisdiction was based on a contract between an investor and the host state, without relying on an IIA. While the investor alleged that the respondent state expropriated its investment, a submission from the investor showed that the latter made a "personal contribution" of US$2 million to the President of the Republic of Kenya in order to contract.[138] In deciding that a contract obtained through acts of bribery prevented an investor claim, the tribunal made the following statement:

> [I]n light of domestic laws and *international conventions relating to corruption*, and in light of the decisions taken in the matter by courts and international tribunals, *this Tribunal is convinced that bribery is contrary to international public policy of most, if not all States, or to use another formula, to transnational public policy*. Thus, *claims based on contracts of corruption or on contracts obtained by corruption cannot be upheld by this Arbitral Tribunal*.[139]

Of particular relevance for present purposes is the fact that the tribunal in *World Duty Free* extensively relied on international treaties and other international instruments addressing the prohibition of corruption to affirm the existence

134 *Southern Pacific Properties (Middle East) Limited v Arab Republic of Egypt* (1992), Dissenting Opinion, 8 ICSID Review 400 (ICSID) at 401.

135 *Ibid* at 462–466.

136 See e.g. *Wena Hotels Ltd v Arab Republic of Egypt* (2000), Award, 41 ILM 896 (ICSID) at para 111; *International Thunderbird Gaming Corporation v United Mexican States* (2005), Separate Opinion, online: italaw www.italaw.com/sites/default/files/case-documents/ita0432.pdf (accessed 26 March 2018) (UNCITRAL) at para 112; *Gustav F W Hamester GmbH& Co KG v Republic of Ghana* (2010), Award, online: italaw www.italaw.com/sites/default/files/case-documents/ita0396.pdf (accessed 26 March 2018) (ICSID) at para 123; *Niko Resources (Bangladesh) Ltd v People's Republic of Bangladesh et al* (2013), Decision on Jurisdiction, online: italaw www.italaw.com/sites/default/files/archive/italaw1561_0.pdf (accessed 26 March 2018) (ICSID) at paras 434 and 440–441; *Fraport AG Frankfurt Airport Services Worldwide v Republic of the Philippines* (2014), Award, online: italaw www.italaw.com/sites/default/files/case-documents/italaw4114.pdf (accessed 26 March 2018) (ICSID) at para 479.

137 *World Duty Free Company Limited v Republic of Kenya* (2006), Award, 46 ILM 339 (ICSID).

138 *Ibid* at para 66.

139 *Ibid* at para 157 [emphasis added].

of an international public policy against corruption.[140] The codification process developed in parallel to international investment law thus played an undeniable role in consolidating an international norm against corruption that reached the status of international public policy and that ultimately led to the dismissal of the foreign investor's claim.

Seven years after *World Duty Free*, *Metal-Tech Ltd v Republic of Uzbekistan* (*Metal-Tech*) demonstrated the influence of the prohibition against corruption in the context of an investment dispute based on an IIA.[141] In that case, the investor claimed that Uzbekistan had breached its obligations with respect to non-discrimination, full protection and security, expropriation, as well as fair and equitable treatment.[142] However, the respondent state challenged the jurisdiction of the tribunal by alleging that the claimant "engaged in corruption and made fraudulent and material misrepresentations to gain approval for its investment."[143] After emphasizing that the prohibition of corruption by the host state remained consistent with international law and the laws of several states,[144] the tribunal found evidence of corruption by the investor and ruled that the investment was implemented in a way that was inconsistent with the legality requirement found in the IIA.[145] Ultimately, these findings entailed a lack of jurisdiction of the tribunal.[146] In the conclusion of the award, the tribunal emphasized the importance of dismissing a claim pertaining to an investment that was made through corruption as follows:

> While reaching the conclusion that the claims are barred as a result of corruption, the Tribunal is sensitive to the ongoing debate that findings on corruption often come down heavily on claimants, while possibly exonerating defendants that may have themselves been involved in the corrupt acts. . . . The idea, however, is not to punish one party at the cost of the other, but *rather to ensure the promotion of the rule of law, which entails that a court or a tribunal cannot grant assistance to a party that has engaged in a corrupt act.*[147]

Allegations of corrupt practices by a foreign investor have played a more nuanced role in *Hesham Talaat M. Al-Warraq v Republic of Indonesia* (*Al-Warraq*).[148] Given the complexity of the allegations at hand, the tribunal initially decided that

140 *Ibid* at paras 143–145.
141 *Metal-Tech Ltd v Republic of Uzbekistan* (2013), Award, online: italaw www.italaw.com/sites/default/files/case-documents/italaw3012.pdf (accessed 26 March 2018) (ICSID).
142 *Ibid* at para 107.
143 *Ibid* at para 110.
144 *Ibid* at paras 290–292.
145 *Ibid* at para 372.
146 *Ibid* at para 373.
147 *Ibid* at para 389 [emphasis added].
148 *Hesham Talaat M. Al-Warraq v Republic of Indonesia* (2014), Final Award, online: italaw www.italaw.com/sites/default/files/case-documents/italaw4164.pdf (accessed 26 March 2018) (UNCITRAL) [*Al-Warraq*, Final Award].

parties' claims regarding allegations of corruption and the solicitation of bribes had to be dealt with at the merits phase of the arbitration.[149] In the final award, the tribunal concluded that the respondent state's failure to comply with basic elements of justice when conducting a criminal proceeding against the foreign investor violated the fair and equitable treatment that the claimant was entitled to receive by virtue of the most-favored-nation treatment provision found in the applicable IIA.[150] Although the final award does not focus directly on the claimant's conviction for corruption under Indonesian law, the tribunal relied on the effect of Article 9 of the *Agreement on Promotion, Protection and Guarantee of Investments Among Member States of the Organisation of the Islamic Conference* to conclude that the claimant's fraudulent acts were prejudicial to the public interest.[151] As a result, the claimant was "prevented from pursuing his claim for fair and equitable treatment" and could not request compensation under the applicable IIA.[152] Put simply, the tribunal emphasized that "the doctrine of '*clean hands*' render[ed] the Claimant's claim inadmissible."[153]

In addition to the three above-mentioned cases, the practice of corruption arguably played an indirect role with respect to the outcome of the *Siemens AG v Argentina* case.[154] Although the investor was awarded more than US$200 million by an international investment tribunal, several allegations of investor corrupt practices were revealed by foreign anti-corruption agencies.[155] While the decision was subject to a revision proceeding under Article 51 of the *Convention on the Settlement of Investment Disputes between States and Nationals of Other States*,[156] Siemens chose to abandon the award. Overall, the agreement reached between the investor and Argentina suggests that the practice of corruption by the private actor would have had an impact on the procedure and that the outcome of the revision process was predictable.

149 *Hesham Talaat M. Al-Warraq v Republic of Indonesia* (2012), Award on Respondent's Preliminary Objections to Jurisdiction and Admissibility, online: italaw www.italaw.com/sites/default/files/case-documents/italaw3174_0.pdf (accessed 26 March 2018) (UNCITRAL) at para 99.

150 *Al-Warraq*, Final Award, *supra* note 148 at paras 555 and 621.

151 *Ibid* at paras 632 and 634–640.

152 *Ibid* at paras 648 and 652.

153 *Ibid* at para 646 [emphasis in the original].

154 *Siemens A.G. v Argentine Republic* (2007), Award, 14 ICSID Reports 518 (ICSID).

155 For the information pertaining to this paragraph, see Jason Webb Yackee, "Investment Treaties and Investor Corruption: An Emerging Defense for Host States" (2012) 52 Va J Int'l L 723 at 724–725; Joe Tirado, Matthew Page & Daniel Meagher, "Corruption Investigations by Governmental Authorities and Investment Arbitration: An Uneasy Relationship" (2014) 29 ICSID Rev 493 at 507–509; Thomas Kendra & Anna Bonini, "Dealing with Corruption Allegations in International Investment Arbitration: Reaching a Procedural Consensus?" (2014) 31 J Int'l Arb 439 at 444–445.

156 *Convention on the Settlement of Disputes between States and Nationals of Other States*, 18 March 1965, 575 UNTS 159 (entered into force 14 October 1966), art 51.

Similarly, allegations of corrupt practices played an indirect but decisive role in the international investment dispute between companies incorporated in the Netherlands and the Republic of Azerbaijan.[157] While the tribunal in *Azpetrol International Holdings B.V., Azpetrol Group B.V. and Azpetrol Oil Services Group B.V. v Republic of Azberijan* (*Azpetrol*) had to determine whether the parties had previously reached an agreement to settle the case,[158] this settlement agreement followed an application by the respondent state to dismiss the proceedings on the grounds of admission of bribery by the claimant.[159] Once the tribunal concluded that the parties had reached a binding settlement agreement, it emphasized that the claimants "did not contest that the terms of the settlement would have finally disposed all matters in dispute."[160] Once again, the outcome of the dispute in *Azpetrol* suggests that admission of corruption by the claimant had a considerable effect with respect to the protection that can be sought by a foreign investor under international investment arbitration.

Of course, one might suggest that the outcome of cases such as *World Duty Free* and *Metal-Tech* neglects the involvement of state officials in corruption and can ultimately be counterproductive in fighting corruption.[161] In line with *Al-Warraq*, some stress the need to consider allegations of corrupt acts perpetrated by the claimant as a question of admissibility of the claim or at the merits stage of the arbitration.[162] While they are crucial to consider when reflecting on the role of international investment arbitration in the fight against corruption, these issues fall beyond the analysis of the normative integration of foreign investors' responsibilities in international investment law.[163]

Overall, the consistency of the approach taken by tribunals when dealing with corrupt practices is striking in contrast to the consideration of human rights and environmental issues. Although this consideration of corrupt practices by

157 *Azpetrol International Holdings B.V., Azpetrol Group B.V. and Azpetrol Oil Services Group B.V. v Republic of Azberijan* (2009), Award, online: italaw www.italaw.com/sites/default/files/case-documents/ita0059.pdf (accessed 26 March 2018) (ICSID).

158 *Ibid* at para 1.

159 *Ibid* at para 7.

160 *Ibid* at para 105.

161 See e.g. Tamar Meshel, "The Use and Misuse of the Corruption Defence in International Investment Arbitration" (2013) 30:3 J Int'l Arb 267 at 274; Kulick, *supra* note 130 at 321.

162 See *Fraport AG Frankfurt Airport Services Worldwide* (2007), Dissenting Opinion of Mr. Bernardo M. Cremades, online: italaw www.italaw.com/sites/default/files/case-documents/ita0340.pdf (accessed 26 March 2018) (ICSID) at paras 37–38 and 40. See also Newcombe, "Investor Misconduct: Jurisdiction", *supra* note 131 at 198–200; Kulick, *ibid* at 332–341.

163 For an analysis of various procedural issues pertaining to allegations of corruption, see generally Richard Kreindler, "Legal Consequences of Corruption in International Investment Arbitration: An Old Challenge with New Answers" in Laurent Lévy & Yves Derain, eds, *Liber Amicorum en l'honneur de Serge Lazareff* (Paris: Editions Pedone, 2011) 383 [Kreindler, "Legal Consequences"]; Newcombe, "Investor Misconduct: Jurisdiction", *ibid*; Cameron A Miles, "Corruption, Jurisdiction and Admissibility in International Investment Claims" (2012) 3:2 J Int'l Disp Settlement 329 at 330 [Miles, "Corruption"]. See also Carolyn B Lamm, Brody K Greenwald & Kristen M Young, "From World Duty Free to Metal-Tech: A Review of International Investment Treaty Arbitration Cases Involving Allegations of Corruption" (2014) 29 ICSID Rev 328 at 342–349; Kendra & Bonini, *supra* note 155.

investment arbitration tribunals extensively depends upon evidentiary issues,[164] the impact of this finding on international investment arbitration is unequivocal: an investor resorting to corruption loses the ability to seek redress.[165] Llamzon summarizes this impact in the following terms:

> For those who maintain that investment arbitration is an unfair system that is skewed in favor of the foreign investors, the idea that corruption has been actively and frequently used by States *against* investors, that this defense can potentially negate any and all claims made by investors if successful, *and* that there would be no such preclusive effect if corruption was invoked by the investor, may come as a surprise.[166]

Even without explicit IIA provisions with respect to the prohibition of corrupt acts by foreign investors, many tribunals have emphasized that such an outcome directly results from the wide consensus with respect to the prohibition of corruption as being an integral part of international public policy, as evidenced by several international instruments codifying the prohibition of corruption.[167] Ultimately, the cases summarized above demonstrate that foreign investors' responsibilities in the area of corruption are more strongly integrated within international investment arbitration than allegations of human rights violations and environmental harms.

Conclusion

Analyzing the normative integration of foreign investors' responsibilities in international investment law goes beyond a consideration of provisions included in IIAs. It is in this regard that Chapter 2 of this book has offered an examination of the extent to which international investment arbitration tribunals demonstrate responsiveness to harms related to foreign investors' conduct when assessing the consistency of a measure adopted by a respondent state with its obligations under international law. Once again, the consideration of areas of foreign investors' responsibilities as functionally differentiated normative orders that evolve in parallel with international investment rules and principles is instructive. In order to provide a more nuanced

164 See e.g. Kreindler, "Legal Consequences", *ibid* at 387; Cecily Rose, "Circumstantial Evidence, Adverse Influences, and Findings of Corruption: Metal-Tech Ltd. v. The Republic of Uzbekistan" (2014) 15 J World Invest & Trade 747 at 754; Tirado et al, *supra* note 155 at 496–498; Lamm et al, *ibid* at 330–341.

165 See e.g. Miles, "Corruption", *supra* note 163 at 330; Aloysius Llamzon, "State Responsibility for Corruption: The Attribution Asymmetry in International Investment Arbitration" (2013) 10:3 TDM 1 at 5; Lamm et al, *ibid* at 239.

166 Llamzon, *ibid* at 38–39 [emphasis in the original and footnotes omitted].

167 See e.g. Pierre Lalive, "Ordre public transnational (ou réellement international) et arbitrage international" (1986) 3 Rev arb 329 at 337 and 357–359; Giorgio Sacerdoti, "Corruption in Investment Transactions: Policy Initiatives, Legal Principles and Arbitral Practice" (2009) 24:2 ICSID Rev 565 at 578; Kreindler, "Legal Consequences", *supra* note 163 at 383 and 388; Kulick, *supra* note 130 at 317.

response when determining whether international investment arbitration tribunals consider the negative impact of foreign investors' activities in local communities in which they operate and the environment, the analysis above has considered the areas of human rights, environmental protection and corruption.

This examination allows a conclusion that contrasts with the perception that international investment arbitration tribunals totally fail to impose responsibilities on foreign investors when deciding a claim. Echoing the findings of Chapter 1 with respect to the content of IIAs, the analysis above suggests that the normative integration of foreign investors' responsibilities in international investment arbitration is fragmented. On the one hand, international tribunals have failed to adopt a consistent approach with respect to the negative impact that foreign investors' activities can have on human rights and the environment. It is plain that several tribunals have taken into consideration the effects of foreign investors' activities on the environment or human rights when assessing the legality of a measure adopted by a respondent state. However, international investment case law includes several examples of decisions in which arbitrators have merely refused to address any issues that reach beyond the protection of investments and investors. Without seeking to neglect the contribution brought by international tribunals that have engaged with this negative impact and that have demonstrated responsiveness, this lack of consistency points toward a weak normative integration of responsibilities in international arbitration for these two areas. On the other hand, when international investment arbitration tribunals are confronted with evidence of corruption on the side of the claimants, these tribunals have more consistently decided that an investor whose activities are tainted with corrupt practices loses the ability to seek redress under international arbitration. Such an approach unambiguously suggests a stronger normative integration.

Taken as a whole, Chapter 1 and Chapter 2 thus demonstrate the fragmented normative integration of foreign investors' responsibilities in international investment law. It is here suggested that this fragmentation is a key characteristic of the evolving codification of foreign investors' responsibilities in a context of neoliberal globalization. Yet, with a view to providing a more complete analysis of this phenomenon, a macro-level analysis of the evolving codification process must also seek to explain the reasons underlying this fragmentation. In other words, having acknowledged that foreign investors' responsibilities in the area of corruption benefit from a stronger normative integration in international investment law than other areas of responsibilities, one must now turn to inherent relations of power between the actors involved in the international investment lawmaking process to explain the differences existing between these areas. It is in this regard that the next chapter provides a critical account of this fragmented normative integration.

3 Inherent Relations of Power and Interests

Introduction

A macro-level analysis of the evolving codification of foreign investors' responsibilities in a context of neoliberal globalization would be incomplete without an explicit consideration of power relations that underlie the elaboration of rules pertaining to international investment and foreign investors. The analysis provided in the previous chapters suggests a weak normative integration of foreign investors' responsibilities in international investment law for the areas of human rights, environmental protection and labour rights. However, references to the necessity of punishing corrupt practices by foreign investors in some international investment agreements (IIAs) as well as the consistency with which international investment arbitration tribunals have dealt with evidence of corrupt practices by claimants remain puzzling. One must go beyond the legal pluralist approach to account for elements driving this fragmented normative integration of foreign investors' responsibilities in international investment law.

Chapter 3 explores inherent relations of power and the interests of powerful actors involved in international investment lawmaking to explain this fragmentation. From the outset, it is widely acknowledged that multiple actors are actively involved in the development of norms pertaining to the regulation of international investment.[1] Even if most countries act as both importers and exporters of foreign direct investment (FDI), the interests of states hosting stocks of foreign capital can clash with the interests of states that are the home of numerous foreign investors. This international investment lawmaking process also includes non-state actors. As emphasized by Muchlinski, "[t]he major investors, in particular [multinational enterprises], are at the heart of legal developments in this field, even if they are not formally its subjects."[2]

1 See e.g. Peter Muchlinski, "Policy Issues" in Peter Muchlinski, Frederico Ortino & Christoph Schreuer, eds, *The Oxford Handbook of International Investment Law* (Oxford: Oxford University Press, 2008) 3 at 7–8 [Muchlinski, "Policy Issues"]; Muthucumaraswamy Sornarajah, *The International Law on Foreign Investment*, 3rd ed (Cambridge: Cambridge University Press, 2010) at 6 and 61 [Sornarajah, *The International Law*].

2 Muchlinski, "Policy Issues", *ibid* at 7.

Furthermore, nongovernmental organizations (NGOs) and intergovernmental organizations also participate in the elaboration and the implementation of rules regulating international investment.

Acknowledging that a plurality of actors can play a role in the international investment lawmaking process must nevertheless come with the recognition that potential conflicts are likely to emerge and that the most powerful actors can disproportionally influence its outcome.[3] It is in this regard that the adoption of a critical approach appears as a useful tool to supplement the analysis presented in the previous chapters. In order to account for inherent relations of power and conflicting interests that underlie the codification of foreign investors, this chapter combines a critical constructivist approach with a critical discourse analysis.[4] In addition to acknowledging the role of non-state actors in international relations, the critical constructivist approach sheds light on the influence of the most powerful actors' interests in the mutual constitution of agents and social structures such as international norms. With a view to examining this mutual constitution, publicly available statements submitted by actors participating in consultation processes led by intergovernmental organizations can be analyzed by using a critical discourse analysis.

The analysis presented below supports the proposition that consultations pertaining to the codification of foreign investors' responsibilities are characterized by attempts from powerful actors to safeguard their interests. After identifying which actors appear as the most powerful protagonists with respect to the elaboration of rules regulating international investment and foreign investors (1), it sheds light on interests and power relations underlying the codification of foreign investors' responsibilities in various areas. While several actors support the adoption of international legal norms codifying foreign investors' responsibilities, other actors that can directly influence the outcome of the international investment lawmaking process seek to discourage the adoption of these initiatives in the areas of human rights, environmental protection and labour rights (2). By contrast, an analysis of the discourse of actors involved in consultations concerning the prohibition of corruption suggests that such efforts are in line with the interests of actors that can exercise direct power over the regulation of international investment, amidst broad support from other actors (3). Combined with the examination provided in the previous chapters, the analysis below shows that the extent to which foreign investors' responsibilities are normatively integrated in international investment law is ***consistent with most powerful actors' interests.***

3 See e.g. A Claire Cutler, "The Privatization of Authority in the Global Political Economy" in Gary Teeple & Stephen McBride, eds, *Relations of Global Power: Neoliberal Order and Disorder* (Toronto: University of Toronto Press, 2011) 41 at 50; Celine Tan, "Navigating New Landscapes: Socio-Legal Mapping of Plurality and Power in International Economic Law" in Amanda Perry-Kessaris, ed, *Socio-Legal Approaches to International Economic Law: Text, Context, Subtext* (New York: Routledge, 2013) 19 at 22 and 28; David Schneiderman, "Power and Production in Global Legal Pluralism: An International Political Economy Approach" in Amanda Perry-Kessaris, ed, *Socio-Legal Approaches to International Economic Law: Text, Context, Subtext* (New York: Routledge, 2013) 98 at 108.

4 See section 3 of the introduction.

1. A Preliminary Step: Relations of Power in International Investment Lawmaking

In order to assess how powerful actors use consultations pertaining to the codification of foreign investors' responsibilities to safeguard their interests, one must first be able to determine which actors can be considered as the most powerful protagonists in the international investment lawmaking process. While some authors are prompt to suggest that markets and multinational enterprises are becoming more powerful than states,[5] scrutinizing the power of the various actors involved in this process requires a more nuanced consideration of different ways actors can influence each other. Drawing from differentiated conceptions of power in international relations elaborated by Barnett and Duvall,[6] this section accounts for various relations of power between actors involved in the elaboration of rules related to international investment.

In line with the core premises of the constructivist approach, Barnett and Duvall define power as "the production, in and through social relations, of effects that shape the capacities of actors to determine their circumstances and fate."[7] More specifically, they provide four different concepts of power.[8] *Compulsory power* is presented as a situation characterized by interactions in which one previously constituted actor has a direct control over another. When international actors exercise an indirect control over others through an institutional intermediary or through diffuse interactions, such situations reflect *institutional power*. Beyond the possibility of describing power as an attribute of particular actors and their interactions, Barnett and Duvall also consider power as a process of constituting what actors are as social beings. Therefore, they refer to the constitution of subjects' capacities in direct relations to one another as *structural power*. When this constitution is socially diffuse and produces subjectivity mainly through systems of knowledge and discursive practices, it can be referred to as *productive power*.

Several examples found in the literature suggest that capital-exporting states exercise *structural power* over capital-importing states. In fact, identities and interests of states are strongly shaped by the social position that they occupy. Acting as the home states of foreign investors, capital-exporting states perceive foreign investment as a means to increase trade with host states, secure procurement in natural resources for their economy and ensure the repatriation of parts of the profits earned by national investors.[9] They are thus particularly active in securing the adoption of IIAs to

5 See e.g. Susan Strange, *The Retreat of the State: The Diffusion of Power in the World Economy* (Cambridge: Cambridge University Press, 1996) at 29.
6 Michael Barnett & Raymond Duvall, "Power in International Politics" (2005) 59:1 Int'l Organization 39.
7 *Ibid* at 42.
8 For the rest of this paragraph, see *ibid* at 43.
9 See e.g. Peter T Muchlinski, *Multinational Enterprises and the Law*, 2nd ed (Oxford: Oxford University Press, 2007) at 82–86 [Muchlinski, *Multinational Enterprises*]; Jeswald W Salacuse, "The Treatification of International Investment Law" (2007) 13 Law & Bus Rev Am 155 at 39–40; Sornarajah, *The International Law*, *supra* note 1 at 5.

safeguard the interests of their national investors.[10] The ability of capital-exporting states to directly negotiate these agreements with capital-importing states that agree to grant protections to foreign investment is widely acknowledged as showing the pressure that the former can exert and the asymmetric nature of their relations with the latter.[11] Arguments found in the literature regarding the extent to which international investment rules reflect the national constitutional systems of capital-exporting states also evidence their structural power.[12]

Structural power also characterizes the relationship of foreign investors over capital-importing states. One crucial element to understand the constitutive relationship between these actors is the need of capital-importing states to create new jobs, bring new technology and skills to their territory, develop their natural resources and strengthen their local industries.[13] While capital-importing states compete to attract foreign investments on their territory,[14] foreign investors often succeed to "make contracts and agreements with agencies in host country governments in order to obtain special privileges and benefits that they would not otherwise have – a dynamic that seems to have existed since the advent of foreign investment."[15] One can even suggest that the economic influence of foreign investors allows them to resist sanctions adopted by host states or that the latter do not have the resources to appropriately monitor corporate conduct.[16] This structural power of foreign investors is also not exercised solely over developing

10 See e.g. José E Alvarez, "The Public International Law Regime Governing International Investment" (2009) 344 Rec des Cours 193 at 264–265 [Alvarez, "The Public International Law"]; Sornarajah, *The International Law*, *supra* note 1 at 5 and 62; Peter Muchlinski, "Multinational Enterprises as Actors in International Law: Creating 'Soft Law' Obligations and 'Hard Law' Rights" in Math Noortmann & Cedric Ryngaert, eds, *Non-State Actors Dynamics in International Law: From Law-Takers to Law-Makers* (Farnham: Ashgate Publishing, 2010) 9 at 15 [Muchlinski, "Multinational Enterprises as Actors"]; Kate Miles, *The Origins of International Investment Law: Empire, Environment and the Safeguarding of Capital* (Cambridge: Cambridge University Press, 2013) at 115–116.

11 See e.g. Muchlinski, *Multinational Enterprises*, *supra* note 9 at 117; Alvarez, "The Public International Law", *ibid* at 253–256 and 267–268; Miles, *ibid* at 118; David Schneiderman, *Resisting Economic Globalization: Critical Theory and International Investment Law* (New York: Palgrave Macmillan, 2013) at 2 [Schneiderman, *Resisting Economic Globalization*].

12 See generally David Schneiderman, *Constitutionalizing Economic Globalization: Investment Rules and Democracy's Promise* (Cambridge: Cambridge University Press, 2008).

13 See e.g. Nathan M Jensen, "Democratic Governance and Multinational Corporations: Political Regimes and Inflows of Foreign Direct Investment" (2003) 57 Int'l Organization 587 at 589; Muchlinski, *Multinational Enterprises*, *supra* note 9 at 85 and 87–88; Salacuse, *supra* note 9 at 38; Schneiderman, *Resisting Economic Globalization*, *supra* note 11 at 132–133; Stephen Wilks, *The Political Power of the Business Corporation* (Cheltenham, UK: Edward Elgar, 2013) at 63.

14 See e.g. Strange, *supra* note 5 at 9; Jensen, *ibid* at 589; Schneiderman, *Resisting Economic Globalization*, *ibid* at 131; Wilks, *ibid* at 46.

15 See Salacuse, *supra* note 9 at 39. See also Vaughan Lowe, "Corporations as International Actors and International Law Makers" (2004) 14 Italian YB Int'l L 23 at 23; Sornarajah, *The International Law*, *supra* note 1 at 5. See generally Julian Arato, "Corporations as Lawmakers" (2015) 56 Harv Int'l L J 229.

16 See e.g. Steven R Ratner, "Corporations and Human Rights: A Theory of Legal Responsibility" (2001) 111:3 Yale LJ 443 at 462; A Claire Cutler, "Transnational Business Civilization, Corporations, and the Privatization of Global Governance" in Christopher May, ed, *Global Corporate Power* (Boulder, CO: Lynne Rienner Publishers, 2006) 199 at 207 [Cutler, "Transnational Business Civilization"].

countries. When facing the proposition of a large investment on its territory, several countries are ready to offer incentives and adopt a legal framework that is consistent with the interests of the foreign investor.[17]

The relationship existing between foreign investors and capital-exporting states is also marked by *structural power* held by the former over the latter. In fact, in addition to the influence of foreign investors in shaping the legal framework of capital-importing states, some authors stress the efforts of these private actors to lobby their home states with a view to ensuring that the development of the law furthers their interests and remains business friendly.[18] Given the aforementioned benefits that home states can gain through investments made by their nationals abroad, some states can fear persistent threats from foreign investors and be reluctant to adopt any sort of legislation that would impose additional costs to these private actors.[19] The often-emphasized active role that these private actors play in commercial diplomacy and the negotiation of IIAs constitutes another aspect of this structural power of foreign investors over capital-exporting states.[20]

What is more, foreign investors' efforts to lobby their home states to ensure that developments pertaining to the regulation of international investment remain consistent with their own interests is accompanied by an indirect influence of foreign investors on normative developments occurring in intergovernmental organizations. In fact, this *productive power* of foreign investors over intergovernmental organizations operates in addition to the more direct influence exercised by these private actors on states. For example, the participation of these private actors in intergovernmental organizations regarding the elaboration of standards applicable to the mining sector has been identified in the literature and echoes this productive power of foreign investors.[21] Muchlinski also pinpoints the role of foreign investors in shaping the international lawmaking process in the following terms:

> [Multinational enterprises] can be seen as 'law-makers' even though the traditional law-making process of international law does not formally accord any status to such entities in that process. However, it is on the process of influencing state policy and state practice, *and the agendas of intergovernmental organizations*, in relation to corporate interests that the law-making function of firms is to be seen.[22]

17 See Salacuse, *supra* note 9 at 39.

18 See e.g. Jonathan I Charney, "Transnational Corporations and Developing Public International Law" (1983) 1983:4 Duke LJ 748 at 751; Muchlinski, "Policy Issues", *supra* note 1 at 7; Muchlinski, "Multinational Enterprises as Actors", *supra* note 10 at 10 and 15–16; Miles, *supra* note 10 at 115.

19 See e.g. Ratner, *supra* note 16 at 463; Cutler, "Transnational Business Civilization", *supra* note 16 at 201; Thomas Risse, "Transnational Actors and World Politics" in Walter Carlsnaes, Thomas Risse & Beth A Simmons, eds, *Handbook of International Relations*, 2nd ed (London: Sage Publications, 2013) 426 at 431.

20 See e.g. Sornarajah, *The International Law*, *supra* note 1 at 62; Miles, *supra* note 10 at 116.

21 See Hevina S Dashwood, "Canadian Mining Companies and Corporate Social Responsibility: Weighing the Impact of Global Norms" (2007) 40:1 Can J Pol Sc 129 at 132.

22 Muchlinski, "Multinational Enterprises as Actors", *supra* note 10 at 10 [emphasis added].

In addition to power emerging from ongoing relationships that shape identities and interests of actors involved in this international lawmaking process, access to an international dispute settlement mechanism granted to foreign investors in several IIAs constitutes an instance of ***institutional power***. In fact, the prior consent to international arbitration that is provided in several IIAs entails that consent of the parties to international investment arbitration occurs whenever a foreign investor whose investment is protected by the treaty submits a request for arbitration.[23] Of course, given that this interaction depends upon the existence of a specific institution, the power that is exercised through this channel remains more diffuse than the aforementioned structural relations. However, the existence of such an avenue to resolve an international investment dispute undoubtedly shifts the balance of power in favor of foreign investors. Furthermore, the fact that foreign investors are considered as full and equal parties in international investment arbitration proceedings implies that these private actors play an undeniable role in shaping international investment law.[24]

Beyond the power held by capital-exporting states and foreign investors, a certain form of ***productive power*** is also acknowledged for NGOs. The present analysis considers both organizations representing business interests and organizations focusing primarily on public interests. While Barnett and Duvall consider the deployment of normative resources by NGOs to compel states or multinational enterprises to alter their policies or conduct as reflecting a compulsory power,[25] the involvement of these NGOs in the international investment lawmaking process is considerably different from these direct interactions. In fact, the power of NGOs on this social process is far more diffuse than power exercised by foreign investors and states. For example, while focusing primarily on the protection of social rights and the environment in an attempt to limit corporate power in international investment law, several public interest NGOs are mostly recognized for their capacity of providing additional expertise and making procedures more transparent.[26] Beside their notorious impact on negotiations around the failed *Multilateral Agreement on Investment*,[27] their role

23 See e.g. Andrew Newcombe & Lluís Paradell, *Law and Practice of Investment Treaties: Standards of Treatment* (Alphen aan den Rijn: Kluwer Law International, 2009) at 44; Sornarajah, *The International Law*, *supra* note 1 at 306–307.

24 See José E Alvarez, "Critical Theory and the North American Free Trade Agreement's Chapter Eleven" (1996) 28 U of Miami Inter-Am L Rev 303 at 305; Patrick Dumberry & Érik Labelle-Easthaugh, "Non-State Actors in International Investment Law: The Legal Personality of Corporations and NGOs in the Context of Investor-State Arbitration" in Jean d'Aspremont, ed, *Participants in the International Legal System: Multiple Perspectives on Non-State Actors in International Law* (New York: Routledge, 2011) 360 at 360.

25 Barnett & Duvall, *supra* note 6 at 50 and 60.

26 See e.g. Robert O'Brien, "NGOs, Global Civil Society and Global Economic Regulation" in Sol Picciotto & Ruth Mayne, eds, *Regulating International Business: Beyond Liberalization* (New York: St. Martin's Press, 1999) 257 at 263–265; Risse, *supra* note 19 at 434.

27 See e.g. O'Brien, *ibid* at 258; Sornarajah, *The International Law*, *supra* note 1 at 67; Miles, *supra* note 10 at 118.

in the field of regulating international investment and foreign investors thus mainly relates to placing certain ideas and issues on the political agenda of states and intergovernmental organizations.[28]

Several intergovernmental organizations – *e.g.* the United Nations (UN), the Organisation for Economic Co-operation and Development (OECD), the International Labour Organization (ILO) and agencies of the World Bank Group – also hold *productive power* over the elaboration of rules regulating international investment and foreign investors. For example, commenting on the UN Global Compact, Barnett and Duvall echo the role of intergovernmental organizations in opening a discursive space "in which various actors are produced as subjects empowered legitimately to comment on their performance."[29] Adopting a critical stance to account for this diffuse influence, Cutler mentions that organizations such as the OECD generate the material and ideological foundations that contribute to the global expansion of capitalism.[30] However, the influence of intergovernmental organizations does not seem to be as robust as the one generated by other actors involved in this process. After stressing the quasi-legislative power of these organizations in the development of norms pertaining to international investment law, Muchlinski recalls their "history of frequent failure in relation to the adoption of international rules in this area," as well as the institutional limits regarding their potential actions.[31]

What the existing literature pertaining to international investment law suggests is that capital-exporting states and foreign investors are perceived as holding enough power to directly shape the lawmaking process. In addition to productive power and institutional power held by foreign investors, both capital-exporting states and foreign investors are the sole actors that can exercise structural power over other protagonists involved in this process. By contrast, while NGOs and intergovernmental organizations hold productive power and are able to bring specific aspects to the forefront of the discussions, their positions appear to be limited to an indirect influence on normative developments if they fail to secure support from other powerful actors. Having noted the ongoing exercise of power that is inherent to the relations between actors involved in the regulation of international investment, it becomes relevant to assess how these power relations operate in the specific context of consultations regarding the codification of foreign investors' responsibilities.

28 See Muchlinski, "Policy Issues", *supra* note 1 at 8; Risse, *supra* note 19 at 436.

29 Barnett & Duvall, *supra* note 6 at 61.

30 A Claire Cutler, "Legal Pluralism as the 'Common Sense' of Transnational Capitalism" (2013) 3:4 Oñati S-L Series 719 at 727.

31 Muchlinski, "Policy Issues", *supra* note 1 at 8. See also Peter Muchlinski, "Human Rights, Social Responsibility and the Regulation of International Business: The Development of International Standards by Intergovernmental Organisations" (2003) 3 Non-St Actors & Int'l L 123 at 124 and 145–151.

2. Conflicting Interests: Human Rights, Environmental Protection and Labour Rights

A closer look at the interests of actors involved in the codification of foreign investors' responsibilities occurring in intergovernmental organizations is a crucial step to provide a macro-level analysis of this codification. Therefore, this section critically analyzes statements provided by various actors during a consultation process that was launched by the UN High Commissioner on Human Rights (UNHCHR) in 2004.[32] Even if these statements were submitted more than ten years ago, they bear a unique relevance for present purposes. While several consultation processes have been held since then, the efforts triggered by the UNHCHR sought to address a broad range of existing initiatives and were not limited to a specific set of standards. Moreover, although the primary focus of the consultations concerned the protection of human rights, several actors expressed their views on issues regarding foreign investors' responsibilities in the areas of environmental protection and labour rights. Most importantly, a critical analysis of these statements sheds light on conflicting interests and relations of power that were inherent in this consultation process. Several NGOs and some states hosting considerable stocks of FDI advocated for the adoption of legal norms to hold foreign investors accountable in the areas of human rights, environmental protection and labour rights (2.1). However, this position encountered the firm opposition of foreign investors, private interest NGOs, capital-exporting states and intergovernmental organizations that backed existing initiatives and advocated for *status quo* (2.2).

2.1 A Push for International Legal Norms

During the consultations launched by the UNHCHR, several public interest NGOs strongly advocated for the development of more stringent standards that could balance the power of foreign investors. Some statements, such as the one provided by the Fédération internationale des ligues des droits de l'Homme, echoed the above-mentioned structural power of foreign investors:

> Every day, human rights are violated with the complicity or the active participation of corporate actors which are ***insufficiently regulated by their home State,*** because the ***States where they operate cannot impose on them effective regulations in the social, environmental or human rights fields.***[33]

32 Office for the United Nations High Commissioner for Human Rights, *Stakeholder Submissions to the Report of the High Commissioner for Human Rights on the Responsibilities of Transnational Corporations and related Business Enterprises with regard to Human Rights*, online: OHCHR https://web.archive.org/web/20140520213840/http://www2.ohchr.org/english/issues/globalization/business/contributions.htm (accessed 26 March 2018). The submissions were also extensively analyzed in Larry Catá Backer, "Multinational Corporations, Transnational Law: The United Nations' Norms on the Responsibilities of Transnational Corporations as a Harbinger of Corporate Social Responsibility in International Law" (2006) 37 Colum Hum Rts L Rev 287.

33 Fédération internationale des ligues des droits de l'Homme, *Contribution of the FIDH to the Consultation of the OHCHR on the Human Rights Responsibilities of Business* (September 2004),

Others appeared to worry about the extent to which foreign investors could hamper the elaboration of legal norms establishing responsibilities for private actors. This aspect was put forward by Christian Aid, which argued that "[b]usiness . . . has consistently used [corporate social responsibility] to block attempts to establish the mandatory international regulation of companies' activities."[34]

Beyond the expression of concerns pertaining to relations of power, public interest NGOs also sought to provide concrete reasons justifying the need for the adoption of legal norms that could steer the conduct of private investors when operating abroad. In addition to statements recalling several negative effects of foreign investors' activities,[35] the need for balancing legal protections granted to foreign investors with legal obligations was recalled on several instances. After highlighting that foreign investors' responsibilities were not established in an enforceable legal framework, a submission provided by MISEREOR and other collaborators thus stressed "an obvious need to match the rights of companies with responsibilities."[36]

Another recurring theme that can be identified from the discourse of public interest NGOs is the strong skepticism of these organizations regarding the effectiveness of voluntary initiatives adopted by private actors. While acknowledging that these private initiatives rendered a certain awareness of businesses regarding their responsibilities, most public interest NGOs maintained that they remained insufficient to address the negative impact of foreign investors' activities and could not be considered as an appropriate substitute for regulation.[37] It is in this regard that Oxfam submitted the following statement:

online: OHCHR https://web.archive.org/web/20140520213840/http://www2.ohchr.org/english/issues/globalization/business/contributions.htm (accessed 26 March 2018) [emphasis added]. See also International Commission of Jurists, *Submission to the United Nations Office if the High Commissioner for Human Rights on Business and Human Rights* (26 October 2004), online: OHCHR https://web.archive.org/web/20140520213840/http://www2.ohchr.org/english/issues/globalization/business/contributions.htm (accessed 26 March 2018).

34 Christian Aid, *Behind the Mask: The Real Face of CSR*, online: OHCHR https://web.archive.org/web/20140520213840/http://www2.ohchr.org/english/issues/globalization/business/contributions.htm (accessed 26 March 2018) at 2.

35 See e.g. Greenpeace, *Responsibilities of Transnational Corporations and related Business Enterprises with regard to Human Rights* (30 September 2004), online: OHCHR https://web.archive.org/web/20140520213840/http://www2.ohchr.org/english/issues/globalization/business/contributions.htm (accessed 26 March 2018).

36 MISEREOR et al, *The Responsibilities of Transnational Corporations and related Business Enterprises with regard to Human Rights* (30 September 2004), online: OHCHR https://web.archive.org/web/20140520213840/http://www2.ohchr.org/english/issues/globalization/business/contributions.htm (accessed 26 March 2018).

37 See e.g. MISEREOR et al, *ibid*; Christian Aid, *supra* note 34 at 15; Human Rights Watch, *Statement on the United Nations Norms on the Responsibilities of Transnational Corporations and other Business Enterprises with regard to Human Rights to the Office of the United Nations High Commissioner for Human Rights* (30 September 2004), online: OHCHR https://web.archive.org/web/20140520213840/http://www2.ohchr.org/english/issues/globalization/business/contributions.htm (accessed 26 March 2018); International Commission of Jurists, *supra* note 33.

> *So far Oxfam remains unconvinced that industry-led voluntary codes can address these issues.* The obvious problem is that they are voluntary. There is little evidence, even where there is good monitoring and verification that the human rights performance of companies has markedly improved as a result. From the point of view of the victims of human rights violations and exploitation by business, *legislative protection backed by action must be preferable to voluntary processes.*[38]

In addition to these public interest NGOs, at least one private interest NGO also appeared to be in favor of adopting legal norms regarding foreign investors' responsibilities in the areas of human rights, environmental protection and labour rights. After recalling the relevance of "mandatory efforts in order to achieve sustainable change and to raise the minimum standard of acceptable behaviour,"[39] the Business Leaders Initiative on Human Rights thus argued the following:

> We see that it is in our *interests*, as well as those of wider society, to better understand the ways in which civil, political, economic, social and cultural rights can be supported within our companies and across our business sectors. The prime responsibility for upholding these rights lie with governments, but *we are also interested in exploring where the boundaries of our responsibility might lie to help implement these rights.* We believe that this does not detract from the central role of government as the main duty bearer for fulfilling human rights, rather it reinforces it.[40]

As far as states are concerned, the support for the adoption of additional international norms pertaining to foreign investors' responsibilities did not clearly emerge as a prime consideration for all capital-importing states. In fact, several net capital importers that participated in the consultations were members of the European Union (EU) and submitted a joint statement that was more in line with the interests of this net capital-exporting entity.[41] No other net capital importers

38 Oxfam, *Submission by Oxfam International under Decision 2004/116 on the 'Responsibilities of Transnational Corporations and related Business Enterprises with regards to Human Rights'* (17 November 2004), online: OHCHR https://web.archive.org/web/20140520213840/http://www2.ohchr.org/english/issues/globalization/business/contributions.htm (accessed 26 March 2018) [emphasis added].

39 See Business Leaders Initiative on Human Rights, *Submission to the Office of the UN High Commissioner for Human Rights relating to the 'Responsibilities of Transnational Corporations and related Business enterprises with regard to Human Rights'* (28 September 2004), online: OHCHR https://web.archive.org/web/20140520213840/http://www2.ohchr.org/english/issues/globalization/business/contributions.htm (accessed 26 March 2018).

40 Business Leaders Initiative on Human Rights, *ibid* [emphasis added].

41 The position of the EU is discussed in the following section. These capital-importing states are Belgium, Czech Republic, Hungary and Poland. For all these states, at the moment of the submission of the statements, their FDI outward stocks were lower than their FDI inward stocks. See OECD StatExtract, *Foreign Direct Investment FDI Series of BOP and IIP Aggregates*, online: OECD http://stats.oecd.org/Index.aspx?DataSetCode=FDI_BOP_IIP# (accessed 26 March 2018).

that submitted a statement to this consultation process appeared to be in favor of adopting legal norms pertaining to foreign investors' responsibilities. However, the position of some net exporters of capital hosting considerable stocks of FDI was far more nuanced. It is in this regard that, to a certain extent, countries such as Norway and Canada supported the development of additional international norms pertaining to foreign investors and human rights.[42] For example, Norway maintained that there was "a need for norms from which directives for concrete actions and omissions by companies can be derived."[43] Similarly, Canada identified the lack of "an authoritative document outlining the full range of human rights considerations or principles companies should take into account when investing" as a gap of the existing framework.[44]

Overall, it is plain that a mix of state and non-state actors sought to show their support for the elaboration of international norms that would hold investors accountable when operating abroad. While the discourse of public interest NGOs reflected manifest concerns with respect to the power that foreign investors hold over states, legal norms were perceived as a more effective way than existing initiatives to balance this power. Although some support can be found in a private interest NGO and some states that host considerable stocks of FDI, this position was mainly advocated by actors that do not exercise direct power in the elaboration of rules governing international investment and foreign investors.

2.2 Strong Reactions and Doubts from Powerful Actors

In striking contrast with proponents of the adoption of additional international norms addressing the general lack of accountability of foreign investors, some actors used the same consultation process to articulate their opposition and doubts. Among these actors, foreign investors and private interest NGOs were prompt to dismiss any form of international legal norms that would directly apply to their activities. Interestingly, it is worth noting that these actors implicitly acknowledged the constitutive role of existing initiatives in shaping their identities and interests. For example, according to Shell:

42 In 2004, at the moment of the submission of the statements, the FDI inward stocks of Canada were of USD 315 billion (in comparison to FDI outward stocks of USD 373 billion). The FDI inward stocks of Norway were of USD 85 trillion (in comparison to FDI outward stocks of USD 89 trillion). See OECD StatExtract, *ibid.*

43 Norway, *Decision 2004/116 – Responsibilities of Transnational Corporations and related Business Enterprises with regard to Human Rights* (4 November 2004), online: OHCHR https://web.archive.org/web/20140520213840/http://www2.ohchr.org/english/issues/globalization/business/contributions.htm (accessed 26 March 2018).

44 Canada, *Submission of Canada to the High Commissioner of Human Rights on the Responsibilities of Business Enterprises with regard to Human Rights*, online: OHCHR https://web.archive.org/web/20140520213840/http://www2.ohchr.org/english/issues/globalization/business/contributions.htm (accessed 26 March 2018) at para 4.3.

> The [Shell General Business Principles] guides the day-to-day business and activities of Shell companies and these need to keep pace with *external principles and codes that help shape our business environment*, for example in relation to human rights these include . . . the UN Global Compact (2000), the *OECD Guidelines for Multinational Enterprises* (2001), the *ILO Tripartite Declaration of Principles concerning Multinational Enterprises and Social Policy* (2000).[45]

Additionally, after citing the *OECD Guidelines for Multinational Enterprises* and the UN Global Compact, the International Chamber of Commerce stated that

> *[s]uch voluntary initiatives serve many constructive and useful purposes*, including setting aspirational goals that organizations can work to achieve, coordinating policies among various organizations, communicating the commitment of an organization to a policy or position, and providing guidance to organizations seeking to improve their own performance.[46]

Further to this recognition of existing initiatives, the discourse of foreign investors and private interest NGOs can be understood as seeking to preserve the structural power of foreign investors over capital-importing states and capital-exporting states. In addition to depicting foreign investors as entities that "can effectively put in practice their voluntary commitment to respecting human rights through the application of their own business principles,"[47] several actors alleged that the protection of human rights had to remain the sole responsibility of states. It is in this regard that BP made the following statement: "In general, *accountability should not be given to an actor who does not have the capacity to fulfill that accountability*. Business cannot and should not be held accountable for what is the role of government."[48] Through such a discourse, foreign investors and

45 Shell, *Request from the Office of the UN High Commissioner for Human Rights* (24 September 2004), online: OHCHR https://web.archive.org/web/20140520213840/http://www2.ohchr.org/english/issues/globalization/business/contributions.htm (accessed 26 March 2018) [emphasis added].

46 International Chamber of Commerce, *Request for Input on Report concerning the 'Responsibilities of Transnational Corporations and related Enterprises with regard to Human Rights* (7 September 2004), online: OHCHR https://web.archive.org/web/20140520213840/http://www2.ohchr.org/english/issues/globalization/business/contributions.htm (accessed 26 March 2018) [emphasis added].

47 See International Chamber of Commerce, *ibid.* See also United States Council for International Business, *Submission to the High Commissioner for Human Rights for the Report on the 'Responsibilities of Transnational Corporations and related Business Enterprises with regard to Human Rights'*, online: OHCHR https://web.archive.org/web/20140520213840/http://www2.ohchr.org/english/issues/globalization/business/contributions.htm (accessed 26 March 2018).

48 BP, *Responsibilities of Transnational Corporations and related Business Enterprises with regard to Human Rights* (1 October 2004), online: OHCHR https://web.archive.org/web/20140520213840/http://www2.ohchr.org/english/issues/globalization/business/contributions.htm (accessed 26 March 2018).

private interest NGOs perpetuated the power imbalance characterizing the structural relations between these private actors and states related to their operations.

In this regard, both foreign investors and NGOs representing the interests of businesses stressed the need to maintain voluntary initiatives. Arguing that no "one size fits all approach" was available to regulate foreign investors' activities, Shell thus maintained that

> there is an important role for voluntary codes of practice that can help create that solid foundation of good practice in the field of human rights and environmental performance and that enable business to push back the boundaries of social and environmental performance and operate at the cutting edge.[49]

Some actors, such as the United States Centre for International Business, argued that "[v]oluntary instruments also help to maintain a process of innovation that is a critical aspect in the development and implementation of corporate responsibility programs and initiatives."[50]

It must also be noted that foreign investors and private interest NGOs benefited from the support of capital-exporting states throughout the consultation process launched by the UNHCHR. In fact, important net exporters of capital have been particularly active in demonstrating their disagreement with the adoption of legal standards seeking to steer the conduct of foreign investors. Of particular relevance for present purposes are the statements that were submitted by the United States and members of the EU.[51] In line with the positions adopted by economic private actors, these states acknowledged the influence of existing initiatives with respect to the codification of foreign investors' responsibilities. For example, discussing the increasing awareness of human rights and business enterprises, the EU member states mentioned that

> [t]his tendency is closely related to the fact that the issue of [corporate social responsibility] acquired importance on the political agenda, and that work to formulate standards, principles, and guidelines has taken place in many fora, including in the United Nations, OECD, and the European Union itself.[52]

49 Shell, *supra* note 45.

50 United States Council for International Business, *supra* note 47.

51 Even if some of its members that submitted a statement were net importers of capital, the EU was a net exporter of capital in 2004. The FDI outward stocks of the EU were of USD 5,263 million, in comparison to FDI inward stocks of USD 4,805 million. See OECD StatExtract, *supra* note 41.

52 Statements submitted by member states of the EU were identical in this regard. See e.g. Netherlands, *Reply of the Netherlands to the OHCHR Questionnaire on Responsibilities of Transnational Corporations and related Business Enterprises with regard to Human Rights* (29 September 2004), online: OHCHR https://web.archive.org/web/20140520213840/http://www2.ohchr.org/english/issues/globalization/business/contributions.htm (accessed 26 March 2018) at para 2.

The structure that was developed regarding the codification of foreign investors' responsibilities was thus considered as having had an undeniable impact on the identities and the interests of several actors.

However, capital-exporting states were also largely in favor of initiatives whose application remained voluntary. One glaring example of such a position can be found in the statement submitted by the United States:

> [I]t is the view of the United States that *voluntary, collaborative efforts* to leverage public-private partnerships are the best means for both encouraging responsible business practices by the private sector in this area and for the promotion and protection of human rights. *Any exercised design to impose artificial 'norms and responsibilities' on business enterprises has . . . no basis in fact, no basis in law and is doomed from the outset.*[53]

Far from merely expressing its support for voluntary initiatives, the extent to which the United States rejected the direct imposition of international legal norms on foreign investors contributed to depict the latter as actors that can hardly be regulated under international law.

Moreover, in a way that mirrors the position of foreign investors and private interest NGOs, several participants recalled that the protection of human rights had to be considered as the sole responsibility of states under international law. After stressing "that the prime responsibility for the protection and promotion of human rights rests with States,"[54] the EU underscored that "*[t]ransnational corporations and other business enterprises shall respect local legislation and regulations*, to the extent that local legislation or regulations do not make business an accomplice to human rights violations."[55] The United States even pushed this argument further: "While it is true that private entities have been alleged to have been complicit in, or even aided, human rights abuses committed by governments, *the fundamental cause of such abuses has been the action or inaction of the government, not the private entity.*"[56] These statements extensively support *status quo* and undeniably preserve the power imbalance existing between foreign investors and capital-importing states.

In the same vein, intergovernmental organizations seemed to express some uncertainty with respect to the extent to which any international instruments codifying foreign investors' responsibilities could depart from voluntary initiatives. Without necessarily positioning themselves against international legal norms that seek to address the general lack of accountability of foreign investors,

53 United States of America, *Re: Note Verbale from the OHCHR of August 3, 2004 (GVA2537)* (30 September 2004), online: OHCHR https://web.archive.org/web/20140520213840/http://www2.ohchr.org/english/issues/globalization/business/contributions.htm (accessed 26 March 2018) [emphasis added].

54 See e.g. Netherlands, *supra* note 52 at para 3.

55 See e.g. *ibid* at para 3 [emphasis added].

56 United States of America, *supra* note 53 [emphasis added].

some intergovernmental organizations questioned their feasibility. For example, the ILO summarized this uncertainty in the following terms:

> It therefore would appear useful to ensure that in further consideration of the issue of human rights and business, attention is paid to both the *possibility* and the *desirability* of attempting to impose international legal obligations on non-state actors, particularly business enterprises, under (1) general international public law and (2) international law in the field of human rights and labour.[57]

In sum, these consultations regarding the codification of foreign investors' responsibilities in the areas of human rights, environmental protection and labour rights were characterized by irreconcilable interests. On the one hand, it is plain that the push for departing from existing initiatives and adopting international legal norms that codify foreign investors' responsibilities mostly came from public interest NGOs, with other actors also demonstrating encouragement for additional international norms on this matter. On the other hand, several foreign investors, private interest NGOs and capital-exporting states backed existing voluntary initiatives, while intergovernmental organization expressed some hesitation regarding the adoption of legal norms.

3. Serving the Interests of Powerful Actors: The Prohibition of Corruption

While the analysis of consultations related to foreign investors' responsibilities in the areas examined above sheds light on strong reactions from powerful actors to counter concerns from other participants, examining consultations regarding the prohibition of corruption reveals a strikingly different picture. Consultations that generally addressed the elaboration and the implementation of anti-corruption initiatives under the auspices of intergovernmental organizations – *i.e.* the 2001 UN *Report of the Meeting of the Intergovernmental Open-Ended Expert Group to Prepare Draft Terms of Reference for the Negotiation of an International Legal Instrument Against Corruption*[58] as well as statements submitted during a broad consultation process launched by the OECD in 2008[59] – are particularly relevant to account for this different context.

Discursive materials emerging from these consultations demonstrate the active participation of state and non-state actors, as well as the constitutive relationship

57 International Labour Office, *Letter from Mr. Zdzislaw Kedzia* (2 August 2004), online: OHCHR https://web.archive.org/web/20140520213840/http://www2.ohchr.org/english/issues/globalization/business/contributions.htm (accessed 26 March 2018) [emphasis added].

58 *Report of the Meeting of the Intergovernmental Open-Ended Expert Group to Prepare Draft Terms of Reference for the Negotiation of an International Legal Instrument Against Corruption*, 2001, UN Doc No A/AC.260/2 [*Intergovernmental Open-Ended Expert Group Report*].

59 OECD, *Review of the OECD Anti-Bribery Instruments: Compilation of Responses to Consultation Papers* (Paris: OECD, 2008) [*OECD Review*].

existing between actors and norms concerning the prohibition of corrupt acts by foreign investors. However, with respect to the interests that were put forward throughout these consultations, one must go beyond the confluence of support from the various actors involved. This section thus shows that foreign investors, private interest NGOs and capital-exporting states mainly perceived corrupt acts as preventing the establishment of a competitive level-playing field (3.1). By contrast, support provided by other actors was chiefly motivated by a will to tackle broader negative effects of corruption on society (3.2).

3.1 Securing a Level-Playing Field

Even if foreign investors and private interest NGOs explicitly sought to discourage the adoption of international legal norms to hold private actors accountable in several areas, these actors nevertheless perceived anti-corruption initiatives as a means to further their interests. During the consultations held under the auspices of the UN and the OECD, several actors acknowledged the relevance of existing initiatives in shaping the identities and the interests of international actors. For example, the International Chamber of Commerce addressed the instruments adopted by the OECD and the work of its Working Group on Bribery and in International Business Transactions in the following terms:

> From a business perspective, it clearly appears that the adoption of the [i]nstruments and the work performed by the Working Group during a period of more than ten years *has produced substantial and irreversible effects on the way international bribery is treated*: the criminalization of bribery of foreign public officials is now general in the OECD area and tax deductions for bribe payments are generally disallowed.[60]

Some actors explicitly recognized the mutual reinforcement between international instruments adopted by the OECD and other initiatives developed by the private sector. In this regard, the International Chamber of Commerce also stated its belief that

> the effectiveness of the [i]nstruments should also be measured by the considerable work accomplished, since the adoption of the [i]nstruments, by the private sector through corporate codes of conduct aiming at complying with the standards, laid down in the [i]nstruments, and through integrity programs.[61]

Beyond the recognition of this effectiveness, the primary reason underlying the commitment of foreign investors and private interest NGOs was the concern

60 See *ibid* at 118 [emphasis added].
61 See *ibid* at 118.

to level the playing field for foreign investors seeking to enter new markets. Such concerns were summarized by the Conseil français des investisseurs en Afrique, according to whom "[t]he fact that companies from emerging countries are not necessarily sued for international contract-related bribes *induces serious competition distortions* (to the detriment of companies that chose integrity) while impeding the reduction of corruption in weak governance countries."[62] In a similar way, the Business and Industry Advisory Committee stressed that "more needs to be done to effectively curb corruption and *provide a real level[-]playing field for international business* across OECD countries and in particular outside the OECD."[63] As a result, foreign investors and private interest NGOs called upon an expansion of existing international norms with a view to improving the enforcement of current instruments, including more effectively major emerging countries, addressing passive corruption and targeting the private-to-private corruption issue.[64]

In contrast to other areas in which foreign investors' conduct can produce a negative impact, capital-exporting states approached the prohibition of corruption from a radically different stance. In addition to emphasizing the need for compatibility with principles found in existing anti-corruption instruments,[65] several concerns articulated by foreign investors and private interest NGOs were echoed in the discourse of capital-exporting states. For example, as far as improving the enforcement of current instruments is concerned, the intergovernmental open-ended expert group reported that "the States members of the European Union expressed the view that the new instrument could be nothing else but a convention, *should contain both preventive and enforcement measures* and follow a multidisciplinary approach."[66] Furthermore, the same report mentions that "the members of the Union underlined that *as many countries as possible* should be able to subscribe to the commitment to be expressed in the new instrument."[67]

Above all, the analysis above shows that one cannot bluntly suggest that foreign investors, private interest NGOs and capital-exporting states constantly sought to hamper the codification of foreign investors' responsibilities. The consultation processes that occurred under intergovernmental organizations regarding the area of corruption were unambiguously anchored in demands from these actors to adopt international legal norms to secure a level-playing field serving their interests. What emerges as the key element from this discourse analysis is thus that these normative developments benefited from a crucially

62 See *ibid* at 113 [emphasis added].
63 See *ibid* at 107 [emphasis added].
64 See *ibid*. See the statements from the Business and Industry Advisory Committee (at 108–109), the Conseil français des investisseurs en Afrique (at 113–114), the International Chamber of Commerce (at 119 and 122) and the International Federation of Consulting Engineers (at 127).
65 See *Intergovernmental Open-Ended Expert Group Report*, *supra* note 58 at para 16.
66 See *ibid* at para 16 [emphasis added].
67 See *ibid* at para 16 [emphasis added].

needed support from actors holding enough power to shape international rules applicable to international investment and foreign investors.

3.2 Addressing the Broader Implications of Corruption

Further to the support of the most powerful actors to develop and implement international legal norms prohibiting corruption, one can hardly be surprised that other participants in these consultations also advocated for such norms. The reasons underlying the backing from public interest NGOs, capital-importing states and intergovernmental organizations nevertheless considerably differed from the focus on securing a competitive level-playing field. In fact, an examination of the discourse from these actors demonstrates that they addressed the influence of existing instruments and that they were concerned about broader effects of corrupt practices perpetrated by foreign investors.

Several public interest NGOs thus implicitly referred to the constitutive role of international norms prohibiting corruption. For example, Public Concern at Work mentioned that the variety of instruments adopted by the OECD "have been extremely important *in changing public and organisational attitudes to bribery* over the last decade."[68] By contrast, Transparency International offered a mixed account of these results:

> The ultimate objective of the Convention is to *change corporate culture and stimulate effective anticorruption compliance programs.* Based on [Transparency International]'s extensive relations with the business community, we do not believe that a sea-change in corporate behaviour has taken place. A considerable number of large multinationals have taken action, but progress is uneven and incomplete. A higher and more consistent level of enforcement will be needed *to change corporate culture.*[69]

Regardless of diverging views pertaining to the effectiveness of existing initiatives, both statements recognized the potential influence of international norms on the identities and interests of agents.

Furthermore, the various aspects put forward by public interest NGOs demonstrated the need to address corporate liability and the broad scope of concerns that were considered to support the adoption and implementation of international legal norms to fight corruption. Particularly relevant for present purposes are statements that unambiguously referred to corporate liability for acts of corruption. Transparency International thus addressed the "increasing recognition that to deal with complex crimes such as foreign bribery, corporations should be held liable not only for affirmative derelictions but for lack of supervision or control."[70] Expressing concerns that some states had not effectively established

68 See *OECD Review*, *supra* note 59 at 93 [emphasis added].
69 See *ibid* at 97 [emphasis added].
70 See *ibid* at 101.

the liability of legal persons for corrupt practices, the Trade Union Advisory Committee recalled that "[b]ribery of a foreign public official is a crime that is almost always committed by employees on behalf of and for the benefit of their companies."[71] Moreover, further to organizations that raised concerns pertaining to the protection of whistleblowers,[72] the Global Organisation of Parliamentarians against Corruption described corruption governance as "the greatest hindrance to the development of prosperity in the world."[73]

As far as capital-importing states are concerned, an important element that can be identified from the discourse of these actors is that it also addressed issues reaching beyond the competitive concerns put forward by other participants. For example, capital-importing states implicitly expressed issues pertaining to the structural power of capital-exporting states. The aforementioned intergovernmental open-ended expert group thus reported that Egypt, speaking on behalf of the Group of 77 and China, stressed the importance of including in a legal instrument a chapter on mutual legal assistance and cooperation that would foster international cooperation.[74] The Group of Asian and Pacific states, represented by Jordan, also "believed that the scope of application of the new convention must be responsive to the concerns of all States, particularly on the sensitive issue of *sovereign equality, territorial integrity and non-interference in the domestic affairs of States*."[75] Furthermore, as reported by the intergovernmental open-ended expert group, Uruguay spoke on behalf of the Group of Latin American and Caribbean states and

> confirmed the commitment of the members of the Group to participate actively in the fight against corruption and stressed the need to codify and strengthen international rules against the phenomenon *in order to ensure transparency in both the public and the private sector*.[76]

Finally, some intergovernmental organizations also participated in these consultations related to the codification of foreign investors' responsibilities in the area of corruption. Echoing the implicit consideration of the constitutive effect of existing international initiatives, the Group of States against Corruption from the Council of Europe argued that "the OECD anti-bribery instruments have no doubt been instrumental in increasing awareness of the fact that bribery of foreign public officials is not a normal way of doing business."[77] What is more, the discourse of at least one intergovernmental organization reflected broader social concerns related to corruption. The intergovernmental open-ended expert group

71 See *ibid* at 141.
72 See *ibid*. See the statements from Public Concern at Work (at 94), Open Democracy Advice Centre (at 95) and Transparency International (at 100–101).
73 See *ibid* at 92.
74 See *Intergovernmental Open-Ended Expert Group Report*, *supra* note 58 at para 14.
75 See *ibid* at para 18 [emphasis added].
76 See *ibid* at para 15 [emphasis added].
77 See *OECD Review*, *supra* note 59 at 78.

thus cited the following statement from the Executive Director of the UN Office for Drug Control and Crime Prevention: "Corruption was as much a reality in industrialized countries as in countries with economies in transition and developing countries. . . . Over time, corrupt practices reinforced poverty by making services available only to those who could afford them."[78]

While the overwhelming majority of state and non-state actors involved in these consultations ultimately agreed on the necessity of international legal norms to prohibit the corruption of public agents by foreign investors, they held somehow different positions. Foreign investors, private interest NGOs and capital-exporting states extensively decried the negative impact that corruption can have on competition between private actors seeking to invest in a host state. By contrast, other actors justified their support by stressing broader implications of corruption. Beyond the mere confluence of support, the prohibition of corruption was perceived as serving the interests of actors holding enough power to exercise a more direct influence on the elaboration of international rules.

Conclusion

The analysis above suggests that capital-exporting states and foreign investors are the only actors involved in the international investment lawmaking process that hold enough structural power to exercise a direct influence on the elaboration of rules regulating international investment. Far from neglecting the productive power held by NGOs and intergovernmental organizations, it is plain that the indirect influence exercised by other actors is generally outweighed by the various types of power held by foreign investors and capital-exporting states. When applied to consultations regarding the codification of foreign investors' responsibilities by intergovernmental organizations, this analysis demonstrates an unavoidable reproduction of power relations and diverging interests. In line with the premises of the critical constructivist approach, the reliance on a critical discourse analysis has proven to be relevant to evidence the role of state and non-state actors in these consultations. Capital-importing states, capital-exporting states, foreign investors, NGOs and intergovernmental organizations have all voiced their concerns with respect to the codification of foreign investors' responsibilities in distinct areas. Furthermore, in light of several references to existing initiatives, their discourse suggests a mutual constitution between the actors and the various instruments seeking to tackle the general lack of accountability of foreign investors under international law.

Most importantly, this mutual constitution of agents and social structures encompasses efforts from the most powerful actors involved in these consultations to safeguard their interests. The examination of statements from various actors evidences clashing interests with respect to the areas of human rights,

78 See *Intergovernmental Open-Ended Expert Group Report*, *supra* note 58 at para 8.

environmental protection and labour rights. Some NGOs and states hosting a considerable level of FDI stocks argued in favor of additional international norms to hold foreign investors accountable. However, several foreign investors, private interest NGOs, capital-exporting states and intergovernmental organizations either seemed to be reluctant to depart from current voluntary initiatives or squarely rejected the potential adoption of legal norms for this purpose. By contrast, all actors involved in consultations pertaining to the codification of foreign investors' responsibilities in the area of corruption stressed the relevance of international legal norms. Amidst various actors that were concerned by the broader negative impact of corrupt acts perpetrated by private actors, foreign investors, private interest NGOs and capital-exporting states mainly asked for the establishment of a competitive level-playing field. At the end of the day, the only area for which the elaboration of international legal norms pertaining to foreign investors' responsibilities was perceived as serving the interests of the most powerful actors is the prohibition of corruption.

This account of power relations and distinct interests bears direct implications in the analysis of the normative integration of foreign investors' responsibilities in international investment law. The consistency between most powerful actors' interests and the extent to which foreign investors' responsibilities are integrated in international investment law is striking. The weak consideration of such responsibilities in the areas of human rights, environmental protection and labour rights echoes the reluctance of foreign investors, private interest NGOs, capital-exporting states and intergovernmental organizations exhibited during previous consultations. Furthermore, the stronger normative integration of the prohibition of corruption reflects the general support for international legal norms in this area by the actors that are able to exercise a more direct influence on the international investment lawmaking process. In other words, the fragmented normative integration of foreign investors' responsibilities in international investment law is consistent with the interests of the most powerful actors involved in the international investment lawmaking process.

Part II

The Normative Character of International Initiatives

A Micro-Level Analysis

After having addressed the normative integration of foreign investors' responsibilities in international investment law, a closer look at specific instruments elaborated and implemented by intergovernmental organizations is necessary to determine whether these instruments have reached the realm of legality. It is in this regard that Part II of this book focuses on normative developments and relations of power occurring within four distinct intergovernmental organizations. Initiatives from the Organisation for Economic Co-operation and Development (Chapter 4), the International Labour Organization (Chapter 5), the United Nations (Chapter 6) and the World Bank Group (Chapter 7) are thus analyzed according to an interdisciplinary approach that extensively draws upon the interactional theory of international law. The application of this theory allows positioning each instrument on a continuum that varies from social norms to legal norms. This part of the book ultimately shows that the majority of intergovernmental organizations' instruments codifying standards of appropriate conduct for private actors operating abroad are social norms that fail to produce a genuine sense of obligation.

4 Organisation for Economic Co-operation and Development

Introduction

This chapter begins the micro-level analysis of the codification of foreign investors' responsibilities by examining international instruments emanating from the Organisation for Economic Co-operation and Development (OECD). With the adoption of the first version of the *OECD Guidelines for Multinational Enterprises* (*OECD Guidelines*) in 1976,[1] this intergovernmental organization has been particularly active in this codification process for more than forty years. In parallel to the numerous areas that are included in this broad instrument, the OECD has also contributed to the elaboration and the implementation of international instruments related to the specific area of corruption. The OECD hosted the negotiation of the *Convention on Combating Bribery of Foreign Public Officials in International Business Transactions* (*OECD Anti-Bribery Convention*)[2] in 1997 and has adopted the *Recommendation of the Council for Further Combating Bribery of Foreign Public Officials in International Business Transactions* (*OECD 2009 Recommendation*)[3] in 2009.

Following a brief analysis of the elaboration and implementation processes of norms under the auspices of the OECD (1), this chapter positions these three international instruments on a continuum varying from social norms to legal norms. With respect to the *OECD Guidelines*, an interactional account[4] of this instrument demonstrates that it remains a widely used social norm that has moved closer to

1 The *OECD Guidelines for Multinational Enterprises* are included in Annex 1 of the *Declaration on International Investment and Multinational Enterprises*. See *Declaration on International Investment and Multinational Enterprises*, 21 June 1976, Doc No C(76)99/FINAL (1976). For the most recent version, see *Declaration on International Investment and Multinational Enterprises*, 25 May 2011, Doc No C/MIN(2011)11/FINAL (2011) [*OECD Guidelines 2011*].

2 *Convention on Combating Bribery of Foreign Public Officials in International Business Transactions*, 17 December 1997, 37 ILM 1 (entered into force 15 February 1999) [*OECD Anti-Bribery Convention*].

3 *Recommendation of the Council for Further Combating Bribery of Foreign Public Officials in International Business Transactions*, 26 November 2009, Doc No C(2009)159/REV1/FINAL (amended on 18 February 2010, Doc No C(2010)19) [*OECD 2009 Recommendation*].

4 See section 3 of the introduction.

the threshold of legal norms, without having entered the realm of legality (2). By contrast, both the *OECD Anti-Bribery Convention* and the *OECD 2009 Recommendation* appear as international norms that have succeeded in generating a genuine sense of obligation and that can be categorized as legal norms (3).

1. The OECD: A Plurality of Norms and the Promotion of Neoliberal Policies

In order to better assess the normative character of international instruments codifying foreign investors' responsibilities that have been elaborated and implemented by the OECD, it is worth considering the broader normative process that usually takes place in this intergovernmental organization. According to the *Convention on the Organisation for Economic Co-operation and Development* (*Convention on the OECD*),[5] this intergovernmental organization can adopt diverse normative acts. Article 5 provides that the OECD can take *decisions*, make *recommendations* to member states and enter into *agreements* with member states, non-member states and intergovernmental organizations.[6] While these three acts are all sources of international norms, only decisions taken by the OECD are expressly "binding on all the Members."[7] Although not explicitly mentioned in the *Convention on the OECD*, the work of this intergovernmental organization has also led to the adoption of other forms of instruments, such as declarations, model conventions, good practice guidance and tools.[8]

An interesting aspect of the OECD is also reflected in the way this organization seeks to ensure the continuing elaboration and implementation of these norms by embedding them in a broader normative process.[9] In fact, the initial adoption of international norms by the OECD is often complemented by subsequent reviews, other instruments to supplement the original initiatives and an implementation process relying on peer review. Pressure exercised by other members of the OECD allows a flexible implementation process that operates even despite the lack of formal international instruments and that relies more on persuasion than sanction.

While maintaining a clear prominence on the role of states, the OECD considerably relies on non-state actors' expertise. As early as 1962, the OECD granted a specific consultative status to both the Business and Industry Advisory Committee (BIAC) and the Trade Union Advisory Committee (TUAC). Furthermore, a

5 *Convention on the Organisation for Economic Co-operation and Development*, 14 December 1960, Can TS 1961 No 18 (entered into force 30 September 1961) [*Convention on the OECD*].

6 *Ibid*, art 5.

7 *Ibid*, art 5(a).

8 See e.g. Alexander Böhmer, "Organisation for Economic Co-operation and Development" in Christian Tietje & Alan Brouder, eds, *Handbook of Transnational Economic Governance Regimes* (Leiden: Martinus Nijhoff Publishers, 2009) 227 at 231; Hervé Ascensio, "Les normes produites à l'OCDE et les formes de normativité" in Hervé Ascensio & Nicola Bonucci, eds, *Le pouvoir normatif de l'OCDE* (Paris: Éditions A. Pedone, 2014) 7 at 8.

9 See Ascensio, *ibid* at 14–15;

more regular participation of non-governmental organizations (NGOs) in the work of the Investment Committee through OECD Watch complements this inclusion of non-state actors since 2003.[10]

Most interestingly, OECD member states participate in consolidating a sense of identity. According to Porter and Webb, thanks to the crucial role played by the peer review mechanism in the activities of the OECD, member states engage with the work of this intergovernmental organization because of their identification with the norms and values that the OECD represents.[11] More specifically, member states devote considerable efforts to promote principles of free market and neoliberal policies.[12] With respect to international investment, this organization is particularly active in promoting free movement of capital and redefining policy choices in regulating investment.[13]

The OECD is thus a highly relevant normative site with respect to the evolving codification of foreign investors' responsibilities in a context of neoliberal globalization. In addition to developing various norms and implementing them through an innovative follow-up mechanism, this intergovernmental organization relies on the participation of state and non-state actors. It is against this institutional context that the analysis of the *OECD Guidelines*, the *OECD Anti-Bribery Convention* and the *OECD 2009 Recommendation* is undertaken.

2. The *OECD Guidelines*

The *OECD Guidelines* are a highly comprehensive instrument in terms of the codification of foreign investors' responsibilities. Currently, the instrument includes chapters that address issues such as disclosure of information, human rights, employment and industrial relations, the environment, bribery, consumer interests, science and technology, competition and taxation.[14] The analysis of the normative character of the *OECD Guidelines* nevertheless requires a closer look at their content and the interactions that they generate between international actors. While it is undeniable that they are taken into account by several actors and have proven to be useful to solve specific issues pertaining to activities of many foreign investors, this section argues that the *OECD Guidelines* generally fail to generate a sense of obligation and have not reached the realm of legality. More specifically, although most actors agree on the aspects included within the

10 See e.g. Böhmer, *supra* note 8 at 230.

11 Tony Porter & Michael Webb, "Role of the OECD in the Orchestration of Global Knowledge Networks" in Rianne Mahon & Stephen McBride, eds, *The OECD and Transnational Governance* (Vancouver: UBC Press, 2008) 43 at 43 and 47. See also Michael Webb, "Defining the Boundaries of Legitimate State Practice: Norms, Transnational Actors and the OECD's Project on Harmful Tax Competition" (2004) 11 Rev Int'l Pol Ecn 787 at 792.

12 See e.g. Böhmer, *supra* note 8 at 228.

13 See Russell Alan Williams, "The OECD and Foreign Investment Rules: The Global Promotion of Liberalization" in Rianne Mahon & Stephen McBride, eds, *The OECD and Transnational Governance* (Vancouver: UBC Press, 2008) 117 at 118.

14 *OECD Guidelines 2011*, *supra* note 1, Chapters III–XI.

scope of this instrument, the analysis below sheds light on the absence of shared understandings with respect to the normative nature of this initiative (2.1). Moreover, beyond tensions with some criteria of legality posited by the interactional theory of international law (2.2), the lack of a practice of legality between the actors involved in the implementation of the *OECD Guidelines* confirms the absence of a sense of obligation (2.3).

2.1 Shared Understandings: Diverging Views on the Nature of the Instrument

With respect to the *OECD Guidelines*, it is widely acknowledged that the OECD member states acted as *norm entrepreneurs* to secure the adoption of an international instrument codifying foreign investors' responsibilities before other intergovernmental organizations.[15] Following the launch of negotiations of a *Code of Conduct on Transnational Corporations* at the United Nations (UN), several capital-exporting states sought to develop an international instrument limited to recommendations formulated by governments to multinational enterprises. More specifically, in line with the promotion of liberal policies that characterizes the OECD, these norm entrepreneurs sought to combine the issue of controlling foreign investors' activities with a desire to liberalize capital export and to protect foreign investment in capital-importing states. Therefore, the *OECD Guidelines* constitute an integral part of a broader *Declaration on International Investment and Multinational Enterprises*,[16] which includes aspects related to national treatment of foreign investment and international investment incentives in addition to the *OECD Guidelines*. It is also worth noting that the *OECD Guidelines* were elaborated by the Committee on International Investment and Multinational Enterprises (now the Investment Committee) between March 1975 and May 1976, with the close collaboration of BIAC and TUAC.[17] Even though some authors report that the governments of Sweden and the Netherlands favored a more formal document to address foreign investors' responsibilities, the majority of the member states opted for an informal and flexible instrument.[18]

An ongoing evolution of the *OECD Guidelines* also characterizes this instrument. So far, these guidelines have been reviewed five times since the adoption of

15 See e.g. Roger Blanpain, "The OECD Guidelines for Multinational Enterprises – The Badger Case" (1978) 126 J Royal Soc'y Arts 326 at 328; Khalil Hamdani & Lorraine Ruffing, *United Nations Centre on Transnational Corporations: Corporate Conduct and the Public Interest* (London: Routledge, 2015) at 84 and 111.

16 For the current version, see *Declaration on International Investment and Multinational Enterprises*, 25 May 2011, C/MIN(2011)11/FINAL (2011).

17 See e.g. Theo W Vogelaar, "The OECD Guidelines: Their Philosophy, History, Negotiation, Form, Legal Nature, Follow-up Procedures and Review" in Norbert Horn, ed, *Legal Problems of Codes of Conduct for Multinational Enterprises* (Hingham: Kluwer Law and Taxation, 1980) 127 at 132.

18 See e.g. Henri Schwamm, "The OECD Guidelines for Multinational Enterprises" (1978) 12 J World Trade L 342 at 343 at 348–349; Vogelaar, *ibid* at 131; Hamdani & Ruffing, *supra* note 15 at 112.

their original version in 1976.[19] For example, these reviews have led to the inclusion of a provision with respect to the establishment of National Contact Points (NCPs) by adhering countries in 1984,[20] a chapter on the environment in 1991[21] and procedural guidance to deal with issues arising from the implementation of the *OECD Guidelines* in specific instances in 2000.[22] Furthermore, the current version includes a chapter on human rights, a new approach to due diligence and responsible supply chain management, as well as a more detailed procedure regarding specific instances of non-compliance with the recommendations stated in the *OECD Guidelines*.[23] However, throughout all these review processes, the explicit "voluntary and not legally enforceable"[24] character of this instrument has remained firmly preserved.

A considerable *community of practice* has also emerged around the subsequent reviews of the *OECD Guidelines*. For example, prior to the latest review of this instrument, the OECD called upon the active involvement of several states and non-state actors. Member states, BIAC, TUAC, OECD Watch, interested non-adhering countries and intergovernmental organizations are thus all cited in the *Terms of Reference* prepared for this review.[25] Scrutinizing various statements provided by these actors during the two most recent reviews of this international instrument, as well as information from participants in semi-structured interviews, is a valuable tool to assess whether these various actors have succeeded in reaching any shared understandings that are necessary to generate a sense of obligation.

It is plain that members of the community of practice have reached solid shared understandings regarding the matters that must be addressed through the *OECD Guidelines*. One example that illustrates this consensus concerns the aspects included in this instrument following its review in 2011. After the adoption of the revised instrument, BIAC mentioned the following:

19 See *Declaration on International Investment and Multinational Enterprises*, 13 June 1979, Doc No C(79)102/FINAL (1979); *Declaration on International Investment and Multinational Enterprises*, 17 May 1984, Doc No C/MIN(84)6(FINAL) (1984); *Declaration on International Investment and Multinational Enterprises*, 5 June 1991, Doc No C/MIN(91)7 (1991) [*OECD Guidelines 1991*]; *Declaration on International Investment and Multinational Enterprises*, 27 June 2000, Doc No C(2000)96/REV1 (2000); *OECD Guidelines 2011*, *supra* note 1.

20 See *Second Revised Decision of the Council on Inter-Governmental Consultation Procedures on the Guidelines for Multinational Enterprises*, June 1984, Doc No C(84)90 (1984) at paras 1–2.

21 See *OECD Guidelines 1991*, *supra* note 19.

22 The Procedural Guidance is attached to the *Decision of the Council on the OECD Guidelines for Multinational Enterprises*, 27 June 2000, Doc No (2000)96/FINAL.

23 *OECD Guidelines 2011*, *supra* note 1, Chapter IV and paras II(A)(10)-II(A)(13); *Decision of the Council on the OECD Guidelines for Multinational Enterprises*, 25 May 2011, Doc No C/MIN(2011)11/FINAL (2011), Procedural Guidance at para I(C)(3) [*Decision on the OECD Guidelines 2011*].

24 This language is still present in the current version of the *OECD Guidelines*. See *OECD Guidelines 2011*, *ibid* at para I(1).

25 See OECD, Investment Division, *Terms of Reference for an Update of the OECD Guidelines for Multinational Enterprises* (Paris: OECD, 2010) at 7–8 [OECD, *Terms of Reference*].

> [T]he process came close to a substantive revision. Although the new text increases the expectations put on business in a number of aspects, the central concerns of business have been addressed in a constructive way. BIAC is therefore in a position to state that it can accept the final text as negotiated by OECD member states.[26]

Along the same lines, OECD Watch "welcome[d] the changes to the *OECD Guidelines* that confirm and broaden the scope of the instrument to the global activities and all business relationships of [multinational enterprises]."[27]

By contrast, a sharp divide has persisted regarding the legal nature of this instrument through the review processes. On the one hand, representatives of the private sector and some member states of the OECD have constantly stressed that such an instrument had to remain voluntary. For example, in the summary of proceedings of a conference that preceded the review of the *OECD Guidelines* in 2000, a representative of BIAC recalled that "[c]onfidence building and trust amongst all adherents to the Guidelines should not be threatened, and suggestions with respect to *making the Guidelines a binding instrument would not be productive* in this regard."[28] On the other hand, several public interest NGOs and some states within the OECD advocated for a formal instrument and a stronger initiative. Following the adoption of the *OECD Guidelines* in 2000, a coalition of NGOs thus mentioned that its members were "disappointed that the OECD Governments chose a combination of voluntary low level standards with a weak implementation mechanism, which in some ways offers the worst of both worlds."[29] Belgium also mentioned that it would have preferred to provide a more strict character to ensure respect of the *OECD Guidelines*.[30] With respect to the most recent review process, EarthRights International published a press release in which it stated that "even if their substance were exactly as human rights and labor organizations wished, the Guidelines would remain simply another aspirational document without a functioning mechanism to encourage compliance and resolve disputes."[31]

26 BIAC, *BIAC Statement on the Adoption of the Update of the OECD Guidelines for Multinational Enterprises at the OECD Ministerial Council Meeting on 25–26 May 2011* (May 2011), online: BIAC http://biac.org/wp-content/uploads/2017/07/FIN-11-05-19-Final-BIAC-statement-on-updated-Guidelines-for-MCM-2011.pdf (accessed 26 March 2018).

27 OECD Watch, *OECD Watch Statement on the Update of the OECD Guidelines for MNEs: Improved Content and Scope, but Procedural Shortcomings Remain* (25 May 2011), online: OECD Watch http://oecdwatch.org/publications-en/Publication_3675 (accessed 26 March 2018).

28 See OECD, Committee on International Investment and Multinational Enterprises, *Conference on the OECD Guidelines for Multinational Enterprises: Summary of Proceedings*, Doc No DAFFE/IME(98)18 (1998) at 28 [emphasis added].

29 See OECD, Directorate for Financial, Fiscal and Enterprise Affairs, *OECD Guidelines for Multinational Enterprises: Statements Made on the Adoption of the Review 2000* (Paris: OECD, 2000) at 22 [OECD, *Statements Review 2000*].

30 See *ibid* at 8.

31 EarthRights International, News Release, "OECD Guidelines Update: Substantive Improvements, Procedural Disappointments" (25 May 2011), online: EarthRights International https://web.archive.org/web/20120418015506/https://www.earthrights.org/campaigns/oecd-guidelines-update-substantive-improvements-procedural-disappointments (accessed 26 March 2018).

These opposing views pertaining to the legal nature of the *OECD Guidelines* have also been echoed by some interviewees. As stated by one of them:

> If I compare the 2000 review with the 2011 update, I think there's no comparison in terms of the level of sophistication. People know a lot more now than they did back in 2000. But there's still – there's this business community that wants us to say this is a voluntary instrument and the NGOs want us to say: "Oh! You got a soft law mediation process . . . Why don't you have a more binding structure, international structure, etc." You know, that's the usual stuff that we get.[32]

Recalling the position of trade unions following the adoption of the first version of the *OECD Guidelines*, another interviewee mentioned that "[b]ecause they were voluntary, the trade unions in the OECD area were very skeptical about it."[33]

One key element that is illuminated through the use of a critical discourse analysis is the *relations of power* between the various members of the community of practice that are emphasized in some statements related to the review of the *OECD Guidelines.* For example, according to several NGOs:

> [g]overnments have accepted the argument *put forcefully by business* during the review that the Guidelines should not be "mandatory in fact or effect". The undersigned NGOs believe that this concession is fundamentally out of step with the experience and expectations of many communities around the world who face enormous obstacles and even dangers in holding multinationals to account for their damaging acts or omissions.[34]

Beyond a mere divergence of views with respect to the nature of the *OECD Guidelines*, the refusal to depart from a voluntary initiative appears to be primarily supported by powerful actors involved in the elaboration of this instrument.

Overall, the fact that the OECD member states acted as norm entrepreneurs that sought to counter normative developments occurring in other intergovernmental organizations by adopting an instrument whose voluntary observance has been preserved through several reviews is particularly instructive to assess the sense of obligation that emanates from the *OECD Guidelines.* Despite a consensus with respect to the expansion of the scope of this initiative, the analysis of discourses submitted in recent review processes and semi-structured interviews strongly suggests that diverging views remain between the members of this community of practice with respect to the legal nature of this instrument. To put it differently, there is a clear lack of shared understandings regarding the possibility of making the *OECD Guidelines* a legally binding instrument.

32 Interview 6.
33 Interview 17.
34 See OECD, *Statements Review 2000, supra* note 29 at 23 [emphasis added].

2.2 Criteria of Legality: A Fairly Legitimate, but Voluntary Initiative

Determining whether the *OECD Guidelines* have evolved toward the realm of legal norms also implies a consideration of their provisions and related commentaries in light of the criteria of legality included in the interactional theory of international law. As shown in the present section, the *OECD Guidelines* meet most of these criteria and thus appear as a fairly legitimate norm. However, a potential contradiction between the objective of the instrument and its explicit voluntary character, as well as a procedural means that can only weakly address conduct of private actors that is inconsistent with the *OECD Guidelines*, create a tension that ultimately affects the emergence of a sense of obligation from this international instrument.

With respect to *promulgation*, it is beyond question that the *OECD Guidelines* are not included in a formal international agreement or any other normative acts authorized by the constituent convention of the OECD. As mentioned above, this instrument is found in Annex 1 of the *Declaration on International Investment and Multinational Enterprises.*[35] As emphasized by the Chair of the drafting group of the first version of the *OECD Guidelines*, declarations at the OECD generally "constitute a solemn form of understanding on principles, without stipulating strict commitments on behalf of the participating parties."[36] These guidelines are nevertheless extensively disseminated and remain accessible to the public. In addition to being published by the OECD, NCPs established by adhering countries distribute brochures on the *OECD Guidelines* and develop promotional tools for various stakeholders, among others.[37]

A particular concern for the *general* application of the *OECD Guidelines* can be found in various provisions of their first chapter, which enunciates the concepts and the principles underlying the whole instrument. Paragraph I(6) mentions that "[g]overnments wish to encourage the widest possible observance of the *Guidelines.*"[38] Moreover, the same paragraph stresses that "[w]hile it is acknowledged that small- and medium-sized enterprises may not have the same capacities as larger enterprises, governments adhering to the *Guidelines* nevertheless encourage them to observe the *Guidelines'* recommendations to the fullest extent possible."[39] In light of the global nature of multinational enterprises' operations, the *OECD Guidelines* also call upon adhering countries "to encourage the enterprises operating on their territories to observe the *Guidelines* wherever they operate, while taking into account the particular circumstances in each host country."[40]

The *OECD Guidelines* also seem to live up to the requirement of *clarity*. Even though some authors argue that the content of this instrument remains broad

35 See *OECD Guidelines 2011*, *supra* note 1.

36 Vogelaar, *supra* note 17 at 132.

37 See e.g. OECD, *Annual Report on the OECD Guidelines for Multinational Enterprises 2014: Responsible Business Conduct by Sector* (Paris: OECD, 2014) at 23–24 [*OECD Guidelines Annual Report 2014*].

38 *OECD Guidelines 2011*, *supra* note 1 at para I(6).

39 *Ibid* at para I(6).

40 *Ibid* at para I(3).

and open to interpretation,[41] it is here submitted that several specifications prevent the *OECD Guidelines* to fall below what would be required to constitute a legitimate norm. Of course, the fact that a specific definition of multinational enterprises is excluded from this instrument can be pointed out as a considerable weakness. However, the additional information provided to emphasize the numerous sectors in which these enterprises can operate, their presence in various states, the potential exercise of influence among the numerous entities and various forms of ownership all contribute to provide a clear sense of these actors.[42] Furthermore, a total of 106 commentaries have been adopted to provide additional information regarding the provisions of this instrument.[43] For example, while some authors maintain that the process and principles underlying the concept of "due diligence" are not adequately defined in the *OECD Guidelines*,[44] the commentaries provide a relatively detailed definition of this term.[45] Where appropriate, several commentaries also refer to other formal and informal international instruments to explain the content of the *OECD Guidelines*.[46]

Another criterion that is included in the interactional theory of international law relates to the *constancy* of norms over time. While important amendments have been introduced to the text of the *OECD Guidelines* through various review processes, such amendments have not profoundly affected their constant character. At least throughout the first three reviews, the constancy of the *OECD Guidelines* has been taken into account "as their effective application depends in part on their stability."[47] With respect to the addition of a chapter on human rights, such an important modification relies primarily on the work undertaken by the UN Special Representative of the Secretary-General on the issue of human rights and transnational corporations and other business enterprises.[48] Rather than attempting to weaken the legitimacy of this international initiative by threatening its stability, the various reviews sought to reflect changes occurring in the international business environment as well as normative developments in other intergovernmental organizations involved in the codification of foreign investors' responsibilities.

Requiring that norms be *non-retroactive* aims to ensure that actors can take them into account in their decision-making processes. Given that nothing in the

41 See e.g. Leyla Davarnejad, "In the Shadow of Soft Law: The Handling of Corporate Social Responsibility Disputes under the OECD Guidelines for Multinational Enterprises" (2011) 2011 J Disp Resol 351 at 352.

42 See *OECD Guidelines 2011*, *supra* note 1 at para I(4).

43 OECD, *OECD Guidelines for Multinational Enterprises, 2011 Edition* (Paris: OECD, 2011), Note by the Secretariat [*OECD Guidelines 2011 – Commentaries*].

44 See e.g. Surya Deva, *Regulating Corporate Human Rights Violations: Humanizing Business* (London: Routledge, 2012) at 86 [Deva, *Regulating*]; Penelope Simons & Audrey Macklin, *The Governance Gap: Extractive Industries, Human Rights, and the Home State Advantage* (New York: Routledge, 2014) at 99 and 103.

45 *OECD Guidelines 2011 – Commentaries*, *supra* note 43 at para 14.

46 *OECD Guidelines 2011 – Commentaries*, *ibid* at paras 7, 10, 29, 36, 39, 48, 49, 51–54, 56–58, 60, 65, 68, 76, 77, 79–81, 87, 96, 99 and 104–106.

47 See OECD, *The OECD Guidelines for Multinational Enterprises*, Doc No OECD/GD(97)40 (1997).

48 See OECD, *Terms of Reference*, *supra* note 25 at 3.

OECD Guidelines explicitly deals with temporal issues, this criterion of legality seems to be easily met. Moreover, at least one NCP that was responsible for the interpretation of these recommendations decided that the application of the 2000 version of the *OECD Guidelines* was inappropriate when considering conduct that occurred before the adoption of this version.[49]

In light of the nature of multinational enterprises' activities and the number of entities upon which they exercise various forms of control, the consideration of feasible requirements is particularly relevant to ensure that international instruments do *not ask the impossible.* In addition to provisions calling upon governments' cooperation when private actors are confronted to conflicting requirements,[50] the commentaries pertaining to the chapter on the disclosure of information unambiguously state that "[d]isclosure recommendations are not expected to place unreasonable administrative or cost burdens on enterprises."[51] Moreover, the concept of due diligence that is included in the latest version of the *OECD Guidelines* ensures a realist character to the recommendations provided in this instrument. While subjecting the conduct of human rights due diligence to several conditions (*i.e.* the size of the private entity, the nature and context of operations and the severity of the risks of adverse human rights impacts),[52] the *OECD Guidelines* expressly provide that seeking to prevent or mitigate an adverse impact directly linked to the activities of multinational enterprises "is not intended to shift responsibility from the entity causing an adverse impact to the enterprise with which it has a business relationship."[53]

While the *OECD Guidelines* do not include any provisions that stand in direct contradiction, there is at least one element that creates a tension regarding the *absence of contradiction.* The Preface of this instrument stresses that "[t]he *Guidelines* aim to ensure that the operations of these enterprises are in harmony with government policies"[54] and that "[g]overnments adhering to the *Guidelines* are committed to continuous improvement of both domestic and international policies with a view to improving the welfare and living standards of all people."[55] Yet, the ubiquitous voluntary character of this initiative may contradict, to a certain extent, such noble objectives.[56] To put it differently, the *OECD Guidelines* recognize the necessity to tackle an important issue, but rely on recommendations whose observance remain strictly voluntary to address it. Although this tension does not equal to imposing contradicting requirements to the same actor, it can be perceived as a certain form of contradiction within this international initiative.

49 See OECD, *Annual Report on the OECD Guidelines for Multinational Enterprises 2008: Employment and Industrial Relations* (Paris: OECD, 2008) at 38 [*OECD Guidelines Annual Report 2008*].
50 *OECD Guidelines 2011*, *supra* note 1 at paras I(2) and I(8).
51 *OECD Guidelines 2011 – Commentaries*, *supra* note 43 at para 30.
52 *OECD Guidelines 2011*, *supra* note 1 at para IV(5).
53 *Ibid* at para II(A)(12).
54 *Ibid*, Preface at para 1.
55 *Ibid*, Preface at para 9.
56 See *ibid* at para I(1).

Finally, when analyzing the extent to which the *OECD Guidelines* are designed to ensure *congruence* between rules and official action, some aspects of this instrument ensure the establishment of a procedure related to this criterion of legality. The *Decision of the Council on the OECD Guidelines for Multinational Enterprises* (*Decision on the OECD Guidelines*) provides that adhering countries shall establish NCPs in order to contribute "to the resolution of issues that arise relating to the implementation of the *Guidelines* in specific instances."[57] According to the procedural guidance attached to the *Decision on the OECD Guidelines*, NCPs are expected to make the results of the procedures they facilitate publicly available, "taking into account the need to protect sensitive business and other stakeholder information."[58] NCPs are thus expected to issue a statement when they decide that issues raised do not merit any further consideration[59] or when no agreement can be reached between the parties involved in a specific instance, including when "one party is unwilling to participate in the procedure."[60] A report must also be prepared when the parties involved reach an agreement on the issues raised.[61] Moreover, the *Decision on the OECD Guidelines* provides that the Investment Committee is responsible for clarification of the *OECD Guidelines.*[62] Ultimately, in order to improve the implementation procedure of the *OECD Guidelines*, the most recent procedural guidance attached to the *Decision on the OECD Guidelines* establishes the facilitation of voluntary peer evaluations by the Investment Committee.[63]

While these procedural devices allow addressing specific instances of non-compliance with the recommendations stated in the *OECD Guidelines*, the extent to which these procedures provide an appropriate response is questionable. In fact, nothing in the *OECD Guidelines* or the *Decision on the OECD Guidelines* expressly requires NCPs or the Investment Committee to determine the compliance of a multinational enterprise with the recommendations stated in this international initiative. The commentary on the procedural guidance for the Investment Committee that is attached to the *Decision on the OECD Guidelines* clearly states the voluntary character of this procedure:

> Statements and reports on the results of the proceedings made publicly available by the NCPs could be relevant to the administration of government programmes and policies. In order to foster policy coherence, NCPs are encouraged to inform these government agencies of their statements and reports when they are known by the NCP to be relevant to a specific agency's policies and programmes. *This provision does not change the voluntary nature of the* Guidelines.[64]

57 *Decision on the OECD Guidelines 2011*, *supra* note 23, at para I(1).
58 *Ibid*, Procedural Guidance at para I(C)(3).
59 *Ibid*, Procedural Guidance at para I(C)(3)(a).
60 *Ibid*, Procedural Guidance at para I(C)(3)(c).
61 *Ibid*, Procedural Guidance at para I(C)(3)(b).
62 *Ibid*, at para II(4).
63 *Ibid*, Procedural Guidance at para II(5)(c).
64 *OECD Guidelines 2011 – Commentaries*, *supra* note 43, Commentary on the Procedural Guidance for the Investment Committee at para 44.

In other words, despite considerable institutional arrangements and details with respect to their functioning, these procedural devices are not intended to specifically determine any breaches of the *OECD Guidelines*.

The assessment of the content of the *OECD Guidelines* through the lens of the criteria of legality provided by the interactional theory of international law thus suggests a fairly legitimate instrument, with some nuances with respect to the criteria of contradiction and congruence. As mentioned above, the express voluntary character of the instrument does not sit well with its objective and remains in tension with the possibility of addressing adequately significant instances of non-compliance. However, such features of the *OECD Guidelines* do not, in themselves, totally prevent the emergence of a genuine sense of obligation. As demonstrated in the following section, it is mostly the reliance on such an express voluntary character by members of the community of practice that ultimately leads to the absence of a sense of obligation. It is in this regard that the analysis now turns to an examination of the practice surrounding this international initiative.

2.3 Practice of Legality: Avoiding a Binding Practice

In order to fully enter the realm of legality, the observance of international norms must be considered as mandatory by a community of actors. In addition to scrutinizing the content of international instruments referring to the *OECD Guidelines*, this section relies on annual reports and transcripts from semi-structured interviews in order to shed light on the type of practice characterizing the implementation of this international initiative.

It is hard to deny that the *OECD Guidelines* have generated a considerable practice. A database provided by the OECD included 389 specific instances that have been brought to NCPs as of March 2018.[65] In an encouraging way, the annual report on the *OECD Guidelines* of 2014 stresses that an "unprecedented number of specific instances involving NCP-facilitated mediation helped parties reach an agreement or create an action plan toward the resolution of the specific instance."[66] Furthermore, other international instruments developed under the auspices of intergovernmental organizations refer to the *OECD Guidelines*.[67]

65 OECD, *Database of Specific Instances*, online: OECD http://mneguidelines.oecd.org/database/ (accessed 26 March 2018).

66 *OECD Guidelines Annual Report 2014*, *supra* note 37 at 16.

67 See e.g. *Norms on the Responsibilities of Transnational Corporations and other Business Enterprises with regard to Human Rights*, 2003, UN Doc E/CN.4//Sub.2/2003/12/Rev.2, Preamble [*UN Norms*]; *Risk Awareness Tool for Multinational Enterprises in Weak Governance Zones*, 8 June 2006, online: OECD www.oecd.org/daf/inv/corporateresponsibility/36885821.pdf (accessed 26 March 2018) at 9; Special Representative of the Secretary-General on the issue of human rights and transnational corporations and other business enterprises, *Guiding Principles on Business and Human Rights: Implementing the United Nations 'Protect, Respect and Remedy' Framework*, 2011, UN Doc A/HRC/17/31, Commentary on Principle 2 and Commentary on Principle 25; *Recommendation of the Council on Due Diligence Guidance for Responsible Supply Chains of Minerals from Conflict-Affected and High-Risk Areas*, 17 July 2012, Doc No C(2012)93 (2012), Preamble [*Recommendation on Due Diligence Guidance*]; *Tripartite Declaration of Principles concerning Multinational Enterprises and Social Policy*, March 2017, online: ILO www.ilo.org/empent/Publications/WCMS_094386/lang--en/index.htm (accessed 26 March 2018), Preamble.

These elements suggest that this international norm undeniably plays a role within the broader codification of standards of appropriate conduct for private firms operating abroad.

Yet, this practice has come under considerable critiques.[68] Submissions from TUAC and OECD Watch included in annual reports on the *OECD Guidelines* often emphasize that the practice of some NCPs is not in line with the procedural guidance attached to the *Decision on the OECD Guidelines*. For example, in 2009, TUAC reported "that the uneven performance of NCPs is severely undermining the effectiveness of the Guidelines as a whole, with improvements in some being negated by the persistently poor performance of a number of laggards, including Japan, Korea and the US."[69] Addressing this issue in harsher terms, OECD Watch maintained that "[t]he NCPs have given themselves such latitude in the way that they operate the Guidelines that NGOs increasingly view the process as an arbitrary, unfair and unpredictable process."[70] Several interviewees also underlined important variations concerning the performance of existing NCPs.[71]

Most importantly, if international actors do not act as if observance of an international instrument is mandatory, it would be inappropriate to conclude that a genuine practice of legality exists. In the case at hand, several discourses demonstrate that the overwhelming majority of interactions within the community of practice are not guided by any sense of obligation. Despite some examples in which NCPs determine violations of the *OECD Guidelines* by a private actor,[72] annual reports on the activities of NCPs abound with examples in which these institutions reiterate the voluntary character of the recommendations included in the *OECD Guidelines*. Several statements from NCPs thus include background information mentioning that the *OECD Guidelines* "establish *non-legally binding principles* covering a broad range of issues in business ethics."[73] In a statement included in the 2005 annual report, the NCP from the United Kingdom stresses that "[t]he purpose of the Guidelines . . . is not to act

68 See e.g. Davarnejad, *supra* note 41 at 366–384; Deva, *Regulating*, *supra* note 44 at 83–85; Elisa Morgera, "From Corporate Social Responsibility to Accountability Mechanisms" in Pierre-Marie Dupuy & Jorge E Viñuales, eds, *Harnessing Foreign Investment to Promote Environmental Protection: Incentives and Safeguards* (Cambridge: Cambridge University Press, 2013) 321 at 346–347; Simons and Macklin, *supra* note 44 at 106–113.

69 See OECD, *Annual Report on the OECD Guidelines for Multinational Enterprises 2009: Consumer Empowerment* (Paris: OECD, 2009) at 83 [*OECD Guidelines Annual Report 2009*].

70 See OECD, *Annual Report on the OECD Guidelines for Multinational Enterprises 2005: Corporate Responsibility in the Developing World* (Paris, OECD: 2005) at 133 [*OECD Guidelines Annual Report 2005*].

71 See e.g. Interview 14: "We have a problem with the National Contact Points in that there's a lot of variation in how well they perform. So we have a couple that are really strong performers and then a couple that are basically just non-existing – I think they don't even have a website or a contact address, things like that."

72 For example, in a statement from the NCP of the United Kingdom, the latter mentioned that "[i]t is usual practice for the NCP to make determinations of compliance and to issue recommendations in respect of a specific instance on those matters which remain unresolved." See *OECD Guidelines Annual Report 2008*, supra note 49 at 78.

73 This formulation can be found in several statements issued by the UK NCP. See e.g. *OECD Guidelines Annual Report 2009*, *supra* note 69 at 31 [emphasis added].

as an instrument of sanction nor to hold any company to account."[74] Rather, this procedure is perceived as "a problem solving mechanism with a view to parties coming to an agreement or for the NCP to make recommendations for future behaviour in similar circumstances."[75]

Other statements from NCPs unambiguously demonstrate that these institutions have no means to oblige a party to engage in the procedure regarding a specific instance. For example, with respect to a statement by the Canadian NCP regarding the activities of a mining company in Myanmar, the 2005 annual report mentions the following:

> While the NCP held a number of discussion and meetings with each party, separately, and offered to facilitate a dialogue between the two sides, it was *unsuccessful in bringing them together to discuss their differences.* The NCP has informed the parties that it has decided to discontinue its efforts to facilitate a dialogue between them. A letter will be sent to the union and the company indicating that the NCP is bringing the specific instance procedure to a close.[76]

Similarly, in a final statement on a specific instance involving a trade union and a business enterprise, the US NCP mentioned that the business enterprise preferred to pursue the issue exclusively under US labor law.[77] As a result, the US NCP "took no immediate action, but indicated to both parties that it would continue monitoring developments in the dispute while considering the preparation of a final report."[78] When facing similar situations, other NCPs merely regretted the unexpected change of commitment of a party.[79]

Beyond these discourses pertaining to the activities of NCPs, the practice related to the *OECD Guidelines* also includes distinct moments in which several actors emphasized the absence of any legal character to this initiative. Responses following a report by the Panel of Experts on the Illegal Exploitation of Natural Resources and other Forms of Wealth of the Democratic Republic of the Congo are a glaring example of the lack of a practice of legality with respect to the *OECD Guidelines.* In its Final Report published in 2002, this panel included a list of business enterprises that were "in violation of the OECD Guidelines for

74 *OECD Guidelines Annual Report 2005, supra* note 70 at 76.

75 *Ibid* at 76.

76 *OECD Guidelines Annual Report 2005, supra* note 70 at 23–24 [emphasis added].

77 See OECD, *Annual Report on the OECD Guidelines for Multinational Enterprises 2007: Corporate Responsibility in the Financial Sector* (Paris, OECD: 2007) at 81–82.

78 See *ibid* at 81–82. Similar examples involving the US NCP can be found in OECD, *Annual Report on the OECD Guidelines for Multinational Enterprises 2012: Mediation and Consensus Building* (Paris: OECD, 2012) at 151; *OECD Guidelines Annual Report 2014, supra* note 37 at 108–109.

79 See e.g. OECD, *Annual Report on the OECD Guidelines for Multinational Enterprises 2011: A New Agenda for the Future* (Paris, OECD: 2011) at 75 [*OECD Guidelines Annual Report 2011*]; OECD, *Annual Report on the OECD Guidelines for Multinational Enterprises 2013: Responsible Business Conduct in Action* (Paris, OECD: 2013) at 95.

Multinational Enterprises."[80] It also stressed that "[h]ome Governments have the *obligation* to ensure that enterprises in their jurisdiction do not abuse principles of conduct that they have adopted as a matter of law."[81]

While the use of the *OECD Guidelines* to assess the conduct of enterprises operating in the Democratic Republic of the Congo could have contributed to foster a practice of legality, it generated numerous critiques from BIAC and the Investment Committee that implicitly refer to the absence of a sense of obligation emanating from the *OECD Guidelines*. In a letter transferred to the UN Secretary-General, the Chair of the Investment Committee felt the need to clarify the nature and the status of this international instrument. More specifically, the Chair of the Investment Committee recalled that

> [w]hile observance of the Guidelines by enterprises is *voluntary and not legally enforceable*, each adhering government has undertaken to establish a National Contact Point that deals with all matters relating to the implementation of the Guidelines in the national context, including specific enquiries regarding the activities of individual enterprises.[82]

BIAC also strongly reacted to this use of the *OECD Guidelines* by maintaining its position "that the NCPs and [the Investment Committee] should continue to clearly reject the use of the Guidelines through the UN 'Panel of Experts' which includes the naming of companies allegedly misbehaving."[83]

The absence of a practice of legality has also been highlighted by many interviewees. After arguing that this international initiative cannot be reduced to a mere voluntary instrument, one of them mentioned the following:

> So, little by little, I think it makes a difference. I don't think there's huge awareness of the Guidelines as an *ex ante* kind of norm thing, among companies, right now. . . . [F]or the time being, that hasn't turned in to: "Oh God, we have to do something to comply with the Guidelines." As a general principle for management, I don't think we're anywhere close to that.[84]

Another participant stressed the concrete consequences that can result from conduct that is inconsistent with the *OECD Guidelines*, while mentioning that the latter fall short of being a legal norm:

80 *Final Report of the Panel of Experts on the Illegal Exploitation of Natural Resources and other Forms of Wealth of the Democratic Republic of the Congo*, 2002, UN Doc S/2002/1146 at paras 175, 177 and Annex III.

81 *Ibid* at 178 [emphasis added].

82 See OECD, *Annual Report on the OECD Guidelines for Multinational Enterprises 2003: Enhancing the Role of Business in the Fight Against Corruption* (Paris, OECD: 2003) at 76–77 [emphasis added].

83 See *ibid* at 90.

84 Interview 6.

> [Y]ou can no longer say there are no consequences, because there are consequences. There are consequences to your reputation; there are consequences in terms of the financial sector asking all kinds of nasty questions; there are consequences in terms of shareholders asking questions; there are consequences when it comes to being allowed to come on trade missions from your government, for example. *It's all rather soft, but the system we have is not a legal system – so there are no appeal mechanisms, there's no legal scrutiny like there is in court. . . . It's not a real legal thing.*[85]

Of course, one could argue that the nature of the practice has evolved since the latest review of the *OECD Guidelines*. In the first annual report following this review, the OECD cited the adoption of the UN *Guiding Principles for Business and Human Rights* and normative developments that occurred at the International Finance Corporation to stress the existence of a "broadly shared view that corporate responsibility is no longer a matter of voluntary goodwill, but at the very least, a duty not to cause harm or actively contribute to economic, environmental and social progress of host economies."[86] However, the apparent departure from the strict voluntary character has not led to the recognition of any binding character to this instrument. In fact, the same annual report describes the *OECD Guidelines* "as the most comprehensive voluntary code of conduct developed by governments in existence today."[87] Even after the most recent amendments to the procedural guidance that ensure the issuance of a statement when no agreement is reached between the parties involved in a specific instance, the OECD has continued to depict such a procedure "as a tool to incentivize cooperation" and as "one factor that might weigh in the cost/benefit analysis of the parties' decision to engage in the NCP procedure."[88] More recently, the 2016 annual report summarizes the normative nature of the *OECD Guidelines* in the following terms: "The Guidelines are recommendations addressed by governments to multinational enterprises. Efforts to confer a binding nature on the Guidelines failed in the early years of their introduction. As such, the instrument is *voluntary in nature.*"[89]

Another interesting element that has been introduced following the review of the *OECD Guidelines* in 2011 and that constitutes an integral part of the practice surrounding this instrument is the peer evaluation of NCPs' activities. Although the assessment by other members of the OECD can definitely contribute to foster a practice of legality, this mechanism has only been weakly used by adhering countries in the case of NCPs. At the time of writing this chapter, only

85 Interview 13 [emphasis added].

86 *OECD Guidelines Annual Report 2011*, *supra* note 79 at 12–13.

87 *Ibid* at 12–13.

88 *Ibid* at 41.

89 OECD, *Annual Report on the OECD Guidelines for Multinational Enterprises 2016* (Paris: OECD, 2016) at 15 [emphasis added].

seven NCPs subjected themselves to such an evaluation process.[90] What is more, the fact that these peer evaluations remain voluntary has been strongly criticized by some members of the community of practice.[91] The difference between such a voluntary evaluation and the more traditional peer review mechanism that is generally found in the OECD is also emphasized in the report related to the peer evaluation of the Japanese NCP:

> Unlike traditional OECD peer reviews, this exercise would not be directed at evaluating the performance of an NCP against established benchmarks but, instead it should allow both the reviewed NCP and the other participating NCPs to learn from each other how best to further the objectives of the Guidelines in light of their individual challenges.[92]

Interestingly, the general absence of a practice of legality that is evidenced through discourse analysis also implies *relations of power* underlying the implementation of the *OECD Guidelines*. According to OECD Watch, "[t]he Guidelines were agreed after lengthy negotiations between all the parties but their scope is constantly being eroded seemingly at the behest of business confederations."[93] A letter from the Chair of the Investment Committee to BIAC dated from 2002 also illuminates the alignment of the *OECD Guidelines*' implementation with the interests of business enterprises. As stated by the Chair of the Investment Committee:

> Recognising the importance of the business community's support and co-operation to the effectiveness of the Guidelines, delegates agreed on the need for additional efforts to cultivate that support and co-operation. They believe that *BIAC and its affiliates' contribution to the promotion of the Guidelines are the most effective means to encourage voluntary observance of the Guidelines* by the broadest spectrum of individual multinational enterprises.[94]

Beyond the absence of shared understandings with respect to the legal nature of this instrument, the lack of a practice of legality thus partly appears as the result of relations of power and reflects the interests of powerful actors involved in the community of practice that surrounds the *OECD Guidelines*.

90 See OECD, *NCP Peer Reviews*, online: OECD https://mneguidelines.oecd.org/ncppeerreviews.htm (accessed 26 March 2018).

91 See e.g. Amnesty International, Press Release, "The 2010–2011 Update of the OECD Guidelines for Multinational Enterprises Has Come to an End: The OECD Must Now Turn Into Effective Implementation" (23 May 2011), online: Amnesty International www.amnesty.org/en/documents/IOR30/001/2011/en/ (accessed 26 March 2018).

92 OECD, *Japanese NCP: Peer Learning and Review* (Paris: OECD, 2012) at 8.

93 See *OECD Guidelines Annual Report 2005*, *supra* note 70 at 133.

94 See OECD, *Annual Report on the OECD Guidelines for Multinational Enterprises 2002: Focus on Responsible Supply Chain Management* (Paris, OECD: 2002) at 36 [emphasis added].

To be clear, nothing in the present argumentation aims to deny the concrete consequences that the *OECD Guidelines* can have on the conduct of international actors. It is plain that refusal to engage in a procedure with an NCP can ultimately lead to negative financial, reputational and other social consequences that are taken into account by international actors. Facing these consequences, several actors can thus decide to participate in such a procedure and seek an agreement to solve an issue arising from the implementation of the *OECD Guidelines.* As a social norm, this international initiative thus undoubtedly plays a role in influencing behavior of several actors. However, a closer analysis of the nature of the interactions between members of this community of practice does not permit a conclusion that the majority of these members act according to a practice of legality. At best, the actual practice is characterized by a will to use this international initiative to solve issues occurring in specific instances, with the existence of recent and sporadic examples that point toward an ambiguous sense of obligation around this international instrument. At worst, it encompasses deliberate efforts to maintain the express voluntary character of the *OECD Guidelines* and avoid the imposition of any direct sanctions to hold private investors accountable for harm caused abroad. Ultimately, while more recent discourses have contributed to slightly depart from the strict voluntary character of the *OECD Guidelines*, nothing from the analysis above allows qualifying this practice as ensuring a genuine sense of obligation.

3. The *OECD Anti-Bribery Convention* and the *OECD 2009 Recommendation*

In addition to the inclusion of a chapter dealing with anti-bribery in the *OECD Guidelines*, the OECD has served as a normative site to develop other initiatives addressing this issue more specifically. Taken as a whole, the *OECD Anti-Bribery Convention* and the *OECD 2009 Recommendation* address aspects such as the definition of bribery of foreign public officials, sanctions, jurisdiction, enforcement, mutual legal assistance, small facilitation payments, reporting of foreign bribery and tax deductibility, among others.[95] In contrast to the *OECD Guidelines*, this section argues that the OECD anti-bribery instruments create a sense of obligation and that they both constitute international legal norms. Notwithstanding some disagreements pertaining to the elements covered within their scope, these instruments are embedded in solid shared understandings to establish international norms addressing the liability of legal persons for the bribery of foreign public officials (3.1). Moreover, when considered together, the *OECD Anti-Bribery Convention* and the *OECD 2009 Recommendation* are entirely consistent with the criteria of legality identified in the interactional theory of international law (3.2). Finally, despite some disappointments pertaining to the number of convictions by domestic courts, the practice surrounding the implementation of

95 See generally *OECD Anti-Bribery Convention*, *supra* note 2; *OECD 2009 Recommendation*, *supra* note 3.

these two international instruments is a practice of legality that fosters a sense of obligation for several international actors (3.3).

3.1 Shared Understandings: Powerful Actors Pushing for the Liability of Legal Persons

Analyzing the emergence of OECD instruments that focus on the bribery of foreign officials in international business transactions inevitably leads to the recognition of the role of the United States as a key *norm entrepreneur*. Following the Watergate scandal and the adoption of the *Foreign Corrupt Practice Act* (*FCPA*),[96] the United States sought to obtain a commitment from other states to effectively address the issue of bribery in transnational business transactions through various intergovernmental organizations. For example, in a memorandum to the President of the United States in 1980, the Secretary of Commerce and the United States Trade Representative maintained that "[d]iscouraging corruption in international business on the part of foreign firms requires a multilateral agreement" and that the United States has "been pursuing such an agreement actively in the UN, with only marginal success."[97] While the United States primarily sought to limit the comparative advantage granted to foreign private entities not subjected to legislation equivalent to the *FCPA*, these efforts were supported by non-state actors who also raised serious concerns regarding the negative impact of corruption for developing countries through the 1980s.[98] In 1989, the United States proposed the creation of an *ad hoc* group under the auspices of the OECD "to examine the feasibility of an international agreement on illicit payments, with a view towards negotiating *a binding agreement* among OECD members on that subject."[99]

Further to the initial push provided by the United States and non-state actors, members of the OECD supported the adoption of a formal international agreement focused on addressing international corruption. After a first recommendation adopted in 1994 and in parallel to a campaign of persuasion led by

96 *Foreign Corrupt Practices Act*, 15 USC § 78 (1977). Many authors link the emergence of formal international agreements prohibiting corruption with the *FCPA*. See e.g. Robert D Tronnes, "Ensuring Uniformity in the Implementation of the 1997 OECD Convention on Combating Bribery of Foreign Public Officials in International Business Transactions" (2000) 33 Geo Wash J Int'l L & Ecn 97 at 100–102; Kenneth W Abbott & Duncan Snidal, "Values and Interests: International Legalization in the Fight against Corruption" (2002) 31:S1 J Legal Stud S141 at S161–S162; Marco Arnone & Leonardo S Borlini, *Corruption: Economic Analysis and International Law* (Northampton: Edward Elgar, 2014) at 209–216; Cecily Rose, *International Anti-Corruption Norms: Their Creation and Influence on Domestic Legal Systems* (Oxford: Oxford University Press, 2015) at 1 and 63–64.

97 United States of America, Department of State, *Foreign Relations of the United States, 1977–1980*, Vol III (Washington, DC: Department of State, 2013) at 740.

98 See e.g. Tronnes, *supra* note 96 at 111; Abbott & Snidal, *supra* note 96 at S159.

99 *United States Proposal on the Issue of Illicit Payments*, 23 March 1989, Doc No C(89)49 (1989), Annex [emphasis added] [*United States Proposal*].

the public interest NGO Transparency International,[100] the OECD member states elaborated "agreed common elements" for an international convention that were included in the Annex of the *Revised Recommendation of the Council on Combating Bribery in International Business Transactions* in 1997.[101] Among the various aspects that were considered to open negotiations on such an international convention, the OECD member states agreed that "[m]onetary or other civil, administrative or criminal penalties on *any legal person involved*, should be provided, taking into account the amounts of the bribe and of the profits derived from the transaction obtained through the bribe."[102] It is on the basis of these elements that the *OECD Anti-Bribery Convention* was negotiated and ultimately signed in 1997.[103] Most importantly, Article 2 of this formal international agreement provides that "[e]ach Party shall take such measures as may be necessary, in accordance with its legal principles, to establish the liability of legal persons for the bribery of a foreign public official."[104]

Another integral part regarding the emergence of the OECD anti-bribery instruments relates to the adoption of the *OECD 2009 Recommendation*. In fact, the initial push for this international instrument resulted from a general will to reaffirm the relevance of the *OECD Anti-Bribery Convention* a decade after its signature. Following the *Statement on a Shared Commitment to Fight Against Bribery* in November 2007[105] and the *Policy Statement on Bribery in International Business Transactions* in June 2009,[106] the *OECD 2009 Recommendation* has been adopted on 26 November 2009.[107] Annex I of this international instrument includes additional details with respect to the responsibility of legal persons for the bribery of foreign public officials in international business transactions.[108] Further to an amendment adopted on 18 February 2010, the *OECD 2009 Recommendation* also includes a second annex entitled *Good Practice Guidance on International Controls, Ethics, and Compliance*.[109]

100 *Recommendation of the Council on Bribery in International Business Transactions*, 27 May 1994, Doc No C(94)75/FINAL (1994). See also Giorgio Sacerdoti, "The 1997 OECD Convention on Combating Bribery of Foreign Public Officials in International Business Transactions: An Example of Piece-Meal Regulation of Globalisation" (1999) 9 Italian YB Int'l L 26 at 32–35; David Metcalfe, "The OECD Agreement to Criminalize Bribery: A Negotiation Analytic Perspective" (2000) 5 Int'l Negotiation 129 at 134; Abbott & Snidal, *supra* note 96 at S165;; Rose, *supra* note 96 at 64–65.

101 *Revised Recommendation of the Council on Combating Bribery in International Business Transactions*, 23 May 1997, Doc No C(97)123/FINAL (1997).

102 *Ibid*, Annex at para 5.

103 *OECD Anti-Bribery Convention*, *supra* note 2.

104 *Ibid*, art 2.

105 OECD, *Shared Commitment to Fight Against Foreign Bribery* (Paris: OECD, 2007) [OECD, *Shared Commitment*].

106 OECD, Working Group on Bribery in International Business Transactions, *Policy Statement on Bribery in International Business Transactions* (Paris: OECD, 2009).

107 *OECD 2009 Recommendation*, *supra* note 3.

108 *Ibid*, Annex I at para B.

109 *Ibid*, Annex II.

Closely related to the liability of legal persons, this good practice guidance is directly addressed to companies and seeks to contribute to the establishment of various measures geared toward the detection of corrupt practices within business activities.[110]

A closer look at the international actors involved in the consultation process that was initiated by the OECD to review the anti-bribery instruments in January 2008 allows identifying a vast *community of practice* surrounding the elaboration of these international norms.[111] In addition to state actors, this community includes members of the private sector, NGOs, trade unions and representatives from intergovernmental organizations, among others.[112] All these actors have been actively involved in discussions related to the reaffirmation of the relevance of the *OECD Anti-Bribery Convention* and have ultimately contributed to the elaboration of the *OECD 2009 Recommendation*. Relying on discourses from members of this community of practice and transcripts from semi-structured interviews, the remaining part of the present section aims to shed light on the existence of shared understandings regarding the elaboration of these two instruments.

Some statements suggest a lack of shared understandings with respect to the inclusion of specific elements within the scope of these two instruments.[113] For example, during the consultation process that occurred ten years after the signature of the *OECD Anti-Bribery Convention*, the Working Group on Bribery in International Business Transactions (Working Group on Bribery) identified some diverging views as far as the inclusion of private sector corruption is concerned:

> [I]n September 2006, the [International Chamber of Commerce] sent a further letter and memorandum repeating its concerns about private sector corruption. . . . It also stated that it would be appropriate to amend the 1997 Revised Recommendation or adopt a new Recommendation that "strongly recommends" that each Party to the Convention "take such legislative and other measures as may be necessary to establish that it is a criminal offence under its law" to engage in bribery in the private sector "and that this crime, as well as its prosecution, be made a high enforcement priority". . . . The Working Group recognises that this issue is not so far in its mandate and is cautious about extending its mandate to cover this issue, a perspective shared by Transparency International.[114]

110 *Ibid*, Annex II, Introduction.

111 OECD, Working Group on Bribery in International Business Transactions, *Consultation Paper: Review of the OECD Instruments on Combating Bribery of Foreign Public Officials in International Business Transactions Ten Years After Adoption* (Paris: OECD, 2008) [OECD, *Consultation Paper*].

112 *Ibid* at 3.

113 For a presentation of issues addressed in the negotiation of the *OECD Anti-Bribery Convention*, see Metcalfe, *supra* note 100 at 136–139.

114 OECD, *Consultation Paper*, *supra* note 111 at paras 19 and 21.

In a way that reflects the position adopted by Transparency International, BIAC also expressed some doubts pertaining to the inclusion of bribery occurring solely in the private sector:

> While we recognize that private-to-private bribery is an issue that needs to be addressed we question whether the OECD anti-bribery instruments are the means that are best suited to tackle this problem. Inclusion of private-to-private bribery would mean a significant expansion of the scope of the OECD anti-bribery instruments and this would bear the risk to lose focus.[115]

Other statements suggest a lack of shared understandings pertaining to the exclusion of small facilitation payments from the scope of the *OECD Anti-Bribery Convention*. While some states initially pushed for maintaining an exception in the international agreement, Transparency International recalled that "other anticorruption conventions, adopted after the OECD Convention, do not exempt facilitation payments [and that] a substantial number of OECD states prohibit facilitation payments."[116] Likewise, TUAC emphasized that "[t]he exception of facilitation payments . . . has long been a *source of controversy*" and it contended "that it is also a source of potential abuse, confusion and reputational damage."[117] In other words, despite support from a considerable number of actors, the opposition of some states prevented the reach of shared understandings with respect to the inclusion of small facilitation payments in the *OECD Anti-Bribery Convention*.

Regardless of these diverging views, one crucial point on which international actors have reached shared understandings is the elaboration of a strong commitment to establish the liability of legal persons for the bribery of foreign public officials in international business transactions. Constituted from state representatives, the Working Group on Bribery thus mentioned in its consultation paper that the focus on the effectiveness of states' systems for the liability of legal persons "is consistent with the overall focus of the Convention on *deterring, detecting and sanctioning the bribery of foreign public officials through a punitive approach*."[118] Non-state actors have also used the consultation process surrounding the OECD anti-bribery instruments to demonstrate their support to establishing the liability of legal persons. For example, Transparency International highlighted an "*increasing recognition* that to deal with complex crimes such as foreign bribery, *corporations should be held liable* not only for affirmative derelictions but for lack of supervision or control."[119]

115 See OECD, *Review of the OECD Anti-Bribery Instruments: Compilation of Responses to Consultation Paper* (Paris: OECD, 2008) at 109 [OECD, *Responses to Consultation*].
116 See *ibid* at 102.
117 See *ibid* at 139 [emphasis added].
118 OECD, *Consultation Paper*, *supra* note 111 at para 24 [emphasis added].
119 See OECD, *Responses to Consultation*, *supra* note 115 at 101 [emphasis added].

Echoing the shared understandings for strong international initiatives dealing with the liability of legal persons for the bribery of foreign public officials, several actors have also emphasized the need to ensure adequate implementation of the OECD anti-bribery instruments. In this regard, representatives of the *OECD Anti-Bribery Convention* member states expressly committed to "[e]nsure that the standards of the Convention remain at the forefront of the global fight against foreign bribery and that *their enforcement continues to be monitored* by a systematic, effective and adequate review mechanism."[120]

With respect to non-state actors, one instance of support for a strong implementation of these instruments can be found in a statement offered by the International Chamber of Commerce:

> The effective, continuous and thorough monitoring of the [i]nstruments' implementation, conducted by the Working Group should guarantee the consolidation and enhancement of what has been achieved up to the present date. *The monitoring process played a determining role in the recognition by State Parties of their obligations and responsibilities under the [i]nstruments.* For its part, business reaffirms its readiness to contribute, in any appropriate capacity, to the success of the monitoring of the Instruments.[121]

Such support is also found in statements from public interests NGOs. Transparency International thus advocated for the "[c]ontinuation of a rigorous and adequately funded monitoring program until there is active enforcement by all parties."[122]

Representatives of intergovernmental organizations have also participated in this consultation process and supported an adequate implementation of the convention. For example, the staff of the International Monetary Fund mentioned that the "fair but rigorous monitoring system" of the *OECD Anti-Corruption Convention* "provides Parties with *incentives to properly implement* the Convention" and thus "strongly support[ed] the plans for continued monitoring."[123] Overall, an effective monitoring of the OECD anti-bribery instruments is firmly grounded in shared understandings between states, business actors, public interest NGOs and intergovernmental organizations.

In addition to the general support to address the liability of legal persons for the bribery of foreign officials and to establish a solid monitoring mechanism, relying on a critical discourse analysis allows emphasizing *relations of power* and interests underlying the elaboration of these instruments. In line with its role as a norm entrepreneur, the United States emphasized the capacity of the OECD to influence other international actors and the common interest of capital-exporting

120 See OECD, *Shared Commitment*, *supra* note 105 [emphasis added].
121 See OECD, *Responses to Consultation*, *supra* note 115 at 118 [emphasis added].
122 See *ibid* at 97.
123 See *ibid* at 83 [emphasis added].

states to adopt an international agreement addressing appropriate sanctions to punish corporations involved in bribery. According to the United States:

> Bribery is a problem of many countries, not just those of the OECD. But as the U.S. Congress recognized, *the OECD has a long history of setting an example for others.* . . . OECD members have a *common interest* in showing they are committed to ethical business practices abroad by their nationals.[124]

Similarly, one interviewee linked the participation of private actors in the elaboration of these international instruments with their own interests:

> Because they see it as being in their interests as well, so that they can have similar standards across the board. They just have to comply with one standard rather than having to comply and change things depending on which country they are doing business in. And I think that's why so many have turned up to these consultations and want to be involved.[125]

In sum, from the very beginning, international actors involved in the elaboration of OECD instruments designed to address the bribery of foreign public officials have agreed on the necessity to embed the liability of legal persons for such acts in binding international initiatives with an effective implementation mechanism. The construction of these shared understandings has also reproduced relations of power, suggesting that a strong commitment to address bribery in international business transactions is in line with the interests of powerful actors involved in the elaboration process. Beyond the general support for such initiatives, the weight of powerful members of the community of practice is evidenced through critical discourse analysis and should not be neglected. Ultimately, these shared understandings constitute a breeding ground for the emergence of a sense of obligation emanating from the *OECD Anti-Bribery Convention* and the *OECD 2009 Recommendation.*

3.2 Criteria of Legality: The Elaboration of Highly Legitimate Norms

In addition to the consideration of interactions among the community of actors surrounding the elaboration of the *OECD Anti-Bribery Convention* and the *OECD 2009 Recommendation*, analyzing the normative character of the OECD anti-bribery instruments requires the examination of their content against criteria of legality. As demonstrated in the following paragraphs, when considering the *OECD Anti-Bribery Convention* and the *OECD 2009 Recommendation* as a whole, these international instruments meet all the criteria characterizing legitimate international norms that can potentially create a sense of obligation.

124 *United States Proposal*, *supra* note 99, Annex [emphasis added].
125 Interview 12.

From the outset, the OECD anti-bribery instruments easily meet the criterion of ***promulgation***. As far as the *OECD Anti-Bribery Convention* is concerned, this international instrument is a formal international agreement that entered into force on 15 February 1999.[126] Moreover, the Working Group on Bribery provides an updated list of the parties to the *OECD Anti-Bribery Convention* in each of its annual reports. This list includes the dates of the deposition of the instrument of ratification, the entry into force of the convention and the entry into force of the implementing legislation for each member state.[127] While the *OECD 2009 Recommendation* falls beyond the scope of the formal sources of international law, this initiative belongs to one of the various types of normative acts that are expressly provided at Article 5 of the *Convention on the OECD*. Ultimately, these OECD anti-bribery instruments are made available to the public and are easily accessible, thus ensuring that the requirement of promulgation is satisfied.

The requirements established in these two international instruments also appear to be ***general***, both with respect to their equal application among member states and to private actors that are indirectly concerned by these instruments. For example, according to the definition of the offence of bribery of foreign public officials included in the *OECD Anti-Bribery Convention*:

> *Each Party* shall take such measures as may be necessary to establish that it is a criminal offence under its law for *any person* intentionally to offer, promise or give any undue pecuniary or other advantage, whether directly or through intermediaries, to a foreign public official, for that official or for a third party, in order that the official act or refrain from acting in relation to the performance of official duties, in order to obtain or retain business or other improper advantage in the conduct of international business.[128]

Similarly, Section I of the *OECD 2009 Recommendation* stresses that it "shall apply to OECD Member countries and other countries party to the OECD Anti-Bribery Convention," without making any additional differences.[129] The importance granted to a general application is also echoed at Article 5 of the *OECD Anti-Bribery Convention*, which emphasizes that investigation and prosecution of bribery "shall not be influenced by considerations of national economic interest, the potential effect upon relations with another State or the identity of the natural or legal persons involved."[130]

While international norms are expected to be *clear* in order to be considered as legitimate, nothing in the *OECD Anti-Bribery Convention* or the *OECD*

126 *OECD Anti-Bribery Convention*, *supra* note 2.

127 See OECD, Working Group on Bribery, *Annual Report 2014* (Paris: OECD, 2014) at 51 [Working Group Report, *Annual Report 2014*].

128 *OECD Anti-Bribery Convention*, *supra* note 2, art 1(1) [emphasis added].

129 *OECD 2009 Recommendation*, *supra* note 3, section i.

130 *OECD Anti-Bribery Convention*, *supra* note 2, art 5.

2009 Recommendation poses a serious concern in this regard. In fact, several terms bearing particular meanings for the purposes of the instrument – *e.g.* "bribery of foreign public official," "complicity," "foreign public official," "foreign country" and "act or refrain from acting in relation to the performance of official duties" – are defined at Article 1 of the *OECD Anti-Bribery Convention.*[131] Furthermore, the latter is accompanied by 37 paragraphs of commentaries adopted by the Negotiating Conference on 21 November 1997 and providing additional definitions of specific terms.[132] Where appropriate, express references to other initiatives in the *OECD Anti-Bribery Convention* commentaries and the *OECD 2009 Recommendation* also contribute to ensure that these two international instruments live up to the requirement of clarity.[133]

These OECD anti-bribery instruments are also *constant* initiatives. While amendments to the *OECD Anti-Bribery Convention* are possible, they must follow a specific procedure set out at Article 16. In this regard, an amendment submitted by any member state must be submitted to a depository and must be adopted by consensus of the parties, or any other means determined by the parties.[134] The fact that withdrawal of a member state from the *OECD Anti-Bribery Convention* is only effective one year after the date of the receipt of such a notification also contributes to strengthening the constancy of this international instrument.[135] Furthermore, the amendment of the *OECD 2009 Recommendation* through the addition of Annex II in 2010 has not led to the modification of any provision of this recommendation and does not seem to have posed any problem with the constant application of this norm.

As far as the fifth criterion of legality is concerned, nothing in the *OECD Anti-Bribery Convention* or the *OECD 2009 Recommendation* expressly addresses temporal issues. As such, it seems appropriate to conclude that these international instruments meet the requirement of *non-retroactivity* included in the interactional theory of international law.

In order to be considered as legitimate, international norms must not establish requirements *asking for impossible* achievements. In this regard, the two international instruments considered for present purposes extensively call upon the need to take into account differences existing between member states when implementing their provisions. One glaring example of this flexibility can be found at Article 2 of the *OECD Anti-Bribery Convention*, which requires each member state to establish the liability of legal persons for the bribery of foreign public officials "in accordance with its legal principles."[136] Through this specification, the member

131 *Ibid*, art 1(4).

132 *Commentaries on the Convention on Combating Bribery of Foreign Public Officials in International Business Transactions*, 21 November 1997 (Paris: OECD, 2011) at paras 5, 12–14, 17–18, 21–22 and 28 [*Commentaries on the OECD Anti-Bribery Convention*].

133 See *ibid* at paras 27, 29, 30, 34; *OECD 2009 Recommendation*, *supra* note 3, Sections III(iii), VII(ii), XI(ii), XI(iii) and XII.

134 *OECD Anti-Bribery Convention*, *supra* note 2, art 16.

135 *Ibid*, art 17.

136 *Ibid*, art 2.

states intend to avoid imposing an impossible requirement on parties for which criminal responsibility is not applicable to legal persons.[137] In such circumstances, these parties "shall ensure that legal persons shall be subject to effective, proportionate and dissuasive non-criminal sanctions, including monetary sanctions, for bribery of foreign public officials."[138] Other elements that expressly refer to constraints imposed by domestic legal principles and international treaties in these two instruments include issues related to mutual legal assistance,[139] extradition,[140] awareness-raising,[141] tax legislation,[142] reporting of foreign bribery,[143] regulation of financial institutions[144] and public procurements,[145] among others.

In light of the abovementioned absence of shared understandings with respect to the inclusion of small facilitation payments under the scope of the *OECD Anti-Bribery Convention*, addressing the extent to which the OECD anti-bribery instruments meet the criterion of the *absence of contradiction* requires some nuances. When considering solely the *OECD Anti-Bribery Convention* and its commentaries, one might be surprised to see an exception authorizing such payments. Paragraph 9 of the commentaries to the convention provides the following:

> Small "facilitation" payments do not constitute payments made "to obtain or retain business or other improper advantage" . . . and, accordingly, are also not an offence. Such payments, which, in some countries, are made to induce public officials to perform their functions, such as issuing licenses or permits, are generally illegal in the foreign country concerned. Other countries can and should address this corrosive phenomenon by such means as support for programmes of good governance. However, criminalisation by other countries does not seem a practical or effective complementary action.[146]

Despite these clarifications, it is plain that authorizing facilitations payments "made to induce public officials to perform their function" is in sharp contradiction with the provision of the *OECD Anti-Bribery Convention* that defines the offence of bribery of foreign public officials as including "*any* undue pecuniary . . . advantage . . . to a foreign public official . . . in order that the official act . . . in relation to the performance of official duties."[147] When considering the *OECD Anti-Bribery Convention* alone, one could thus conclude that it fails to meet the criterion of the absence of contradiction.

137 See *Commentaries on the OECD Anti-Bribery Convention*, *supra* note 132 at para 20.
138 See *OECD Anti-Bribery Convention*, *supra* note 2, art 3(2).
139 See *ibid*, art 9(1).
140 See *ibid*, art 10(4).
141 See *OECD 2009 Recommendation*, *supra* note 3, Section III.
142 See *ibid*, Section III.
143 See *ibid*, Sections III and IX(i) –IX(ii).
144 See *ibid*, Section III.
145 See *ibid*, Section III.
146 *Commentaries on the OECD Anti-Bribery Convention*, *supra* note 132 at para 9.
147 *OECD Anti-Bribery Convention*, *supra* note 2, art 1(1) [emphasis added].

Yet, such a failure is considerably diluted when taking into account the content of the *OECD 2009 Recommendation*. In fact, according to Section VI of this instrument, member states should "undertake to periodically review their policies and approach on small facilitation payments in order to effectively combat the phenomenon" and "encourage companies to prohibit or discourage the use of small facilitation payments in internal company controls, ethics and compliance programmes or measures."[148] What is more, through the *OECD 2009 Recommendation*, the Council of the OECD "urges all countries to raise awareness of their public officials on their domestic bribery and solicitation laws with a view to stopping the solicitation and acceptance of small facilitation payments."[149] At the end of the day, in light of normative developments that occurred after the adoption of the *OECD Anti-Bribery Convention*, the articulation of the offence of bribery of foreign public officials and the issue of small facilitation payments is more coherent since the adoption of the *OECD 2009 Recommendation* than under the sole consideration of the convention.

Given that the OECD anti-bribery instruments at hand require states to establish the liability of legal persons, two different aspects with respect to *congruence* between rules and official action must be discussed. First, the implementation of the *OECD Anti-Bribery Convention* and the *OECD 2009 Recommendation* is subjected to a peer review mechanism. Article 12 of the *OECD Anti-Bribery Convention* thus stipulates that, through the work of the Working Group on Bribery, "[t]he Parties shall co-operate in carrying out a programme of systematic follow-up to monitor and promote the full implementation of this Convention."[150] Even if recommendations adopted under the auspices of the OECD are not expressly considered as formal obligations under the *Convention on the OECD*, the *OECD 2009 Recommendation* is also monitored by the same mechanism. According to Section XIV of this recommendation, the Council thus instructs the Working Group on Bribery to continue the monitoring of these OECD anti-bribery instruments.[151] More specifically, the Working Group on Bribery is tasked with the following:

> Continuation of the programme of rigorous and systematic monitoring of Member countries' implementation of the OECD Anti-Bribery Convention and this Recommendation to promote the full implementation of these instruments, including through an ongoing system of mutual evaluation, where each Member country is examined in turn by the Working Group on Bribery, on the basis of a report which will provide an objective assessment of the progress of the Member country in implementing the OECD Anti-Bribery Convention and this Recommendation, and which will be made publicly available.[152]

148 *OECD 2009 Recommendation*, *supra* note 3, Section VI.
149 *Ibid*, Section VII.
150 *OECD Anti-Bribery Convention*, *supra* note 2, art 12.
151 *OECD 2009 Recommendation*, *supra* note 3, Section XIV.
152 *Ibid*, Section XIV(i).

In other words, significant instances of non-compliance by a member state with the rules elaborated in these instruments can thus be addressed through a procedure that is expressly provided in the *OECD Anti-Bribery Convention* and reaffirmed in the *OECD 2009 Recommendation.*

Second, as far as the relationship between member states and private firms is concerned, these international instruments seek to foster the enforcement of sanctions by state officials in order to punish the bribery of foreign public officials in international business transactions. The *OECD Anti-Bribery Convention* thus requires such punishment by "effective, proportionate and dissuasive" criminal or non-criminal sanctions.[153] With respect to enforcement, the same convention stresses that "[i]nvestigation and prosecution of the bribery of a foreign public official shall be subject to the applicable rules and principles of each Party."[154] Additional details regarding investigation and prosecution are also provided in Annex I of the *OECD 2009 Recommendation.*[155] In other words, while the OECD anti-bribery instruments do not provide any international procedural devices that directly allow addressing an act of corruption by a private actor, the provisions dealing with sanctions and enforcement demonstrate an additional layer of congruence between rules and official action.

In sum, the ongoing normative developments under the auspices of the OECD have led to the elaboration of international norms on the bribery of foreign public officials in international business transactions that easily meet the criteria of legality. Both the *OECD Anti-Bribery Convention* and the *OECD 2009 Recommendation* thus emerge as legitimate norms that, if applied according to a practice of legality, can generate a strong sense of obligation that characterizes legal norms.

3.3 Practice of Legality: The Consolidation of a Sense of Obligation

In addition to the consideration of shared understandings regarding the liability of legal persons for the bribery of foreign public officials and the extent to which the OECD anti-bribery instruments meet a set of criteria of legality, determining the normative character of these instruments requires a closer analysis of the practice according to which international actors implement them. Beyond the mere references to the OECD anti-bribery instruments in other international instruments codifying foreign investors' responsibilities, the present analysis applies a critical discourse analysis to reports, documents and transcripts from semi-structured interviews.

One component that suggests the emergence of a practice of legality surrounding the *OECD Anti-Bribery Convention* and the *OECD 2009 Recommendation* is the extensive reference to these instruments in other

153 *OECD Anti-Bribery Convention, supra* note 2, art 3(1) and 3(2).
154 *Ibid*, art 5.
155 *OECD 2009 Recommendation, supra* note 3, Annex I, D.

formal and informal international initiatives. While the most recent version of the commentaries accompanying the *OECD Guidelines* expressly mentions the *OECD 2009 Recommendation*,[156] the *OECD Anti-Bribery Convention* benefits from a broader consideration. In addition to references in informal instruments elaborated under the auspices of the OECD,[157] formal and informal initiatives developed by the UN and the European Union also refer to this convention.[158]

When considering solely the number of convictions by member states for the bribery of foreign public officials, one could be tempted to conclude that the legal character of the practice surrounding the implementation of these international instruments is somewhat weak. For example, the consultation paper prepared by the Working Group on Bribery to discuss the first ten years of the *OECD Anti-Bribery Convention* emphasizes that "regrettably few convictions have been obtained as yet by most Parties."[159] In a response to this consultation process, the Asian Development Bank argued that "the effectiveness of the instrument in terms of the number of actual convictions has been unfortunately low."[160] "Notable differences in the way State Parties enforce their national anti-foreign bribery laws" were also pointed out by the International Chamber of Commerce.[161] The data provided by the Working Group on Bribery in a more recent annual report nevertheless suggests that 333 individuals and 111 entities have been sanctioned under criminal proceedings in 17 states since the *OECD Anti-Bribery Convention* entered into force, thus hinting toward the development of a stronger practice.[162]

Most importantly, when analyzing discourses related to the implementation of the OECD anti-bribery instruments, it is plain that members of the community of practice acknowledge a sense of obligation inherent to these international norms. For example, in previous annual reports, the Working Group on Bribery presented the *OECD Anti-Bribery Convention* in the following terms:

> The Anti-Bribery Convention is the only *legally binding instrument* globally to focus primarily on the supply of bribes to foreign public officials in international business transactions. All Convention countries *must* make the bribery of foreign public officials a criminal offence. They are

156 *OECD Guidelines 2011 – Commentaries*, *supra* note 43 at paras 76, 77 and 80.

157 See *Recommendation of the Council on Bribery and Officially Supported Export Credits*, 14 December 2006, Doc No C(2006)163 (2006), Preamble and II(a); *Recommendation of the Council on Tax Measures for Further Combating Bribery of Foreign Public Officials in International Business Transactions*, 25 May 2009, Doc No C(2009)64 (2009), Preamble; *Recommendation on Due Diligence Guidance*, *supra* note 67, Preamble.

158 See *UN Norms*, *supra* note 67, Preamble; *United Nations Convention Against Corruption*, 31 October 2003, 2349 UNTS 41 (entered into force 14 December 2005), Preamble; *Criminal Law Convention on Corruption*, 27 January 1999, 2216 UNTS 225, STE 173 (entered into force 1 July 2002), Preamble; EC, *Council Framework Decision 2003/568/JHA of 22 July 2003 on Combating Corruption in the Private Sector*, [2003] OJ, L 192/54, Preamble.

159 OECD, *Consultation Paper*, *supra* note 111 at 5.

160 See OECD, *Responses to Consultation*, *supra* note 115 at 77.

161 See *ibid* at 118.

162 Working Group Report, *Annual Report 2014*, *supra* note 127 at 15.

> *obligated* to investigate credible allegations and, where appropriate, to prosecute those who offer, promise or give bribes to foreign public officials and to subject those who bribe to effective, proportionate and dissuasive penalties.[163]

Similar statements can also be found regarding the *OECD 2009 Recommendation*, which was depicted as providing "a series of targeted measures to *enhance Parties' implementation of their Convention obligations* including to better prevent, detect, investigate and prosecute credible allegations of foreign bribery."[164]

In a subtler way, the discourse of the Working Group on Bribery is also instructive to understand the character of the practice surrounding Annex II of the *OECD 2009 Recommendation*. While it is turned toward private actors, the good practice guidance included in this annex is expressly not intended to be legally binding.[165] However, when addressing the role of this international initiative included in the *OECD 2009 Recommendation*, the Working Group on Bribery explicitly acknowledged its contribution to ultimately create a sense of responsibility for compliance with anti-bribery norms:

> The advice that the Good Practice Guidance offers is meant to be flexible and can be adapted by companies of all sizes and from any industry. It emphasizes that, first and foremost, effective internal controls, ethics and compliance programmes are based on a risk assessment that is regularly monitored, re-assessed and adapted according to changing circumstances. It also emphasises the need for strong, explicit and visible support from senior management, and adoption of a clear and visible anti-bribery policy. Effective measures should also instil in all employees *a sense of responsibility for compliance.*[166]

In other words, in addition to the inherent legal character of the practice emanating from the *OECD 2009 Recommendation*, the Working Group on Bribery recognizes a certain sense of obligation to a guidance that is not expressly expected to be legally binding.

The peer review mechanism that is used to monitor the implementation of OECD anti-bribery instruments has also often been linked to the existence of states' commitments and obligations to fight the bribery of foreign public officials. As expressed by the Chairperson of the Working Group on Bribery:

163 *Ibid* at 8 [emphasis added]. For similar statements, see also OECD, Working Group on Bribery, *Annual Report 2010* (Paris: OECD, 2010) at 11 [Working Group Report, *Annual Report 2010*]; OECD, Working Group on Bribery, *Annual Report 2011* (Paris: OECD, 2011) at 6 [Working Group Report, *Annual Report 2011*]; OECD, Working Group on Bribery, *Annual Report 2013* (Paris: OECD, 2013) at 6 [Working Group Report, *Annual Report 2013*].

164 See Working Group Report, *Annual Report 2014*, *ibid* at 10 [emphasis added].

165 *OECD 2009 Recommendation*, *supra* note 3, Annex II, Introduction.

166 Working Group Report, *Annual Report 2010*, *supra* note 163 at 13 [emphasis added].

> In 2010, we began a new, third-round of intense peer review monitoring evaluations that examine whether and how Convention countries are fulfilling this promise by enforcing the Convention. It is also the first opportunity to examine how countries are transforming the new Anti-Bribery Recommendation and the Good Practice Guidance into action. Through this exercise, we ensure that all . . . Parties to the Convention *are serious about their commitments and held accountable to their obligations to fight foreign bribery.*[167]

Similarly, the Secretary General of the OECD maintained that "[t]he Working Group's peer reviews—which Transparency International calls the 'gold standard' of monitoring—holds Parties *accountable* to their Convention *obligation* to prevent, detect, investigate and prosecute this crime."[168]

The way member states consider recommendations found in peer review reports also suggests the existence of a practice of legality. Of course, one can identify some instances where member states have refused to fully integrate recommendations resulting from the peer review process.[169] However, in the aforementioned consultation paper, the Working Group on Bribery maintained the following:

> These reports include *stringent recommendations* for ensuring the full impact of the anti-bribery instruments. . . . The number and nature of legislative amendments and institutional changes that have been made by Parties in response to the Working Group's recommendations demonstrate the *strength of the peer review process and the commitment of the Parties.*[170]

While these reports only lead to the adoption of recommendations, it is here submitted that the successive monitoring and reporting on the implementation of these recommendations through different phases can considerably improve the sense of obligation that characterizes this practice.

Other aspects of the practice emanating from the *OECD Anti-Bribery Convention* and the *OECD 2009 Recommendation* demonstrate its legal character. For example, discussions pertaining to the accession to the OECD by non-member states have often been related to a commitment from these countries to comply with the *OECD Anti-Bribery Convention*. When addressing the potential accession of five countries to the OECD in 2007, the Working Group on Bribery maintained that:

167 See *ibid* at 4 [emphasis added].

168 See Working Group Report, *Annual Report 2013*, *supra* note 163 at 2 [emphasis added].

169 See e.g. OECD, Directorate for Financial, Fiscal and Enterprise Affairs, *Mid-Term Study of Phase 2 Reports: Application of the Convention on Combating Bribery of Foreign Public Officials in International Business Transactions and the 1997 Recommendation on Combating Bribery in International Business Transactions* (Paris: OECD, 2006) at paras 75 and 123 [OECD, *Mid-Term Study*].

170 OECD, *Consultation Paper*, *supra* note 111 at 5.

> [e]ach candidate country will follow an "accession roadmap," which includes the following anti-corruption principles: ***compliance with the OECD Anti-Bribery Convention***; a legal framework for combating bribery; criminalisation of bribery of foreign officials; adequate accounting, auditing and tax systems to fight bribery; ability to co-operate with Parties to the Convention; and readiness to participate in the peer review process.[171]

Conditioning accession to the OECD to compliance with an OECD anti-bribery instrument and some requirements that it includes clearly strengthens the sense that members of the community of practice have to act according to this international norm.

The legal character of the practice surrounding the OECD anti-bribery instruments is also an important component of the discourse from individuals working in intergovernmental organizations that are involved in the broader codification process of foreign investors' responsibilities. More specifically, several interviewees discussed the efforts of the OECD in the area of corruption as creating concrete "obligations" for states and effectively departing from "voluntary" initiatives.[172] The perspectives offered by some interviewees with respect to the peer review mechanism also demonstrate the sense of obligation that accompanies this procedure to implement the *OECD Anti-Bribery Convention* and the *OECD 2009 Recommendation*. One interviewee thus presented this mechanism in the following terms:

> It's very hard-hitting – it's much harder hitting in a way than the peer reviews of the Guidelines. . . . It's very structured and they're trying to push countries forward. . . . These issues relate to what the Working Group on Bribery views as being non-implementation – let's say non-compliance with certain commitments made in the Anti-Bribery Convention or in the Recommendation. . . . Slowly but surely, it works. Slowly, but surely.[173]

Another interviewee stressed that

> the fact that all these countries are engaged in this ongoing, very rigorous peer review mechanism shows that they are committed to the process and that they are serious about putting in place the laws and processes to prevent bribery. . . . I think there's enormous power in terms of peer pressure that brings about real positive change as a result of this mechanism.[174]

171 OECD, Working Group on Bribery, *Annual Report 2007* (Paris: OECD, 2007) at 26 [emphasis added].
172 See Interview 6; Interview 11.
173 Interview 6.
174 Interview 12.

Interestingly, one participant provided some characteristics of the community of practice involved in this peer review in a way that also suggests the existence of a practice of legality: "The people that attend the Working Group on Bribery are *law enforcement people*. . . . They are adversarial lawyers, they're prosecutors, they're mean – some of them. You know, it's a different kind of mindset. *It's a different community*."[175]

In addition to highlighting that the *OECD Anti-Bribery Convention* and the *OECD 2009 Recommendation* are implemented according to a practice of legality, the critical analysis of statements from the members of this community of practice allows identifying some examples in which the implementation of these instruments is subjected to inherent *relations of power*. While Transparency International maintained that "the Working Group has had the courage to criticize even the most powerful governments,"[176] the Corner House emphasized that the peer review mechanism "appears particularly vulnerable when faced with certain Parties that claim the best interest of the [n]ation, either to stop investigations, or to not adapt their legislation accordingly."[177] Moreover, in response to the consultation process that occurred in 2008, representatives from the private sector implicitly suggested that the implementation of the OECD anti-bribery instruments would not be the same without their considerable support. For example, BIAC put forward that "[t]he initiatives undertaken by business are crucial to the success of the Convention" and that "[o]nly the combined effort of business and governments can lead to a significant reduction in the occurrence of bribery."[178] In other words, in addition to aforementioned relations of power that are inherent to the elaboration of the *OECD Anti-Bribery Convention* and the *OECD 2009 Recommendation*, the sense of obligation that characterizes the practice surrounding these instruments extensively depends upon the support of powerful members of the community of practice.

Overall, while the OECD anti-bribery instruments are anchored in solid shared understandings and meet the criteria of legality's requirements, the previous analysis demonstrates that members of the community of practice surrounding these instruments have also adopted a practice of legality. Through their interactions, these international actors implicitly acknowledge an inherent legal character to these international norms and seem to perceive the recommendations resulting from the peer review mechanism as something that member states ought to act accordingly. Inevitably, the legal character of this practice also appears to be subjected to the support of powerful actors among the community of practice.

175 Interview 6 [emphasis added].

176 See OECD, *Responses to Consultation*, *supra* note 115 at 97.

177 See *ibid* at 130.

178 See *ibid* at 107.

Conclusion

In parallel to fostering a sense of identity revolving around the promotion of neoliberal policies and foreign investment, the OECD provides a normative site that has been particularly active in the elaboration and the implementation of international initiatives seeking to codify foreign investors' responsibilities. Offering a more nuanced analysis of the normative character of the *OECD Guidelines*, the *OECD Anti-Bribery Convention* and the *OECD 2009 Recommendation* thus provides a better understanding of the contribution of this intergovernmental organization within the broader codification process of foreign investors' responsibilities.

Even if the *OECD Guidelines* are not a formal source of international law, they establish standards of appropriate behavior that can be considered by various international actors. The analysis of the elaboration and the implementation of this international norm also demonstrates that the *OECD Guidelines* have evolved. However, these guidelines fail to generate any sense of obligation that characterizes international legal norms. More specifically, norm entrepreneurs and powerful members of the community of practice have constantly sought to confirm the voluntary character of this instrument, thus preventing the emergence of shared understandings with respect to the elaboration of an instrument whose observance would be mandatory. While the content of the *OECD Guidelines* meets several criteria of legality, their express voluntary character appears to be in tension with its explicit goals and is in line with procedural devices that only allow weak responses to significant instances of non-compliance. Moreover, the overwhelming majority of interactions between members of the community of practice that have emerged around the *OECD Guidelines* evidence a practice according to which the implementation of this instrument is perceived as merely voluntary and non-binding.

By contrast, the analysis above allows concluding that both the *OECD Anti-Bribery Convention* and the *OECD 2009 Recommendation* are characterized by a strong sense of obligation and can thus be considered as international legal norms. Regardless of their different relationship with the formal sources of international law, both instruments have fully entered the realm of legality. Further to an initial push by the United States, several international actors have contributed to the emergence of shared understandings regarding the necessity of establishing the liability of legal persons for the bribery of foreign pubic officials in international business transactions. Further to the emergence of these shared understandings, the content of the *OECD Anti-Bribery Convention* and the *OECD 2009 Recommendation* meets all the criteria of legality that ensure the legitimacy of international norms. Moreover, the sense of obligation emanating from these two international instruments is constantly consolidated through a practice of legality between the numerous international actors involved in their implementation process. Cross-references to these OECD anti-bribery instruments in other international initiatives, general statements regarding their inherent sense of obligation and the acknowledgment of the contribution of peer review to influence the decisions of member states unambiguously demonstrate the existence of a community of practice that feels bounded by these international norms. Finally, the fact that the elaboration and the implementation of these instruments are perceived as being in line with the interests of the most powerful members of the community of practice is a key element that must be taken into account when examining the normative character of these instruments.

5 International Labour Organization

Introduction

A micro-level analysis of the normative character of international instruments elaborated and implemented under the auspices of intergovernmental organizations to codify foreign investors' responsibilities calls upon the consideration of the International Labour Organization's (ILO) work. While this organization is a specialized agency of the United Nations (UN),[1] its relative autonomy from the main organs of the UN entails a different normative process that justifies its consideration as a separate intergovernmental organization. In parallel with normative developments that occurred in other organizations in the 1970s, the ILO initiated the elaboration of an international instrument that includes norms pertaining to the conduct of foreign investors with a primary focus on labour rights and social policy. Further to an initial version adopted in 1977, this organization still commits considerable efforts to implement the *Tripartite Declaration of Principles concerning Multinational Enterprises and Social Policy* (*ILO Tripartite Declaration*).[2]

With a view to positioning the *ILO Tripartite Declaration* on a continuum that varies from social norms to legal norms, Chapter 5 relies on the interactional theory of international law.[3] The analysis below suggests that, despite more than forty years of efforts to implement this informal international instrument, the *ILO Tripartite Declaration* has failed to reach the threshold of legality. After contextualizing the elaboration of norms within the ILO's unique tripartite structure (1), this chapter argues that the *ILO Tripartite Declaration* appears as a weak social norm that still struggles to influence the behavior of international actors, let alone to induce any sense of obligation (2).

1 See United Nations, *The United Nations Today* (New York: United Nations, 2008) at 22.

2 For the first version, see *Tripartite Declaration of Principles concerning Multinational Enterprises and Social Policy*, November 1977, 17 ILM 422 [*ILO Tripartite Declaration 1977*]. For the most recent version, see *Tripartite Declaration of Principles concerning Multinational Enterprises and Social Policy*, March 2017, online: ILO www.ilo.org/empent/Publications/WCMS_094386/lang--en/index.htm (accessed 26 March 2018) [*ILO Tripartite Declaration 2017*].

3 See section 3 of the introduction.

1. The ILO: Tripartite Norms in a Context of Neoliberal Globalization

Considering the institutional features of the intergovernmental organization from which the *ILO Tripartite Declaration* has emerged ensures a more contextualized analysis of its normative character. Article 19 of the *Constitution of the International Labour Organization* (*ILO Constitution*)[4] allows the General Conference of representatives of member states (Conference) to adopt *conventions* as well as *recommendations* "where the subject . . . is not considered suitable or appropriate at that time for a [c]onvention."[5] While conventions require ratification by member states and enactment of legislation,[6] recommendations must be communicated to all member states "for their consideration with a view to effect being given to it by national legislation or otherwise."[7] Furthermore, through representations of non-observance formulated by industrial associations[8] and complaints filed by member states,[9] several provisions of the *ILO Constitution* intend to foster the implementation of conventions that are adopted by the Conference. By contrast, *declarations* are not expressly addressed in the *ILO Constitution* and are considered as resolutions generally adopted by the Conference with a view to providing an authoritative statement that reaffirms the importance of certain principles and values, without relying on any specific mechanism to foster their implementation.[10]

What underlies this normative function of the ILO is a unique tripartite structure. In contrast to other organizations that have chosen to rely on the expertise of non-state actors after their initial constitution, the *ILO Constitution* established a tripartite Governing Body from its very beginning. Considered as the executive council of the ILO, the Governing Body includes representatives from member states, employers' associations and workers' associations that elaborate proposals before submitting them to the Conference.[11] By placing the representatives of employers and workers on an "equal footing" with government representatives in decision making, the composition allows a social dialogue that ensures the elaboration and implementation of legitimate labour standards reflecting deliberations between these various parties.[12] From a historical perspective, this tripartite structure is also considered as having

4 *Constitution of the International Labour Organization*, 1 April 1919, 15 UNTS 40 (entered into force 28 June 1919) [*ILO Constitution*].
5 *Ibid*, art 19(1).
6 See *ibid*, art 19(5).
7 See *ibid*, art 19(6).
8 See *ibid*, art 24.
9 See *ibid*, art 26.
10 See ILO, *ILO Declarations*, online: ILO www.ilo.org/global/about-the-ilo/how-the-ilo-works/departments-and-offices/jur/legal-instruments/WCMS_428589/lang--en/index.htm (accessed 26 March 2018) [ILO, "ILO Declarations"].
11 See *ILO Constitution*, *supra* note 4, art 7(1).
12 See Francis Maupain, *The Future of the International Labour Organization in the Global Economy* (Oxford: Hart Publishing, 2013) at 8 and 38.

played a decisive role in the development and the dissemination of international standards produced by the ILO.[13]

While the *ILO Tripartite Declaration* was elaborated in the 1970s, it is worth addressing how this intergovernmental organization has evolved in a context of neoliberal globalization before delving into the analysis of this instrument's normative character. One can identify competing effects produced by the end of the Cold War on the capacity of the ILO to elaborate and implement international norms. According to Maupain, the pluralistic model of the ILO that sought to strike a balance between the interests of workers and employers was opposed to the monolithic conception in the Soviet Bloc countries that focused on the interests of the proletariat.[14] In this regard, the "collapse of the ILO's rival model [deprived] the organisation of an ideological counterweight that had proven to be an essential element of its persuasive powers not only vis-à-vis employers, but with a number of governments as well."[15] While the exacerbation of competition between states with the advent of globalization has arguably increased the need to agree on some international labour standards, such a declining capacity of persuasion has led to a sharp decrease in the will of employers and some governments to engage in the elaboration of international norms under the auspices of this intergovernmental organization. Except in exceptional cases, employers have thus limited their support to international norms geared toward the revision of pre-existing instruments and several governments have appeared to be reluctant to adopt new conventions. In other words, the ILO can be perceived as a normative site that is increasingly struggling to elaborate and implement standards in the context of neoliberal globalization in which it currently operates.

The elaboration and the implementation of an international instrument to address potential violations of labour rights through foreign investors' activities such as the *ILO Tripartite Declaration* must be analyzed by taking into account the institutional context from which it emerges. In addition to conventions and recommendations that can be adopted by the Conference, this tripartite intergovernmental organization can issue declarations on specific matters. Moreover, amidst doubts pertaining to the extent to which these norms are well-suited to influence the conduct of international actors in a context of neoliberal globalization, an assessment of the normative character of the *ILO Tripartite Declaration* appears as an interesting test in this regard.

2. The *ILO Tripartite Declaration*

While focusing primarily on labour rights, the *ILO Tripartite Declaration* covers crucial aspects pertaining to foreign investors' activities. In this regard, the

13 See Sandrine Kott & Joëlle Droux, "Introduction: A Global History Written from the ILO" in Sandrine Kott & Joëlle Droux, eds, *Globalizing Social Rights: The International Labour Organization and Beyond* (New York: Palgrave Macmillan, 2013) 1 at 7.

14 For the rest of this paragraph, see Maupain, *supra* note 12 at 17, 24 and 43–44.

15 *Ibid* at 29.

principles that are included in this informal international instrument address issues of general policies, employment, training, conditions of work and life, as well as industrial relations.[16] The *ILO Tripartite Declaration* nevertheless appears as a weak social norm that bears a limited capacity to influence the behavior of international actors. With respect to shared understandings underlying the elaboration of this instrument, various resolutions and reports demonstrate that several actors have sought to avoid the elaboration of an instrument whose observance would have been mandatory since its inception (2.1). While the provisions of the *ILO Tripartite Declaration* fall short of meeting several criteria of legality (2.2), the analysis below also suggests that the practice according to which this instrument is implemented remains weak and cannot be characterized as implying any legal character (2.3).

2.1 Shared Understandings: Seeking a Non-Mandatory Instrument from the Beginning

In a way that reflects the elaboration of the *Guidelines for Multinational Enterprises* by the Organisation for Economic Co-operation and Development (*OECD Guidelines*),[17] several actors within the ILO appear as *norm entrepreneurs* that initially pushed for the elaboration of an international instrument addressing the activities of multinational enterprises in parallel with normative developments occurring at the UN. While the preamble of previous versions of the *ILO Tripartite Declaration* mentions that "various Industrial Committees, Regional Conferences, and the International Labour Conference since the mid-1960s have requested appropriate action by the Governing Body in the field of multinational enterprises and social policy,"[18] the active role of capital-importing states and workers' representatives is specifically put forward by several authors.[19] In November 1975, the Governing Body decided to hold a Tripartite Advisory Meeting on the relationship of Multinational Enterprises and Social Policy (Tripartite Advisory Meeting) that "should give policy advice on the usefulness of international principles and possibly make suggestions as regards the form and the actual content of a text embodying such principles."[20]

16 See the main parts of the *ILO Tripartite Declaration 2017*, *supra* note 2.

17 See *Declaration on International Investment and Multinational Enterprises*, 21 June 1976, Doc No C(76)99/FINAL (1976), Annex 1.

18 See e.g. *Tripartite Declaration of Principles concerning Multinational Enterprises and Social Policy*, March 2006, online: ILO www.ilo.org/empent/Publications/WCMS_211136/lang--en/index.htm (accessed 26 March 2018), Preamble [*ILO Tripartite Declaration 2006*].

19 See e.g. Hans Günter, *The Tripartite Declaration of Principles concerning the Multinational Enterprises and Social Policy (History, Contents, Follow-up and Relationship with Relevant Instruments of Other Organizations)*, Multinational Enterprises Programme Working Paper 18 (Geneva, 1981) at 1; Peter Muchlinski, "Corporate Social Responsibility" in Peter Muchlinski, Frederico Ortino & Christoph Schreuer, eds, *The Oxford Handbook of International Investment Law* (Oxford: Oxford University Press, 2008) 637 at 646.

20 See ILO, *Progress of ILO Activities on Multinational Enterprises*, 198th Sess, GB.198/5/6 (1975) at para 70.

Further to an initial meeting held in 1976, the Tripartite Advisory Meeting recommended to make arrangements in order to elaborate a "non-mandatory" tripartite declaration of principles concerning multinational enterprises and social policy of a "voluntary character" that could be transmitted to the UN "for incorporation in the proposed Code of Conduct."[21] After the preparation of a draft declaration, the Governing Body decided to reconvene the Tripartite Advisory Meeting[22] and to adopt the *ILO Tripartite Declaration* in November 1977.[23]

Further to the adoption of its initial version, and after recognizing that procedures established under the *ILO Constitution* for the application of ratified conventions were "neither directly nor by analogy applicable to the follow-up of a *non-mandatory Declaration*,"[24] a follow-up procedure was established in order to invite governments to report periodically on the effect given to the Declaration.[25] With respect to disputes arising from the application of the *ILO Tripartite Declaration*, a specific procedure was adopted by the Governing Body in 1986.[26] Moreover, the text of the *ILO Tripartite Declaration* was amended in 2000, 2006 and 2017.[27]

Stated according to the terms employed by the interactional theory of international law, participants in the Tripartite Advisory Meeting and other members of the Governing Body that participated in discussions pertaining to subsequent amendments of this instrument are members of a *community of practice* involved in the elaboration of the *ILO Tripartite Declaration*. For example, the Tripartite Advisory Meeting was composed of twenty-four "specialists" from governments, workers' and employers' circles, as well as the Director-General of the ILO and the Executive Director of the UN Centre on Transnational Corporations.[28] With a view to assessing the existence of shared understandings underlying the elaboration of the *ILO Tripartite Declaration*, the remainder of this section critically analyzes the content of the reports that were submitted by the Tripartite Advisory Meeting in 1976 and 1977,[29] as well as semi-structured interviews that

21 ILO, *Tripartite Advisory Meeting on the Relationship of Multinational Enterprises and Social Policy – Report of the Meeting*, 1976, MNE/1976/D.12, Appendix I at paras 1, 2(a) and 5 [*Tripartite Advisory Meeting – 1976*].

22 See ILO, *Reconvened Tripartite Advisory Meeting on the Relationship of Multinational Enterprises and Social Policy*, 1977, MNE/1977/D.8 at para 1 [*Tripartite Advisory Meeting – 1977*].

23 *ILO Tripartite Declaration 1977*, *supra* note 2.

24 See ILO, *Tripartite Declaration of Principles concerning Multinational Enterprises and Social Policy: Possibilities of a Follow-up Procedure*, 205th Sess, GB.205/10/2 (1978) at para 2 [emphasis added] [ILO, *Possibilities of a Follow-up*].

25 See *ibid* at para 9.

26 ILO, *Procedure for the Examination of Disputes concerning the Application of the Tripartite Declaration*, 233th Sess, Official Bulletin, Vol LXIX, Series A, No 3 (1986) at 196–197 [ILO, *Procedure for the Examination of Disputes*].

27 *Tripartite Declaration of Principles concerning Multinational Enterprises and Social Policy*, November 2000, 41 ILM 186; *ILO Tripartite Declaration 2006 supra* note 18; *ILO Tripartite Declaration 2017*, *supra* note 2.

28 *Tripartite Advisory Meeting – 1976*, *supra* note 21 at paras 2 and 9.

29 *Ibid*; *Tripartite Advisory Meeting – 1977*, *supra* note 22.

were conducted with individuals working for intergovernmental organizations involved in the codification of foreign investors' responsibilities.

Despite some disagreements pertaining to the content of the international instrument,[30] it is plain from the discourses of various members of the community of practice that the crucial point on which the Tripartite Advisory Meeting failed to reach any agreement relates to the legal nature of the *ILO Tripartite Declaration.* Several capital exporting states and representatives of employers recalled that they would only support a non-mandatory initiative. For example, according to the first report of the Tripartite Advisory Meeting, the representative of the United States "had serious reservations concerning a proposal that the ILO should prepare guidelines directed at multinational enterprises" and stressed that he would only support a statement of principles that would be "(i) non-discriminatory with regard to international and domestic enterprises; (ii) *voluntary*; (iii) in consonance with relevant national and international law; and (iv) even-handed in assigning responsibilities to multinational enterprises, labour, and governments."[31] Similarly, the employer members of the advisory meeting appeared to be convinced that a tripartite declaration would be harmful unless its principles "*do not bind multinationals* to observance of ILO standards not ratified or accepted by the host country, or introduce a system of standards making existing ILO Conventions and Recommendations applicable only to multinational enterprises," among others.[32]

By contrast, capital-importing states and workers' associations generally supported the elaboration of a formal convention that would bear a mandatory character. A member of the Mexican government thus stressed that "[a] code of conduct should be in harmony with present international law, as laid down in the new International Economic Order and the Charter of the Rights and Duties of States" and was in favor of "a declaration of principles providing for the control of multinationals, *which would lead up to an ILO Convention.*"[33] Along the same lines, the Tripartite Advisory Meeting reported that a worker member "stressed the need in the Latin American context to establish principles which would lead to control of the multinational enterprises through *effective and legally binding* machinery enforceable at the international level."[34] A worker member of the reconvened Tripartite Advisory Meeting even abstained from the adoption of the *ILO Tripartite Declaration*, because the instrument "did not conform to ILO practice, besides being of a *purely voluntary nature* and devoid of influence on any subsequent adoption of a *binding instrument* governing multinational enterprises."[35]

30 See e.g. *Tripartite Advisory Meeting – 1976*, *supra* note 21 at paras 39 and 41; *Tripartite Advisory Meeting – 1977*, *supra* note 22 at para 9.
31 *Tripartite Advisory Meeting – 1976*, *ibid* at para 75 [emphasis added].
32 *Ibid* at paras 84–85 [emphasis added].
33 *Ibid* at para 77 [emphasis added].
34 *Ibid* at para 78 [emphasis added].
35 See *Tripartite Advisory Meeting – 1977*, *supra* note 22 at para 72 [emphasis added].

These elements of the Tripartite Advisory Meeting's discussions are also echoed in the discourses of several interviewees. One of them thus underscored that while "the workers group, supported by the developing countries, were pushing . . . for an international legal convention, . . . [t]hey were strongly opposed by the employers group and also less than enthusiastic positions by the OECD governments."[36] A similar issue was also summarized by another interviewee in the following terms:

> [Employers] are very much willing to engage in the whole process, but it depends under which terms, I would say. So if this is a purely *voluntary enterprise driven process*, then they don't have any problems to be involved in this process. From the moment that you start to talk about increasing and making that concrete instruments and procedures to talk about responsibilities of private sector, then yes, private sector is more reluctant there.[37]

The same interviewee stressed that the avoidance of a mandatory instrument by employers can also be found in their attempts at "not including procedural mechanisms that make it possible to be held accountable."[38]

One aspect that is particularly explicit in the work of the Tripartite Advisory Meeting is that the discourses of several participants reproduce *relations of power* underlying the elaboration of the international instrument. For example, the representative of the Union of Soviet Socialist Republics underscored that

> [o]wing to their *economic power* the transnational corporations occupy a *stronger and even predominant position* as compared to the trade unions, and in a number of cases in comparison with governments. Hence responsibility in the social sphere should rest primarily and mainly on the transnational corporations.[39]

The extent to which such relations of power impeded the emergence of shared understandings was particularly manifest at the reconvened Tripartite Advisory Meeting, where a worker representative justified his abstention in a vote pertaining to the *ILO Tripartite Declaration* by expressly relying on the power of multinational enterprises. As reported by the ILO:

> [A worker member] considered that the draft conclusions revealed practically no trace of the original joint views of the Workers' group. The tribute to a positive role of the multinational enterprises in the preamble was ideological and unacceptable. The decisive factor for opposing the *multinationals which in the capitalist world had economic, political and ideological power*, was the

36 Interview 17.
37 Interview 3.
38 *Ibid.*
39 *Tripartite Advisory Meeting – 1976*, *supra* note 21 at para 76 [emphasis added].

> mass struggle of the workers, but it was also desirable to elaborate an international instrument to control them; this would be done most appropriately in the United Nations, with the ILO playing its part under UN guidance.[40]

In sum, the elaboration process of the *ILO Tripartite Declaration* reflects a serious lack of shared understandings to elaborate a mandatory instrument from the very beginning. While the absence of such an agreement can be found in the conclusions of the Tripartite Advisory Meeting and the decisions pertaining to the adoption of a follow-up procedure, the discourses of the members of the community of practice unambiguously demonstrate divergent views with respect to the legal nature of the *ILO Tripartite Declaration*. Amidst relations of power underlying the elaboration of this instrument, the development of a non-mandatory initiative primarily reflects the interests of some powerful states and representatives of the employers, thus seriously impeding any sense of obligation that could emanate from this initiative.

2.2 Criteria of Legality: Tensions and Failures

Regardless of an international instrument's relation with the formal sources of international law, the interactional theory of international law posits that an instrument has to meet a set of criteria of legality in order to be considered as a legal norm. While failure to meet this component of the interactional theory affects the legitimacy of an international initiative, the conclusion that the *ILO Tripartite Declaration* has not entered into the realm of legality is partly grounded in tensions and failures that characterize the relation between this initiative and several criteria of legality.

From the outset, suggesting that the informal character of the *ILO Tripartite Declaration* entails a failure to meet the criterion of *promulgation* would be grossly inconsistent with the analysis of the *OECD Guidelines* presented in the previous chapter.[41] In fact, even if the form of this declaration differs from a convention or a recommendation that can be adopted by the Conference, the *ILO Tripartite Declaration* is published by the ILO and is undeniably available to the public. Yet, there is at least one aspect related to the promulgation of this initiative that hints toward the generation of a weak sense of obligation. While the Conference regrouping all states representatives has adopted various declarations that "contain symbolic and political undertakings by the member States,"[42] the *ILO Tripartite Declaration* is the only declaration that was adopted by the Governing Body.[43] Amidst the various forms that norms elaborated by the ILO can take, the *ILO Tripartite Declaration* thus appears as a *sui generis* instrument that does not sit well with the other initiatives emanating from this intergovernmental organization.

40 *Tripartite Advisory Meeting – 1977*, *supra* note 22 at para 99 [emphasis added].
41 See section 2.2 of Chapter 4.
42 See ILO, "ILO Declarations", *supra* note 10.
43 See *ibid.*

The content of this international instrument suggests a fairly broad application that is in line with the criterion of *generality*. Paragraph 8 of the *ILO Tripartite Declaration* thus stipulates that "*[a]ll the parties* concerned by this Declaration should respect the sovereign rights of States, obey the national laws and regulations, give due consideration to local practices and respect relevant international standards."[44] Another aspect echoing this general character is the inclusion of several provisions that seek to avoid discrimination between multinational enterprises and domestic firms. While paragraph 5 mentions that "[t]hese principles do not aim at introducing or maintaining inequalities of treatment between multinational and national enterprises,"[45] other provisions expressly establish similar requirements for both types of enterprises.[46]

To a certain extent, the terms of the *ILO Tripartite Declaration*'s provisions can also be considered as providing sufficient *clarity* to live up to the requirements of the criteria of legality. Despite the absence of a definition of "multinational enterprises," the various aspects that are covered in paragraph 6 allow a fairly clear understanding of these private firms, at least from an economic perspective.[47] The numerous references to ILO conventions and recommendations also contribute to improve the overall clarity of this informal international instrument.[48] However, compromises made during the negotiation of some specific provisions have considerably affected this clarity in some instances. For example, paragraph 35 reads as follows: "Arbitrary dismissal procedures should be avoided."[49] In addition to the absence of information on the meaning of such procedures and the extent to which they "should be avoided," this provision does not include any specific addressees. According to the report of the reconvened Tripartite Advisory Meeting, this phrasing resulted from a proposal of the representative of the United Kingdom as a response to a wish from the employers "to avoid any implication that special *obligations* were being placed on multinational enterprises."[50] While such an evasive provision considerably affects the clarity of the instrument, the justification underlying its formulation unambiguously demonstrates a will to limit the sense of obligation resulting from the instrument.

Two other criteria do not pose any particular problem with respect to the *ILO Tripartite Declaration*. Given that the amendments adopted since the initial version of this instrument primarily aim to reflect other instruments emanating from this intergovernmental organization, nothing in the subsequent versions of the *ILO Tripartite Declaration* seriously impedes its *constancy*.[51] Moreover, as

44 *ILO Tripartite Declaration 2017, supra* note 2 at para 8 [emphasis added].
45 *Ibid* at para 5.
46 See e.g. *ibid* at paras 27 and 62.
47 See *ILO Tripartite Declaration 2017, ibid* at para 6. See also Hans Günter, "The Tripartite Declaration of Principles (ILO): Standards and Follow-Up" in *Legal Problems of Codes of Conduct for Multinational Enterprises* (Hingham: Kluwer Law and Taxation, 1980) 155 at 158.
48 See *ILO Tripartite Declaration 2017, ibid*, Annex I.
49 *Ibid* at para 35.
50 *Tripartite Advisory Meeting – 1977, supra* note 22 at para 32 [emphasis added].
51 See *ILO Tripartite Declaration 2017, supra* note 2, Preamble.

far as the requirement of *non-retroactivity* is concerned, it is worth noting that nothing in the provisions of this international instrument relates to its temporal application. Therefore, the *ILO Tripartite Declaration* appears to live up to the requirements of these two criteria.

Another criterion that seems to be met by this informal international instrument relates to the establishment of requirements that can be achieved within its subjects' activities *without asking the impossible.* Of course, several provisions of the *ILO Tripartite Declaration* encapsulate enough flexibility to ensure that their demands are feasible. For example, paragraph 17 mentions that "[b]efore starting operations, multinational enterprises should, *wherever appropriate*, consult the competent authorities and the national employers' and workers' organizations in order to keep their manpower plans, *as far as practicable*, in harmony with national social development policies."[52] However, the absence of an explicit recognition of potential conflicting requirements imposed by domestic legislation and international standards can lead to a tension with respect to this criterion of legality. While the *OECD Guidelines* specify that the observance of this international instrument is not intended to place enterprises in situations where they face conflicting requirements with domestic law,[53] such an articulation is not expressly included in the *ILO Tripartite Declaration.* The aforementioned paragraph 8 thus calls upon multinational enterprises to obey national law and regulations, as well as to respect relevant international standards.[54] Without asking the impossible, it must be noted that such a provision creates a tension to the extent that it fails to recognize that conflicting requirements may emerge.

When considering the tension between the noble aim of an instrument and its express voluntary character, the issue raised in the previous chapter pertaining to the criterion of *non-contradiction* appears to be even more apparent in the case of the *ILO Tripartite Declaration* than in the *OECD Guidelines.*[55] In the first paragraph of this initiative, it is acknowledged that "the advances made by multinational enterprises in organizing their operations beyond the national framework may lead to *abuse* of concentrations of economic power and to *conflicts* with national policy objectives and with the interest of the workers."[56] Yet, such abuse of economic power and potential conflicts are solely addressed through principles, "which governments, employers' and workers' organizations and multinational enterprises are *recommended to observe on a voluntary basis.*"[57] This situation creates a tension regarding the criterion of non-contradiction and can entail a considerable impact on the normative character of the instrument when international actors rely on this aspect to avoid a binding practice.

52 *Ibid* at para 17 [emphasis added]. Similar provisions can be found at paras 19, 20, 30, 31, 32 and 37, for example.

53 *Declaration on International Investment and Multinational Enterprises*, 25 May 2011, Doc No C/MIN(2011)11/FINAL (2011), Annex 1 at para I(2).

54 *ILO Tripartite Declaration 2017*, *supra* note 2 at para 8.

55 See section 2.2 of Chapter 4.

56 *ILO Tripartite Declaration 2017*, *supra* note 2 at para 1 [emphasis added].

57 *Ibid* at para 7 [emphasis added].

Finally, with respect to the criterion of *congruence*, neither of the two aforementioned follow-up mechanisms adopted by the Governing Body constitutes a procedural mechanism that allows addressing significant instances of non-compliance. Regarding the procedure to invite governments to report periodically on the effect given to the *ILO Tripartite Declaration* that was established in 1978, the Governing Body clearly stated that the non-mandatory nature of this initiative prevented the adoption of a procedure pertaining to particular instances of non-compliance.[58] It is also worth noting that these periodical reports have been set aside in 2008[59] and replaced by a different information-gathering process occurring at the regional level that also avoids addressing instances of non-compliance.[60] The absence of consideration for non-compliance can also be found in the *Procedure for the Examination of Disputes concerning the Application of the Tripartite Declaration of Principles concerning Multinational Enterprises and Social Policy by Means of Interpretation of its Provisions* (*Procedure for the Examination of Disputes*) that was adopted in 1986.[61] Given that the purpose of the procedure "is to interpret the provisions of the Declaration when needed to resolve a disagreement on their meaning, arising from an actual situation, between parties to whom the Declaration is commended,"[62] several authors emphasize that this mechanism is not geared toward determining whether a party has failed the meet the requirements of the *ILO Tripartite Declaration*.[63] Interestingly, the most recent version of the *ILO Tripartite Declaration* lists "operational tools" that pertain to the promotion of the instrument, the facilitation of company–union dialogue and the *Procedure for the Examination of Disputes*, without expressly addressing instances of non-compliance.[64]

Even if the *ILO Tripartite Declaration* meets the requirements of some criteria of legality, unavoidable issues remain with a majority of them and affect

58 ILO, *Possibilities of a Follow-up*, *supra* note 24 at para 14.

59 See ILO, *Proposal for Evaluating the Effect Given to the Tripartite Declaration of Principles concerning Multinational Enterprises and Social Policy*, 301th Sess, GB.301/MNE/4 (2008) at para 13. For an account of the weak participation of states in these periodic reports, see Alice De Jonge, *Transnational Corporations and International Law: Accountability in the Global Business Environment* (Northampton: Edward Elgar, 2011) at 30–31.

60 See ILO, *Update on the Implementation of the Promotional Framework and Follow-up to the Tripartite Declaration of Principles concerning Multinational Enterprises and Social Policy, Including ILO Collaboration with other Intergovernmental and International Organizations*, 325th Sess, GB.325/POL/9 (2015) at para 16.

61 ILO, *Procedure for the Examination of Disputes*, *supra* note 26.

62 *Ibid* at para 1.

63 See e.g. Jennifer A Zerk, *Multinationals and Corporate Social Responsibility: Limitations and Opportunities in International Law* (Cambridge: Cambridge University Press, 2006) at 257; Jernej Letnar Černič, "Corporate Responsibility for Human Rights: Analyzing the ILO Tripartite Declaration of Principles concerning Multinational Enterprises and Social Policy" (2009) 6 Miskolc J Int'l L 24 at 30–31; Emily Sims, "The ILO Declaration of Principles concerning Multinational Enterprises and Social Policy: Strengths & Provisions" in Roger Blanpain & Michele Colucci, eds, *International Encyclopedia for Labour Law and Industrial Relations* (Alphen aan den Rijn: Kluwer Law International, 2013) 1 at para 19; Khalil Hamdani & Lorraine Ruffing, *United Nations Centre on Transnational Corporations: Corporate Conduct and the Public Interest* (London: Routledge, 2015) at 116.

64 *ILO Tripartite Declaration 2017*, *supra* note 2, Annex II.

the legitimacy of this international initiative. The uncommon promulgation, the lack of clarity regarding some provisions, the tension pertaining to unaddressed potential conflicting requirements, the contradiction between the acknowledgment of the power of multinational enterprises and the voluntary observance of the principles the instrument encapsulates, as well as the absence of a procedural mechanism to address specific instances of non-compliance all represent tensions and failures regarding the criteria of legality. Taken as a whole, these aspects constitute lacunas that are inherent to the content of the *ILO Tripartite Declaration* and that impede its evolution toward the realm of legality.

2.3 Practice of Legality: A Weak and Non-Binding Practice

In addition to considering shared understandings and criteria of legality, a thorough analysis of the *ILO Tripartite Declaration's* normative character requires an examination of the practice according to which it is implemented. With a view to assessing the sense of obligation that emanates from the *ILO Tripartite Declaration*, this section demonstrates that the practice surrounding this initiative is highly problematic in several respects. While references to this international instrument and use of its procedure pertaining to disputes are relatively scarce, several discourses demonstrate a weak practice that cannot be considered as bearing any legal character.

The commentaries accompanying the *OECD Guidelines* include some paragraphs that expressly refer to the *ILO Tripartite Declaration*, stressing that the provisions on employment and industrial relations echo several aspects addressed in the ILO instrument.[65] This practice is also strengthened by a memorandum of understanding pertaining to the implementation of each instrument agreed between the ILO and the OECD in 2011.[66] Moreover, the UN *Norms on the Responsibilities of Transnational Corporations and other Business Enterprises with Regard to Human Rights* refer to the *ILO Tripartite Declaration* in their preamble.[67] However, the fact that other international initiatives – *e.g.* the UN *Guiding Principles on Business and Human Rights*[68] – do not mention the *ILO Tripartite Declaration* suggests that the latter plays a more limited role in contributing to the codification of foreign investors' responsibilities than other initiatives.

Another element pointing toward a weak practice surrounding this international initiative is the limited use of the aforementioned *Procedure for the*

65 OECD, *OECD Guidelines for Multinational Enterprises, 2011 Edition* (Paris: OECD, 2011), Commentaries at paras 48, 49 and 56.

66 See ILO, *ILO Collaboration with Other Intergovernmental and International Organizations in Promoting the Principles of the Tripartite Declaration of Principles concerning Multinational Enterprises and Social Policy*, 322th Sess, GB.322/POL/8 (2014) at para 27.

67 *Norms on the Responsibilities of Transnational Corporations and other Business Enterprises with regard to Human Rights*, 2003, UN Doc E/CN.4//Sub.2/2003/12/Rev.2, Preamble.

68 Special Representative of the Secretary-General on the issue of human rights and transnational corporations and other business enterprises, *Guiding Principles on Business and Human Rights: Implementing the United Nations 'Protect, Respect and Remedy' Framework*, 2011, UN Doc A/HRC/17/31.

Examination of Disputes. According to an internal document provided by an interviewee, only three requests for interpretation that explicitly identified provisions of the *ILO Tripartite Declaration* have resulted in the approval of an interpretation by the Governing Body.[69] What is more, no interpretation has been formally approved by the Governing Body since 1998, suggesting that this procedure has been largely unemployed and that members of the community of practice have almost given up on relying on this procedure to contribute to the implementation of this international instrument.

At first sight, some discourses related to the implementation of the *ILO Tripartite Declaration* can send a confusing signal pertaining to the legal character of the practice surrounding this international instrument. In fact, some summaries of reports on the effect given to the *ILO Tripartite Declaration* hint toward a practice of legality. For example, Mexico is considered as having "*observed* the principles of the Declaration and used them as guidelines for the drawing up of investment-related plans and programmes."[70] Along the same lines, the Federated Unions of Employers of Ireland stated that "the vast majority of multinational companies in Ireland act in a manner which is *entirely consistent with the principles in the Declaration*."[71] A stronger sense of obligation granted to the instrument at hand can also be found in some discourses. One summary of reports thus mentions that a Swiss multinational enterprise "has stated that it considers it of *great importance* that its subsidiaries *should respect the principles set out in the industrial relations chapter of the Declaration*."[72] When reporting on the regulation of multinational enterprises that are operating in their home states, several actors thus submit that national legislation and general actions are largely consistent with the requirements of the declaration.

Such a consistency with the requirements of the *ILO Tripartite Declaration* must nevertheless not be conflated with measures induced by this international

69 For the interpretations that were approved by the Governing Body, see ILO, *Report of the Committee on Multinational Enterprises*, 229th Sess, Official Bulletin, Vol LXVIII, Series A, No 3 (1985) at 113–114; ILO, *Report of the Committee on Multinational Enterprises*, 239th Sess, Official Bulletin, Vol LXXI, Series A, No 3 (1988) at 138; ILO, *Report on the Subcommittee on Multinational Enterprises*, 272th Sess, Official Bulletin, Vol LXXXI, Series A, No 2 (1998) at 49 Černič 50. Two other requests for interpretation were submitted. However, one request was declared non-receivable and the other was submitted to the Governing Body for information only, given that the Subcommittee on Multinational Corporations was unable to approve one of the two conflicting interpretations.

70 See ILO, *Summary of Reports Submitted by Governments and by Employers' and Workers' Organisations for the Fifth Survey on the Effect Given to the Tripartite Declaration of Principles concerning Multinational Enterprises and Social Policy Submitted to the Committee on Multinational Enterprises*, 1992, TDME/REP 5 (Rev.) at 21 [ILO, *Summary of Fifth Government Reports*] [emphasis added].

71 See ILO, *Summary of the Reports on the Effect Given to the Tripartite Declaration of Principles concerning Multinational Enterprises and Social Policy*, 1980, GB/MNE/1980/D.1 at 10 [ILO, *Summary of First Government Reports*] [emphasis added]. Some workers' associations also put forward similar conclusions. See ILO, *Summary of Second Government Reports on the Effect Given to the Tripartite Declaration of Principles concerning Multinational Enterprises and Social Policy Submitted to the Committee on Multinational Enterprises*, 224th Sess, GB.224/MNE/1/1/D.1 (1983) at 15 [ILO, *Summary of Second Government Reports*].

72 ILO, *Summary of Second Government Reports*, *ibid* at 114 [emphasis added].

instrument *per se*. Given that the *ILO Tripartite Declaration* refers to several conventions and recommendations that have previously required legislative changes, these summaries of reports might reflect a practice of legality that relates more to these other international instruments than to the informal international instrument at hand. In this regard, the Government of Italy stated that "the principles embodied in the Declaration are applied in the country since most of the international labour [c]onventions cited in this instrument have been ratified."[73] Similarly, the Government of Panama reported to have "generally adopted measures to promote secure and stable employment, but not specifically within the framework advocated by the [*ILO Tripartite Declaration*]."[74] This nuance was also mentioned by some workers' associations. According to the Swiss Federation of Trade Unions, "[t]here have been no legal provisions established in Switzerland on the basis of the [*ILO Tripartite Declaration*]."[75] In other words, the few examples hinting toward a practice that implicitly acknowledge a legal character to the *ILO Tripartite Declaration* should not be considered as a proof that the members of the community of practice feel bounded to act according to this initiative.

What is more, the legal character of this practice has often been unambiguously rejected when specifically addressing the application of the *ILO Tripartite Declaration* to multinational enterprises operating outside their home country. The situation in Finland was thus described in the following terms:

> Finnish enterprises have expanded their international activities, even to the extent that the management of certain branches has been transferred abroad. Expansion has taken place through investment, mergers and take-overs, and it is linked to the changes in the structure of the European economy. Regrettably, *little attention continues to be paid in this process by either the enterprises or government authorities to key principles in the ILO Tripartite Declaration.*[76]

Similarly, the Danish Employers' Organization observed "that neither the ILO Declaration nor the OECD Guidelines gave employees a legal right to demand formal negotiations across national borders."[77]

Comments by various members of the community of practice depicting the *ILO Tripartite Declaration* as a voluntary instrument that primarily seeks to improve a social dialogue also render the general absence of a practice of legality.

73 See ILO, *Summary of Fifth Government Reports*, *supra* note 70 at 35.

74 See ILO, *Seventh Survey on the Effect Given to the Tripartite Declaration of Principles concerning Multinational Enterprises and Social Policy: Summary of Reports Submitted by Governments and by Employers' and Workers' Organizations*, 280th Sess, GB.280/MNE/1/2 (2001) at 150.

75 See *ibid* at 51.

76 See ILO, *Summary of Fourth Government Reports on the Effect Given to the Tripartite Declaration of Principles concerning Multinational Enterprises and Social Policy Submitted to the Committee on Multinational Enterprises*, 244th Sess, GB.244/MNE/1/1/D.1 (1989) at 25 [ILO, *Summary of Fourth Government Reports*] [emphasis added].

77 See *ibid* at 164.

Such a position was summarized during a symposium that was held in 2003 in the following terms:

> Today, the [*ILO Tripartite Declaration*] represents a unique set of guidelines for *voluntary action* on labour issues and the only one agreed to by the social partners on the basis of universal standards. The [*ILO Tripartite Declaration*] seeks to *inspire good policy and practice* in international investment and to promote partnerships based on *social dialogue*.[78]

Since the adoption of the initial version, the voluntary nature of this international instrument has also been often considered as a crucial aspect for the support from employers' associations[79] and some states,[80] while being sharply criticized by workers' associations.[81]

In addition to the weak use of the *Procedure for Examination of Disputes*, discourses pertaining to the functioning of this procedure also offer important elements that tend to suggest the absence of a practice of legality. For example, the Danish Federation of Trade Unions reportedly stated that "it is extremely difficult to bring to the ILO, and have settled, complaints concerning cases in which a multinational enterprise has failed to comply with the principles of the Declaration."[82] When scrutinizing documents related to deliberations of requests of interpretation under this procedure, it is also plain that several actors sought to avoid any form of practice that would approach a legal setting. During one of these deliberations, the representative of the Government of the United States emphasized that "the Subcommittee was *not a 'quasi-judicial' body* and that it was not the practice of the ILO to issue conclusions relating to the *conduct of individual enterprises*."[83] "Bearing in mind its voluntary character," the same representative stressed that "[t]he Subcommittee should look at the scope and aim of the Tripartite Declaration and not go beyond them."[84]

78 ILO, *Follow-up on the Symposium on the Tripartite Declaration of Principles concerning Multinational Enterprises and Social Policy and related Multilateral Initiatives*, 291th Sess, GB.291/MNE/1 (2004) at para 3.

79 See e.g. ILO, *Summary of First Government Reports*, *supra* note 71 at 9; ILO, *Summary of Fourth Government Reports*, *supra* note 76 at 17–18; ILO, *Summary of Reports Submitted by Governments and by Employers' and Workers' Organisations for the Sixth Survey on the Effect Given to the Tripartite Declaration of Principles concerning Multinational Enterprises and Social Policy*, 268th Sess, GB.268/MNE/1/1B (1997) [ILO, *Summary of Sixth Government Reports*]; ILO, *Tripartite Forum on Promoting the Tripartite Declaration of Principles concerning Multinational Enterprises and Social Policy: Summary of Proceedings*, 2002, TFTDME/2002/1 at 3 [ILO, *Tripartite Forum – Proceedings*].

80 See e.g. ILO, *Summary of Second Government Reports*, *supra* note 71 at 17–18; ILO, *Summary of Fifth Government Reports*, *supra* note 70 at 28–29.

81 See e.g. ILO, *Summary of First Government Reports*, *supra* note 71 at 12–13; ILO, *Summary of Second Government Reports*, *ibid* at 8 and 12.

82 See ILO, *Summary of Fifth Government Reports*, *supra* note 70 at 15, 26 and 330–331.

83 ILO, *Report of the Subcommittee on Multinational Enterprises*, 264th Sess, GB.264/13 (1995) at paras 28–29 [emphasis added].

84 *Ibid* at paras 28–29.

The recognition of the absence of a "legal recourse for failure to comply with the [*ILO Tripartite Declaration*]"[85] and that the role of this instrument is limited to "build up the capacity . . . to deal with issues"[86] by some interviewees are also in line with the discourses of actors that stressed the absence of a legal character to this procedure.

Another problematic aspect of the practice surrounding this informal international instrument is that several international actors are simply not aware of the *ILO Tripartite Declaration*. For example, in the early years following the adoption of this instrument, the Norwegian Confederation of Trade Unions stated that it does "not have the impression that there is a great deal of interest in the ILO guidelines among Norwegian enterprises," stressing that such a situation is "due to the voluntary nature of the rules."[87] Similarly, the American Federation of Labor and Congress of Industrial Organizations noted that "the Tripartite Declaration is 'virtually unknown' in the US and many enterprises adopt codes of conduct which make no reference to this instrument."[88] Beyond these statements, other activities organized under the auspices of the ILO highlighted the lack of awareness for the *ILO Tripartite Declaration*.[89] Even a regional report resulting from the new information-gathering process regarding the implementation of this informal international instrument includes several excerpts recalling the low level of knowledge pertaining to its existence, "particularly in contrast to the OECD Guidelines for Multinational Enterprises and the United Nations Guiding Principles on Business and Human Rights."[90] One interviewee echoed this weak awareness in the following terms: "I must confess I'm not sure that many people know about the [*ILO Tripartite Declaration*]. So, to claim it has had a huge contribution would be wishful thinking."[91] In other words, the absence of a practice of legality is partly rooted in the fact that the *ILO Tripartite Declaration* remains in the shadow of other initiatives.

The critical component of the discourse analysis performed for present purposes also allows shedding light on *relations of power* that underlie the implementation of the *ILO Tripartite Declaration* and that are in line with the overall lack of a practice of legality. An explanation of the failure to appropriately address instances of non-compliance with the principles of the declaration can be found in the following statement from the General Union of Workers in Spain:

85 Interview 1.
86 Interview 1. See also Interview 3.
87 See ILO, *Summary of First Government Reports*, *supra* note 71 at 12–13.
88 See ILO, *Summary of Sixth Government Reports*, *supra* note 79.
89 See ILO, *Tripartite Forum – Proceedings*, *supra* note 79 at 5–7 and 9.
90 See ILO, *Multinational Enterprises, Development and Decent Work: Report on the Promotion and the Application of the Tripartite Declaration of Principles concerning Multinational Enterprises and Social Policy in the Americas* (Geneva: ILO, 2014) at 47.
91 Interview 1.

> The non-application of the Tripartite Declaration in Spain is widespread and it would require general political and economic measures to change this situation. . . . The Government has not responded to these developments for fear that enterprises would relocate."[92]

Along the same lines, the Unitary Confederation of Workers in Costa Rica added that

> while the intention behind the Tripartite Declaration is good, it is *difficult to apply in practice, precisely because of the nature, practices and employment policies of MNEs*, which are guided by the profit motive which leads them to show scant respect for laws, governments and the workers.[93]

The absence of a binding practice related to the *ILO Tripartite Declaration* is thus often linked to the position of powerful foreign investors amidst the other members of the community of practice.

Despite some discourses that indirectly reflect a practice of legality related to the *ILO Tripartite Declaration* and some isolated instances of commitment toward the principles that this instrument includes, it would be inappropriate to conclude that the practice according to which international actors implement this initiative reflects a general legal character. The limited number of references in other international instruments, the scarce use of the *Procedure for the Examination of Disputes*, the rejection of an application outside the home state, the constant emphasis on its voluntary character, the avoidance of characterizing the dispute procedure as a legal setting, the low level of awareness and the avowed difficulties regarding its application to powerful actors all suggest that the practice related to this informal international instrument faces crucial problems. While the mere existence of a practice surrounding the *ILO Tripartite Declaration* is weak, it would be inaccurate to conclude that such a practice bears any legal character and contributes to the emergence of a sense of obligation.

Conclusion

Amidst the various international initiatives that emerged in the 1970s, the unique tripartite structure of the ILO allowed an interesting contribution to the evolving codification of foreign investors' responsibilities. In line with the struggle of this intergovernmental organization to elaborate and implement labour standards in a context of neoliberal globalization, the analysis above demonstrates that this informal international instrument has led to a weak social norm that falls short of meeting several requirements to enter the realm of legality. In light of the inherent relations of power underlying the attempt

92 See ILO, *Summary of Sixth Government Reports*, *supra* note 79.

93 See ILO, *Summary of Second Government Reports*, *supra* note 71 at 8 [emphasis added].

to embed this norm in shared understandings, it is plain that powerful actors that participated in the elaboration of the *ILO Tripartite Declaration* were opposed to the adoption of principles whose observance would have been mandatory. Moreover, the tensions and failures pertaining to the relationship between several provisions of the *ILO Tripartite Declaration* and the criteria of legality impede a form of legitimacy that characterizes international legal norms. A consideration of other international instruments and discourses of the members of the community of practice that emerged around the *ILO Tripartite Declaration* also hints toward an initiative that remains in the shadow of other instruments and whose voluntary character is constantly repeated, thus preventing a genuine practice of legality. While it might appear as a useful instrument to reaffirm the legal character of ILO conventions and recommendations, the *ILO Tripartite Declaration* ultimately fails to generate a sense of obligation of its own with respect to the extraterritorial regulation of foreign investors' activities.

6 United Nations

Introduction

The United Nations (UN) has been created with a view to, among others, "achiev[ing] international cooperation in solving international problems of an economic, social, cultural or humanitarian character, and in promoting and encouraging respect for human rights."[1] The efforts deployed by this intergovernmental organization related to the general lack of accountability of foreign investors at the international level seek to achieve this purpose in a context where powerful private actors operate in various countries. Beyond the specialized agencies that are involved in this codification process and that are analyzed elsewhere in this book,[2] Chapter 6 continues the micro-level analysis of international instruments that seek to regulate foreign investors' conduct by focusing on initiatives resulting from the work of UN organs.

Since the failed attempt at adopting a *Code of Conduct on Transnational Corporations*[3] in the early 1990s, the UN has been involved in the elaboration and the implementation of four initiatives that are particularly relevant for present purposes. Shortly after the launch of the UN Global Compact by the UN Secretary-General in 2000,[4] the Sub-Commission on the Promotion and the Protection of Human Rights (Sub-Commission) deployed considerable efforts to adopt a draft version of the *Norms on the Responsibilities of Transnational Corporations and other Business Enterprises with Regard to Human Rights* (*UN Norms*)[5] in 2003. Although the Commission on Human Rights did not support this initiative, it nevertheless triggered the work of a Special Representative of the Secretary-General on the issue of human rights and transnational corporations and other business enterprises (Special

1 See *Charter of the United Nations*, 26 June 1945, Can TS 1945 No 7 (entered into force 24 October 1945), art 1 [*UN Charter*].

2 See Chapter 5 and Chapter 7.

3 *Code of Conduct on Transnational Corporations (Draft)*, 1990, UN Doc E/1990/94. See also generally Karl P Sauvant, "The Negotiations of the United Nations Code of Conduct on Transnational Corporations: Experience and Lessons Learned" (2015) 16 J World Invest & Trade 11.

4 See United Nations Global Compact, online: United Nations Global Compact www.unglobalcompact.org/what-is-gc/mission/principles (accessed 26 March 2018) [UN Global Compact].

5 *Norms on the Responsibilities of Transnational Corporations and other Business Enterprises with Regard to Human Rights*, 2003, UN Doc E/CN.4/Sub.2/2003/12/Rev.2 [*UN Norms*].

Representative) that led to the endorsement by the Human Rights Council of the *United Nations Guiding Principles on Business and Human Rights* (*UN Guiding Principles*) in 2011.[6] In parallel with the elaboration of these informal international instruments, the *United Nations Convention Against Corruption* (*UNCAC*) was negotiated under the auspices of the UN and adopted in October 2003.[7]

Considering that these efforts to regulate private firms ultimately find their roots in a historical will to establish a new international economic order, the initiatives adopted under the auspices of the UN have emerged from a particular institutional context that departs from a general commitment to neoliberal policies (1). Yet, the UN has elaborated and implemented international initiatives that can only be considered as international norms that fail to fully generate a sense of obligation. Intended as a learning platform to influence the conduct of business enterprises, the UN Global Compact is a widely disseminated social norm that unambiguously remains outside the realm of legality (2). Similarly, even if they have been extensively discussed after their adoption by the Sub-Commission, the *UN Norms* have remained a social norm that is now rarely taken into account to steer private firms' conduct (3). With respect to the *UN Guiding Principles*, although they possess key elements suggesting a potential evolution toward the threshold of legality, this informal instrument is currently a social norm (4). Finally, despite its formal character under international law, the *UNCAC* generally appears as a social norm that faces notable issues and fails to fully generate a sense of obligation (5).

1. The UN: Multiple Sources of Norms to Change the Economic Order

Contextualizing the analysis of the normative character of international initiatives elaborated and implemented under the auspices of the UN calls for a consideration of the multiple sources of norms that are found within this intergovernmental organization. Even if the *Charter of the United Nations* (*UN Charter*) only requires member states to agree to the decisions adopted by the UN Security Council,[8] other UN entities can adopt resolutions that encompass standards of appropriate conduct for international actors.[9] For example, Article 10 of the *UN Charter* provides that the UN General Assembly "may discuss any questions or any matters within the scope of the present Charter . . . and may make recommendations to the Members of the United Nations or the Security Council."[10] With respect to the UN Economic and Social Council,

6 Special Representative of the Secretary-General on the issue of human rights and transnational corporations and other business enterprises, *Guiding Principles on Business and Human Rights: Implementing the United Nations 'Protect, Respect and Remedy' Framework*, 2011, UN Doc A/HRC/17/31 [*UN Guiding Principles*].

7 *United Nations Convention Against Corruption*, 31 October 2003, 2349 UNTS 41 (entered into force 14 December 2005) [*UNCAC*].

8 *UN Charter*, *supra* note 1, art 25.

9 For a description of the UN principal organs, see United Nations, *The United Nations Today* (New York: United Nations, 2008) at 6–18 [United Nations, *UN Today*].

10 *UN Charter*, *supra* note 1, art 10.

Article 62 mentions that its functions include the possibility of making recommendations for the purpose of promoting human rights, as well as preparing draft conventions for submission to the UN General Assembly.[11] The UN Economic and Social Council is also authorized to invite to its deliberation, or consult with, various international actors such as member states, representatives of specialized agencies and non-governmental organizations (NGOs).[12] Finally, Article 98 stipulates that the UN Secretary-General "shall act [as the chief administrative officer of the UN] in all meetings of the General Assembly, of the Security Council [and] of the Economic and Social Council, . . . and shall perform such other functions as are entrusted to him by these organs."[13]

While the Organisation for Economic Co-operation and Development (OECD) shapes the identity of its member states as promoters of liberal and neoliberal policies,[14] the development of international norms related to the misconduct of foreign investors by the UN emerges from a drastically different institutional context. In fact, in addition to the elaboration of two reports addressing the impact of transnational corporations,[15] the UN General Assembly adopted several resolutions affirming the right of states to regulate foreign investors' activities during the 1970s. In the *Declaration on the Establishment of a New International Economic Order*, the UN General Assembly mentioned that such an economic order should be founded on the "regulation and supervision of the activities of transnational corporations by taking measures in the interest of the national economies of the countries where such transnational corporations operate on the basis of the full sovereignty of those countries."[16] Similarly, the *Charter of Economic Rights and Duties of States* stated that

> [e]ach State has the right: (a) [t]o regulate and exercise authority over foreign investment within its national jurisdiction in accordance with its laws and regulations and in conformities with its national objectives and priorities[; and] (b) [t]o regulate and supervise the activities of transnational corporations within its national jurisdiction and take measures to ensure that such activities comply with its laws, rules and regulations and conform with its economic and social policies.[17]

11 *Ibid*, art 62.
12 See *ibid*, art 69–71.
13 *Ibid*, art 98.
14 See section 1 of Chapter 4.
15 Department of Economic and Social Affairs, *Multinational Corporations in World Development* (New York: United Nations, 1973); *The Impact of Transnational Corporations on the Development Process and on International Relations: Report of the Group of Eminent Persons to Study the Role of Multinational Enterprises on Development and on International Relations*, 1974, UN Doc E/5500/Add.1.
16 *Declaration on the Establishment of a New International Economic Order*, GA Res 3201(S-VI), UNGAOR, 6th Ext Sess, Supp No 1, UN Doc A/9559, (1974) 3 at para 4(g).
17 *Charter of Economic Rights and Duties of States*, GA Res 3281(XXIX), UNGAOR, 29th Sess, Supp No 31, UN Doc A/9631, (1974) 50 at para 2(2).

The concerns raised through these resolutions ultimately led to the establishment of an intergovernmental information and research Centre on Transnational Corporations,[18] operating under the guidance of the Commission on Transnational Corporations.[19] The Centre was created in 1974 and conducted its activities in three principal areas (*i.e.* research and information on transnational corporations, technical assistance and intergovernmental support). Of particular relevance for present purposes, the Centre on Transnational Corporations' expertise supported the work of the Commission on Transnational Corporations, which was initially tasked to assist the UN Economic and Social Council "in evolving a set of recommendations which, taken together, would represent the basis for a code of conduct dealing with transnational corporations."[20] However, due to the lack of agreement between international actors with respect to legal nature of the instrument and a considerable shift in the ideological context,[21] such a code of conduct was never adopted. Amidst a broader reform of the UN, the Centre on Transnational Corporations and the Commission on Transnational Corporations were abolished in the early 1990s, and their activities were integrated to the United Nations Conference on Trade and Development.[22]

Despite the demise of these agencies and the failure to adopt a code of conduct on transnational corporations, the UN has remained an interesting normative site when it comes to international initiatives related to the conduct of foreign investors. Several organs – the UN Secretary-General, the UN General Assembly and the UN Economic and Social Council – can adopt recommendations that contribute to the emergence of international norms. Furthermore, such recommendations emerge within an institutional context historically marked by an undeniable support for the regulation of foreign investors. Taken as a whole, these aspects provide a breeding ground for the elaboration and the implementation of initiatives such as the UN Global Compact, the *UN Norms*, the *UN Guiding Principles* and the *UNCAC*.

2. The UN Global Compact

The first contribution to the codification of foreign investors' responsibilities by the UN since the failure of the *Code of Conduct on Transnational Corporations* is reflected in ten principles enunciated by the UN Secretary-General. More specifically, the UN Global Compact concisely addresses responsibilities of business enterprises in the areas of human rights, labour

18 *The Impact of Transnational Corporations on the Development Process and on International Relations*, ESC Res 1908(LVII), UNESCOR, 1974, UN Doc E/5570, 13 at para 6.

19 *The Impact of Transnational Corporations on the Development Process and on International Relations*, ESC Res 1913(LVII), UNESCOR, 1974, Supp No 1A, UN Doc E/5570/Add.1, 3 at para 4.

20 See *ibid* at para 3(e).

21 See e.g. Sauvant, *supra* note 3 at 38–62.

22 See Khalil Hamdani & Lorraine Ruffing, *United Nations Centre on Transnational Corporations: Corporate Conduct and the Public Interest* (London: Routledge, 2015) at 20–23.

rights, the environment and anti-corruption.[23] Despite the large network of participants that have committed to implement it, the UN Global Compact remains a social norm that fails to generate any sense of obligation. In fact, the UN Secretary-General has explicitly considered this initiative as a voluntary forum for dialogue since its inception, a characteristic strongly supported by powerful international actors commenting on its elaboration (2.1). Furthermore, a closer look at the provisions of this instrument shows that the UN Global Compact fails to meet several criteria of legality, thus seriously impeding its legitimacy (2.2). Ultimately, in addition to the disengagement of several participants beyond the initial commitment to implement them, the absence of a sense of obligation to comply with the UN Global Compact's principles is found in several discourses from the members of the community of practice (2.3).

2.1 Shared Understandings: Establishing a Voluntary Forum for Dialogue

In a way that sharply contrasts with a state-centric view of the international law-making process, the emergence of the UN Global Compact primarily results from the efforts of the UN Secretary-General and a limited number of non-state actors who acted as *norm entrepreneurs*. More specifically, this initiative finds its roots in a speech delivered by Kofi Annan at the World Economic Forum in which he called upon business enterprises "to embrace, support and enact a set of core values in the areas of human rights, labour standards, and environmental practices."[24] In order to elaborate this set of core values, the UN Secretary-General relied on the work of a Special Adviser to the UN Secretary-General on the Global Compact.[25] Further to the official launch of this initiative in July 2000,[26] the elaboration of the UN Global Compact also included a tenth principle with respect to the area of anti-corruption in 2004,[27] as well as the elaboration of integrity measures in 2005.[28]

23 UN Global Compact, *supra* note 4, Principles 1–10.

24 United Nations, Press Release, SG/SM/6881, "Secretary-General Proposes Global Compact on Human Rights, Labour, Environment, in Address to World Economic Forum in Davos" (1 February 1999) online: United Nations www.un.org/press/en/1999/19990201.sgsm6881.html (accessed 26 March 2018) [United Nations, "SG Proposes Global Compact"].

25 United Nations, *The Global Compact Leaders Summit 2004: Final Report* (New York: United Nations Global Compact Office, 2004) at 25 [United Nations, *Leaders Summit 2004*].

26 See United Nations, Press release, SG/SM/7495, "Secretary-General Welcomes International Corporate Leaders to Global Compact Meeting" (26 July 2000) online: United Nations www.un.org/press/en/2000/20000726.sgsm7495.doc.html (accessed 26 March 2018) [United Nations, "SG Welcomes"].

27 See United Nations, *Leaders Summit 2004*, *supra* note 25 at 5.

28 United Nations Global Compact, *Integrity Measures* (June 2016), online: United Nations Global Compact www.unglobalcompact.org/docs/about_the_gc/Integrity_measures/Integrity_Measures_Note_EN.pdf (accessed 26 March 2018) [UN Global Compact, *Integrity Measures*].

In addition to the work of the UN Secretary-General and his Special Adviser, the UN Global Compact relies on a vast *community of practice* that includes representatives of private companies, government entities, intergovernmental organizations, international business organizations, public interest NGOs, academics and labour organizations, among others.[29] Critically analyzing statements made by these actors shortly after the launch of this initiative and transcripts from semi-structured interviews allows an assessment of the existence of shared understandings with respect to the elaboration of the UN Global Compact.

It is plain from these discourses that the members of the community of practice failed to reach any shared understandings pertaining to the legal nature of this instrument. While the UN Secretary-General initially sought to establish "a forum for dialogue"[30] and a "learning network that provides a framework through which its participants are able to publicly support a set of universally agreed values,"[31] he was firmly supported by private interest NGOs and several states that stressed the voluntary character of the UN Global Compact. For example, in a joint statement from the UN Secretary-General and the International Organization of Employers, these actors "agreed that the Global Compact is not a substitute for other approaches, such as regulation, and that it is a *voluntary initiative* that seeks to motivate employers to act within their sphere of influence."[32] This approach was also expressly supported by several member states during a plenary meeting of the UN General Assembly that was held shortly after the launch of the UN Global Compact.[33]

By contrast, public interest NGOs "call[ed] on the United Nations to deliver real corporate accountability in a legal framework" and deplored that the UN Global Compact was defined "neither as a *binding set of regulations* nor as a code of conduct for companies."[34] These criticisms are also recalled in the discourses of individuals working for intergovernmental organizations that are involved in the codification of foreign investors' responsibilities. One participant in the research project thus compellingly stated the following: "[T]here are some civil society actors that would like to see binding instruments that are enforceable. . . . So

29 See e.g. United Nations, *The Global Compact Leaders Summit 2007 – Facing Realities: Getting Down to Business* (New York: United Nations Global Compact Office, 2007) at 7 [United Nations, *Leaders Summit 2007*].

30 United Nations, "SG Welcomes", *supra* note 26.

31 Secretary-General, *Cooperation between the United Nations and All Relevant Partners, in Particular the Private Sector*, 2001, UN Doc A/56/323 at para 86.

32 United Nations, Press Release, SG/SM/8212-ECO/24, "United Nations Joint Statement on Global Compact by Secretary-General and President of International Organization of Employers (IOE)" (26 April 2002) online: United Nations www.un.org/press/en/2002/sgsm8212.doc.htm (accessed 26 March 2018) [emphasis added].

33 See *Towards Global Partnership – 37th Plenary Meeting*, 2001, UN Doc A/56/PV.37.

34 EarthRights International, *Joint Civil Society Statement on the Global Compact and Corporate Accountability* (23 June 2004), online: EarthRights International https://web.archive.org/web/20101223032244/https://www.earthrights.org/campaigns/joint-civil-society-statement-global-compact-and-corporate-accountability (accessed 26 March 2018) [emphasis added].

that is one criticism – you know, possible blue washing, if you want. But, I think we're very clear that our mission is not to be sort of a watchdog organization of companies but more a learning initiative."[35]

It is also worth emphasizing that the absence of shared understandings regarding the legal nature of the UN Global Compact is anchored in discourses that reproduce *relations of power* between international actors. While the UN Secretary-General justified the elaboration of its initiative by emphasizing that "power [of big investors] brings with it great opportunities – and great responsibilities,"[36] public interest NGOs maintained that "governments should work together more effectively to reduce corporate influence on government and intergovernmental decision-making processes."[37] Ultimately, critically analyzing the existence of shared understandings between international actors that elaborated or commented on the UN Global Compact demonstrates the most powerful actors' unwillingness to grant any legal character to this initiative.

In sum, several international actors involved in the discussions that followed the elaboration and the launch of the UN Global Compact failed to agree on the nature of this initiative. The UN Secretary-General initially depicted it as a voluntary learning forum and this position found support from private interest NGOs and several states. Despite a clear contrast with the position of public interest NGOs, the convergence of views between the main norm entrepreneurs and powerful representatives of the private sector led to the elaboration of an international social norm.

2.2 Criteria of Legality: Multiple Roadblocks

Even if it is plain that several international actors agreed to elaborate the UN Global Compact as a voluntary forum geared toward dialogue from its inception, the analysis of the normative character of this initiative would be incomplete without an assessment of the relation between its provisions and the criteria of legality advanced in the interactional theory of international law.[38] As emphasized in the present section, the failure of the UN Global Compact to meet the requirements of several criteria thus becomes an additional obstacle that separates this international initiative from the realm of legality.

With respect to *promulgation*, the fact that the UN Global Compact remains an informal instrument that was not expressly provided by the *UN Charter* is undeniable. However, some aspects related to this international initiative ensure that it is made available to the public. Not only is the UN Global Compact widely disseminated through a website,[39] but the UN General Assembly has also

35 Interview 10.
36 United Nations, "SG Proposes Global Compact", *supra* note 24.
37 EarthRights International, *supra* note 34.
38 See section 3 of the introduction.
39 UN Global Compact, *supra* note 4.

constantly referred to and supported this initiative since 2002.[40] Such dissemination and recognition thus ensure that the principles of the UN Global Compact are promulgated to a certain extent.

Moreover, nothing in this international initiative poses any significant issues with respect to the criterion of *generality*. With a Preamble stressing that "[t]he Global Compact asks *companies* to embrace, support and enact . . . a set of core values,"[41] the content of this initiative does not expressly limit its application to any specific entities. This general application is also reflected in the broad range of participants in the initiative. As of April 2018, the UN Global Compact was represented by a network of 10,689 active participants that included business enterprises, private interest NGOs, public interest NGOs, academic institutions and public sector organizations.[42] Moreover, given that nothing in the principles enshrined in the UN Global Compact expressly deals with temporal requirements, this international initiative easily meets the requirements related to the criterion of *non-retroactivity*.

However, despite additional information that is made available on its website,[43] several authors emphasize that the lack of details provided in the UN Global Compact's principles considerably affects its *clarity*.[44] In contrast to other international instruments, each provision of this initiative is summarized in a single sentence or less. For example, the two principles pertaining to the area of human rights read as follows: "Principle 1: Business should support and respect the protection of internationally proclaimed human rights; and Principle 2: make sure that they are not complicit in human rights abuses."[45] Another element raising issues with respect to the clarity of the UN Global Compact is its reliance on the concept of "sphere of influence" in its Preamble.[46] While the use of a relatively vague term in a provision does not necessarily entail an unclear international norm, the absence of any express attempts at clarifying this concept is troublesome.

Furthermore, while all the other instruments analyzed in this book easily meet the criterion of *constancy*, the UN Global Compact is the only one facing issues in this regard. In fact, when one considers the various publications from the UN with respect to this initiative, the Preamble of the UN Global Compact has not always been included with its principles. For example, in the annual review that

40 See e.g. *Towards Global Partnerships*, GA Res 56/76, UNGAOR, 56th Sess, Supp No 49, UN Doc A/RES/56/76, (2002), Preamble. More recently, see *Towards Global Partnerships: A Principle-Based Approach to Enhanced Cooperation between the United Nations and All Relevant Partners*, GA Res 70/224, UNGAOR, 70th Sess, Supp No 49, UN Doc A/RES/70/224, (2016).

41 UN Global Compact, *supra* note 4, Preamble [emphasis added].

42 See United Nations Global Compact, *Our Participants*, online: United Nations Global Compact www.unglobalcompact.org/what-is-gc/participants (accessed 16 April 2018) [United Nations Global Compact, *Our Participants*].

43 UN Global Compact, *supra* note 4.

44 See e.g. Surya Deva, "Global Compact: A Critique of the U.N.'s Public–Private Partnership for Promoting Corporate Citizenship" (2006) 34 Syracuse J Int'l L & Com 107 at 129 [Deva, "Global Compact"]; Evaristus Oshionebo, "The U.N. Global Compact and Accountability of Transnational Corporations: Separating Myth from Realities" (2007) 19 Fla J Int'l L 1 at 23.

45 UN Global Compact, *supra* note 4, Principle 1 and Principle 2.

46 *Ibid*, Preamble.

was published in 2010, the ten principles of the UN Global Compact are preceded by the following sentence: "[T]he Global Compact asks companies to embrace, support and enact, within their sphere of influence, a set of core values in the areas of human rights, labour standards, the environment and anti-corruption."[47] However, previous and subsequent publications neglect this Preamble.[48] Given that the latter provides important elements pertaining to the scope of the requirements that are asked to companies, such a lack of constancy is highly problematic as far as the legitimacy of the instrument is concerned.

Strongly related to the failure to meet the two previous criteria, the UN Global Compact can also be perceived as *asking impossible requirements* to its adherents. In fact, the inadequacy of the "sphere of influence" to clearly define the business relations for which the participants have to implement the content of the UN Global Compact's principles has often been considered as providing a requirement reaching beyond the normal activities of business enterprises.[49] Interestingly, the failure to include the wording of the Preamble in recent publications of the UN Global Compact hints toward a desire to depart from the use of these terms. However, its sporadic inclusion in the UN Global Compact impedes this instrument from ensuring that it remains realistic.

Without encompassing plain *contradictions* between its provisions, the wording chosen in the Preamble of the UN Global Compact does not sit well with the pressing issues that this initiative seeks to address. In his speech to the World Economic Forum, the UN Secretary-General summarized the issues at hand in the following terms:

> The problem is this. The spread of markets outpaces the ability of societies and their political systems to adjust to them, let alone to guide the course they take. History teaches us that such an imbalance between the economic, social and political realms can never be sustained for very long. The industrialized countries learned that lesson in their bitter and costly encounter with the Great Depression.[50]

Unfortunately, an international initiative that merely "asks companies"[51] to behave according to a set of core values is ill-suited to tackle a problem of this magnitude. As mentioned with respect to instruments analyzed in previous chapters, the weakness of the requirements included in the UN Global Compact can ultimately create a tension with this criterion of legality.

47 United Nations, *United Nations Global Compact: Annual Review 2010* (New York: United Nations Global Compact Office, 2011) at 10 [United Nations, *Annual Review 2010*].

48 See e.g. United Nations, *United Nations Global Compact: Annual Review 2008* (New York: United Nations Global Compact Office, 2009) at 68; United Nations, *Global Corporate Sustainability Report 2013* (New York: United Nations Global Compact Office, 2013) at 26 [United Nations, *Sustainability Report 2013*].

49 See e.g. Deva, "Global Compact", *supra* note 44 at 132.

50 United Nations, "SG Proposes Global Compact", *supra* note 24.

51 UN Global Compact, *supra* note 4, Preamble.

Finally, even if integrity measures were adopted after the initial launch of the UN Global Compact, the latter fails to meet the criterion of *congruence*.[52] From the outset, a note on the integrity measures published by the UN Global Compact expressly provides that this initiative "is not designed, nor does it have the mandate or resources, to monitor or measure participants' performance."[53] In fact, most of these integrity measures relate to either the use of the UN Global Compact's logo or to changes in the participation status of business enterprises that fail to submit a "Communication on Progress."[54] Furthermore, a dialogue facilitation process has been established to address allegations of systematic and egregious abuses.[55] Although this process is geared toward the provision of guidance and assistance to a participating company that is the subject of such allegations, the note on the integrity measures specifies that the "Global Compact Office will not involve itself in any way in any claims of a legal nature that a party may have against a participating company."[56] Even if the integrity measures provide that a participant refusing to engage in the dialogue facilitation process can see its participation in the UN Global Compact changes,[57] the fact that such a process expressly avoids determining compliance with the principles of this initiative remains a crucial impediment to congruence.

Overall, the numerous issues posed by the provisions of the UN Global Compact with respect to the majority of the criteria of legality advanced in the interactional theory of international law strongly suggest that this international instrument fails to generate a sentiment of legitimacy that characterizes legal norms. Despite its consistency with some requirements (*i.e.* promulgation, generality and non-retroactivity), the failure to sufficiently meet other crucial criteria (*i.e.* clarity, constancy, not asking the impossible, absence of contradiction and congruence) suggests that the UN Global Compact is unlikely to generate any sense of obligation.

2.3 Practice of Legality: A Vast, but Weak and Non-Binding Practice

Beyond the consideration of interactions that occurred around the elaboration of the UN Global Compact and the consistency of its provisions with the criteria of legality, several aspects related to the implementation of this initiative shed light on an impressive practice that nevertheless lacks a legal character. In addition to the large number of active participants, other international instruments elaborated by intergovernmental organizations expressly refer to the UN Global Compact. The *UN Norms*[58] and the *Principles for Responsible Investment*

52 See generally UN Global Compact, *Integrity Measures*, *supra* note 28.
53 *Ibid* at 1.
54 *Ibid* at 1–2.
55 *Ibid* at 2–5.
56 *Ibid* at 2.
57 *Ibid* at 3.
58 *UN Norms*, *supra* note 5, Preamble.

in Agriculture and Food Systems (*UN PRAI*)[59] thus all point to the UN Global Compact as a relevant normative development. This practice is also reflected in other initiatives that are supported by the UN Global Compact itself, such as the Principles for Responsible Investment and the Principles for Responsible Management Education.[60] Moreover, the various reports summarizing the activities of the UN Global Compact emphasize the existence of a large network – *e.g.* Global Compact Local Networks – that provides crucial resources and organizes multiple events related to this initiative.[61]

Despite such a vast practice, other elements pertaining to the implementation of the UN Global Compact hide crucial issues. As of April 2018, the database provided on the official website of the UN Global Compact indicates 2,245 "non-communicative participants" among 10,689 "active" participants.[62] Furthermore, the response rate to an implementation survey that has been conducted on an annual basis since 2007 roughly oscillates between 15% and 25% of all participants.[63] Beyond the initial enthusiasm to join the UN Global Compact that is demonstrated by the overall number of participants, this quantitative data thus demonstrates a rather weak participation through time.

Moreover, a closer look at the discourses from the members of the community of practice strongly suggests that the practice surrounding the implementation of this international initiative lacks a legal character. Interestingly, the participation in the UN Global Compact is often depicted as a "commitment." For example, participants are considered as making a "[l]eadership *commitment* to mainstream the Global Compact Principles into strategies and operations and to take action in support of broader UN goals in a transparent way."[64] Various declarations issued after the triennial Global Compact Leaders Summits also stressed a will from the participants to "*commit* to continuously advance the implementation of the UN Global Compact and its principles."[65] The requirement to produce a Communication of Progress was even considered as a "*mandatory* disclosure policy" and "a critical component of the Global Compact Integrity Measures."[66]

59 Committee on World Food Security, *Principles for Responsible Investment in Agriculture and Food Systems*, 2014, CFS 2014/41/4/Rev.1 at para 19(A)(v) [*Principles for Responsible Investment in Agriculture*].

60 These two initiatives were acknowledged by the UN General Assembly. See *Towards Global Partnerships*, GA Res 64/223, UNGAOR, 64th Sess, Supp No 49, UN Doc A/RES/64/223, (2010).

61 See e.g. United Nations, *Annual Review 2010*, supra note 47 at Annex A and Annex D; United Nations, *Sustainability Report 2013*, *supra* note 48 at 22–23.

62 United Nations Global Compact, *Our Participants*, *supra* note 42.

63 See e.g. United Nations, *UN Global Compact Annual Review – 2007 Leaders Summit* (New York: United Nations Global Compact Office, 2007) at 9; United Nations, *Sustainability Report 2013*, *supra* note 48 at 6.

64 See United Nations, *United Nations Global Compact Annual Review: Anniversary Edition* (New York: United Nations Global Compact Office, 2010) at 18 [emphasis added] [United Nations, *Annual Review 2009*].

65 See e.g. the *Shanghai Declaration* at para 6 in United Nations, *Global Compact Summit: China – Building Alliances for a Sustainable Global Economy: Final Report* (New York: United Nations Global Compact Office, 2006) at 31 [emphasis added] [United Nations, *Global Compact Summit: China*].

66 See United Nations, *Annual Review 2010*, supra note 47 at 18 [emphasis added].

Despite these semantic choices, the community of practice surrounding the UN Global Compact does not seem to recognize any sense of obligation to specifically act according to the principles that this initiative encapsulates. While the voluntary nature of the instrument was considered as a "crucial success factor" justifying the participation of several actors that attended the Global Compact Leaders Summit in 2004,[67] the same report underscores that public interest NGOs and trade unions "criticized the initiative for what they said was a fundamental *lack of accountability and governance mechanisms to ensure companies follow through on their commitments to the principles*."[68] During a subsequent Global Compact Leaders Summit, the foreign minister of France stressed the need to rethink the UN Global Compact because of the "limits of voluntary engagements," adding that "eventually these principles will have to be made obligatory for those companies that do not comply."[69]

Beyond the constant emphasis on the UN Global Compact's voluntary character, other elements found in several discourses hint toward the lack of a practice of legality. While considering the dialogue facilitation process as "a transparent means to handle credible allegations of systematic or egregious abuse of the Global Compact's overall aims and principles by a participating organization,"[70] some annual reports also reiterate "the Global Compact's nature as a learning, dialogue and partnership platform as distinct from a certification scheme, compliance-based initiative or adjudicatory body."[71] The failure to ensure that the principles of the UN Global Compact are effectively implemented by the various actors through their supply chains is another recurring theme that demonstrates the absence of a practice of legality.[72]

The social rather than legal nature of the practice surrounding the UN Global Compact was discussed at great length by some interviewees who participated in this research project. In this regard, one participant recalled that the continuous support of the UN General Assembly to the UN Global Compact was primarily related to its voluntary nature:

> The Global Compact, as an initiative, has been recognized by the General Assembly. . . . It started as an initiative of the [Secretary-General], but it has got the intergovernmental stamp of approval as an initiative – but again, *as a voluntary initiative that is a learning platform* and that is engaging and involving companies in the affairs of the UN.[73]

67 United Nations, *Leaders Summit 2004*, *supra* note 25 at 6.
68 *Ibid* at 3 [emphasis added].
69 United Nations, *Leaders Summit* 2007, *supra* note 29 at 13.
70 See United Nations, *United Nations Global Compact Activity Report 2013* (New York: United Nations Global Compact Office, 2014) at 28.
71 United Nations, *Annual Review 2009*, *supra* note 64 at 20.
72 See United Nations, *Leaders Summit 2004*, *supra* note 25 at 7; United Nations, *Sustainability Report 2013*, *supra* note 48 at 7.
73 Interview 16 [emphasis added].

When asked whether business enterprises feel bounded to act according to the principles included in this international initiative, another participant answered the following:

> [B]ecause they are voluntary initiatives, I wouldn't say they feel it directly from being a part of our initiative, but . . . once there's a critical mass of companies that do think in a way, then, you know . . . So, I think it's a lot of the actors working in concert that really changes these norms that it becomes unacceptable to do something else even if it's not legally binding.[74]

Consistent with the definition of an international social norm, such statements stress the ability of the UN Global Compact to set standards of appropriate conduct, without generating any sense of obligation to act according to its principles.

As far as *relations of power* between members of the community of practice are concerned, the characterization of the UN Global Compact as a forum for dialogue that is geared toward a learning process relies on an implicit recognition of the power of private business enterprises. In a declaration that was adopted at the UN Global Compact Summit in China, several participants thus advanced that "[b]usiness can be an influential and practical force for good" and that "responsible businesses have proven to be a positive force in spurring development and improving human conditions."[75] By contrast, a representative of Oxfam International stressed that the "tremendous power of corporations" implies that "voluntary codes and initiatives are not a substitute for international and national law."[76] While some international actors emphasize that the current practice surrounding the UN Global Compact remains largely insufficient to address the general lack of accountability of powerful business enterprises at the international level, it is plain that these powerful actors are most likely to influence the normative character of this practice.

In line with the efforts of the norm entrepreneurs and powerful members of the community of practice to stress the voluntary character of the UN Global Compact, as well as the inadequacies between its provisions and the criteria of legality, the absence of a practice of legality surrounding this initiative is quite unsurprising. Of course, the UN Global Compact is well-known and can undoubtedly lead to the inclusion of more sustainable practices in the strategies and operations of business enterprises. However, this international norm struggles to keep its participants active and does not seek to ensure compliance of powerful business actors with the principles that it encompasses. Ultimately, the UN Global Compact is a widely disseminated, but weak and non-binding norm.

74 Interview 10.

75 United Nations, *Global Compact Summit: China*, *supra* note 65 at para 3.

76 See United Nations, *Leaders Summit 2004*, *supra* note 25 at 21.

3. The *UN Norms*

In parallel with the launch and the implementation of the UN Global Compact, a Sub-Commission operating under the UN Economic and Social Council deployed substantial efforts to elaborate another international instrument. With a view to ensuring that the activities of transnational corporations and other business enterprises are consistent with the promotion and the protection of international human rights law, the *UN Norms* include 23 paragraphs that provide requirements for these private actors in various areas,[77] specifications pertaining to their implementation[78] and definitions.[79] However, with respect to their normative character, the *UN Norms* emerge as a social norm whose brief practice has considerably faded away. The avowed intent of the experts from the Sub-Commission to elaborate a binding instrument clashed with the position of powerful international actors and failed to reach any shared understandings with respect to the legal nature of this initiative (3.1). What is more, tensions and failures of the *UN Norms*' provisions regarding several criteria of legality – *i.e.* confusing promulgation, impossible requirements, inherent contradictions and lack of concrete congruence devices – affect the legitimate character of this international instrument (3.2). Although some actors sought to build on the *UN Norms* to develop a genuine legal norm, powerful members of the community of practice impeded this evolution and ultimately prevented any form of practice surrounding this initiative (3.3).

3.1 Shared Understandings: Powerful Actors Opposing an Epistemic Community

One particularity of the *UN Norms* is that their elaboration relied on a group of experts that constituted an *epistemic community* without acting as representatives of states. After the establishment of a sessional working group of the Sub-Commission "to examine the working methods and activities of transnational corporations"[80] in 1998, this working group's mandate was extended with a view to drafting relevant human rights norms concerning transnational corporations and other business activities in 2001.[81] In a resolution adopted in 2003, the Sub-Commission approved the *UN Norms* and decided to transmit this instrument to the Commission on

77 *UN Norms*, *supra* note 5 at paras 1–14.
78 *Ibid* at paras 15–19.
79 Ibid at paras 20–23.
80 See *The Relationship between the Enjoyment of Economic, Social and Cultural Rights and the Right to Development, and the Working Methods and Activities of Transnational Corporations*, CHR Res 1998/8, 1998, UN Doc E/CN.4/SUB.2/1998/45, 30 at para 4.
81 See *The Effects of the Working Methods and Activities of Transnational Corporations on the Enjoyment of Human Rights*, CHR Res 2001/3, 2001, UN Doc E/CN.4/SUB.2/2001/40, 17 at para 4. The sessional working group was later invited to continue its work in this regard: *The Relationship between the Enjoyment of Economic, Social and Cultural Rights and the Right to Development, and the Working Methods and Activities of Transnational Corporations*, CHR Res 2002/8, 2002, UN Doc E/CN.4/SUB.2/2002/46, 24 at para 5.

Human Rights.[82] However, in 2004, the emergence of this initiative came to an abrupt end. After emphasizing that the *UN Norms* "contain useful elements and ideas for consideration by the Commission,"[83] the Commission on Human Rights mentioned that they had "no legal standing, and that the Sub-Commission should not perform any monitoring function in this regard."[84]

In addition to the work of the epistemic community that pushed for their adoption by the Sub-Commission, the elaboration of the *UN Norms* required the involvement of a broad *community of practice*. In this regard, several reports suggest that this initiative results from the work of the members of the sessional working group, other experts from the Sub-Commission, public interest NGOs, intergovernmental organizations, as well as some private interest NGOs that were involved later in the elaboration process.[85] The content of these reports, statements submitted to the UN and transcripts from semi-structured interviews can all be considered as relevant sources of discourses to critically assess the extent to which the *UN Norms* are anchored in shared understandings with respect to their legal nature.

Even if the members of the community of practice were aware that the Sub-Commission was not mandated to elaborate a formal international treaty, several excerpts from the reports of the sessional working group point toward a firm intent to elaborate an international norm that would have been binding or constituted the basis of a legally binding instrument. For example, in its first report, the sessional working group "stressed the fact that the new code of conduct should have a *binding character* and require TNCs to prepare 'human rights impact assessments' on a regular basis."[86] Along these lines, the working group reported that "a number of members . . . strongly urged that [the *UN Norms*] should be the basis for a *legally binding code of conduct* for the regulation of the activities of companies."[87] Later in the elaboration process, the main drafter of the *UN Norms* reportedly stated that this instrument "was *binding* in the sense

82 *Responsibility of Transnational Corporations and other Business Enterprises with regard to Human Rights*, CHR Res 2003/16, 2003, UN Doc E/CN.4/Sub.2/2003/L.11, 52 at paras 1–2.

83 *Responsibilities of Transnational Corporations and Related Business Enterprises with regard to Human Rights*, ESC Dec 2004/116, 2004, Supp No 3, UN Doc E/CN.4/2004/127, 332, Preamble [*Responsibilities of Transnational Corporations*].

84 *Ibid* at para (c).

85 *Report of the Sessional Working Group on the Working Methods and Activities of Transnational Corporations on its First Session*, 1999, UN Doc E/CN.4/Sub.2/1999/9 at paras 1–8 [*Sessional Working Group – First Session*]; *Report of the Sessional Working Group on the Working Methods and Activities of Transnational Corporations on its Second Session*, 2000, UN Doc E/CN.4/Sub.2/2000/12 at paras 2–8 [*Sessional Working Group – Second Session*]; *Report of the Sessional Working Group on the Working Methods and Activities of Transnational Corporations on its Third Session*, 2001, UN Doc E/CN.4/Sub.2/2001/9 at paras 2–7; *Report of the Sessional Working Group on the Working Methods and Activities of Transnational Corporations on its Fourth Session*, 2002, UN Doc E/CN.4/Sub.2/2002/13 at paras 2–7 [*Sessional Working Group – Fourth Session*].

86 *Sessional Working Group – First Session*, *supra* note 85 at para 26 [emphasis added].

87 *Sessional Working Group – Second Session*, *supra* note 85 at para 37 [emphasis added].

that it applied human rights law under ratified conventions to the activities of transnational corporations and other business enterprises."[88]

The members of the sessional working group also emphasized the support that they received from public interest NGOs, recalling that "[a] large majority of NGOs stressed the urgent need for a *legally binding instrument* to regulate the activities of TNCs" and that "[a] voluntary code of conduct was not sufficient."[89] Similarly, the contribution of the *UN Norms* to "codify and distil existing *obligations* under international law as they apply to companies" was applauded in a joint statement signed by 51 public interest NGOs.[90] Some of these actors even advanced the need to establish robust implementation mechanisms to strengthen the normative character of this international initiative. It is in this regard that Human Rights Advocates urged the Sub-Commission to pursue the work of the sessional working group after the adoption of this initiative "to develop complaint procedures independent of the host or home states of transnational corporations to consider the abuses and remedies of violations of the Draft Norms."[91]

However, as the elaboration process evolved, representatives of the private sector vigorously opposed the adoption of a legally binding instrument imposing responsibilities on transnational corporations and other business enterprises. In addition to disagreeing with "assertions of company obligations in doubtful contexts," the International Chamber of Commerce and the International Organization of Employers maintained that the "binding and legalistic approach of the draft norms will not meet the diverse needs and circumstances of companies and will limit the innovation and creativity shown by companies in addressing human rights issues."[92]

Interviews conducted with individuals working for intergovernmental organizations involved in the codification of foreign investors' responsibilities also highlighted the lack of shared understandings underlying the *UN Norms.* Although some interviewees stressed the support from various public interest NGOs,[93] one participant referred to diverging positions among international actors in the following terms:

> There was clearly unhappiness about the process – on how the norms were adopted, or at least proposed. There was also a lot of unhappiness about their content and sort of the structural rigor of the *UN Norms.* So, business

88 *Sessional Working Group – Fourth Session*, *supra* note 85 at para 14.

89 *Sessional Working Group – Second Session*, *supra* note 85 at paras 52–53 [emphasis added].

90 See Fédération internationale des ligues des droits de l'homme, *Statement of Support for the UN Human Rights Norms for Business* (18 March 2004), online: FIDH www.fidh.org/en/issues/globalisation-human-rights/business-and-human-rights/Statement-of-Support-for-the-UN (accessed 26 March 2018) [emphasis added].

91 *Written Statement Submitted by Human Rights Advocates, a Non-Governmental Organization in Special Consultative Status*, 2003, UN Doc E/CN.4/Sub.2/2003/NGO/13 at para 10.

92 *Joint Written Statement Submitted by the International Chamber of Commerce and the International Organization of Employers, Non-Governmental Organizations in General Consultative Status*, 2003, UN Doc E/CN.4/Sub.2/2003/NGO/44.

93 Interview 2.

> associations – particularly . . . the International Organization of Employers, the International Chamber of Commerce and other business organizations – really took a series of objections to the *UN Norms*. . . . Trying to elevate the responsibilities of companies to the level of obligations and to the level of duties to protect and to undertake positive obligations and things like that – which I think, upset them. And then there was, as usual, the typical disagreement between the states – you know, the capital-exporting states and the capital-importing states. The consequence, of course, was that there was not enough consensus.[94]

Similarly, another interviewee emphasized "a number of very fundamental flaws to [the *UN Norms*] in process and in product"[95] that seriously impeded the success of this initiative.

Not only did the members of the community of practice struggle to reach any shared understandings with respect to the legal nature of the *UN Norms*, but the elaboration process of this international norm was characterized by inherent *relations of power*. For example, the members of the sessional working group mentioned that "the integrated international production systems and the mobility of TNCs had increased their power of negotiation and reduced the decision-making power of States, particularly that of developing countries."[96] While public interest NGOs explicitly acknowledged that the political and social influence of transnational corporations "constitute obstacles to an effective control of TNCs activities,"[97] one interviewee stressed that the representatives of the private sector that opposed the elaboration of the *UN Norms* were "a very strong opponent to have."[98] The reproduction of such relations of power in the discourses of various international actors suggests that the opposition from powerful private actors to a legally binding instrument was likely to prevent the emergence of shared understandings with respect to the normative character of the *UN Norms*.

Despite the initial attempt by members of the sessional working group of the Sub-Commission and public interest NGOs to adopt a binding instrument, the elaboration process of the *UN Norms* was thus characterized by strong opposition from powerful actors. Beyond this lack of shared understandings among all the members of the community of practice, the fact that powerful representatives of the private sector vigorously opposed the adoption of a legally binding instrument extensively impedes the characterization of the *UN Norms* as an international legal norm.

94 Interview 9.
95 Interview 19.
96 *Sessional Working Group – Second Session*, *supra* note 85 at para 13.
97 *Joint Written Statement Submitted by Europe-Third World Centre, a Non-Governmental Organization in General Consultative Status, and American Association of Jurists a Non-Governmental Organization in Special Consultative Status*, 2003, UN Doc E/CN.4/Sub.2/2003/NGO/37 at 2.
98 Interview 16.

3.2 Criteria of Legality: Several Issues Affecting Legitimacy

According to the interactional theory of international law, an international instrument whose provisions meet criteria of legality is a legitimate norm that can potentially generate a sense of obligation. With respect to the *UN Norms*, an examination of their provisions in light of these criteria suggests several lacunas. The ambiguous promulgation of the *UN Norms*, the inclusion of requirements that seem to be impossible to meet, inherent contradictions and the absence of concrete devices to address instances of non-compliance all affect the legitimacy of this instrument and impact its potential to emerge as an international legal norm.

Even when considering that informal international instruments can meet the requirement of *promulgation* under specific circumstances, some aspects pertaining to the adoption of the *UN Norms* point toward an important tension. Of course, the approval of the *UN Norms* by the Sub-Commission ensures that this instrument is included in a resolution and available to the public. However, it must be kept in mind that the mandate of the Sub-Commission was limited to the initiation of studies on the development of legal rules rather than the elaboration of international norms.[99] Combined with the ultimate refusal of the Commission to recognize any legal character to the *UN Norms*,[100] it is difficult to maintain that this initiative has been properly promulgated.

By contrast, the provisions included in the *UN Norms* ensure a *general* character to its requirements. For example, the first paragraph of this instrument provides a general obligation regarding human rights that applies to "transnational corporations and other business enterprises."[101] Furthermore, the definitions that are included in the last section of this instrument emphasize that "other business enterprises" refers to "*any* business entity, regardless of the international or domestic nature of its activities, including a transnational corporation, contractor, subcontractor, supplier, licensee or distributor; the corporate, partnership, or other legal form used to establish the business entity; and the nature of the ownership of the entity."[102] As a result, the *UN Norms* undoubtedly avoid carving out any specific enterprises that would fall beyond the scope of its application.

International norms are also expected to be *clear* in order to induce legitimacy. In this regard, some provisions of the *UN Norms* encompass fairly vague requirements. For example, paragraph 10 of this initiative provides the following:

> Transnational corporations and other business enterprises shall recognize and respect applicable norms of international law, national laws and regulations, as well as administrative practices, the rule of law, the public interest,

99 See United Nations, *UN Today*, *supra* note 9 at 248.
100 *Responsibilities of Transnational Corporations*, *supra* note 83 at para (c).
101 *UN Norms*, *supra* note 5 at para 1.
102 *Ibid* at para 21 [emphasis added].

> development objectives, social, economic and cultural policies including transparency, accountability and prohibition of corruption, and authority of the countries in which the enterprises operate.[103]

Moreover, the use of the ambiguous concept of "sphere of activity and influence" that is found in the Preamble of the UN Global Compact raises notable concerns.[104] Notwithstanding these issues, it must be noted that additional information pertaining to the sense of these provisions is included in a commentary prepared by the sessional working group of the Sub-Commission.[105] Without offering a response to all ambiguities that can be identified in the *UN Norms*, such a commentary ensures a certain level of clarity that can satisfy this criterion of legality.

Two other criteria do not pose any specific issues with respect to the content of the *UN Norms*. The absence of any change with respect to the formulation of their provisions after the adoption by the Sub-Commission guarantees the *constancy* of this international instrument. Moreover, given that the *UN Norms* do not expressly deal with temporal issues, this initiative also easily meets the requirement of *non-retroactivity* that is included in the interactional theory of international law.

With that being said, the three remaining criteria are far more problematic. It has been suggested that the reliance on the concept of "sphere of influence" effectively allows limiting the requirements for transnational corporations and business enterprises to their activities and thus avoiding *asking the impossible*.[106] However, a provision that expressly requires these private actors to "provide workers with remuneration that ensures an adequate standard of living for them *and their families*"[107] can entail responsibilities for transnational corporations that reach beyond their direct control. Along the same lines, a requirement of not being "solicited or expected to give a bribe or other improper advantage to any [public officials]"[108] ultimately seek to impose an obligation on transnational corporations and business enterprises that depends upon the actions of a third party.[109]

To the extent that they seek to compile human rights derived from international agreements that must be taken into account by transnational corporations

103 *Ibid* at para 10.

104 *Ibid* at para 1. On the perception of the notion of "sphere of influence" as being vague, see e.g. Surya Deva, "UN's Human Rights Norms for Transnational Corporations and Other Business Enterprises: An Imperfect Step in the Right Direction" (2004) 10 ILSA J Int'l & Comp L 493 at 502–503.

105 *Commentary on the Norms on the Responsibilities of Transnational Corporations and other Business Enterprises with regard to Human Rights*, 2003, UN Doc E/CN.4/Sub.2/2003/38/Rev.2 [*UN Norms Commentary*].

106 See e.g. Andrew Clapham, *Human Rights Obligations of Non-state Actors* (Oxford: Oxford University Press, 2006) at 230.

107 *UN Norms*, *supra* note 5 at para 8 [emphasis added].

108 *Ibid* at para 11.

109 Other examples are mentioned in Rebecca M M Wallace & Olga Martin-Ortega, "The UN Norms: A First Step to Universal Regulation of Transnational Corporations' Responsibilities for Human Rights?" (2004) 26 Dublin U L J 304 at 311.

and other business enterprises in their activities,[110] the majority of paragraphs included in this instrument are not *contradictory*. However, some provisions go further by implicitly suggesting that transnational corporations and other business enterprises already hold obligations to respect human rights under formal international treaties. For example, a paragraph of the Preamble refers to a realization "that transnational corporations and other business enterprises, their officers and persons working for them *are also obligated to respect generally recognized responsibilities and norms contained in United Nations treaties*."[111] A similar tension can be found at paragraph 14, which provides that "transnational corporations and other business enterprises shall carry out their activities . . . *in accordance with relevant international agreements*."[112] Considering that such provisions seek to establish obligations for non-state actors by claiming that these actors already have obligations under existing formal international agreements, one can argue that the *UN Norms* rely on an inherent contradiction.

While reaching beyond the UN Global Compact in terms of addressing the necessity to tackle significant instances of non-compliance, the *UN Norms* also fall short of meeting the criterion of *congruence*. In this regard, paragraph 16 of this instrument provides the following:

> Transnational corporations and other business enterprises shall be subject to periodic monitoring and verification by United Nations, other international and national mechanisms already in existence or yet to be created, regarding application of the Norms. This monitoring shall be transparent and independent and take into account input from stakeholders (including non-governmental organizations) and as a result of complaints of violations of these Norms.[113]

Expressly opening the door to address complaints of violations departs from mere requirements to report that can be found in other international initiatives. However, other provisions and elements of the commentary suggest that a specific mechanism as yet to be determined amidst a plurality of options.[114] The absence a clear procedure to examine compliance of business enterprises' conduct with the *UN Norms* thus seriously impedes congruence between rules and official action.

In addition to a failure to be properly promulgated by the UN Commission on Human Rights, the content of the *UN Norms* falls below the requirements of several criteria of legality. Provisions related to conduct that reach beyond the direct control of transnational corporations and other business enterprises,

110 See *UN Norms*, *supra* note 5 at paras 2–12.

111 *Ibid*, Preamble [emphasis added].

112 *Ibid* at para 14 [emphasis added].

113 *Ibid* at para 16.

114 *UN Norms Commentary*, *supra* note 105 at para 16(b). See also David Weissbrodt & Muria Kruger, "Norms on the Responsibilities of Transnational Corporations and Other Business Enterprises with Regard to Human Rights" (2003) 97:4 Am J Int'l L 901 at 917–921; Surya Deva, *Regulating Corporate Human Rights Violations: Humanizing Business* (London: Routledge, 2012) at 105.

some contradictions between a need to establish obligations for private actors and assumptions that international treaties currently include such obligations, as well as the absence of a concrete mechanism to address significant instances of non-compliance all bear a notable impact on the legitimacy that can be derived from this international instrument.

3.3 Practice of Legality: An Ephemeral and Non-Binding Practice

Despite its express aim to impede any monitoring of the *UN Norms* by the Sub-Commission, Decision 2004/116 of the UN Commission on Human Rights did not totally prevent the emergence of a practice around this instrument.[115] In fact, this decision was accompanied by a request to the Office of the High Commissioner for Human Rights (OHCHR) to compile a report on the legal status of various international instruments codifying foreign investors' responsibilities.[116] The numerous submissions to the OHCHR thus demonstrate a fairly ephemeral practice surrounding the *UN Norms.*[117] With a view to assessing the character of this practice, this section relies on an analysis of the content of other international instruments codifying foreign investors' responsibilities, as well as a critical discourse analysis of these submissions to the OHCHR, reports emanating from the UN that specifically address the nature of the *UN Norms* and semi-structured interviews.

From the outset, the content of other intergovernmental organizations' instruments codifying foreign investors' responsibilities points toward a weak practice as far as the *UN Norms* are concerned. In fact, none of the instruments adopted by the UN or any other intergovernmental organizations considered for present purposes expressly refers to this initiative. The absence of such references strongly suggests that intergovernmental organizations have tended to neglect the contribution of the *UN Norms* in the evolving codification process of foreign investors' responsibilities after the refusal of the UN Commission on Human Rights to recognize any legal standing to this instrument.

When considering the submissions to the OHCHR, two contradictory trends emerge. On the one hand, several public interest NGOs considered this instrument as an initiative that had not yet reached the realm of legality, but that could potentially develop as a legal norm. For example, it is in this regard that the Australian Human Rights Centre maintained that "[t]he Norms provide the basis of a global compliance framework that should over time become *legally binding.*"[118] "Although

115 *Responsibilities of Transnational Corporations, supra* note 83 at para (c).

116 *Ibid* at para (b).

117 These statements are also considered in Chapter 3 of the book. However, given the timing of this consultation process, the *UN Norms* tended to be discussed in greater details in several submissions. To that extent, it is here submitted that these statements can be considered as discourses regarding the practice of legality of the *UN Norms.*

118 Australian Human Rights Centre, *Submission concerning the United Nations Norms on the Responsibilities of Transnational Corporations and Other Business Enterprises with regard to Human Rights* (29 September 2004), online: OHCHR https://web.archive.org/web/20140520213840/http://www2.ohchr.org/english/issues/globalization/business/contributions.htm (accessed 26 March 2018) [emphasis added].

the Norms are not a *binding set of standards* and do not themselves have the force of law," Human Rights Watch also considered that "[t]heir analysis and commentary could . . . provide the conceptual basis for a *binding international instrument* on corporate responsibility since the Norms are an authoritative interpretation of the responsibilities of corporations under international human rights law."[119]

A small group of business enterprises also supported the development of a stronger practice around the *UN Norms*. The Business Leaders Initiative on Human Rights thus initiated a "road-testing of the content of the Norms" in order "to show ways in which the implementation of human rights might be demonstrated to [their] fellow businesses around the world."[120] GAP Inc. referred to its participation in this initiative as a way to test "the feasibility and appropriateness of the provisions of the *UN Norms* in order to identify concrete and appropriate ways to integrate human rights into business decision-making and to empower and strengthen existing initiatives that are working toward the same goal."[121] Despite a clear attempt at contributing to the implementation of this instrument, the Business Leaders Initiative on Human Rights ceased its activities in 2009.[122]

On the other hand, the majority of representatives of the private sector and states denied any legal character to the *UN Norms*, thus preventing the emergence of a practice of legality. For example, the United States Council of International Business argued that "the Sub-Commission's draft obfuscated the line between legal requirements and voluntary actions, making it impossible for any company to comply with its requirements."[123] As far as states are concerned, the United States strongly expressed its refusal to consider any form of legal character to the *UN Norms*, mentioning that "[t]he Sub-Commission had no authority to create a set of 'norms', the clearly stated purpose of which is to bind or guide the action

119 Human Rights Watch, *Statement on the United Nations Norms on the Responsibilities of Transnational Corporations and other Business Enterprises with regard to Human Rights to the Office of the United Nations High Commissioner for Human Rights* (30 September 2004), online: OHCHR https://web.archive.org/web/20140520213840/http://www2.ohchr.org/english/issues/globalization/business/contributions.htm (accessed 26 March 2018) [emphasis added].

120 Business Leaders Initiative on Human Rights, *Submission to the Office of the UN High Commissioner for Human Rights relating to the 'Responsibilities of Transnational Corporations and related Business enterprises with regard to Human Rights'* (28 September 2004), online: OHCHR https://web.archive.org/web/20140520213840/http://www2.ohchr.org/english/issues/globalization/business/contributions.htm (accessed 26 March 2018) at 2.

121 GAP, *Letter from Wilma Walace* (28 September 2004), online: OHCHR https://web.archive.org/web/20140520213840/http://www2.ohchr.org/english/issues/globalization/business/contributions.htm (accessed 26 March 2018).

122 See Business and Human Rights Resource Centre, "Business Leaders Initiative on Human Rights", online: Business and Human Rights Resource Centre http://business-humanrights.org/company-policysteps/other/business-leaders-initiative-on-human-rights-blihr (accessed 26 March 2018).

123 United States Council for International Business, *Submission to the High Commissioner for Human Rights for the Report on the 'Responsibilities of Transnational Corporations and related Business Enterprises with regard to Human Rights'* online: OHCHR https://web.archive.org/web/20140520213840/http://www2.ohchr.org/english/issues/globalization/business/contributions.htm (accessed 26 March 2018) at 4.

of States or of non-State actors."[124] Other states depicted the resources of the UN human rights system as "over-stretched" and inadequate to ensure an appropriate monitoring of the *UN Norms*.[125]

A similar tension can be noted in two reports that followed the consultation process operated by the OHCHR. The first one was intended to compile the submissions to the OHCHR and stressed that the views on this initiative were considerably divided.[126] Without acknowledging any legal character to the *UN Norms*, the OHCHR concluded that they deserved encouragement and recommended "to the Commission to maintain the draft Norms among existing initiatives and standards on business and human rights, with a view to their further consideration."[127] In other words, despite the refusal of the UN Commission on Human Rights to authorize any monitoring of this initiative by the Sub-Commission, such a report left the door open for the development of a practice surrounding the *UN Norms*.

By contrast, a report prepared by the Special Representative during the elaboration of the *UN Guiding Principles* characterized the *UN Norms* as an impractical initiative.[128] Instead of further considering their contribution with respect to its own mandate, the Special Representative provided the following:

> [T]he Norms exercise became engulfed by its own doctrinal excesses. Even leaving aside the highly contentious though largely symbolic proposal to monitor firms and provide for reparation payments to victims, its *exaggerated legal claims* and conceptual ambiguities created confusion and doubt even among many mainstream international lawyers and other impartial observers. Two aspects are particularly problematic in the context of this mandate. One concerns the legal authority advanced for the Norms and the other the principle by which they propose to allocate human rights responsibilities between States and firms.[129]

124 United States of America, *Re: Note Verbale from the OHCHR of August 3, 2004 (GVA2537)* (30 September 2004), online: OHCHR https://web.archive.org/web/20140520213840/http://www2.ohchr.org/english/issues/globalization/business/contributions.htm (accessed 26 March 2018).

125 See e.g. Canada, *Submission of Canada to the High Commissioner of Human Rights on the Responsibilities of Business Enterprises with regard to Human Rights*, online: OHCHR https://web.archive.org/web/20140520213840/http://www2.ohchr.org/english/issues/globalization/business/contributions.htm (accessed 26 March 2018)at para 2.6.

126 Sub-commission on the Promotion and Protection of Human Rights, *Report of the United Nations High Commissioner on Human Rights on the Responsibilities of Transnational Corporations and related Business Enterprises with regard to Human Rights*, 2005, UN Doc E/CN.4/2005/91, paras 22 and 52.

127 *Ibid* at para 52.

128 Special Representative of the Secretary-General on the Issue of Human Rights and Transnational Corporations and Other Business Enterprises, *Interim Report of the Special Representative of the Secretary-General on the Issue of Human Rights and Transnational Corporations and other Business Enterprises*, 2006, UN Doc E/CN.4/2006/97 [*Special Representative – Interim Report*].

129 *Ibid* at para 59 [emphasis added].

Along these lines, the Special Representative justified the adoption of a new approach by maintaining that "the divisive debate over the Norms obscure[d] rather than illuminate[d] promising areas of consensus and cooperation among business, civil society, governments and international institutions with respect to human rights."[130] Taken as a whole, the discourse of the Special Representative strongly discouraged the use of the *UN Norms*, let alone a practice of legality.

Another source of discourses that demonstrates the absence of a practice of legality related to the *UN Norms* can be found in the semi-structured interviews that were conducted for the present research. Of course, some participants acknowledged a certain normative contribution from this instrument with respect to the evolving codification of foreign investors' responsibilities.[131] Despite the refusal of the Special Representative to rely on this instrument for his mandate, one participant even suggested that some concepts of the *UN Norms* had had an appreciable impact on the *UN Guiding Principles*.[132] By contrast, the reference to the practice surrounding the *UN Norms* as "a pretty much disaster"[133] suggests a weak practice that definitely failed to reflect any legal character.

Several discourses that followed the elaboration of the *UN Norms* also reproduce *relations of power* whose consideration contributes to explain the lack of a practice of legality.[134] For example, Christian Aid stressed that representatives of the private sector "have the power to delay the establishment of binding regulation."[135] Fearing that the implementation of the *UN Norms* by NGOs would be "arbitrary, unjustified and discriminatory," BASF maintained that "the draft norms appear to be driven by an ideological anti-corporate spirit, particularly regarding transnational corporations."[136] Any account of the absence of a practice of legality surrounding this instrument must acknowledge that such an outcome is consistent with the position advanced by the most powerful members of the community of practice.

Overall, despite the initial will of the Sub-commission and support from public interest NGOs to establish a legally binding instrument, the *UN Norms* have

130 *Ibid* at para 69.

131 Interview 2: "[T]here is sort of a gradual process. Each of the standards slowly improves the game. So I think the Norms had an important role to play in taking steps towards the elaboration of standards and identifying the various implementation mechanisms that were then being discussed. The subsequent work of the OECD, the UN Human Rights Council, can be said to develop those ideas further."

132 Interview 9.

133 *Ibid.*

134 On the role of relations of power in the failure of the *UN Norms*, see e.g. Daniel Augenstein & David Kinley, "Beyond the 100 Acre Wood: In which International Human Rights Law Finds New Ways to Tame Global Corporate Power" (2015) 19 Int'l J Hum Rights 828 at 831.

135 Christian Aid, *Behind the Mask: The Real Face of CSR*, online: OHCHR https://web.archive.org/web/20140520213840/http://www2.ohchr.org/english/issues/globalization/business/contributions.htm (accessed 26 March 2018) at 20.

136 BASF, *Comments on the UN Draft Norms*, online: OHCHR https://web.archive.org/web/20140520213840/http://www2.ohchr.org/english/issues/globalization/business/contributions.htm (accessed 26 March 2018).

fallen short of entering the realm of legality. In addition to a failure to meet several criteria of legality, the opposition of powerful actors and subsequent reports from the UN have played a decisive role in preventing the emergence of shared understandings and a genuine practice of legality. Even if some members of the community of practice initially considered them as providing the basis for a binding instrument, the *UN Norms* have belonged to the realm of social norms and are now an international initiative that has faded away.

4. The *UN Guiding Principles*

Shortly after the brief practice emerging from the *UN Norms*, a Special Representative undertook the elaboration of another initiative related to the codification of foreign investors' responsibilities. In this regard, the *UN Guiding Principles* include 31 paragraphs and rest on three different pillars: a state duty to protect human rights, a corporate responsibility to respect human rights and access to remedy.[137] The analysis below suggests that the *UN Guiding Principles* currently exist as a social norm, with a stronger potential to evolve toward the realm of legality than instruments previously elaborated and implemented under the auspices of the UN. From the outset, it is plain that support from powerful international actors for this initiative has depended upon the recognition that the *UN Guiding Principles* do not enshrine any new legal obligations (4.1). However, the legitimacy of this international norm is extensively strengthened by its fulfillment of several criteria of legality (4.2). Furthermore, even if these principles are not currently compulsory, the practice surrounding this instrument contributes to make the *UN Guiding Principles* harder to circumvent and could potentially evolve toward a practice of legality (4.3).

4.1 Shared Understandings: More than Voluntary, Less than Legal

The *UN Guiding Principles* are characterized by a relatively long period of elaboration that was initiated by the Commission on Human Rights in 2005.[138] By adopting Resolution 2005/69, a group of states requested the UN Secretary-General to appoint a Special Representative with a mandate to "identify and clarify standards of corporate responsibility and accountability for transnational corporations and other business enterprises with regard to human rights."[139] In a way that recalls the *epistemic community* that elaborated the *UN Norms*,

137 See *UN Guiding Principles*, *supra* note 6.

138 See *Human Rights and Transnational Corporations and other Business Enterprises*, CHR Res 2005/69, UNESCOR, 2005, Supp No 3, UN Doc E/2005/23, 268 [*CHR Resolution 2005/69*]. This resolution was led by the United Kingdom and four other core sponsors, namely Argentina, India, Nigeria and the Russian Federation: John Gerard Ruggie, *Just Business: Multinational Corporations and Human Rights* (New York: W. W. Norton & Company, 2013) at xlvii.

139 *CHR Resolution 2005/69*, *ibid* at para 1(a).

the *UN Guiding Principles* also result from the work of a group of experts who did not act as representatives of member states.[140] After the presentation of "a principles-based conceptual and policy framework"[141] that was welcomed by the Human Rights Council in 2008, the mandate of the Special Representative was extended with a view to operationalizing further this framework.[142] As a result, the Special Representative presented the *UN Guiding Principles* to the Human Rights Council for consideration in March 2011.[143] Ultimately, in addition to emphasizing the role played by the Special Representative "in generating greater shared understanding of business and human rights challenges among all stakeholders,"[144] the Human Rights Council endorsed this informal instrument and decided to establish a Working Group on the Issue of Human Rights and Transnational Corporations and other Business Enterprises (Working Group) in order to implement the *UN Guiding Principles.*[145]

In addition to the Special Representative and his team, the *community of practice* that contributed to the elaboration of this initiative includes a broad variety of international actors. When introducing the *UN Guiding Principles*, the Special Representative emphasized that these principles have been informed by discussions conducted with representatives of governments, business enterprises and associations, public interest NGOs, as well as experts related to various areas.[146] The Special Representative thus identified "an emerging community of actors who, while approaching the challenges from different perspectives, nevertheless are working to improve current practices."[147] More specifically, several

140 See e.g. John Gerard Ruggie & John F Sherman III, "Adding Human Rights Punch to the New Lex Mercatoria : The Impact of the UN Guiding Principles on Business and Human Rights on Commercial Legal Practice" (2015) 6 J Int'l Disp Settlement 455 at 456.

141 Special Representative of the Secretary-General on the Issue of Human Rights and Transnational Corporations and Other Business Enterprises, *Promotion and Protection of All Human Rights, Civil, Political, Economic, Social and Cultural Rights, Including the Right to Development – Protect, Respect and Remedy: A Framework for Business and Human Rights*, 2008, UN Doc A/HRC/8/5 at para 1 [*Special Representative – 2008a Report*].

142 See *Mandate of the Special Representative of the Secretary-General on the Issue of Human Rights and Transnational Corporations and other Business Enterprises*, HRC Res 8/7, 2008, UN Doc A/HRC/8/52, 30 at paras 1 and 4.

143 *UN Guiding Principles*, *supra* note 6.

144 *Human Rights and Transnational Corporations and other Business Enterprises*, HRC Res 17/4, 2011, UN Doc A/HRC/RES/17/4 at para 2 [*HRC Resolution 17/4*].

145 *Ibid* at paras 1 and 6. The mandate of the Working Group was renewed in 2014 and in 2017. See *Human Rights and Transnational Corporations and other Business Enterprises*, HRC Res 26/22, 2014, UN Doc A/HRC/RES/26/22 at para 10 [*HRC Resolution 26/22*]; *Business and Human Rights: Mandate of the Working Group on the Issue of Human Rights and Transnational Corporations and other Business Enterprises*, HRC Res 35/7, 2017, UN Doc A/HRC/RES/35/7 at para 11 [*HRC Resolution 35/7*].

146 *UN Guiding Principles*, *supra* note 6, Introduction at para 10.

147 See Special Representative of the Secretary-General on the Issue of Human Rights and Transnational Corporations and Other Business Enterprises, *Report of the Special Representative of the Secretary-General on the Issue of Human Rights and Transnational Corporations and other Business Enterprises – Addendum – Summary of Five Multi-Stakeholder Consultations*, 2008, UN Doc A/HRC/8/5/Add.1 at para 66 [*Special Representative – 2008 Report – Addendum 1*].

actors seized the opportunity to join the consultation process by submitting statements during the mandate of the Special Representative and shortly after the endorsement of the *UN Guiding Principles* by the Human Rights Council. In addition to these submissions, reports prepared by the Special Representative and transcripts from semi-structured interviews are considered as discourses that can be critically analyzed to assess the shared understandings on which the *UN Guiding Principles* rely.[148]

One aspect that strikingly distinguishes the elaboration of the *UN Guiding Principles* from previous instruments of the UN is the reliance on extensive consultations and an incremental process that ultimately allowed support from several types of actors.[149] Despite diverging views with respect to issues such as states' extraterritorial obligations,[150] the *UN Guiding Principles* are often considered as relying on a broad consensus. For example, according to the Special Representative, "there was broad acceptance of the underlying premise of the consultation, that companies have a responsibility to respect human rights, and of due diligence as a useful overarching concept enabling companies to operationalize the responsibility to respect."[151] Moreover, the UN Global Compact Human Rights Working Group commended the Special Representative for his inclusive approach and mentioned that the result of his work enjoyed "the legitimacy and widespread support that is essential for sustainable progress in

148 For another study related to the *UN Guiding Principles* that also relies on discourse analysis, see Karin Buhmann, "Navigating from 'Train Wreck' to being 'Welcomed': Negotiation Strategies and Argumentative Patterns in the Development of the UN Framework" in Surya Deva & David Bilchitz, eds, *Human Rights Obligations of Business: Beyond the Corporate Responsibility to Protect?* (Cambridge: Cambridge University Press, 2013) 29.

149 See e.g. Karin Buhmann, "The Development of the 'UN Framework': A Pragmatic Process Towards a Pragmatic Output" in Radu Mares, ed, *The UN Guiding Principles on Business and Human Rights: Foundations and Implementation* (Leiden: Martinus Nijhoff Publishers, 2012) 85 at 103; Surya Deva, "Treating Human Rights Lightly: A Critique of the Consensus Rhetoric and the Language Employed by the Guiding Principles" in Surya Deva & David Bilchitz, eds, *Human Rights Obligations of Business: Beyond the Corporate Responsibility to Protect?* (Cambridge: Cambridge University Press, 2013) 78 at 81 [Deva, "Treating Human Rights"]; Michael K Addo, "The Reality of the United Nations Guiding Principles on Business and Human Rights" (2014) 14 Hum Rts L Rev 133 at 136.

150 See e.g. International Organisation of Employers et al, *Joint IOE-ICC-BIAC Comments on the Draft Guiding Principles on Business and Human Rights* (26 January 2011), online: Business and Human Rights Resource Centre http://business-humanrights.org/en/un-secretary-generals-special-representative-on-business-human-rights/un-protect-respect-and-remedy-framework/guiding-principles/submissions-to-consultation-on-draft-guiding (accessed 26 March 2018) at 5 [International Organisation of Employers et al, *Special Representative Submission*]; Amnesty International et al, *Joint Civil Society Statement on the Draft Guiding Principles on Business and Human Rights* (14 January 2011), online: Business and Human Rights Resource Centre http://business-humanrights.org/en/un-secretary-generals-special-representative-on-business-human-rights/un-protect-respect-and-remedy-framework/guiding-principles/submissions-to-consultation-on-draft-guiding (accessed 26 March 2018) at 1.

151 *Special Representative – 2008 Report – Addendum 1, supra* note 147 at para 152.

ensuring respect for human rights in business activities around the world."[152] In other words, the absence of stark opposition from any members of the community of practice suggests that the *UN Guiding Principles* are anchored in solid shared understandings.

Yet, when looking more closely at the statements submitted during the elaboration of this instrument, such an apparent consensus for the *UN Guiding Principles* hides notable divergences with respect to their legal character. As a starting point, it is plain that the Special Representative did not seek to establish any new international legal obligations for either states or business enterprises. Of course, when considering the corporate responsibility to respect human rights as a "baseline expectation"[153] or a "universally applicable human rights responsibility for all companies, in all situations,"[154] it is plain that the epistemic community behind the *UN Guiding Principles* seeks to depart from an instrument whose observance is merely voluntary. However, in his introduction to this instrument, the Special Representative underscored that "[t]he Guiding Principles' normative contribution lies *not in the creation of new international law obligations* but in elaborating the implications of existing standards and practices for [s]tates and business."[155]

This absence of new legal obligations is the primary reason explaining the support of several states and business enterprises for this international instrument. For example, a joint statement from the International Organisation of Employers, the International Chamber of Commerce and the Business and Industry Advisory Committee linked the support of business to the *UN Guiding Principles* to the recognition that they were "not a scheme for attributing legal liability or setting *legal norms*, and [that] the corporate responsibility to respect is a *social expectation* but has *no legal implications*."[156] Along the same lines, several representatives of business enterprises emphasized the relevance of non-judicial grievance mechanisms to address allegations of human rights violations.[157] Finally, while the European

152 United Nations Global Compact, *Statement by the UN Global Compact Human Rights Working Group to the Special-Representative of the Secretary-General on Business and Human Rights* (January 2011), online: Business and Human Rights Resource Centre http://business-humanrights.org/en/un-secretary-generals-special-representative-on-business-human-rights/un-protect-respect-and-remedy-framework/guiding-principles/submissions-to-consultation-on-draft-guiding (accessed 26 March 2018).

153 See *Special Representative – 2008a Report*, *supra* note 141 at para 55.

154 See Special Representative of the Secretary-General on the Issue of Human Rights and Transnational Corporations and Other Business Enterprises, *Business and Human Rights: Further Steps Toward the Operationalization of the 'Protect, Respect and Remedy' Framework*, 2010, UN Doc A/HRC/14/27 at para 65.

155 *UN Guiding Principles*, *supra* note 6, Introduction at para 14 [emphasis added].

156 International Organisation of Employers et al, *Special Representative Submission*, *supra* note 150 at 2 [emphasis added].

157 See e.g. United States Chamber of Commerce, *Comments of the United States Chamber of Commerce on the Draft Guiding Principles on Business and Human Rights* (31 January 2011), online: Business and Human Rights Resource Centre http://business-humanrights.org/en/un-secretary-generals-special-representative-on-business-human-rights/un-protect-respect-and-remedy-framework/guiding-principles/submissions-to-consultation-on-draft-guiding (accessed 26 March 2018) at 3.

Union limited its consideration of the *UN Guiding Principles* to an "authoritative policy framework,"[158] the United Kingdom mentioned that they "are policy guidelines, not all of which necessarily reflect the current state of international law."[159]

By contrast, while demonstrating considerable dissatisfaction with the lack of a legal character to this initiative, several public interest NGOs and some states perceived the work of the Special Representative as a step that could pave the way to the adoption of international legal norms to hold business enterprises accountable. For example, after acknowledging that they constitute "a significant step towards strengthening corporate accountability for human rights abuses," Oxfam International considered that the wording of the *UN Guiding Principles* was "ambiguous in parts and tend[ed] to obscure the mandatory nature of State and business obligations."[160] Along the same lines, the Scottish Human Rights Commission maintained that "the principles must be seen as a foundation from which we can build" and "that nothing in the [*UN Guiding Principles*] should be seen as limiting the further development and application of international human rights law or national law."[161] The need for stronger grievance mechanisms that depart from non-judicial initiatives to specifically address human rights violations was also mentioned in several submissions.[162]

158 European Union, *EU Comments on the Draft Guiding Principles for the Implementation of the UN 'Protect, Respect and Remedy' Framework* (31 January 2011), online: Business and Human Rights Resource Centre http://business-humanrights.org/en/un-secretary-generals-special-representative-on-business-human-rights/un-protect-respect-and-remedy-framework/guiding-principles/submissions-to-consultation-on-draft-guiding (accessed 26 March 2018) at 1.

159 United Kingdom, *UK Government Comments on the Draft UN Guiding Principles for the Implementation of the 'Protect, Respect and Remedy' Framework* (January 2011), online: Business and Human Rights Resource Centre http://business-humanrights.org/en/un-secretary-generals-special-representative-on-business-human-rights/un-protect-respect-and-remedy-framework/guiding-principles/submissions-to-consultation-on-draft-guiding (accessed 26 March 2018) at 1.

160 Oxfam International, *Oxfam International's Perspective on the Draft Guiding Principles for the Implementation of the United Nations 'Protect, Respect and Remedy' Framework* (31 January 2011), online: Business and Human Rights Resource Centre http://business-humanrights.org/en/un-secretary-generals-special-representative-on-business-human-rights/un-protect-respect-and-remedy-framework/guiding-principles/submissions-to-consultation-on-draft-guiding (accessed 26 March 2018).

161 International Co-ordinating Committee of National Institutions for the Promotion and Protection of Human Rights, Scottish Human Rights Commission, *UN Representative on Business and Human Rights' Draft Guiding Principles for the Implementation of the UN 'Protect, Respect, and Remedy' Framework'* (January 2011), online: Business and Human Rights Resource Centre http://business-humanrights.org/en/un-secretary-generals-special-representative-on-business-human-rights/un-protect-respect-and-remedy-framework/guiding-principles/submissions-to-consultation-on-draft-guiding (accessed 26 March 2018) at 39.

162 See e.g. *Written Statement Submitted by Human Rights Advocates Inc., a Non-Governmental Organization in Special Consultative Status*, 2011, UN Doc A/HR/17/NGO/3 at para 6; International Federation of Human Rights et al, *Joint Civil Society Statement on Business and Human Rights to the 17th Session of the UN Human Rights Council* (15 June 2011), online: Business and Human Rights Resource Centre http://business-humanrights.org/en/un-secretary-generals-special-representative-on-business-human-rights/reports-to-un-human-rights-council/2011 (accessed 26 March 2018).

Interviews conducted for the present research project also highlighted the absence of shared understandings regarding the legal nature of the *UN Guiding Principles*. As summarized by one participant:

> I think one of the contentious points – and I think it still exists to this day – has to do with the binding nature of the Guiding Principles. And this was more of an issue from the perspective of some NGOs who wanted a binding treaty that would directly impose binding legal obligations on businesses that would be a treaty that countries would ratify and then would become law.[163]

Another interviewee considered this division as “the continuation of the polarized bit that sat at the start of [the Special Representative]’s mandate.”[164]

Furthermore, the discourses emanating from the elaboration of the *UN Guiding Principles* reproduce inherent *relations of power* between the international actors involved. The Special Representative himself thus noted that a

> rationale for engaging the transnational corporate sector has emerged in the past few years: the sheer fact that it has global reach and capacity and that it is capable of acting at a pace and scale that neither [g]overnments nor international agencies can match.[165]

Along the same lines, one interviewee explained the power held by private economic actors in the following terms: “There’s a whole sort of movement in civil society on that, but the problem is that business is very influential – not just at the UN, but more importantly at the national level.”[166] Power imbalances between states were also acknowledged in at least one statement from the Kenya National Commission on Human Rights, which mentioned that “[d]eveloping countries that are negotiating bilateral trade and/or investment agreements may not be in a position to retain their domestic policy space due to power imbalances and development aid conditionalities.”[167] Despite the inclusive character of the consultations driven by the Special Representative, this recognition of inherent power relations suggests that the position advocated by representatives of the private sector and capital-exporting states were more likely to influence their outcome.

163 Interview 4.

164 Interview 19.

165 *Special Representative – Interim Report*, *supra* note 128 at para 16 [emphasis omitted].

166 Interview 16.

167 International Co-ordinating Committee of National Institutions for the Promotion and Protection of Human Rights, Kenya National Commission on Human Rights, *UN Representative on Business and Human Rights’ Draft Guiding Principles for the Implementation of the UN ‘Protect, Respect, and Remedy’ Framework’* (January 2011), online: Business and Human Rights Resource Centre http://business-humanrights.org/en/un-secretary-generals-special-representative-on-business-human-rights/un-protect-respect-and-remedy-framework/guiding-principles/submissions-to-consultation-on-draft-guiding (accessed 26 March 2018) at 8.

Notwithstanding broad support for this instrument and the efforts of the epistemic community to elaborate an instrument whose observance cannot be considered as merely voluntary, a critical analysis of discourses from international actors involved in the elaboration of the *UN Guiding Principles* suggests two clashing views with respect to their legal character. Although some actors wished for the elaboration of an instrument that could have led to the imposition of concrete obligations for states and business enterprises, powerful actors rallied behind the Special Representative only to the extent that the *UN Guiding Principles* would remain a social norm that would not add any legal obligations. As a result, the elaboration process of the *UN Guiding Principles* failed to reach shared understandings for a legally binding instrument that would impose obligations to states and business enterprises.

4.2 Criteria of Legality: More Legitimacy than Previous Initiatives

Although shared understandings in which the *UN Guiding Principles* are embedded point toward an international social norm, one crucial element suggesting a potential evolution toward the realm of legality stems from the legitimacy that this initiative generates. The fact that the provisions of this international instrument meet almost all the criteria of legality articulated in the interactional theory of international law is a key element to the emergence of the sense of obligation that characterizes international legal norms.

With respect to *promulgation*, it is unquestionable that the *UN Guiding Principles* remain an informal instrument under international law. As mentioned above, the Special Representative presented this initiative to the Human Rights Council, a subsidiary organ of the UN General Assembly whose mandate is limited to making "recommendations . . . for the further development of international law in the field of human rights."[168] Despite the unambiguous role of this council in the elaboration of human rights norms, nothing in the elaboration of this instrument amounted to the negotiation of a formal international agreement. However, the fact that the Human Rights Council "[w]elcome[d] the work and contributions of the Special Representative . . . and endorse[d] the Guiding Principles on Business and Human Rights"[169] demonstrates support from the members of the UN and has contributed to the promulgation of the initiative.

Another aspect that contributes to foster the legitimacy of the *UN Guiding Principles* relates to their *general* character. The general principles preceding the main paragraphs of the instrument provide that "[t]hese Guiding Principles apply to *all States* and to *all business enterprises*, both transnational and others, regardless of their size, sector, location, ownership and structure."[170] In addition

168 See *Human Rights Council*, GA Res 60/251, UNGAOR, 60th Sess, Supp No 49, UN Doc A/RES/60/251 (2006) at para 5(c).
169 See *HRC Resolution 17/4*, *supra* note 144 at para 1 [emphasis omitted].
170 *UN Guiding Principles*, *supra* note 6, General Principles [emphasis added].

to extending the duty to protect human rights to all states, the drafters of this instrument chose to avoid any distinction between transnational corporations and other business enterprises pertaining to the corporate responsibility to respect human rights.[171] The general principles also call upon the implementation of the *UN Guiding Principles* "in a non-discriminatory manner," with a specific consideration of the most vulnerable groups.[172]

Several elements of the *UN Guiding Principles* also ensure that this informal instrument lives up to the requirement of *clarity*. The Special Representative cautiously included a commentary for each principle, with a view to "further clarifying its meaning and implications."[173] More specifically, even if several authors consider the application of the concept of due diligence as confusing or requiring clarification,[174] the process through which business enterprises should carry out due diligence is explained at great length in Guiding Principles 17 to 21 and their related commentaries.[175] Some reports prepared by the Special Representative to present the framework that preceded the *UN Guiding Principles* also provide additional information with respect to human rights due diligence.[176] While a certain level of flexibility around this concept remains, it is here submitted that the efforts deployed by the Special Representative through his mandate contribute to providing enough clarity to meet this criterion of legality.

In a way that echoes the application of the criteria of legality to the majority of instruments codifying foreign investors' responsibilities, the criterion of *constancy* does not encounter any specific obstacles with respect to the *UN Guiding Principles*. The recent elaboration of this instrument has not led to any revision so far, thus avoiding a lack of constancy with respect to its content. Likewise, the absence of temporal considerations throughout the provisions of the *UN Guiding Principles* allows circumventing potential issues pertaining the *retroactive application* of this international norm.

The legitimate character of the *UN Guiding Principles* also results from its provisions that *avoid asking the impossible* to states and business enterprises. In fact, the wording of several provisions found in this instrument demonstrates an express consideration of the variety of situations in which states and business enterprises can operate, without jeopardizing the universal character of the state duty to protect and the corporate responsibility to respect human rights.

171 See *ibid*, Guiding Principle 14.

172 *Ibid*, General Principles.

173 *Ibid*, Introduction, at para 14.

174 See e.g. Radu Mares, "Global Corporate Social Responsibility, Human Rights and Law: An Interactive Regulatory Perspective on the Voluntary–Mandatory Dichotomy" (2010) 1 Transn'l Legal Theory 221 at 265; Deva, "Treating Human Rights", *supra* note 149 at 98–101. See generally Sabine Michalowski, "Due Diligence and Complicity: A Relationship in Need of Clarification" in Surya Deva & David Bilchitz, eds, *Human Rights Obligations of Business: Beyond the Corporate Responsibility to Protect?* (Cambridge: Cambridge University Press, 2013) 218.

175 *UN Guiding Principles*, *supra* note 6, Guiding Principles 17–21.

176 See e.g. *Special Representative – 2008a Report*, *supra* note 141 at paras 56–64.

For example, as far as state-owned enterprises and export credit agencies are concerned, Guiding Principle 4 provides that states "should take additional steps to protect against human rights abuses . . . including, *where appropriate*, by requiring human rights due diligence."[177] Guiding Principle 15 also stipulates that "[i]n order to meet their responsibility to respect human rights, business enterprises should have in place policies and processes *appropriate to their size and circumstances.*"[178] The recognition of situations in which conflicting requirements between domestic legislation and international human rights can emerge constitutes another element from the *UN Guiding Principles* that is in line with this criterion of legality. After maintaining that business enterprises should "[c]omply with all applicable laws and respect internationally recognized human rights, wherever they operate,"[179] Guiding Principle 23 stipulates that they should "[s]eek ways to honour the principles of internationally recognized human rights when faced with conflicting requirements."[180]

The extent to which the *UN Guiding Principles* meet the criterion pertaining to the *absence of contradiction* is particularly noteworthy. Not only does this instrument exclude any direct contradictions between its provisions, but the tension observed in other initiatives between the pressing need to hold business enterprises accountable and the reliance on a voluntary instrument is obviated. After acknowledging that "[n]othing in these Guiding Principles should be read as creating new international law obligations,"[181] this instrument does not rely on an express voluntary observance of its principles. In this regard, Guiding Principle 11 provides the following:

> The responsibility to respect human rights is a global standard of expected conduct for all business enterprises wherever they operate. It exists independently of States' abilities and/or willingness to fulfil their own human rights obligations, and does not diminish those obligations. And it exists over and above compliance with national laws and regulations protecting human rights. . . . Business enterprises may undertake other commitments or activities to support and promote human rights, which may contribute to the enjoyment of rights. But this does not offset a failure to respect human rights throughout their operations.[182]

While the absence of an express voluntary character to the observance of the corporate responsibility to respect human rights allows a stronger consistency with the criteria of legality, it also implies that international actors cannot rely on any provisions of this instrument to easily circumvent such a responsibility.

177 *UN Guiding Principles*, *supra* note 6, Guiding Principle 4 [emphasis added].
178 *Ibid*, Guiding Principle 15.
179 *Ibid*, Guiding Principle 23(a).
180 *Ibid*, Guiding Principle 23(b).
181 *Ibid*, General Principles.
182 *Ibid*, Guiding Principle 11.

The only criterion of legality that is not fulfilled by the *UN Guiding Principles* relates to *congruence*. Of course, the inclusion of several provisions that specifically concern the access to remedy hints toward a consideration of significant instances of non-compliance with the *UN Guiding Principles*.[183] Guiding Principle 25 thus mentions that

> [a]s part of their duty to protect against business-related human rights abuse, [s]tates must take appropriate steps to ensure, through judicial, administrative, legislative or other appropriate means, that when such abuses occur within their territory and/or jurisdiction those affected have access to effective remedy.[184]

Other provisions and commentaries address the role of state-based judicial mechanisms, state-based non-judicial grievance mechanisms and non-state-based grievance mechanisms in this regard.[185] However, nothing in the *UN Guiding Principles* amounts to a specific procedural mechanism to determine compliance by business enterprises with the corporate responsibility to respect human rights.

Another element of the failure to fulfill this criterion of congruence stems in the silence of the *UN Guiding Principles* on the establishment of a procedural device to examine the compliance of states with their duty to protect human rights. Even if the Working Group was established to implement this international instrument, the mandate of this entity is not geared toward the investigation of non-compliance. Rather, as provided in Resolution 17/4 of the Human Rights Council, the Working Group is primarily tasked with the general dissemination and promotion of the *UN Guiding Principles*, the dissemination of good practices and lessons learned on their implementation, as well as the promotion of capacity-building and the use of the *UN Guiding Principles*, among others.[186] While part of the mandate of the Working Group involves the conduct of country visits, these visits are not intended to focus on any allegations of human rights violations.

In sum, despite a failure to fulfill the criterion of congruence, an assessment of the provisions of the *UN Guiding Principles* shows that this instrument meets most of the criteria of legality that characterize international legal norms. Of particular interest when considering the potential evolution of this norm is that it implicitly shuts the door to the voluntary observance of its requirements. Bearing in mind that such features are insufficient to guarantee the emergence of a sense of obligation, the analysis of the normative character of *UN Guiding Principles* now turns to the interactions between the members of the community of practice with respect to their implementation.

183 *Ibid*, Guiding Principles 25–31.
184 *Ibid*, Guiding Principles 25.
185 *Ibid*, Guiding Principles 26–28.
186 *HRC Resolution 17/4*, *supra* note 144 at para 6.

4.3 Practice of Legality: Making the UN Guiding Principles *Unavoidable*

The analysis of the interactions between international actors that have implemented the *UN Guiding Principles* since 2011 is crucial to determine whether the work of the Special Representative has resulted in a social norm or a legal norm. In addition to references to this international instrument included in other initiatives, these interactions can be analyzed through a critical analysis of discourses from members of the community of practice. Along with the actors previously involved in the elaboration of this instrument, the members of the Working Group established further to the endorsement of the *UN Guiding Principles* by the Human Rights Council constitute an integral part of this community. More specifically, submissions made to the Working Group, reports prepared by the Working Group, National Action Plans elaborated by states and transcripts from semi-structured interviews all constitute discourses that provide insights with respect to the practice surrounding the *UN Guiding Principles.*

Considering that this instrument is relatively recent, the extent to which the *UN Guiding Principles* have been mentioned in other international initiatives codifying foreign investors' responsibilities demonstrates a fairly impressive uptake. In this regard, express references to the work of the Special Representative can be found in the commentaries of the *OECD Guidelines*,[187] the *OECD Due Diligence Guidance for Responsible Supply Chains of Mineral from Conflict-Affected and High-Risk Areas*,[188] the Guidance Notes of the *Performance Standards on Environmental and Social Sustainability* of the International Finance Corporation,[189] and the *Tripartite Declaration of Principles concerning Multinational Enterprises and Social Policy* of the International Labour Organization.[190] Under the auspices of the UN, the *UN PRAI* adopted by the Committee on World Food Security also refers to the *UN Guiding Principles.*[191] One can thus witness a form of convergence toward the *UN Guiding Principles* in the elaboration and the revision of standards concerning extraterritorial activities of private actors by intergovernmental organizations.[192]

187 OECD, *OECD Guidelines for Multinational Enterprises, 2011 Edition* (Paris: OECD, 2011), Commentaries at para 36 [*OECD Guidelines 2011 – Commentaries*].

188 OECD, *OECD Due Diligence Guidance for Responsible Supply Chain of Minerals from Conflict-Affected and High-Risk Areas* (Paris: OCDE, 2013) at 13 and 70.

189 *International Finance Corporation's Guidance Note: Performance Standards on Environmental and Social Sustainability*, 1 January 2012, online: IFC www.ifc.org/wps/wcm/connect/e280ef804a0256609709ffd1a5d13d27/GN_English_2012_Full-Document.pdf?MOD=AJPERES (accessed 26 March 2018) at Guidance Note 45.

190 *Tripartite Declaration of Principles concerning Multinational Enterprises and Social Policy*, March 2017, online: ILO www.ilo.org/empent/Publications/WCMS_094386/lang--en/index.htm (accessed 26 March 2018), Preamble and at para 10.

191 *Principles for Responsible Investment in Agriculture, supra* note 59 at paras 19(A)(v) and 33.

192 See *Report of the Working Group on the Issue of Human Rights and Transnational Corporations and other Business Enterprises*, 2015, UN Doc A/70/216 at para 7 [*Working Group – 2015 General Assembly Report*].

Other initiatives have contributed to strengthen the practice around this instrument. In addition to the publication of an interpretative guide on the corporate responsibility to respect human rights by the OHCHR,[193] the Working Group prepared some guidance for states regarding the elaboration of National Action Plans to implement the *UN Guiding Principles* in 2014.[194] The *UN Guiding Principles Reporting Framework* was also launched in February 2015, with a view to providing "clarity, for the first time, on how companies can report in a meaningful and coherent way on their progress in implementing their responsibility to respect human rights."[195] More recently, the *Guide to Implementing the UN Guiding Principles on Business and Human Rights in Investment Policymaking* was published in March 2016 in order to better implement the state duty to protect human rights through any measures related to foreign direct investment.[196] While these tools do not directly address the issue of accountability for a failure to meet the corporate responsibility to respect or the state duty to protect human rights, they nevertheless contribute to expand the practice surrounding this international norm.

Beyond these references in international instruments and the elaboration of subsequent means to further the implementation of the *UN Guiding Principles*, discourses from the members of the community of practice nevertheless demonstrate that the current interactions around this instrument do not reflect a practice of legality. Of course, with respect to the state duty to protect human rights, several statements suggest the existence of obligations that states hold to address human rights violations by business enterprises. The United Kingdom thus considered its National Action Plan as "set[ing] out how the Government has responded to the [*UN Guiding Principles*] and [its] plans for further work to . . . implement UK Government ***obligations*** to protect human rights within UK jurisdiction where business enterprises are involved."[197] Lithuania presented its plan as a document specifying "actions, planned or implemented measures and ***legislative provisions intended to consolidate Lithuania's duty to***

193 OHCHR, *The Corporate Responsibility to Respect Human Rights: An Interpretative Guide* (Geneva: United Nations, 2012).

194 For the most recent version, see Working Group on Business and Human Rights, *Guidance on National Action Plans on Business and Human Rights* (November 2016), online: OHCHR www.ohchr.org/Documents/Issues/Business/UNWG_NAPGuidance.pdf (accessed 26 March 2018).

195 *UN Guiding Principles Reporting Framework* (February 2015), online: UN Guiding Principles Reporting Framework www.ungpreporting.org/reporting-framework/ (accessed 26 March 2018).

196 LSE Investment and Human Rights Project & Laboratory for Advanced Research on the Global Economy, *Guide to implementing the UN Guiding Principles on Business and Human Rights in Investment Policymaking* (March 2016), online: LSE http://blogs.lse.ac.uk/investment-and-human-rights/files/2016/02/3689_LSE_UNGPs_Guide_En_FIN_NEW_Web.pdf (accessed 26 March 2018).

197 United Kingdom, *Good Business: Implementing the UN Guiding Principles on Business and Human Rights* (September 2013), online: OHCHR www.ohchr.org/EN/Issues/Business/Pages/NationalActionPlans.aspx (accessed 26 March 2018) at 6 [emphasis added].

protect, defend and respect human rights, as well as to ensure effective remedies."[198] Moreover, Sweden stressed that it "acts to ensure that state-owned companies set a good example . . . and that their conduct in general instils public confidence, for example by striving to *comply with* international guidelines such as the UN Guiding Principles."[199]

However, this sense of obligation is generally owed to formal human rights international agreements rather than to the *UN Guiding Principles.* For example, without mentioning the *UN Guiding Principles*, the National Action Plan adopted by Denmark emphasizes that this country "is fully *committed to human rights obligations* – both nationally and internationally – and has signed and ratified *many legal instruments*, which belong to various organs, especially the United Nations, the European Union and the Council of Europe."[200] In the same vein, after highlighting the "*obligation* to provide effective remedies when a company has committed human rights abuses" that is found in the *UN Guiding Principles*, Sweden emphasized that "legal remedies available in the Swedish legal system are *in line with the international human rights conventions* that Sweden has acceded to."[201]

The lack of recognition of a binding character to the corporate responsibility to respect human rights is even more striking. Even if some representatives of the private sector stress a commitment to this responsibility,[202] several submissions from business enterprises to the Working Group aimed to emphasize the absence of legal obligations in the *UN Guiding Principles.* A joint statement from the International Employers Organisation, the International Chamber of Commerce and the Business and Industry Advisory Committee thus stressed that these principles "elaborate existing standards and do *not seek to create new international legal obligations or to assign legal liability.*"[203] These organizations also recalled the necessity of relying on "dialogue and consultation"[204] in order to sustain the engagement of business enterprises in the implementation of this instrument.

198 Lithuania, *Lithuania's National Action Plan on the Implementation of the United Nations Guiding Principles on Business and Human Rights* (February 2015), online: OHCHR www.ohchr.org/EN/Issues/Business/Pages/NationalActionPlans.aspx (accessed 26 March 2018) at 1[emphasis added].

199 Sweden, *Action Plan for Business and Human Rights* (August 2015), online: OHCHR www.ohchr.org/EN/Issues/Business/Pages/NationalActionPlans.aspx (accessed 26 March 2018) at 9 [emphasis added].

200 Denmark, *Danish National Action Plan – Implementation of the UN Guiding Principles on Business and Human Rights* (April 2014), online: OHCHR www.ohchr.org/EN/Issues/Business/Pages/NationalActionPlans.aspx (accessed 26 March 2018) at 12 [emphasis added].

201 Sweden, *supra* note 199 at 15 [emphasis added].

202 See e.g. International Organisation of Employers et al, *Joint Recommendation to the United Nations Working Group on Business and Human Rights* (8 December 2011), online: OHCHR www.ohchr.org/EN/Issues/Business/Pages/Submissions.aspx (accessed 26 March 2018) at 1.

203 *Ibid* at 2 [emphasis added].

204 *Ibid* at 2.

Submissions from states and National Action Plans also hint toward the absence of a legal character with respect to the second pillar of the *UN Guiding Principles*. Rather than emphasizing the existence of an obligation, the European Union mentioned "its *expectation* that all European enterprises should meet the corporate responsibility to respect human rights as set out in the Guiding Principles."[205] Similarly, when addressing the potential establishment of "a new statutory obligation on due diligence . . . for companies when implementing the UN principles on a national level," Finland maintained that "[t]ransforming . . . due diligence . . . into a *legally binding obligation* is difficult to envisage."[206] Others, such as the Netherlands, expressly referred to the corporate responsibility to respect human rights as a "social responsibility."[207] Employing more explicit terms, Nicaragua considered the "*[n]on-binding* nature of the Framework and Guiding Principles" as an obstacle to the dissemination and implementation of this instrument.[208] It rather suggested to "[d]evelop a universal, legally binding framework that is applicable in the same way to all companies without exception" and to "[i]ncorporate 'the process of due diligence' as part of a universal, legally binding human rights framework for business."[209]

Other aspects of the practice surrounding the *UN Guiding Principles* demonstrate that compliance with this instrument is not perceived as being compulsory. Although the mandate of the Working Group includes the conduct of country visits, the latter are often considered as a means to discuss best practices and lessons learned.[210] Rather than providing an opportunity to investigate individual cases of alleged business-related human rights abuses, the Working Group reported that such country visits constituted "an opportunity to help to move a country forward in managing cases of negative impact of business activities."[211] Several members of the community of practice expressed

205 European Union, *Contribution of the European Union before the First Session of the UN Working Group on Human Rights and Transnational Corporations and other Business Enterprises* (6 January 2012), online: OHCHR www.ohchr.org/EN/Issues/Business/Pages/Submissions.aspx (accessed 26 March 2018) at 2 [emphasis added].

206 Finland, *National Action Plan for the Implementation of the UN Guiding Principles on Business and Human Rights* (October 2014), online: OHCHR www.ohchr.org/EN/Issues/Business/Pages/NationalActionPlans.aspx (accessed 26 March 2018) at 25 [emphasis added].

207 Netherlands, *National Action Plan on Business and Human Rights* (December 2013), online: OHCHR www.ohchr.org/EN/Issues/Business/Pages/NationalActionPlans.aspx (accessed 26 March 2018) at 1.

208 International Co-ordinating Committee of National Institutions for the Promotion and Protection of Human Rights, Nicaragua, *Submissions to the United Nations Working Group on Transnational Corporations and other Business Enterprises* (December 2011), online: OHCHR www.ohchr.org/EN/Issues/Business/Pages/Submissions.aspx (accessed 26 March 2018) at 49 [emphasis added].

209 *Ibid* at 49–50.

210 See *Report of the Working Group on the Issue of Human Rights and Transnational Corporations and other Business Enterprises*, 2012, UN Doc A/HRC/20/29 at para 86.

211 *Report of the Working Group on the Issue of Human Rights and Transnational Corporations and other Business Enterprises*, 2013, UN Doc A/HRC/23/32 at para 60.

their concerns regarding the absence of consideration for allegations of human rights violations during these country visits.[212]

Although it is plain that the *UN Guiding Principles* are not compulsory for the time being, there are some aspects that contribute to make this international instrument harder to circumvent with respect to the state duty to protect and the corporate responsibility to respect human rights. In a report that was submitted in 2014, the Working Group mentioned that it had sent a number of communications to states and business enterprises "to introduce the core concepts, ***obligations***, responsibilities and expectations set out in the Guiding Principles."[213] These communications are geared toward obtaining clarifications in response to allegations of violations and are not intended to specifically examine compliance with the *UN Guiding Principles*.[214] However, they have been considered as important tools to obtain a response from international actors on alleged violations.[215] Although they were not expressly mentioned in the initial mandate of the Working Group, these communications have become an integral part of the practice related to the implementation of this instrument and have been specifically mentioned in the resolutions of the Human Rights Council that extended the mandate of the Working Group in 2014 and 2017.[216] Combined with the absence of an express voluntary character to the observance of this instrument, this procedure at least ensures that compliance with the *UN Guiding Principles* cannot be easily circumvented. The consideration by the Working Group of the opportunity for states to report on the implementation of the *UN Guiding Principles* to UN treaty bodies is also an interesting avenue that could consolidate a practice of legality around this instrument.[217]

The discourses of individuals working for intergovernmental organizations involved in the codification of foreign investors' responsibilities also suggest a practice around the *UN Guiding Principles* that currently lacks a legal character, but that nevertheless includes some room for evolution. One interviewee thus acknowledged that "even though the Guiding Principles themselves are not binding directly – they aren't law – they are increasingly reflected in policy and in law and in adjudication and many NGOs are using it in their advocacy."[218] Along the same lines, another participant mentioned that

212 See e.g. Human Rights Watch, *'Moving from Guidance to Compliance': Human Rights Watch Recommendations to the UN Expert Body on Business and Human Rights* (December 2011), online: OHCHR www.ohchr.org/EN/Issues/Business/Pages/Submissions.aspx (accessed 26 March 2018).

213 *Report of the Working Group on the Issue of Human Rights and Transnational Corporations and other Business Enterprises*, 2014, UN Doc A/HRC/26/25 at para 67 [*Working Group – 2014 Report*] [emphasis added].

214 *Ibid* at para 68.

215 *Ibid* at para 74.

216 *HRC Resolution 26/22*, *supra* note 145 at para 11; *HRC Resolution 35/7*, supra note 145 at para 13.

217 *Working Group – 2015 General Assembly Report*, *supra* note 192 at para 83.

218 Interview 4.

> while the Guiding Principles themselves do not impose legal obligations, the area they cover will either a) already be covered in part or in full – mostly in part – of laws at the national level; or b) if the Guiding Principles' potential is realized, will increasingly be covered at the national level by effective norms and regulations – if and when states start doing their job.[219]

In addition to stressing the avowed intent to exclude a voluntary observance of the *UN Guiding Principles*,[220] several participants depicted this instrument as being part of an "evolutionary process."[221] One interviewee even implicitly suggested that the practice related to this international instrument has already produced appreciable effects on the perceptions of international actors:

> [W]e are still at that stage where we have to give some hearing to seemingly conflicting social values. Which is why the Guiding Principles could go so far, but not beyond that. Now, of course, that was 2011. If in 2015 we had to reinvent the Guiding Principles, the question would be: 'Would it be the same?'. I suspect not, because I think we have learnt a lot more in four years and the companies are now prepared to understand and give a little bit more room.[222]

In addition to bearing crucial insights with respect to the nature of this practice, the discourses of international actors pertaining to the implementation of the *UN Guiding Principles* demonstrate inherent *relations of power*. Amnesty International thus identified obstacles to remedies that should be taken into account by the Working Group, namely "challenges presented by the complexity of corporate structures and how these are often used to evade accountability," as well as "imbalances in power and influence between corporate actors and victims and the overall impact that this has on justice."[223] Similarly, when reporting on the effectiveness of non-judicial grievance mechanisms, the Working Group acknowledged some concerns with respect to "structural power imbalances that impair victims' ability to effectively represent themselves."[224] Commenting on the development of initiatives to measure the implementation of the *UN Guiding Principles*, the Working Group warned that "[i]f the process of developing measurement tools is limited to a small number of experts or institutions, it runs the risk of *replicating existing power relationships* in which potential victims remain

219 Interview 16.

220 Interview 19: "The Guiding Principles are not a voluntary thing you sign up to or choose not to sign up to. They are a statement of existing responsibilities that all companies have. It's not a membership proposition."

221 Interview 4.

222 Interview 9.

223 Amnesty International, *Letter from Seema Joshi to the Working Group on Human and Transnational Corporations and other Business Enterprises* (8 December 2011), online: OHCHR www.ohchr.org/EN/Issues/Business/Pages/Submissions.aspx (accessed 26 March 2018) at 4.

224 *Working Group – 2014 Report*, *supra* note 213 at para 37.

voiceless and powerless."[225] Given that foreign investors and business enterprises are perceived as being more powerful than other members of the community of practice, the stronger influence that these actors can have on preventing the emergence of a practice of legality must be taken into account.

The analysis of the normative character of the *UN Guiding Principles* according to the interactional theory of international law demonstrates that this instrument is an international norm that has not entered the realm of legality. The support granted by powerful actors in the elaboration of this instrument is strongly related to the express recognition by the Special Representative that it does not impose any new legal obligations for states and business enterprises. Considering the position of some actors that perceived them as a first step toward a binding instrument, the *UN Guiding Principles* are not anchored in shared understandings regarding their legal nature. Moreover, even if references to the *UN Guiding Principles* in other international instruments and the elaboration of various tools to facilitate their implementation contribute to the emergence of a vast practice, discourses from the members of the community of practice suggest that powerful actors often recall the absence of new legal obligations from this instrument. Such a practice seriously prevents the emergence of a practice of legality and the generation of any sense of obligation.

However, the adherence to the *UN Guiding Principles* that results from its consistency with almost all the criteria of legality, combined with some practices that contribute to making the observance of these principles unavoidable, sharply contrast with other informal international instruments. To a certain extent, suggesting that an international norm whose support from powerful actors specifically relies on its social nature could potentially evolve toward the realm of legality can appear as a paradox. In fact, the generation of a sense of obligation would require extensive changes with respect to the shared understandings underlying this informal instrument. Yet, given the wide practice surrounding this instrument and the absence of any provisions expressly mentioning that the observance of this instrument remains voluntary, it is here submitted that these changes are more probable with respect to the *UN Guiding Principles* than any other social norms embedded in informal instruments.

5. The *UNCAC*

The last instrument elaborated and implemented under the auspices of the UN that is considered in this book specifically relates to the area of corruption. Adopted by the UN General Assembly in October 2003 and entered into force in December 2005, the *UNCAC* is a formal international agreement that also codifies responsibilities related to foreign investors.[226] Amidst the various aspects included in the scope of this instrument, the latter establishes

225 *Working Group – 2015 General Assembly Report*, *supra* note 192 at para 59.
226 *UNCAC*, *supra* note 7.

several offences – *e.g.* bribery of foreign public officials,[227] trading of influence,[228] bribery in the private sector,[229] laundering of proceeds of crime[230] and concealment[231] – that can apply to private actors operating outside their home state. Moreover, the *UNCAC* includes a requirement for states to establish the liability of legal persons for participating in these offences[232] and expressly provides states' jurisdiction for offences that are committed by a national having his habitual residence in their territory.[233] However, despite its formal character under international law, an interactional account of the *UNCAC* suggests that it fails to generate a genuine sense of obligation. Even if international actors reached shared understandings with respect to the elaboration of a formal international instrument, several states opted for the adoption of flexible provisions and a vague implementation mechanism (5.1). The social character of this international norm also results from tensions with specific criteria of legality (5.2) and a practice that fails to ensure a proper follow-up on lack of compliance with the requirements of the *UNCAC* (5.3).

5.1 Shared Understandings: Agreeing to a Formal, but Weak Instrument

Several resolutions adopted under the auspices of the UN demonstrate a long history of attempts at tackling the issue of corruption, from the perspectives of both international business transactions and crime prevention.[234] For example, when adopting the *United Nations Declaration against Corruption and Bribery in International Commercial Transactions*,[235] the UN General Assembly requested the examination of ways to promote the criminalization of corruption and bribery in international commercial transactions, "including through legally binding international instruments."[236] Concrete efforts to elaborate an international agreement on this specific matter emerged in parallel with the negotiation of the *United Nations Convention Against Transnational Organized Crime* (*UNCATOC*).[237] In December 1999, the UN General Assembly requested the

227 *Ibid*, art 16(1).
228 *Ibid*, art 18.
229 *Ibid*, art 21.
230 *Ibid*, art 23.
231 *Ibid*, art 24.
232 *Ibid*, art 26(1).
233 *Ibid*, art 42(2)(b).
234 For a general overview of these efforts, see United Nations Office on Drugs and Crime, *Travaux Préparatoires of the Negotiations for the Elaboration of the United Nations Convention Against Corruption* (New York: United Nations, 2010) at ix–xliii [*Travaux Préparatoires*].
235 *United Nations Declaration against Corruption and Bribery International Commercial Transaction*, GA Res 51/191, UNGAOR, 51st Sess, Supp No 49, UN Doc A/RES/51/191, (1997), Annex.
236 *Ibid* at para 4.
237 *United Nations Convention Against Transnational Organized Crime*, 15 November 2000, 2225 UNTS 209 (entered into force 29 September 2003).

ad hoc committee tasked with the negotiation of this international agreement "to explore the desirability of an international instrument against corruption, either ancillary to or independent of the [*UNCATOC*]."[238]

Echoing diplomatic efforts that occurred at the OECD, early attempts to address the issue of corruption under the auspices of the UN benefited from a strong push from the United States, which acted under domestic pressure from private actors further to the adoption of the *Foreign Corrupt Practice Act*.[239] However, given that the resolution recognizing the desirability of "an effective international *legal* instrument against corruption, independent of the [*UNCATOC*]" was adopted without a vote,[240] the member states of the UN General Assembly can all be considered as *norm entrepreneurs* that pushed forward the idea of elaborating the *UNCAC*. More specifically, in its Resolution 55/161, the UN General Assembly requested the UN Secretary-General to convene an intergovernmental open-ended expert group to elaborate the draft terms of reference for the negotiation "of the future *legal* instrument against corruption"[241] and decided to establish an *ad hoc* committee for the negotiation of such an instrument.[242] After the report of the intergovernmental open-ended expert group in 2001,[243] the UN General Assembly adopted the terms of reference for the *UNCAC* and specifically requested the consideration by the *ad hoc* committee of the liability of legal persons, among others.[244] At the end of its seventh session, the *ad hoc* committee approved a draft version of the *UNCAC* and submitted it to the UN General Assembly for consideration.[245] Building on a constant will to elaborate a formal instrument under international law expressly addressing the liability of legal persons for corruption throughout the whole negotiation process, this formal international agreement was adopted on 31 October 2003.[246]

238 *Action against Corruption*, GA Res 54/128, UNGAOR, 54th Sess, Supp No 49, UN Doc A/RES/54/128, (2000) at para 6.

239 See United States of America, Department of State, *Foreign Relations of the United States, 1977–1980*, Vol III (Washington, DC: Department of State, 2013) at 176. See also Philippa Webb, "The United Nations Convention Against Corruption: Global Achievement or Missed Opportunity?" (2005) 8 J Int'l Ecn L 191 at 192; Anita Ramasastry, "Closing the Governance Gap in the Business and Human Rights Arena: Lessons from the Anti-Corruption Movement" in Surya Deva & David Bilchitz, eds, *Human Rights Obligations of Business: Beyond the Corporate Responsibility to Protect?* (Cambridge: Cambridge University Press, 2013) 162 at 163 and 174–176.

240 *An Effective Legal Instrument Against Corruption*, GA Res 55/61, UNGAOR, 55th Sess, Supp No 49, UN Doc A/RES/55/61, (2001) at para 1 [emphasis added].

241 *Ibid* at para 5 [emphasis added].

242 *Ibid* at para 7.

243 *Report of the Meeting of the Intergovernmental Open-Ended Expert Group to Prepare Draft Terms of Reference for the Negotiation of an International Legal Instrument against Corruption*, 2001, UN Doc A/AC.260/2.

244 *Terms of Reference for the Negotiation of an International Legal Instrument Against Corruption*, GA Res 56/260, UNGAOR, 56th Sess, Supp No 49, UN Doc A/RES/56/260, (2002) at para 3.

245 *Report of the Ad Hoc Committee for the Negotiation of a Convention against Corruption on the Work of its First to Seventh Sessions*, 2003, UN Doc A/58/422 at para 90.

246 *United Nations Convention Against Corruption*, GA Res 58/4, UNGAOR, 58th Sess, Supp No 49, UN Doc A/RES/58/4, (2003).

The elaboration of the *UNCAC* also includes efforts that were deployed after its entry into force to establish a mechanism for the review of its implementation. The Conference of the State Parties to the *UNCAC* thus decided to institute an open-ended intergovernmental expert working group tasked with making recommendations on this matter in 2006.[247] From the outset, the Conference of the State Parties underlined that this review mechanism should "[b]e transparent, efficient, non-intrusive, inclusive and impartial" and "provide opportunities to share good practices and challenges," among others.[248] In a subsequent resolution, the Conference of the State Parties decided that the mechanism should be non-adversarial and non-punitive, and that it should be geared toward the promotion of universal adherence to the *UNCAC*.[249] The *Terms of Reference of the Mechanism for the Review of Implementation of the United Nations Convention against Corruption* were adopted in 2009 and established an Implementation Review Group.[250] *Guidelines for the Governmental Experts and the Secretariat in the Conduct of Country Reviews* were also adopted in 2011.[251]

Beyond the resolutions that can be used to trace the emergence of this international norm, the discourses of the members of the *community of practice* involved in its elaboration provide crucial information with respect to the shared understandings that underlie the *UNCAC*. In fact, representatives of states, intergovernmental organizations, public interest NGOs and private interest NGOs constitute a community of actors that contributed to the elaboration of the *UNCAC* and its review mechanism.[252] In this regard, the reports emanating from the sessions of the *ad hoc* committee on the negotiations of the *UNCAC*, the reports of the open-ended intergovernmental working group on the review of the implementation and the transcripts of semi-structured interviews are all relevant sources of discourses that shed light on the shared understandings in which this norm is embedded.

It is plain from the analysis of these discourses that the states involved in the elaboration of the *UNCAC* supported the elaboration of a formal instrument from the very beginning. For example, the importance of a "*binding international legal instrument* against corruption that embodied a comprehensive

247 *Review of Implementation*, CAC Res 1/1, 2006, UN Doc CAC/COSP/2006/12 at para 2.

248 *Ibid* at para 3.

249 *Review of Implementation*, CAC Res 2/1, 2008, UN Doc CAC/COSP/2008/15 at para 3.

250 *Review Mechanism*, CAC Res 3/1, 2009, UN Doc CAC/COSP/2009/15 at para 2 [*Resolution 3/1*]. For the establishment of the Implementation Review Group, see paras 42–44 of the *Terms of Reference of the Mechanism for the Review of Implementation of the United Nations Convention against Corruption* [*Terms of Reference – Review Mechanism*]. The *Terms of Reference – Review Mechanism* are included in the annex of the *Resolution 3/1*.

251 *Mechanism for the Review of Implementation of the United Nations Convention against Corruption*, CAC Res 4/1, 2011, UN Doc CAC/COSP/2011/14 at para 6.

252 See e.g. *Report of the Ad Hoc Committee for the Negotiation of a Convention against Corruption on its Seventh Session, Held in Vienna from 29 September to 1 October 2003*, 2003, UN Doc A/AC.261/25 at para 24.

approach" was mentioned by the Group of 77 and China at the first meeting of the *ad hoc* committee.[253] However, several representatives also aimed at maintaining a high level of flexibility in the provisions of this instrument. As summarized by the *ad hoc* committee, "[m]any representatives expressed the view that the future convention against corruption should be *binding*, effective, efficient and universal and that it should be a *flexible and balanced instrument* that would take into account the legal, social, cultural, economic and political differences of countries, as well as their different levels of development."[254] Some state representatives even implicitly referred to various "degree[s] to which the measures should be obligatory."[255] Along the same lines, one interviewee emphasized that the negotiation process led to the adoption of some provisions that are "not mandatory."[256] In other words, beyond the avowed intent to elaborate a formal instrument under international law, several states agreed to limit the impact of the requirements included in the *UNCAC*.

As far as the elaboration of the mechanism for the review of implementation of the *UNCAC* is concerned, some non-state actors pushed for an initiative that would allow an effective assessment of states' compliance with the requirements found in the agreement. Representatives of the business sector thus "expressed strong support for the Convention and called for the establishment of an effective and robust review mechanism by the Conference."[257] However, several capital-importing states advocated for a review mechanism that would primarily serve as a way to support states in the implementation of this instrument rather than assessing their compliance. For example, the Group of Latin American and Caribbean States "were of the view that the assumption of obligations by States through the ratification of the new convention would require sustained technical assistance."[258] Other states emphasized that the review mechanism should not be intrusive and should respect the sovereignty of states.[259] Overall, it was assumed that "the mechanism would have a progressive and gradual approach[,] was to be based

253 *Report of the Ad Hoc Committee for the Negotiation of a Convention against Corruption on its First Session, Held in Vienna from 21 January to 1 February 2002*, 2002, UN Doc A/AC.261/4 at para 26 [emphasis added] [*Ad Hoc Committee – First Session Report*].

254 *Ibid* at para 33 [emphasis added].

255 See the information related to the Group of Latin American and Caribbean States in *Report of the Ad Hoc Committee for the Negotiation of a Convention against Corruption on its Fifth Session, Held in Vienna from 10 to 21 March 2003*, 2003, UN Doc A/AC.261/16 at para 15.

256 Interview 20.

257 See *Report on the Meeting of the Open-Ended Intergovernmental Working Group on Review of the Implementation of the United Nations Convention against Corruption Held in Vienna from 11 to 13 May 2009*, 2009, UN Doc CAC/COSP/WG.1/2009/3 at para 8.

258 See *Report of the Informal Preparatory Meeting of the Ad Hoc Committee for the Negotiation of a Convention Against Corruption, Held in Buenos Aires from 4 to 7 December 2001*, 2001, UN Doc A/AC.261/2 at para 24.

259 See the information related to the Group of 77 and China in *Report of the Ad Hoc Committee for the Negotiation of a Convention against Corruption on its Sixth Session, Held in Vienna from 21 July to 8 August 2003*, 2003, UN Doc A/AC.261/22 at para 10.

on consensus and negotiation," and that "the review mechanism should serve to identify and disseminate best practices."[260]

Interestingly, the discourses emanating from the *ad hoc* committee and the open-ended intergovernmental working group reproduce *relations of power* in a far subtler way than for other instruments. Even if the disappointment expressed by the African Group concerning the lack of funds at the Secretariat to ensure the participation of all the least developed countries in the work of the *ad hoc* committee suggests a weaker position of these countries throughout the elaboration of this international norm,[261] the discourses do not explicitly reproduce relations of power. Yet, taking into account the large number of capital-importing states at the UN General Assembly, it can nevertheless be suggested that these actors generally benefited from a form of institutional power during the negotiations of the *UNCAC*.[262] In this regard, the intent of several capital-importing states to include more flexibility with respect to its provisions and the review mechanism played an important role in shaping the shared understandings that underlie this agreement.

Overall, it is plain that the elaboration of the *UNCAC* relies on an initial will from norm entrepreneurs to elaborate a formal instrument under international law to address various offences related to corruption and contribute to the establishment of the liability of legal persons. However, a closer look at the resolutions adopted by the Conference of the State Parties and the discourses from actors involved in the elaboration process demonstrates a will from several states to limit the normative character of this instrument. Ultimately, in line with the position adopted by a large number of capital-importing states, the community of practice agreed on the elaboration of an international initiative with a flexible mandatory character for several provisions and a review mechanism that is primarily oriented toward a learning process. Although some core issues of this international norm probably rely on a stronger consensus, the shared understandings emerging from the elaboration of the *UNCAC* considerably affect the sense of obligation that can be generated from this international norm as a whole.

5.2 *Criteria of Legality: Inherent Contradictions and Weak Congruence*

Beyond its adoption as a formal international agreement, the *UNCAC*'s normative character also depends upon the extent to which this international initiative meets specific criteria of legality. While the majority of these criteria do not pose any particular issues, two aspects negatively affect the ability of the *UNCAC* to generate legitimacy and a sense of obligation. The attempt at elaborating a flexible instrument ultimately led to the adoption of weak provisions that contradict the

260 See *Report on the Meeting of the Open-Ended Intergovernmental Working Group on Review of the Implementation of the United Nations Convention against Corruption Held in Vienna from 15 to 17 December 2008*, 2008, UN Doc CAC/COSP/WG.1/2008/8 at para 20.

261 See *Ad Hoc Committee – First Session Report*, *supra* note 253 at para 28.

262 For a discussion on institutional power, see section 1 of Chapter 3.

aim of fighting corruption at the international level. Moreover, the mechanism for the review of implementation of the *UNCAC* does not provide an appropriate procedural device to determine the lack of compliance of states.

From the outset, the *UNCAC* sharply contrasts with the other initiatives elaborated and implemented under the auspices of the UN to the extent that it is a formal international agreement. While the criterion of *promulgation* can also be fulfilled by informal international instruments, the adoption of this initiative as an international treaty ensures that it easily meets this criterion of legality. Moreover, relying on the ratification from 183 states as of the seventh Conference of the State Parties in 2017,[263] this international agreement is unambiguously approaching a universal character and is made available to various international actors.

The *UNCAC* does not discriminate with respect to the states that must implement its requirements nor the legal persons that are concerned by the offences that it establishes. For example, regarding the bribery of foreign public officials and officials of pubic international organizations, Article 16(1) provides the following:

> *Each State Party* shall adopt such legislative and other measures as may be necessary to establish as a criminal offence, when committed intentionally, the promise, offering or giving to a foreign public official or an official of a public international organization, directly or indirectly, of an undue advantage, for the official himself or herself or another person or entity, in order that the official act or refrain from acting in the exercise of his or her official duties, in order to obtain or retain business or other undue advantage in relation to the conduct of international business.[264]

Without including any distinction among the legal persons concerned, Article 26(1) also provides that "*[e]ach state* shall adopt such measures as may be necessary . . . to establish the liability of legal persons for participation in the offences established in accordance with this Convention."[265] Therefore, the *UNCAC* lives up to the requirement of *generality* that characterizes international legal norms.

Several aspects of this agreement also ensure that it meets the criterion of *clarity*. Despite the absence of a specific definition of corruption among the terms expressly defined in the *UNCAC*,[266] the chapter focusing on criminalization and law enforcement provides sufficient details regarding the offences that must be criminalized by states.[267] As exemplified by the citation of Article 16 above, the information included in the articles of the *UNCAC* extensively contributes to the clarity of this international instrument. Furthermore, even if this instrument is not accompanied

263 *United Nations Convention against Corruption: Status of Ratifications as at 18 October 2017*, 2017, UN Doc CAC/COSP/2017/CRP.2.
264 *UNCAC*, *supra* note 7, art 16(1) [emphasis added].
265 *Ibid*, art 26(1) [emphasis added].
266 *Ibid*, art 2.
267 *Ibid*, Chapter III.

by any set of official commentaries that could provide additional information on the meaning of its provisions, the publication of the *travaux préparatoires* resulting from the negotiation process of the *UNCAC*[268] and a legislative guide[269] are particularly useful to interpret each article of this instrument.

Not only has the *UNCAC* not been amended so far, some features of this international agreement suggest particular attention from the negotiators with respect to its *constancy*. Article 69(1) provides a detailed procedure requiring any proposed amendments to be submitted to the UN Secretary-General prior to its transmission to the member states and the Conference of the State Parties for its adoption by consensus or a two-thirds majority vote.[270] In a way that also contributes to a constant application of the *UNCAC*, Article 70(1) includes a procedure stipulating that a "denunciation shall become effective one year after the date of receipt of the notification by the Secretary-General."[271]

Moreover, none of the instruments elaborated and implemented under the auspices of intergovernmental organizations that are considered in this book supposes a *retroactive application*. Likewise, given that the *UNCAC* does not expressly address any temporal issues, this international instrument unambiguously meets the requirement of this criterion of legality.

Even if the Chairman of the *ad hoc* committee responsible for the *UNCAC* negotiations expressed his concerns with respect to the repeated references to the conformity of its provisions with domestic legislation,[272] such references are particularly relevant to ensure that the *UNCAC* does *not ask impossible requirements* to its member states. For example, regarding the liability of legal persons, Article 26(2) provides that "[s]ubject to the legal principles of the [s]tate [p]arty, the liability of legal persons may be criminal, civil or administrative."[273] Without allowing states to circumvent the requirement to establish such liability, this provision takes into account the limits that can be imposed by different legal systems and contributes to the legitimacy of the *UNCAC*.

With respect to *contradiction*, it is worth mentioning that the absence of an exception for facilitation payments allows the *UNCAC* to avoid a contradiction that was initially found in the OECD *Convention on Combating Bribery of Foreign Public Officials in International Business Transactions*.[274] However, while many provisions echo the intent of elaborating a flexible legal instrument, the

268 *Travaux Préparatoires*, *supra* note 234.

269 United Nations Office on Drugs and Crime, *Legislative Guide for the Implementation of the United Nations Convention Against Corruption* (New York: United Nations, 2006).

270 *UNCAC*, *supra* note 7, art 69(1).

271 *Ibid*, art 70(1).

272 See *Report of the Ad Hoc Committee for the Negotiation of a Convention against Corruption on its Third Session, Held in Vienna from 30 September to 11 October 2002*, 2002, UN Doc A/AC.261/9 at para 33. This element is also criticized in the literature: Marco Arnone & Leonardo S Borlini, *Corruption: Economic Analysis and International Law* (Northampton: Edward Elgar, 2014) at 254; Cecily Rose, *International Anti-Corruption Norms: Their Creation and Influence on Domestic Legal Systems* (Oxford: Oxford University Press, 2015) at 114.

273 *UNCAC*, *supra* note 7, art 26(2).

274 This contradiction is discussed in section 3.2 of Chapter 4.

weakness of several requirements can ultimately be perceived as being in tension with the overarching aim of the *UNCAC*. According to its Preamble, states are "[c]oncerned about the seriousness of problems and threats posed by corruption to the stability and security of societies, undermining the institutions and values of democracy, ethical values and justice and jeopardizing sustainable development and the rule of law."[275] By contrast, the means that are considered to tackle these problems and threats are sometimes notably limited. Several articles thus merely require that states "shall consider" or "may consider" adopting specific measures. For example, such a requirement is included in the provision addressing the demand of bribes by foreign pubic officials:

> Each State Party *shall consider* adopting such legislative and other measures as may be necessary to establish as a criminal offence, when committed intentionally, the solicitation or acceptance by a foreign public official or an official of a public international organization, directly or indirectly, of an undue advantage, for the official himself or herself or another person or entity, in order that the official act or refrain from acting in the exercise of his or her official duties.[276]

Although these provisions do not amount to asking contradictory requirements to member states, the adoption of such weak provisions does not ensure a sufficient contribution to tackle a problem that is depicted as being of the utmost seriousness.

Finally, in line with the attempt of states to focus on building their capacity to implement the requirements of the *UNCAC*, the mechanism to review implementation of this agreement is not entirely appropriate to address significant instances of non-compliance and fulfill the criterion of *congruence*. Although Article 30(1) underscores that "[e]ach State Party shall make the commission of an offence established in accordance with this Convention liable to sanctions that take into account the gravity of that offence,"[277] the existence of a procedural mechanism to tackle the reluctance of states to implement the agreement is less straightforward. In fact, Article 66(2) establishes a state-to-state dispute settlement mechanism regarding the interpretation and the implementation of the *UNCAC*.[278] This provision also mentions that any disputes that cannot be settled through negotiation can be submitted to arbitration and, ultimately, to the International Court of Justice.[279] However, pursuant to Article 66(3), several member states made a reservation concerning this dispute settlement mechanism.[280]

275 *UNCAC*, *supra* note 7, Preamble.
276 *Ibid*, art 16(2) [emphasis added].
277 *Ibid*, art 30(1).
278 *Ibid*, art 66(2).
279 *Ibid*, art 66(2).
280 For the list of reservations, see United Nations Treaty Collection: online United Nations https://treaties.un.org/Pages/ViewDetails.aspx?src=TREATY&mtdsg_no=XVIII-14&chapter=18&clang=_en (accessed 26 March 2018).

The lack of congruence is also reflected in the review process that was established further to the adoption of the *UNCAC*. In fact, the terms of reference summarize the goals of this process in the following terms:

> (a) Promote the purposes of the Convention as set out in its article 1; (b) Provide the Conference with information on the measures taken by States parties in implementing the Convention and the difficulties encountered by them in doing so; (c) Help States parties to identify and substantiate specific needs for technical assistance and to promote and facilitate the provision of technical assistance; (d) Promote and facilitate international cooperation in the prevention of and the fight against corruption, including in the area of asset recovery; (e) Provide the Conference with information on successes, good practices and challenges of States parties in implementing and using the Convention; (f) Promote and facilitate the exchange of information, practices and experiences gained in the implementation of the Convention.[281]

Above all, the review process culminates with the elaboration of a report that "shall be finalized upon agreement between the reviewing States parties and the State party under review."[282] While such a review can be useful to foster the implementation of the *UNCAC*, it is here submitted that it is not adapted to provide an independent assessment of a state's compliance with the requirements included in this agreement.

Assessing the provisions of the *UNCAC* and the instruments related to the mechanism to review its implementation against criteria of legality sheds light on some issues that can affect the sense of obligation generated by this international norm. Even if this international instrument meets most of these criteria of legality, several provisions remain weak and suggest a tension with the avowed intent to tackle the threat of corruption. Furthermore, the review mechanism adopted after the entry into force of the *UNCAC* is a way to foster dialogue around good implementation practices rather than a procedural device to fully address the lack of compliance by states.

5.3 Practice of Legality: Watering Down the Normative Character of the UNCAC

Interactions between the members of the community of practice to implement the *UNCAC* is another key element to consider when assessing the normative character of this instrument. In order to shed light on the nature of the practice surrounding the *UNCAC*, the present section combines an examination of the provisions of other instruments codifying foreign investors' responsibilities with discourses from members of the community of practice that devote efforts to implement the agreement. Reports and other documents from the Conference of the State Parties,

281 *Terms of Reference – Review Mechanism*, *supra* note 250 at para 11.
282 *Ibid* at para 34.

reports on the sessions of the Implementation Review Group, NGOs' statements submitted to the Implementation Review Group and transcripts of semi-structured interviews thus all constitute relevant discourses that ultimately suggest the absence of a proper legal character to the practice surrounding the *UNCAC*.

Several aspects point toward a vast practice characterizing the implementation of the *UNCAC* since its entry into force. Express references to this agreement in other international instruments adopted under the auspices of intergovernmental organizations suggest a key role of this initiative in the evolving codification of foreign investors' responsibilities.[283] It is also plain that states are extensively engaged in the implementation of the *UNCAC*. As mentioned by the Conference of the State Parties, more than 120 executive summaries, 160 self-assessment checklists and almost 150 country visits and joint meetings have been completed during the first cycle of the review mechanism.[284] This vast participation was also highlighted by an interviewee in the following terms:

> [I]t is amazing how seriously countries are taking this and how much they engage. And it is even more rewarding to see how much developing countries are engaging with this. And how important they consider, how seriously they take the entire affair. And how much they invest limited resources – both human and financial – in engaging both as countries under review but also as countries reviewing others.[285]

Interestingly, some excerpts of the reports related to the implementation of the *UNCAC* include express references to obligations resulting from this instrument. For example, the Vice-President of a Conference of the State Parties called upon states "to adapt their legislation and regulations in order to ***comply with the obligation*** to establish as criminal offences the acts described in the Convention as ***mandatory offences***, without prejudice to other criminalization provisions."[286] Similarly, "[s]peakers reported on national efforts and initiatives to implement the provisions of the Convention and described domestic legislative, administrative and judicial measures to incorporate into their legal systems the requirements

283 See *Recommendation of the Council for Further Combating Bribery of Foreign Public Officials in International Business Transactions*, 26 November 2009, Doc No C(2009)159/REV1/FINAL (amended on 18 February 2010, Doc No C(2010)19), Preamble; *Recommendation of the Council on Due Diligence Guidance for Responsible Supply Chains of Minerals from Conflict-Affected and High-Risk Areas*, 17 July 2012, Doc No C(2012)93 (2012), Preamble; *OECD Guidelines 2011 – Commentaries*, *supra* note 187 at para 79; *Principles for Responsible Investment in Agriculture*, *supra* note 59 at para 19(B)(iii). The principles of the UN Global Compact are also partly "derived" from the *UNCAC*. See UN Global Compact, *supra* note 4.

284 *Report of the Conference of the State Parties to the United Nations Convention against Corruption on its Sixth Session Held in St. Petersburg, Russian Federation, from 2 to 6 November 2015*, 2015, UN Doc CAC/COSP/2015/10 at para 6.

285 Interview 20.

286 See *Report of the Conference of the State Parties to the United Nations Convention against Corruption on its Second Session, Held in Nusa Dua, Indonesia, from 28 January to 1 February 2008*, 2008, UN Doc CAC/COSP/2008/15 at para 63.

set forth in the Convention" during a previous conference.[287] Yet, some of these discourses were provided with a view to identifying best practices regarding the implementation of the *UNCAC* rather than establishing a sense of having to comply with the requirements found in this international instrument.[288]

Most significantly, other statements from members of the community of practice suggest that this international norm is not perceived as generating a general sense of obligation. One key element in this regard relates to discourses that expressly acknowledge the existence of non-mandatory provisions in the *UNCAC*. Addressing the preparation of thematic reports by the Implementation Review Group, some speakers suggested that "future reports could more clearly differentiate between mandatory and non-mandatory provisions."[289] Similarly, the consideration of "non-mandatory provisions and evolving good practices" in the country reviews was raised by several states.[290] By shedding light on the consideration of some provisions of the *UNCAC* as being non-mandatory, such discourses suggest that the practice surrounding this international instrument cannot be considered as a general practice of legality.

Even if some discourses related to the implementation of this international norm demonstrate the ability of the country reviews to influence the behavior of states when it comes to adopting measures to tackle corruption, it remains unclear whether the amendments to their legislation were made pursuant to a will to comply with the conclusions of the country review reports. According to the Implementation Review Group, "some speakers referred to the observations made in the country review reports or during the dialogue phase and reported that *some of those observations* had since been addressed within the domestic systems of their countries."[291] Similarly, other states mentioned that such reports "had been *beneficial* for their domestic reforms,"[292] while others merely "noted the importance, usefulness and positive impact of the country reviews."[293] The same Implementation Review Group reported that "in designing national reform

287 See *Report of the Conference of the State Parties to the United Nations Convention against Corruption on its Fourth Session, Held in Marrakech, Morocco, from 24 to 28 October 2011*, 2011, UN Doc CAC/COSP/2011/14 at para 40 [*Conference of the State Parties – Fourth Session Report*].

288 See *Report of the Conference of the State Parties to the United Nations Convention against Corruption on its Fifth Session, Held in Panama City from 25 to 29 November 2013*, 2014, UN Doc CAC/COSP/2013/18 at para 49.

289 See *Report of the Implementation Review Group on its Resumed Third Session, Held in Vienna from 14 to 16 November 2012*, 2012, UN Doc CAC/COSP/IRG/2012/6/Add.1 at para 30 [*Implementation Review Group – Third Resumed Session Report*].

290 See *Report of the Implementation Review Group on its Second Session, Held in Vienna from 30 May to 2 June 2011*, 2011, UN Doc CAC/COSP/IRG/2011/4 at para 39.

291 *Ibid* at para 39 [emphasis added].

292 See *Implementation Review Group – Third Resumed Session Report*, *supra* note 289 at para 26 [emphasis added].

293 See *Report of the Implementation Review Group on its Fifth Session, Held in Vienna from 13 to 15 October 2014*, 2014, UN Doc CAC/COSP/IRG/2014/11/Add.1 at para 34 [*Implementation Review Group – Fifth Session Report*].

measures, a number of [s]tates parties had been oriented by the *good practices and lessons learned* in other countries as identified through the reviews."[294]

Several statements also emphasized the perception of country reviews as a means to identify areas where technical assistance is needed rather than a thorough assessment of compliance. At the first session of the Implementation Review Group, the Group of Latin American and Caribbean States reportedly

> encouraged States parties to submit their technical assistance needs through the self-assessment checklist and was of the view that the Secretariat should submit periodic reports on technical assistance to the Implementation Review Group in order to systematically identify regional and thematic tendencies.[295]

The identification of technical assistance needs was also depicted by the same group of states as "one of the crucial aspects of the work of the Review Mechanism."[296] The prevalence of technical assistance over the evaluation of compliance was even reported by the Conference of the State Parties, which mentioned that some states "expressed the view that compliance with the Convention should not be a prerequisite for technical assistance and that no conditions should be attached to the provision of assistance."[297]

Another element that extensively prevents the emergence of a practice of legality can be found in the refusal from several states to elaborate a concrete follow-up procedure to the country reviews. Reports of the Implementation Review Group highlight a clear divide among the member states on this matter. For example, the representative of the European Union and other states regretted the absence of "an appropriate follow-up to the problems identified through the Mechanism and to implement lessons learned throughout the process."[298] As an alternative, the Implementation Review Group reported that states had developed national action plans based on the outcome of the review process "on a *voluntary* basis,"[299] while others suggested "the compilation of *non-binding recommendations* for the implementation of the Convention and of common best practices into a document to serve as a reference."[300] Without suggesting that

294 *Report of the Implementation Review Group on its Resumed Sixth Session, Held in St. Petersburg, Russian Federation, on 3 and 4 November 2015*, 2015, UN Doc CAC/COSP/IRG/2015/5/Add.1 at para 12 [emphasis added].

295 *Report of the Implementation Review Group on its First Session, Held in Vienna from 28 June to 2 July 2010*, 2010, UN Doc CAC/COSP/IRG/2010/7 at para 13.

296 See *ibid* at para 22.

297 *Report of the Conference of the State Parties to the United Nations Convention against Corruption on its First Session, Held in Amman from 10 to 14 December 2006*, 2006, UN Doc CAC/COSP/2006/12 at para 90.

298 See *Implementation Review Group – Fifth Session Report*, *supra* note 293 at para 5.

299 *Report of the Implementation Review Group on its Third Session, Held in Vienna from 18 to 22 June 2012*, 2012, UN Doc CAC/COSP/IRG/2012/6 at para 56 [emphasis added].

300 *Report of the Implementation Review Group on its Resumed Fifth Session, Held in Vienna from 13 to 15 October 2014*, 2014, UN Doc CAC/COSP/IRG/2014/11/Add.1 at para 43 [emphasis added].

reliance on these national action plans is useless to encourage compliance, the fact that the member states currently rely on these non-binding alternatives demonstrates that the practice surrounding the country reviews does not bear a strong legal character.

These discourses sharply contrast with attempts from public interest NGOs to strengthen the legal character of the *UNCAC*. A declaration of the Coalition of the Civil Society Friends against Corruption depicted the agreement as encompassing "legal, political and moral obligations" and called upon governments to "show the ambition required to ensure that *UNCAC* has a real and lasting impact on global corruption."[301] Along the same lines, representatives of the business sector and public interest NGOs called upon the deployment of efforts to monitor the implementation by states of the recommendations provided in country reviews. For example, Transparency International supported the establishment of a follow-up process to address these recommendations, recalling that it would "help ensure that the findings of the reviews are given priority and that momentum for Convention against Corruption implementation is maintained."[302]

Relations of power are also at play in the implementation process of this international norm. However, instead of the traditional cleavage between international actors observed in the implementation of other instruments, the tensions that are reproduced in the discourses of the members of the community of practice primarily concern capital-importing states and non-state actors. In fact, Resolution 4/6 adopted by the Conference of the State Parties limits the participation of NGOs in the mechanism for the review of implementation to briefings held in the margins of the review process.[303] In this regard, a representative of the group of African states stressed the intergovernmental nature of the implementation mechanism.[304] While the representative of the European Union advocated for a more transparent mechanism,[305] another speaker reportedly "regretted that the potential of the Review Mechanism could not be exploited to the fullest by providing NGOs with an opportunity to contribute specific knowledge in the fight against corruption while leaving decision-making power to States parties."[306] Similarly, Transparency International and the Transparency and Accountability Network stated that

301 See *Civil Society and Private Sector Forum, Forum for Anti-Corruption Activities and Forum for Parliamentarians: Side Events Held on the Occasion of the First Session of the Conference of the State Parties to the United Nations Convention against Corruption*, 2006, UN Doc CAC/COSP/2006/CRP.6 at 4.

302 *Statement Submitted by Transparency International, a Non-Governmental Organization in Consultative Status with the Economic and Social Council*, 2013, UN Doc CAC/COSP/IRG/2013/NGO/3 at 5.

303 *Non-Governmental Organizations and the Mechanism for the Review of Implementation of the United Nations Convention against Corruption*, CAC Res 4/6, 2011, UN Doc CAC/COSP/2011/14 at paras 1–2.

304 See *Report of the Implementation Review Group on its Sixth Session, Held in Vienna from 1 to 5 June 2015*, 2015, UN Doc CAC/COSP/IRG/2015/5 at para 6.

305 See *ibid* at para 5.

306 See *Conference of the State Parties – Fourth Session Report*, *supra* note 287 at para 93.

> [t]he restrictions placed on NGO written and oral statements to the [Intergovernmental Review Group] briefing limit [its] ability to report on [its] anti-corruption activities and assessments, [thus restricting] meaningful dialogue and exchange of information between governments and other stakeholders about the UNCAC review process and UNCAC implementation.[307]

Recalling the institutional power of capital-importing states at the UN, the weaker position of public interest NGOs and representatives of the private sector in contrast to these states in the activities of the Implementation Review Group suggests a limited impact of their calls for a practice of legality.

Despite the formal character of the *UNCAC* under international law, the application of the interactional theory of international law suggests that it is a strong social norm that nevertheless fails to generate a general sense of obligation. Although the UN General Assembly initially supported the adoption of a formal instrument under international law to establish the liability of legal persons for various corruption offences, the shared understandings characterizing the elaboration of the *UNCAC* rely on an avowed intent by a majority of states to adopt an instrument including several flexible provisions with an implementation mechanism geared toward a learning process. These negotiations led to several weak provisions that fail to meet the criteria of non-contradiction and congruence that usually characterize international legal norms. Finally, even if one could be tempted to suggest that some provisions of the *UNCAC* remain mandatory, the interactions between the members of the community of practice highlight a practice that primarily seeks to build the capacity of states. Such a practice fails to establish any form of follow-up with respect to the country reviews, thus preventing the emergence of a practice bearing an overarching legal character. Without denying the ability of this instrument to influence the behavior of states with respect to the measures that they adopt to address corruption, the analysis above stresses that such influence relies on the social character of the *UNCAC* rather than on a general sense of obligation to act accordingly.

Conclusion

The UN has hosted a rich normative process related to the codification of foreign investors' responsibilities that is rooted in a historical will to change the international economic order. While the initiatives elaborated and implemented by various organs of this intergovernmental organization include both formal and informal international instruments, they all constitute international norms whose normative character is better assessed through a consideration of their provisions and the interactions that they generate between international actors.

307 *Statement Submitted by Transparency International, a Non-Governmental Organization in Consultative Status with the Economic and Social Council, and by the Transparency and Accountability Network, a Non-Governmental Organization not in Consultative Status with the Economic and Social Council*, 2013, UN Doc CAC/COSP/IRG/2013/NGO/1 at 3.

Only through such an account can one position the UN Global Compact, the *UN Norms*, the *UN Guiding Principles* and the *UNCAC* on a continuum that varies from social norms to legal norms.

Initially intended as a platform for dialogue and a learning process for the adoption of sustainable conduct by business enterprises, it is plain that the UN Global Compact has never been considered as a legal norm. The UN Secretary-General benefited from the support of powerful actors when launching an initiative that relies on a voluntary commitment of private actors to take into account their impact on human rights, labour rights, environmental protection and corruption. This absence of shared understandings for a legal initiative is combined to a failure to meet several criteria of legality – namely clarity, constancy, not asking the impossible, absence of contradiction and congruence – that usually characterize international legal norms. Ultimately, despite a high number of participants and a broad dissemination of this initiative, the practice surrounding the UN Global Compact faces important problems and an express avoidance of assessing compliance with the principles that it includes. As a result, the UN Global Compact is a fairly weak social norm.

While the epistemic community that initiated the elaboration of the *UN Norms* avowedly intended to adopt a binding instrument, this instrument never reached the threshold of legality and can hardly be considered as an international norm nowadays. More specifically, the working group tasked with their elaboration became the target of numerous critics from several states and representatives of the private sector, preventing the emergence of shared understandings with respect to the legal nature of this instrument. The confusion that persists with respect to their promulgation, the inclusion of requirements reaching beyond the direct control of business enterprises, the presence of inherent contradictions and the absence of a fully developed procedure to address congruence all constitute tensions and failures of the *UN Norms* to meet criteria of legality. What is more, even if some actors perceived it as a starting point to impose obligations on foreign investors, the ephemeral practice of this initiative was characterized by a manifest opposition from powerful actors to implement the *UN Norms* according to a practice of legality.

The weak practice regarding the UN Global Compact and the brief existence of the *UN Norms* sharply contrast with the impressive uptake that characterizes the fairly recent *UN Guiding Principles*. Although it remains unquestionable that the *UN Guiding Principles* are currently a social norm that does not produce a genuine sense of obligation, this informal international instrument has a stronger potential than other informal instruments to evolve toward the realm of legality. Of course, while the Special Representative was never tasked with the elaboration of a legal instrument, the support provided by powerful actors was conditioned to the absence of any new obligations in this initiative. Similarly, the current practice surrounding the *UN Guiding Principles* is characterized by discourses emphasizing the absence of any legal character. Yet, given that this instrument is anchored in shared understandings that the corporate responsibility to respect human rights is not strictly voluntary, that its provisions meet almost all the criteria of legality and that some aspects of the practice contribute to make it unavoidable, it is here submitted that the *UN Guiding Principles* could eventually generate a sense of obligation despite its informal character.

The adoption of a formal international agreement does not guarantee the elaboration and the implementation of a legal norm as understood by the interactional theory of international law. In fact, despite its formal character, the *UNCAC* is a strong social norm that remains below the threshold of legality on various points. Even if the UN General Assembly initially opted for the adoption of a formal international instrument, the shared understandings in which this agreement is embedded are characterized by a will to adopt flexible requirements and a review mechanism that does not concretely assess the compliance of states. The elaboration of the *UNCAC* thus resulted in the adoption of some provisions that are in tension with the aim to fully tackle the scourge of corruption, as well as a mechanism to review implementation that is insufficient to ensure congruence between the rules and official action. The absence of a sense of obligation emanating from the *UNCAC* also results from a practice focusing on providing opportunities for dialogue on best practices, rather than appropriately following-up on significant instances of non-compliance.

7 World Bank Group

Introduction

The last multilateral intergovernmental organization involved in the codification of foreign investors' responsibilities that is considered for the purposes of this micro-level analysis is the World Bank Group. Acting as both a development agency and an investment promoter, the institutions that constitute this organization have developed several instruments that articulate standards of behavior related to the activities of private investors operating abroad. A key instrument that specifically concerns the responsibilities of clients operating projects financed by one of these institutions is the *Performance Standards on Social & Environmental Sustainability* (*Performance Standards*), which were elaborated by the International Finance Corporation (IFC) in 2006 and revised in 2012.[1] Similar standards have subsequently been adopted by the Multilateral Investment Guarantee Agency (MIGA) in 2007,[2] as well as the International Bank for Reconstruction and Development (IBRD) and the International Development Association (IDA) in 2013.[3]

Given the similarity of these performance standards, a detailed analysis of each instrument would only be redundant. Accordingly, this chapter focuses on the

1 *International Finance Corporation's Performance Standards on Social & Environmental Sustainability*, 30 April 2006, online: IFC www.ifc.org/wps/wcm/connect/Topics_Ext_Content/IFC_External_Corporate_Site/IFC+Sustainability/Our+Approach/Risk+Management/Performance+Standards/ (accessed 26 March 2018) [*IFC Performance Standards 2006*]; *International Finance Corporation's Performance Standards on Environmental and Social Sustainability*, 1 January 2012, online: IFC www.ifc.org/wps/wcm/connect/Topics_Ext_Content/IFC_External_Corporate_Site/IFC+Sustainability/Our+Approach/Risk+Management/Performance+Standards/ (accessed 26 March 2018) [*IFC Performance Standards 2012*].

2 *Multilateral Investment Guarantee Agency's Performance Standards on Social & Environmental Sustainability*, 1 October 2007, online: MIGA www.miga.org/documents/performance_standards_social_and_env_sustainability.pdf (accessed 26 March 2018). These standards were also revised in 2013. See *Multilateral Investment Guarantee Agency Performance Standards on Environmental and Social Sustainability*, 1 October 2013, online: MIGA www.miga.org/documents/performance_standards_env_and_social_sustainability.pdf (accessed 26 March 2018).

3 *Operational Policy 4.03 – Performance Standards for Private Sector Activities*, May 2013, online: World Bank https://policies.worldbank.org/sites/ppf3/PPFDocuments/Forms/DispPage.aspx?docid=1566 (accessed 26 March 2018) [*World Bank Performance Standards*].

IFC Performance Standards and contextualizes the assessment of their normative character by considering the broader activities of the World Bank Group. After a brief overview of its institutional features and the identity shift toward sustainability that has occurred in the World Bank Group (1), an application of the interactional theory of international law[4] suggests that the *IFC Performance Standards* unambiguously generates a sense of obligation for the IFC and its clients (2). Despite its informal character under international law, this instrument thus constitutes a legal norm.

1. The World Bank Group: Several Activities and a Major Identity Shift

A consideration of the normative site from which the *IFC Performance Standards* emanate is relevant to contextualize the analysis of their normative character. According to the World Bank Group, its role is to use financial resources to support various projects with a view to diminishing poverty, increasing economic growth and improving the quality of life.[5] In 2017, the World Bank Group thus committed $61.4 billion in loans, grants, equity investments and guarantees to their members and private businesses.[6] More specifically, this intergovernmental organization consists of five institutions that undertake different aspects related to this use of financial resources.[7] While the IBRD lends resources to governments of middle-income and low-income countries, the activities of the IDA focuses on interest-free loans and grants to the poorest countries. As far as relations with the private sector are concerned, the IFC seeks to stimulate investments from private actors in developing countries and the MIGA provides guarantees against losses caused by non-commercial risks in these countries. Finally, although this institution does not strictly relate to the use of financial resources to partner with developing countries, the International Centre for Settlement of Investment Disputes provides international facilities regarding the conciliation and arbitration of international investment disputes.

In contrast to other intergovernmental organizations considered in this book, the institutions that constitute the World Bank Group do not have explicit power to elaborate international norms. For example, instead of enunciating specific normative acts that can be adopted by the IFC, the *Articles of Agreement* of this organization focus primarily on its functioning.[8] Section 2(a) of Article IV thus

4 See section 3 of the introduction.

5 World Bank, *A Guide to the World Bank*, 3rd ed (Washington: The World Bank, 2011) at 3 [World Bank, *A Guide*].

6 See World Bank, *Annual Report 2017: End Extreme Poverty, Boost Shared Prosperity* (Washington: The World Bank, 2017).

7 For a brief overview of these five institutions, see World Bank, *A Guide*, *supra* note 5 at 2 and 10–29.

8 *International Finance Corporation Articles of Agreement*, 27 June 2012, online: IFC www.ifc.org/wps/wcm/connect/1c95b500484cb68d9f3dbf5f4fc3f18b/IFC_Articles_of_Agreement.pdf?MOD=AJPERES (accessed 26 March 2018) [*IFC Articles of Agreement*].

mentions that "all the powers of the Corporation shall be vested in the Board of Governors,"[9] which can delegate the authority to exercise some of its powers to the Board of Directors.[10] In this regard, the latter is "responsible for the conduct of the general operations of the Corporation, and for this purpose shall exercise all the powers given to it by this Agreement or delegated to it by the Board of Governors."[11] Among other powers, the Board of Directors considers and approves projects submitted for funding by the IFC.[12] As far as votes are concerned, they are determined by the equal distribution of the aggregate sum of the voting power of all members as well as the allocation of the share of stock held by each member.[13] As of March 2018, the Director appointed by the United States thus held 20.99%, followed by the Directors of Japan (6.01%) and Germany (4.77%).[14]

Of particular relevance for an analysis that partly draws on a constructivist analytical framework is the consideration of an identity shift that occurred within the World Bank Group. Despite an undeniable focus on the protection of foreign investment, this intergovernmental organization responded to criticisms pertaining to the negative impact of its activities on local communities and the environment by adopting various policies that seek to foster sustainable development. Some authors stress a change in the identity of the World Bank Group through reforms of its policies that were triggered by pubic interest nongovernmental organizations (NGOs) and the United States.[15] Several scholars have also identified an increasing consideration of environmental and social sustainability throughout the operations of the IFC since the late 1990s.[16] Of course, the IFC's purpose primarily relates to the advancement of "economic development by encouraging the growth of productive private enterprise in member countries, particularly in the less developed areas."[17] Yet, Park argues that transnational advocacy networks socialized the IFC, a process that led to a change in the mandate and bureaucratic culture of this organization.[18] In other words, although

9 *Ibid*, Article IV, Section 2(a).
10 *Ibid*, Article IV, Section 2(c).
11 See *ibid*, Article IV, Section 4(a).
12 See World Bank, *A Guide, supra* note 5 at 9 and 97–98.
13 See *IFC Articles of Agreement, supra* note 8, Article IV, Section 3.
14 See IFC, *Subscriptions and Voting Power of Member Countries* (10 April 2018), online: The World Bank http://siteresources.worldbank.org/BODINT/Resources/278027-1215524804501/IFCCountryVotingTable.pdf (accessed 11 April 2018).
15 See generally Susan Park, "Norm Diffusion within International Organizations: A Case Study of the World Bank" (2005) 8 J Int'l Rel & Dev 111. See also David B Hunter, "Civil Society Networks and the Development of Environmental Standards at International Financial Institutions" (2008) 8 Chi J Int'l L 437 at 457.
16 See e.g. Susan Park, "How Transnational Environmental Advocacy Networks Socialize International Financial Institutions: A Case Study of the International Finance Corporation" (2005) 5 Global Envtl Politics 95 at 109 [Park, "How Transnational Advocacy"]; Hunter, *ibid* at 443–445; Adebola Adeyemi, "Changing the Face of Sustainable Development in Developing Countries: The Role of the International Finance Corporation" (2014) 16 Envtl L Rev 91 at 95–97.
17 See *IFC Articles of Agreement, supra* note 8, Article I.
18 See generally Park, "How Transnational Advocacy", *supra* note 16. See also Susan Park, "The World Bank Group: Championing Sustainable Development Norms?" (2007) 13 Global Governance 535 at 545–552.

the focus on financial viability and protection of private investors fits the context of neoliberal globalization, this identity shift has opened the door to the consideration of foreign investors' responsibilities and the development of international norms in this regard.

Although the various institutions of the World Bank Group are ultimately managed by their member states,[19] it is also worth noting that their operations extensively rely on the work of experts and professionals. While the elaboration of environmental and social standards in international finance institutions "has been accompanied by the emergence of an epistemic community that committed to the creation and implementation of these standards," Hunter emphasizes that these sustainable standards differ considerably from the outcome of the typical state-to-state negotiation process.[20] The level of expertise related to the elaboration and the implementation of international norms to limit the negative impact of projects financed by the World Bank Group thus requires the participation of non-state actors to a great extent.

This brief analysis of the World Bank Group demonstrates that this intergovernmental organization can play an important role with respect to the codification of foreign investors' responsibilities. Through its institutions, the World Bank Group is involved in various activities that seek to both increase economic development and promote foreign investment. While the entities within the institutions constituting this intergovernmental organization are vested with powers that broadly relate to this role, the identity shift toward a more sustainable development has prepared the ground for the development of international norms whose elaboration and implementation extensively rely on the participation of non-state actors.

2. The *IFC Performance Standards*

It is in this particular institutional context that the *IFC Performance Standards* must be analyzed. Combined with the *IFC Policy on Environmental and Social Sustainability* (*IFC Sustainability Policy*)[21] and the *IFC Access to Information Policy* (*IFC Information Policy*),[22] the *IFC Performance Standards* are part of a broader framework on sustainability.[23] While the two policies primarily concern responsibilities of the IFC, the *IFC Performance Standards* "are directed towards clients, providing guidance on how to identify risks and impacts, and are designed to help avoid, mitigate, and manage risks and impacts as a way of doing business

19 See World Bank, *A Guide, supra* note 5 at 3.

20 See Hunter, *supra* note 15 at 462–465.

21 *International Finance Corporation's Policy on Environmental and Social Sustainability*, 1 January 2012, online: IFC www.ifc.org/wps/wcm/connect/7540778049a792dcb87efaa8c6a8312a/SP_English_2012.pdf?MOD=AJPERES (accessed 26 March 2018) [*IFC Sustainability Policy 2012*].

22 *International Finance Corporation Access to Information Policy*, 1 January 2012, online: IFCpwww.ifc.org/wps/wcm/connect/98d8ae004997936f9b7bffb2b4b33c15/IFCPolicyDisclosureInformation.pdf?MOD=AJPERES (accessed 26 March 2018).

23 IFC, *IFC Sustainability Framework* (Washington: IFC, 2012) [IFC, *Sustainability Framework*].

in a sustainable way, including stakeholder engagement and disclosure obligations of the client in relation to project-level activities."[24] Further to requiring the assessment and management of environmental and social impacts, these standards cover the following issues: labour and working conditions; resource efficiency and pollution prevention; community health, safety and security; land acquisition and involuntary resettlement; biodiversity conservation and sustainable management of living natural resources; Indigenous peoples; and cultural heritage.[25]

The analysis below suggests that the *IFC Performance Standards* generate a genuine sense of obligation for the IFC and its clients, thus constituting an international legal norm. The epistemic community that initiated the elaboration of this international instrument benefited from the support of powerful actors and succeeded in reaching shared understandings regarding the adoption of an instrument whose observance is mandatory to obtain funding from the IFC (2.1). Moreover, the consistency of the *IFC Performance Standards* with the criteria of legality articulated in the interactional theory of international law fosters the legitimacy of this instrument (2.2). The extent to which the members of the community of practice seek to disseminate the *IFC Performance Standards* and ensure compliance with their content also constitutes a strong practice of legality (2.3).

2.1 Shared Understandings: Developing Mandatory Standards for Private Actors

In line with the general influence of specialists in the work of the World Bank Group discussed above, the intent to develop a set of standards for the assessment of projects' environmental and social risks was initially advanced by an *epistemic community* related to the IFC. Prior to the elaboration of the *IFC Performance Standards*, this organization relied on a set of *Safeguard Policies* that were inspired by the *Operational Policies*, which were applied within the World Bank Group for loans to public entities.[26] Further to an assessment of these policies that was published by the Office of the Compliance Advisor Ombudsman (CAO) in 2003, several experts acknowledged the need for the elaboration of a clear set of standards that specifically apply to private actors' activities.[27] As a result, the IFC staff prepared the first version of the *IFC Performance Standards*, which was approved by the Board of Directors in February 2006.[28] The central role of

24 *IFC Performance Standards 2012, supra* note 1, Overview at para 1.

25 *Ibid*, Performances Standards 1–8.

26 See IFC, *Safeguard Policies*, online: IFC www.ifc.org/wps/wcm/connect/Topics_Ext_Content/IFC_External_Corporate_Site/IFC+Sustainability/Our+Approach/Risk+Management/Performance+Standards/#pre2006 (accessed 26 March 2018).

27 CAO, *A Review of IFC's Safeguard Policies – Core Business: Achieving Consistent and Excellent Environmental and Social Outcomes* (Washington: World Bank, 2003) at 46; CAO, *Safeguard Policy Review Revisited: Has IFC Addressed the Recommendations of the CAO Safeguard Policy Review?*, online: CAO www.cao-ombudsman.org/howwework/advisor/documents/FINALCAOSafeguardPolicyReviewRevisited-Aug19.pdf (accessed 26 March 2018) at para 1 [CAO, *Safeguard Policy Review Revisited*].

28 *IFC Performance Standards 2006, supra* note 1.

experts is also evidenced through several assessments that led to the revision of this international instrument.[29] In a progress report on the revision process that was held from 2009 to 2011, the IFC stressed that

> [o]ngoing engagement with IFC staff has been a central part of the update process since its beginning and has helped to ensure that the proposed changes reflect the realities of IFC's business activities and incorporate lessons learned from the four years of experience.[30]

Ultimately, the current version of the *IFC Performance Standards* was submitted to the Board of Directors in April 2011[31] and became effective on January 1st, 2012.[32]

In addition to in-house experts and the necessary approval from the IFC Board of Directors, a broader *community of practice* participated in the elaboration of this instrument. In a document elaborated prior to launching the review of the *IFC Performance Standards*, the IFC referred to the participation of clients, business organizations, trade unions, public interest NGOs, United Nations (UN) agencies and other institutions of the World Bank Group in the consultation process.[33] A critical analysis of the discourses from the epistemic community and the members of this community of practice is a key step to assess the existence of shared understandings that underlie the *IFC Performance Standards*. Reports provided by the CAO and the IFC, various statements from international actors involved in the consultations that preceded the two versions of the standards and transcripts of semi-structured interviews conducted for the present research constitute a pool of discourses that are particularly relevant in this regard.

From the outset, the intent of experts involved in the elaboration of the *IFC Performance Standards* was to develop a flexible and "outcome-focused approach"

29 See e.g. IFC, *IFC's Policy and Performance Standards on Social and Environmental Sustainability and Policy on Disclosure of Information: Report on the First Three Years of Application* (29 July 2009), online: IFC www.ifc.org/wps/wcm/connect/90f2d88046b63bdaa9f7abb254bfb7d4/IFC_Third_Year_Report_PS_DP_.pdf?MOD=AJPERES (accessed 26 March 2018) [IFC, *Report on the First Three Years*]. A report provided by the Independent Evaluation Group is also mentioned in IFC, *Progress Report on IFC's Policy and Performance Standards on Social and Environmental Sustainability, and Policy on Disclosure of Information* (14 April 2010), online: IFC www.ifc.org/wps/wcm/connect/d29bff0049800841a2a0f2336b93d75f/Compounded%2BCODE_Progress%2BReport%2Bon%2BIFC%2527s%2BSustainability%2BFramework_Review%2Band%2BUpdate.pdf?MOD=AJPERES (accessed 26 March 2018) at paras 21–24 [IFC, *Progress Report – April 2010*].

30 IFC, *Progress Report – April 2010, ibid* at para 8.

31 IFC, *Update of IFC's Policy and Performance Standards on Environmental and Social Sustainability, and Access to Information Policy* (14 April 2011), online: IFC www.ifc.org/wps/wcm/connect/fca42a0049800aaaaba2fb336b93d75f/Board-Paper-IFC_SustainabilityFramework-2012.pdf?MOD=AJPERES (accessed 26 March 2018) at vi [IFC, *Update*].

32 *IFC Performance Standards 2012, supra* note 1.

33 IFC, *IFC Policy and Performance Standards on Social and Environmental Sustainability: Review and Update* (26 August 2009), online: IFC www.ifc.org/wps/wcm/connect/d9f9008049800946a606f6336b93d75f/PPS%2BOverview%2Bof%2BConsultation%2Band%2BEngagement_English.pdf?MOD=AJPERES (accessed 26 March 2018) at 6.

to assess clients' impact on the environment and society.[34] Nevertheless, several discourses point toward a will to elaborate a mandatory instrument for private actors. In this regard, the CAO expressly supported the position of the IFC, which "publicly stated that provisions of the [IFC Sustainability Policy] and the Performance Standards will be *mandatory.*"[35] When providing a response to NGOs that attended a consultation held in Turkey, the IFC also mentioned that "[w]hile developing the [*IFC Performance Standards*], the aim was to create a system that *holds clients accountable* for the impacts on the ground."[36]

Other members of the community of practice also emphasized the mandatory character of the *IFC Performance Standards* by underscoring the need to condition the IFC's funding to compliance with these standards and to elaborate an effective accountability mechanism in this regard. For example, with respect to the elaboration of the first version of this instrument, Friends of the Earth Japan and other public interest NGOs stressed that the IFC should clearly state that it "will not finance projects which do not meet the requirements of all Performance Standards."[37] An explicit support for the elaboration of a mandatory requirement beyond national frameworks was also mentioned during a consultation held in Russia to revise the *IFC Performance Standards.*[38] Even the United States emphasized

> the need for assurance of compliance at the time of Board consideration and strong client commitment to continued compliance, coupled with continued IFC oversight and the *availability of appropriate and timely remedies in the event of non-compliance, including possible IFC disengagement.*[39]

However, an important tension between capital-importing states and other members of the community of practice was discussed at great length by a participant in the research project:

34 See CAO, *IFC's Review of Safeguard Policies & Policy on Disclosure of Information*, online: CAO www.cao-ombudsman.org/howwework/advisor/documents/CAOcommentsonthefinalPPSdraftsFINAL-February22006.pdf (accessed 26 March 2018) at para 1.3; IFC, *Update, supra* note 31 at 14.

35 CAO, *Safeguard Policy Review Revisited, supra* note 27 at para 54 [emphasis added].

36 IFC, *Review and Update of the Policy and Performance Standards on Social and Environmental Sustainability and Policy on Disclosure of Information: Consultations' Report – Istanbul, Turkey* (22 June 2010), online: IFC www.ifc.org/wps/wcm/connect/8138608049800964a676f6336b93d75f/PS_Consultations_Istanbul.pdf?MOD=AJPERES (accessed 26 March 2018) at 2 [emphasis added].

37 Friends of the Earth Japan et al, *Comments on the IFC's Draft Policy on and Performance Standards on Social & Environmental Sustainability and the Draft Policy on Disclosure of Information* (25 November 2005), online: JACSES.org www.jacses.org/sdap/mof/gijiroku/CommentsonIFCSafeguard&Disclosure.pdf (accessed 26 March 2018).

38 See IFC, *Review and Update of the Policy and Performance Standards on Social and Environmental Sustainability and Policy on Disclosure of Information* (9 July 2010), online: IFC www.ifc.org/wps/wcm/connect/15cd8200498007f0a1cff3336b93d75f/Moscow%2BOpen%2BHouse%2BSummary.pdf?MOD=AJPERES (accessed 26 March 2018) at 3.

39 United States of America, *US Comments on IFC Policy and Performance Standards on Social and Environmental Sustainability and Policy on Disclosure of Information* (January 2010), online: US Department of the Treasury www.treasury.gov/resource-center/international/development-banks/Documents/jan2010_policy.pdf (accessed 26 March 2018) at 14 [emphasis added].

> It is in the interests of the donor countries to have a strict requirement on what we now consider international good practice – whether it is on financial management, procurement, environmental and social standards, anti-corruption, etc. – as possible. So, those who represent that constituency would like to have very strict conditionality on the lending. The borrowing countries often feel that. . . this imposes huge transaction costs and implementation challenges and delays, and requires things of them where they don't yet have the policy environment or the institutional capacity to implement them properly. . . . And, one of the political divisions, more generally, in our board was precisely along those lines. So there was a general group of member countries and their executive directors that have pushed for stronger requirements. And this was met with resistance by many from developing countries who said: "You're just overcomplicating things and making the finance almost impossible."

Such concerns ultimately point toward the existence of *relations of power* between the members of the community of practice. For example, a submission from a group of public interest NGOs mentioned that "IFC's approach to measuring effectiveness demonstrates a bias towards responding to the needs of IFC's private sector clients rather than, and perhaps to the detriment of, the concerns of local communities and the environment."[40] Similarly, one interviewee implicitly referred to such relations of power by underscoring that "[i]f only the wealthiest or the best functioning countries or companies can afford or be able to implement this type of standards, then you are effectively discriminating against lower capacity clients."[41] Considered in addition to the advantage granted to some capital-exporting states through the voting system of this organization, these statements expressly recognize the power held by private actors and some members of the IFC. Support from these powerful actors is an element that must thus be factored in when explaining the emergence of shared understandings regarding the mandatory character of the *IFC Performance Standards.*

The consideration of the process through which this instrument was elaborated, as well as the critical discourse analysis of various statements and reports that emanated from this elaboration process, demonstrate that the *IFC Performance Standards* rely on shared understandings with respect to their mandatory character. Despite a certain degree of reluctance from some capital-importing states, the epistemic community that initiated the elaboration process was supported by powerful actors involved in a community of practice to develop environmental and social standards that must be followed by foreign investors operating projects funded by the IFC.

40 Center for International Environmental Law, *Submission by Civil Society Organizations to the International Finance Corporation: Commenting on the Social and Environmental Sustainability Policy, Performance Standards and Disclosure* (11 March 2010), online: Halifax Initiative www.halifaxinitiative.org/sites/halifaxinitiative.org/files/Civil%20Society%20Submission%20to%20IFC%2011Mar10.pdf (accessed 26 March 2018) at 2.

41 Interview 7.

2.2 Criteria of Legality: Provisions Fostering the Instrument's Legitimacy

In addition to observing the interactions between international actors that participated in the elaboration of the *IFC Performance Standards*, a consideration of the extent to which their content meets a set of criteria of legality is an integral part of a nuanced analysis of their normative character. This section demonstrates that the *IFC Performance Standards*, when considered with the *IFC Sustainability Policy* and other documents elaborated under the auspices of the IFC, meet all the criteria of legality included in the interactional theory of international law. This international norm thus induces a high level of legitimacy that undoubtedly contributes to the sense of obligation that it generates.

Like several instruments included in Part II of this book, the *IFC Performance Standards* can be considered as meeting the criterion of *promulgation* without being adopted as a formal international agreement. As mentioned above, these standards were approved by the IFC's Board of Directors before becoming applicable to investments and advisory clients of the IFC. Moreover, in addition to being included in a publication that details the sustainability framework applied by this organization,[42] a summary of the IFC's environmental and social due diligence process mentions that a copy of the *IFC Performance Standards* is provided to each client of this organization.[43] Despite their informal character under international law, the *IFC Performance Standards* are thus available to the public and the private actors that they concern.

Even if the *IFC Sustainability Policy* stipulates that the application of the *IFC Performance Standards* relies on a categorization based on the magnitude of risks and impacts of each project,[44] nothing in the content of this international instrument amounts to a failure to meet the criterion of *generality*. In fact, when describing its overall approach, the *IFC Sustainability Policy* provides that "environmental and social due diligence applies to *all IFC investment activities.*"[45] Moreover, the *IFC Performance Standards* stress that the requirement to assess and manage environmental and social risks included in Performance Standard 1 "applies to *all projects* that have environmental and social risks and impacts" and that "[t]he requirements section of each Performance Standard applies to *all activities financed under the project*, unless otherwise noted in the specific limitations described in each paragraph."[46] In other words, despite the categorization that is used to differentiate the application of the *IFC Performance Standards*, there is a presumption that no client can avoid the requirement to address the environmental and social impact of its project.

42 See IFC, *Sustainability Framework*, *supra* note 23.

43 IFC, *Understanding the IFC's Environmental and Social Due Diligence Process*, online: IFC www.ifc.org/wps/wcm/connect/b58ead804942ee5da7a5ff4f5ddda76e/IFC+Process.pdf?MOD=AJPERES (accessed 26 March 2018).

44 *IFC Sustainability Policy 2012*, *supra* note 21 at paras 40–44.

45 *Ibid* at para 20 [emphasis added].

46 *IFC Performance Standards 2012*, *supra* note 1, Overview at para 4 [emphasis added].

Several provisions of the *IFC Performance Standards*, combined with the elaboration of other documents by this intergovernmental organization, also contribute to the *clarity* of this international instrument. While the application of these standards relies on broad concepts such as "area of influence" and "Free, Prior, and Informed Consent," these terms are extensively described in the standards themselves.[47] Another aspect of the *IFC Performance Standards* that contributes to the clarity of this instrument is the express reference to international agreements.[48] Furthermore, the IFC developed a set of Guidance Notes with a view to offering "helpful guidance on the requirements contained in the Performance Standards, including reference materials, and on good sustainability practices to improve project performance."[49] The *Environmental, Health and Safety Guidelines* were also elaborated by the IFC as technical reference documents with general and industry-specific examples of good international industry practice.[50] Taken as a whole, these elements undeniably enhance the clarity of the *IFC Performance Standards.*

While unanticipated changes in the provisions of an international instrument can affect its legitimacy, the application of a revised version of the *IFC Performance Standards* since January 2012 does not pose any serious issues as far as the criterion of *constancy* is concerned. Of course, the revision process has led to the inclusion of important elements within the provisions of the *IFC Performance Standards* such as climate change, human rights, supply chain management, stakeholder engagement, as well as Free, Prior, and Informed Consent for Indigenous peoples.[51] However, according to the IFC, "most of the revised language represents either clarifications or more explicit reference to approaches that have become recognized as standard practice in recent years."[52] The adoption of the revised version of the *IFC Performance Standards* must thus be seen as reflecting the evolution of the practice surrounding this instrument rather than a threat to the criterion of constancy.

None of the instruments that are analyzed in Part II of this book encounters any specific issue with respect to the *avoidance of a retroactive application.* The absence of provisions that relate to the temporal application of the *IFC Performance Standards* thus echoes a feature that is found in other international instruments and ensures that these standards live up to the requirements of this

47 For "area of influence," see *ibid*, Performance Standard 1 at para 8. For "Free, Prior, and Informed Consent," see *ibid*, Performance Standard 7 at paras 13–17.

48 See *ibid*, Performance Standard 2 at para 2; Performance Standard 6 at para 1; Performance Standard 8 at para 1.

49 *International Finance Corporation's Guidance Note: Performance Standards on Environmental and Social Sustainability*, 1 January 2012, online: IFC www.ifc.org/wps/wcm/connect/e280ef804a0256609709ffd1a5d13d27/GN_English_2012_Full-Document.pdf?MOD=AJPERES (accessed 26 March 2018). These guidance notes are mentioned in *IFC Performance Standards 2012, ibid*, Overview at para 8.

50 *Environmental, Health, and Safety General Guidelines*, 30 April 2007, online: IFC www.ifc.org/wps/wcm/connect/554e8d80488658e4b76af76a6515bb18/Final%2B-%2BGeneral%2BEHS%2BGuidelines.pdf?MOD=AJPERES (accessed 26 March 2018). See also *IFC Performance Standards 2012, ibid*, Overview at para 6.

51 For a summary of these changes, see IFC, *Update, supra* note 31 at 6–13 and Annex A.

52 *Ibid* at 4.

criterion. Moreover, the IFC explicitly provides that the application of the 2012 version of the *IFC Performance Standards* is limited to investments and advisory clients whose projects went through the initial credit review process after 1 January 2012.[53] Along the same lines, the first version of this international instrument only concerns investments and advisory clients that went through the same process between 30 April 2006 and 31 December 2011.[54]

Although the identification of "all relevant environmental and social risks and impacts of the project"[55] can appear as a daunting task, at least four elements of the *IFC Performance Standards* ensure that this international norm does *not ask the impossible*. First, the use of a fairly detailed concept of "area of influence" at Performance Standard 1 contributes to limit the scope of the requirements to aspects that are related to clients' activities.[56] Second, the requirement to elaborate an environmental and social management system is balanced with an explicit recognition that clients cannot control the actions of governments and third parties.[57] In this regard, clients are required to "identify the different entities involved and the roles they play, the corresponding risks they present to the client, and opportunities to collaborate with these third parties in order to help achieve environmental and social outcomes that are consistent with the Performance Standards."[58] Third, several provisions of this instrument seek to ensure that its requirements are commensurate with the nature and the scale of the project. For example, such a concern is included in provisions pertaining to the establishment of an environmental and social management system,[59] the elaboration of management programs,[60] monitoring requirements[61] and stakeholder engagement.[62] Fourth, the *IFC Performance Standards* expressly acknowledge potential conflicts between these standards and national legislation, without requiring clients to simultaneously comply with two conflicting norms. For example, with respect to labour standards, Performance Standard 2 encourages clients to carry out their operations in a way that remains consistent with the standard's intent, "without contravening applicable law."[63] Taken as a whole, these elements prevent the imposition of requirements that cannot realistically be met by the IFC's clients.

53 IFC, *Environmental and Social Performance Standards and Guidance Notes*, online: IFC www.ifc.org/wps/wcm/connect/topics_ext_content/ifc_external_corporate_site/ifc+sustainability/our+approach/risk+management/performance+standards/environmental+and+social+performance+standards+and+guidance+notes (accessed 26 March 2018).
54 See *ibid*.
55 See *IFC Performance Standards 2012, supra* note 1, Performance Standard 1 at para 7.
56 *Ibid*, Performance Standard 1 at para 8.
57 *Ibid*, Performance Standard 1 at para 2.
58 *Ibid*, Performance Standard 1 at para 2.
59 *Ibid*, Performance Standard 1 at para 5.
60 *Ibid*, Performance Standard 1 at paras 14–15.
61 *Ibid*, Performance Standard 1 at para 22.
62 *Ibid*, Performance Standard 1 at para 25.
63 *Ibid*, Performance Standard 2 at para 16.

The legitimacy of the *IFC Performance Standards* is also strengthened by the *avoidance of an inherent contradiction* that characterizes several informal international instruments previously analyzed. In addition to the absence of any direct contradictions between its provisions, the application of the *IFC Performance Standards* appears as a coherent means to achieve the IFC's goal of enhancing sustainable development. According to the *IFC Sustainability Policy*, the "IFC believes that an important component of achieving positive development outcomes is the environmental and social sustainability of these activities."[64] In this regard, paragraph 24 of this policy ensures that the *IFC Performance Standards* are used in a way that contributes to this overarching belief:

> IFC's agreements pertaining to the financing of clients' activities include specific provisions with which clients undertake to comply. *These include complying with the applicable requirements of the Performance Standards* and specific conditions included in action plans, as well as relevant provisions for environmental and social reporting, and supervision visits by IFC staff or representatives, as appropriate. If the client fails to comply with its environmental and social commitments as expressed in the legal agreements and associated documents, IFC will work with the client to bring it back into compliance, and if the client fails to reestablish compliance, IFC will exercise its rights and remedies, as appropriate.[65]

To put it differently, the absence of an express voluntary character to the observance of the *IFC Performance Standards* ensures a higher level of consistency with the ambit of the IFC than what is found in several informal international instruments codifying foreign investors' responsibilities.

Finally, the existence of various procedural devices to ensure the consideration of significant instances of non-compliance with the *IFC Performance Standards* is in line with the criterion of *congruence*. Beyond the requirement for each client to establish a grievance mechanism "to receive and facilitate resolution of affected Communities' concerns and grievances about the client's environmental and social performance,"[66] the IFC is closely involved in determining compliance of its clients' operations with the *IFC Performance Standards*.[67] Among other tools, the IFC relies on the *Environmental and Social Review Procedures Manual*, which "provides a structured approach for [IFC's Environment, Social and Governance Department] to monitoring and recording client performance."[68]

64 *IFC Sustainability Policy 2012, supra* note 21 at para 1.

65 *Ibid* at para 24 [emphasis added].

66 See *IFC Performance Standards 2012, supra* note 1, Performance Standard 1 at para 35. Grievance mechanisms established by clients are also mentioned at Performance Standard 2 (at para 20), Performance Standard 4 (at para 12) and Performance Standard 5 (at para 11).

67 See *IFC Sustainability Policy 2012, supra* note 21 at para 45.

68 *Environmental and Social Review Procedures Manual*, October 2016, online: IFC www.ifc.org/wps/wcm/connect/d0db8c41-cfb0–45e9-b66a-522c88f270a5/ESRP_Oct2016.pdf?MOD=AJPERES (accessed 26 March 2018), 1 at 1.1.

The work of the CAO is also a key element that contributes to congruence with respect to the *IFC Performance Standards*. Constituted as an independent recourse and accountability mechanism of the IFC and the MIGA for environmental and social concerns, the CAO assumes three interdependent roles (*i.e.* dispute resolution, compliance and advisor).[69] Of course, it must be noted that this entity "is not an appeals court or a legal enforcement mechanism, nor is CAO a substitute for international court systems or court systems in host countries."[70] Moreover, the *CAO Operational Guidelines* recall that engaging in the dispute resolution process that it provides to communities and individuals affected by IFC's projects is "a voluntary decision [requiring] agreement between the complainant and client."[71] While such restraints fail to adequately determine compliance with the *IFC Performance Standards* in a way that would meet this criterion of legality, the compliance role of the CAO nevertheless contributes to congruence between the provisions of this instrument and official action. More specifically, without focusing primarily on clients' operations, the CAO compliance mechanism assesses how the IFC assures itself "of the performance of its business activity or advice, as well as whether the outcomes of the business activity or advice are consistent with the intent of the relevant policy provisions."[72] According to the *CAO Operational Guidelines*, the compliance investigation criteria include "policies, *Performance Standards*, guidelines, procedures, and requirements whose violation might lead to adverse environmental and/or social outcomes."[73] In other words, in addition to the monitoring of each project that is conducted by the IFC, the CAO ensures that the IFC effectively applies the *IFC Performance Standards* to tackle significant instances of non-compliance.

By meeting all the criteria of legality that are included in the interactional theory of international law, the *IFC Performance Standards* appear as a highly legitimate international norm. Even if they are not enshrined in a formal international agreement, these standards can generate a considerable level of adherence from international actors. While such legitimacy is a necessary condition for any international norm to evolve as a legal norm, the *IFC Performance Standards* are in a good standing to be considered as such.

2.3 Practice of Legality: Interactions Geared Toward Compliance

An international instrument relying on shared understandings with respect to its mandatory character and meeting a whole set of criteria of legality is in a good position to be applied according to a practice of legality. Interestingly, the IFC depicts

69 See *CAO Operational Guidelines*, March 2013, online: CAO www.cao-ombudsman.org/documents/CAOOperationalGuidelines_2013.pdf (accessed 26 March 2018) at para 1.2.
70 See *ibid* at para 1.1.
71 *Ibid* at para 3.1.
72 See *ibid* at para 4.1.
73 *Ibid* at para 4.3 [emphasis added].

itself as being at the "centre of a global *community of practice* in an effort to promote consistent implementation of the Performance Standards by all users."[74] With a view to assessing the nature of the practice that has emerged from the *IFC Performance Standards*, this section examines the extent to which this instrument has been included in other initiatives that seek to codify foreign investors' responsibilities. Furthermore, a critical discourse analysis of various reports from the IFC and the CAO, as well as transcripts from semi-structured interviews, allows concluding that the community of practice surrounding the *IFC Performance Standards* implements this international instrument in a way that is binding for the IFC and its clients.

This initiative is not extensively referred to in other international instruments adopted by intergovernmental organizations that are considered in this book. In fact, beyond a vague reference to "performance standards required by institutions that support overseas investments" in a commentary of the *Guiding Principles on Business and Human Rights*,[75] intergovernmental organizations are not expressly taking into account the contribution of the *IFC Performance Standards* with respect to the broader codification process of foreign investors' responsibilities. However, an important part of the practice that characterizes the implementation of the *IFC Performance Standards* is the uptake of these standards within the World Bank Group and international financial institutions. In fact, the *Operational Policy 4.03 – Performance Standards for Private Sector Activities* (*Operational Policy 4.03*) provides that

> [t]he eight IFC Performance Standards have been adopted by the Bank . . . for application to Bank support for projects (or components thereof) that are designed, owned, constructed and/or operated by a Private Entity . . . in lieu of the World Bank's safeguard policies.[76]

The inclusion of the *IFC Performance Standards* as Exhibit III of the *Equator Principles* also suggests a wide practice amidst the financial industry.[77]

Beyond these references, the discourses of the community of practice related to the *IFC Performance Standards* strongly support the idea that this international norm is implemented according to a practice of legality. In fact, several reports from the IFC focus on the need for its clients to comply with these standards. For example, the IFC considered the Environmental and Social Review Procedure as describing "steps to be taken in case of *noncompliance with the Performance Standards* during the implementation phase."[78] As far as

74 IFC, *Update, supra* note 31 at vi [emphasis added].

75 Special Representative of the Secretary-General on the issue of human rights and transnational corporations and other business enterprises, *Guiding Principles on Business and Human Rights: Implementing the United Nations 'Protect, Respect and Remedy' Framework*, 2011, UN Doc A/HRC/17/31, Guiding Principle 2, Commentary.

76 *World Bank Performance Standards, supra* note 3 at para 2.

77 *Equator Principles*, 4 June 2013, online: Equator Principles http://equator-principles.com/wp-content/uploads/2017/03/equator_principles_III.pdf (accessed 26 March 2018), Exhibit III.

78 IFC, *Report on the First Three Years, supra* note 29 at 6 [emphasis added].

the reports of the CAO are concerned, several excerpts unambiguously underscore its role to ensure that the IFC applies the *IFC Performance Standards* as a binding international norm. In its annual report published in 2007, the CAO mentioned that

> [t]he compliance role has responsibility to make *judgments* about whether IFC and MIGA are in *compliance with relevant standards* and guidelines on projects that have prompted complaints or have raised concerns with the World Bank President, IFC/MIGA management, or the CAO.[79]

In another annual report, the CAO addressed the IFC's assessment of a project in Kazakhstan by stressing "IFC's *obligations* to assure itself of project performance."[80] Moreover, with respect to a mining project in Peru, the CAO emphasized that "although efforts were made by IFC to supervise Quellaveco's *compliance with evolving environmental and social standards*, the lack of clarity around the company's *obligations* made it difficult to deal with issues that emerged during IFC's supervision of the project."[81]

The legal character of the practice surrounding the *IFC Performance Standards* is also mentioned in the discourses of individuals working for intergovernmental organizations involved in the codification of foreign investors' responsibilities. Interestingly, one interviewee warned against the lack of flexibility that the inclusion of the *IFC Performance Standards* in a formal source of international law would entail:

> I would gather that this is one of the challenges in translating it into formalized law. Because, internally, when we engage with our clients, we build an enormous amount on case practice, and consistency of professional judgments across regions and across sectors. And we have internal peer review meetings and discussions. I get called in . . . to essentially advise on interpretation issues, quite frequently. And this would be difficult to replicate, I think, in a legal framework.[82]

While depicting the IFC's approach as avoiding a "legalistic approach,"[83] the same interviewee nevertheless claimed that the practice surrounding the *IFC Performance Standards* remains "legally binding":

79 CAO, *2006–07 Annual Report* (Washington: CAO, 2007) at 3 [emphasis added].

80 CAO, *2008–09 Annual Report* (Washington: CAO, 2009) at 19 [emphasis added].

81 CAO, *Advisory Note: IFC's Policy and Performance Standards on Social and Environmental Sustainability and Disclosure Policy – Commentary on IFC's Progress Report on the First 18 Months of Application* (17 December 2007), online: CAO www.cao-ombudsman.org/howwework/advisor/documents/CAOpublicstatementIFCperformancestandards121707.pdf (accessed 26 March 2018) at 4 [emphasis added].

82 Interview 7.

83 *Ibid.*

> When we invest in a company or lend to a company, [the *IFC Performance Standards*] become *legally binding contractual obligations*. So we have our lawyers who write legal contracts with the companies we invest in. They commit to following these standards. And if they don't, well there's obviously different ways in which we try to bring them back into *compliance*. Sometimes, that's a gradual process, sometimes it's more absolute. . . . If it's absolutely not working, we can withdraw and require a repayment of the loan.[84]

Along the same lines, another interviewee mentioned that "all institutional lenders are *obliged* to comply with [the *IFC Performance Standards*]," despite their "soft law" character.[85]

In line with the other international instruments considered in this book, the discourses pertaining to the implementation of the *IFC Performance Standards* also reproduce inherent *relations of power*. For example, regarding its role as an ombudsman that addresses complaints from communities and individuals affected by a project, the CAO recognized that "[l]ack of trust, respect, and *imbalances of power* often lay at the heart of the problem, rather than evidence presented by one side or the other."[86] An audit of IFC's environmental and social due diligence in a specific project conducted by the CAO also emphasized that "commercial pressures were allowed to prevail and overly influence the categorization of the project."[87] Beyond this implicit recognition that private actors often hold more power than other members of the community of practice, the IFC expressly acknowledged that providing a comprehensive view of performance requirements early in the engagement process "is of critical importance for private sector clients that need a high level of certainty on roles, responsibilities, and performance expectations before entering into a financial transaction."[88] In other words, the practice of legality that has emerged around the *IFC Performance Standards* is ultimately perceived as being in line with the interests of powerful private actors that enter into contractual relations with the IFC.

The reference to the *IFC Performance Standards* in the contracts that are signed between the IFC and its clients is a key element of the practice of legality surrounding this instrument. This inclusion sharply contrasts with the practice of other initiatives analyzed in this book. Of course, given that the terms of these contractual agreements do not imply any requirements for other international actors, an instance of non-compliance with the standards by an actor that is not a client of the IFC cannot be addressed by this institution. Nevertheless, this should not be considered as a reason to diminish the legal character of the

84 *Ibid* [emphasis added].
85 Interview 8 [emphasis added].
86 CAO, *The CAO at 10: Annual Report FY2010 and Review FY2000–10* (Washington: CAO, 2010) at 28 [emphasis added].
87 See CAO, *Annual Report 2011* (Washington: CAO, 2011) at 34–35.
88 IFC, *Report on the First Three Years, supra* note 29 at 21.

practice surrounding the *IFC Performance Standards*. Regardless of the scope of actors to whom these standards are applicable, it is the fact that members of the community of practice perceive observance of these standards as being mandatory in order to operate a project funded by the IFC that shows the legal character of this practice. Moreover, recalling the references to the *IFC Performance Standards* in the *Operational Policy 4.03* and the *Equator Principles*, it is here submitted that the practice regarding the *IFC Performance Standards* somehow reaches beyond these contractual agreements and that this instrument exists as an international norm.

In sum, in addition to a considerable uptake by the World Bank Group and international financial institutions, the discourses pertaining to the implementation of the *IFC Performance Standards* suggest that members of the community of practice perceive this instrument as bearing a binding character. Observance of these standards is constantly considered as mandatory for IFC's clients and several discourses acknowledge an obligation for the IFC to ensure that private actors comply with them. While this implementation process inevitably encompasses relations of power between actors involved, the recognition that predictable performance expectations remain in the interests of powerful clients of the IFC contributes to perpetuate the practice of legality that characterizes the *IFC Performance Standards*.

Conclusion

Even if their application is limited to the private actors that operate projects funded by the IFC, the *IFC Performance Standards* remain an integral part of the evolving codification of foreign investors' responsibilities by intergovernmental organizations. Within a broader context of neoliberal globalization, this normative development emerges from an important shift of identity that paved the way to the consideration of environmental and social sustainability in the World Bank Group's operations. Moreover, without being considered as a formal source of international law, an interactional account of the *IFC Performance Standards* demonstrates that this instrument has been elaborated and implemented as an international legal norm that generates a sense of obligation for the IFC and its clients. The initial intent of an epistemic community to elaborate standards applicable to private actors and whose observance is mandatory to obtain funding from the IFC has benefited from the support of powerful members of the community of practice. In addition to these shared understandings, the *IFC Performance Standards* meet all the criteria of legality that contribute to enhance the legitimacy of international norms. Finally, while a predictable application of such standards can be perceived as being in line with the interests of the IFC's powerful clients, several discourses related to the implementation of the *IFC Performance Standards* evidence a practice of legality.

Conclusion

A contextualized assessment of foreign investors' responsibilities that reaches beyond the formal character of instruments under international law and that expressly takes into account the interactions of actors involved in the international lawmaking process provides a mixed response to the question that was asked in the introduction of this book. In a context of neoliberal globalization, the extent to which the processes of elaboration and implementation of foreign investors' responsibilities by intergovernmental organizations have reached the realm of legality is uneven and extensively driven by the interests of the most powerful actors.

This book relies on the assumption that an analysis of the international phenomenon at hand requires a consideration of normative developments and relations of power between international actors. The previous chapters thus rely on an analytical framework that explicitly combines legal pluralism from international law and critical constructivism from international relations theory. This framework ensures a consideration of the normative character of initiatives adopted beyond the strict control of states, as well as relations of power involved in the mutual constitution of international actors and international norms. An interdisciplinary character is also present in the methodology, which expressly draws on interpretation in international law and critical discourse analysis. In addition to scrutinizing the content of various international instruments and decisions from international investment arbitration tribunals, this methodology provides concrete evidence of relations of power inherent to normative developments that relate to the codification of foreign investors' responsibilities.

A macro-level analysis advances some elements of the mixed response to the research question. With a view to situating this evolving codification process within the broader context of neoliberal globalization, this analysis focuses on the normative integration of foreign investors' responsibilities in international investment law. Functionally differentiated normative orders covering different areas of foreign investors' responsibilities – *i.e.* human rights, environmental protection, labour rights and anti-corruption – have emerged in parallel to efforts to protect foreign investment. However, the extent to which these responsibilities are included in international investment agreements and considered in decisions from international investment arbitration tribunals remains fragmented. These responsibilities are often included in international investment agreements only through hortatory provisions with respect to human rights, environmental protection and labour rights. Moreover, the consideration of the negative impact of foreign investors' activities in these areas by international investment arbitration tribunals has been marked by an inconsistent approach, thus suggesting a rather weak normative integration. By contrast, the stronger provisions pertaining to the prohibition of corruption in international investment agreements and the consistent recognition that foreign investors resorting to corruption lose their ability to seek redress under international investment arbitration point toward a stronger normative integration of foreign investors' responsibilities for this area.

Enter relations of power and diverging interests that are inherent to the international investment lawmaking process. The macro-level analysis presented in this book emphasizes that foreign investors and capital-exporting states hold structural power over other actors involved in the elaboration of rules governing international investment. Moreover, a critical analysis of statements submitted through consultation processes piloted by intergovernmental organizations suggests that discourses of international actors reproduce relations of power. Discourses pertaining to the elaboration of foreign investors' responsibilities in the areas of human rights, environmental protection and labour rights are characterized by hardly reconcilable positions. While public interest nongovernmental organizations (NGOs) and states hosting considerable levels of foreign direct investment stocks generally support the elaboration of international instruments whose observance is not merely voluntary, their demands meet a strong opposition from the majority of private interest NGOs, foreign investors, capital-exporting states and some intergovernmental organizations. By contrast, foreign investors, private interest NGOs and capital-exporting states unambiguously support the elaboration of effective legal norms to prohibit corruption in order to level the playing field and prevent undue commercial advantages to actors that resort to corruption. Although the support for anti-corruption initiatives from public interest NGOs, capital-importing states and intergovernmental organizations is also notable, this support is primarily marked by concerns that reach beyond competitive issues.

In other words, this macro-level analysis suggests that foreign investors' responsibilities are not totally absent from international investment law. Even if the integration of these responsibilities remains generally weak and uneven, provisions found in some international investment agreements and the consideration of the negative impact of foreign investors' activities by some tribunals when assessing the legality of a measure adopted by a respondent state must be acknowledged. It is thus more accurate to address the normative integration of foreign investors' responsibilities in international investment law as being fragmented rather than non-existent. Supplementing a legal pluralist approach and the interpretation of primary sources with a critical constructivist approach and a critical discourse analysis also suggests that this fragmentation remains consistent with the interests of the most powerful actors involved in the international investment lawmaking process.

The analysis of the extent to which international norms setting foreign investors' responsibilities have evolved from social norms to legal norms is conducted in previous chapters through a micro-level analysis of instruments elaborated and implemented under the auspices of intergovernmental organizations. By drawing on the interactional theory of international law – which also combines legal pluralism and (critical) constructivism – and an interdisciplinary methodology, this book allows positioning each instrument on a continuum that varies from social norms to legal norms. With a view to determining which instruments currently produce a sense of obligation and have reached the threshold of legality, these findings are here presented from the instrument that carries the weakest normative character to the initiative that generates the strongest sense of obligation.

Among all the norms considered for present purposes, the instrument that bears the lowest normative character is the *Norms on the Responsibilities of Transnational Corporations and other Business Enterprises with Regard to Human Rights* (*UN Norms*)[1] that were adopted by the Sub-Commission on the Promotion and the Protection of Human Rights (Sub-Commission) of the United Nations (UN). Even if the experts from the Sub-Commission initially intended to develop a binding instrument to address the issue of business and human rights, the strong opposition from powerful foreign investors and capital-exporting states prevented the emergence of shared understandings with respect to the legal character of this instrument. Aspects related to their promulgation and their content also fail to meet several criteria of legality, thus negatively impacting the ability of the *UN Norms* to be considered as a legitimate instrument. The brief practice that occurred shortly after the refusal of the UN Commission on Human Rights to acknowledge any legal standing to this initiative was also marked by efforts from powerful actors to prevent the use of the *UN Norms* as the basis for a binding instrument, thus keeping this initiative far below the threshold of legality. Now, given the absence of a current practice regarding the *UN Norms*, one wonders if this instrument is still considered as enunciating standards of appropriate behavior and constituting an international norm at all.

The contribution of the International Labour Organization (ILO) to the evolving codification of foreign investors' responsibilities has also led to the elaboration and the implementation of an instrument that appears as a relatively weak social norm. From the outset, the norm entrepreneurs that pushed for the elaboration of the *Tripartite Declaration of Principles concerning Multinational Enterprises and Social Policy* (*ILO Tripartite Declaration*)[2] sought to adopt an instrument whose observance would remain non-mandatory. Even if capital-importing states and workers' associations generally supported the negotiation of a formal international agreement on this matter, the opposition from several capital-exporting states and representatives of employers posed a major obstacle to reach shared

1 *Norms on the Responsibilities of Transnational Corporations and other Business Enterprises with Regard to Human Rights*, 2003, UN Doc E/CN.4/Sub.2/2003/12/Rev.2.

2 For the current version, see *Tripartite Declaration of Principles concerning Multinational Enterprises and Social Policy*, March 2017, online: ILO www.ilo.org/empent/Publications/WCMS_094386/lang--en/index.htm (accessed 26 March 2018).

understandings with respect to the *ILO Tripartite Declaration*'s legal nature. Lack of clarity related to some provisions, requirements that can be perceived as asking the impossible of foreign investors, an inherent contradiction between the aim of the instrument and its express voluntary character, as well as the absence of a procedural mechanism to properly determine lack of compliance with the provisions of the declaration all constitute inconsistencies with the criteria of legality. At the end of the day, even if the *ILO Tripartite Declaration* provides standards of appropriate behavior, the weakness of this social norm is evidenced through a practice characterized by the rejection of its legal character by many powerful actors and a general lack of awareness.

The analysis provided in the previous chapters also allows identifying some widely disseminated international norms that nevertheless fail to generate a sense of obligation. In this regard, the UN Global Compact[3] has always been considered as a voluntary initiative primarily geared toward dialogue. Shared understandings in which this initiative is anchored were shaped by private interest NGOs and some states that joined the UN Secretary-General to support the elaboration of a voluntary initiative. The provisions of the UN Global Compact also imply considerable issues with most of the criteria of legality (*i.e.* clarity, constancy, not asking the impossible, absence of contradiction and congruence). While the broad awareness of the UN Global Compact ensures a stronger normative character than the *ILO Tripartite Declaration*, the worrisome disengagement of participants beyond their initial commitment and the repeated voluntary character of the initiative prevent the emergence of a practice of legality and lead to a fairly weak social norm.

A more recent initiative endorsed by the Human Rights Council of the UN bears a stronger normative character than the UN Global Compact. Even if the *Guiding Principles on Business and Human Rights* (*UN Guiding Principles*)[4] undeniably constitute an international social norm, some aspects of their provisions and the interactions that they generate suggest a strong potential to evolve closer to the threshold of legality. In fact, while some public interest NGOs and capital-importing states advocated for the elaboration of a formal international agreement, the support provided by foreign investors and capital-exporting states extensively depended upon the initial intent of the Special Representative of the Secretary-General on the issue of human rights and transnational corporations and other business enterprises not to adopt any new legal obligations. The overwhelming majority of interactions within the community of practice implementing this international instrument also demonstrates an unambiguous will to avoid establishing a practice of legality for the moment. However, the highly legitimate character of the *UN Guiding Principles* that results from their consistency with almost all the criteria of legality, the absence

3 United Nations Global Compact, online: United Nations Global Compact www.unglobalcompact.org/AboutTheGC/TheTenPrinciples/index.html (accessed 26 March 2018).

4 Special Representative of the Secretary-General on the issue of human rights and transnational corporations and other business enterprises, *Guiding Principles on Business and Human Rights: Implementing the United Nations 'Protect, Respect and Remedy' Framework*, 2011, UN Doc A/HRC/17/31.

of an express voluntary character to the corporate responsibility to respect human rights that they establish and some aspects of their surrounding practice that make the consideration of this instrument unavoidable can be considered as the foundation of a potential sense of obligation.

An interactional account of the *Guidelines for Multinational Enterprises* (*Guidelines*)[5] adopted by the Organisation for Economic Co-operation and Development (OECD) also suggests that this instrument embodies a widely disseminated international social norm whose normative character is even stronger than the *UN Guiding Principles*. The constant disagreement between the various international actors involved in the elaboration and revision of these guidelines with respect to their legal nature demonstrates the absence of shared understandings to establish a legal norm. What is more, despite an express voluntary character that remains in tension with the ambit of this instrument and the absence of a procedure that requires the determination of a lack of compliance with the *OECD Guidelines*, this instrument meets most of the criteria that characterize legitimate international norms. Even if the practice surrounding the *OECD Guidelines* is characterized by a persistent emphasis on the voluntary observance of the recommendations included in this instrument and generally fails to generate a practice of legality, the extensive reliance on the National Contact Points to address specific instances pertaining to the application of these guidelines contributes to make this instrument a stronger social norm than the *UN Guiding Principles*.

The last international instrument considered as a social norm in the previous chapters is the *United Nations Convention Against Corruption* (*UNCAC*).[6] Despite its formal character under international law, the *UNCAC* fails to generate a general sense of obligation and thus cannot be considered as a proper international legal norm according to an interactional account. Although the norm entrepreneurs and the international actors that contributed to the elaboration of this instrument agreed to negotiate a formal international agreement to hold legal persons liable for various offences related to corruption, the shared understandings underlying the *UNCAC* are marked by a will from several states to establish flexible standards. The legitimacy of this international agreement is also negatively impacted by several weak provisions that do not sit well with the ambit of tackling the scourge of corruption and a mechanism for the review of implementation that fails to adequately address significant instances of non-compliance. The emergence of a practice that is primarily oriented toward learning and sharing of best practices also points toward the absence of a sense of obligation emanating from this international norm. Even if the *UNCAC* is promulgated as a formal international agreement and relies on a vast practice, this instrument can only be perceived as a strong, yet social international norm.

5 For the most recent version, see *Declaration on International Investment and Multinational Enterprises*, 25 May 2011, Doc No C/MIN(2011)11/FINAL (2011), Annex 1.

6 *United Nations Convention Against Corruption*, 31 October 2003, 2349 UNTS 41 (entered into force 14 December 2005).

By contrast, three initiatives considered in this book appear as proper international legal norms in the sense of the interactional theory of international law. The first initiative lies in an informal instrument adopted under the auspices of the International Finance Corporation (IFC), namely the *International Finance Corporation's Performance Standards on Environmental and Social Sustainability* (*IFC Performance Standards*).[7] These standards result from the work of an epistemic community that intended to elaborate an instrument whose observance is mandatory for clients operating projects funded by this institution of the World Bank Group. Despite some opposition from capital-importing states, these mandatory standards were supported by more powerful actors and thus rely on strong shared understandings with respect to their mandatory character. When considered in light of accompanying documents, the *IFC Performance Standards* also meet all the criteria of legality advanced in the interactional theory of international law. Furthermore, the various discourses related to the implementation of these standards render a practice of legality that focuses on the need to ensure that IFC's clients comply with these standards. Despite their informal character under international law, the *IFC Performance Standards* thus appear as an international legal norm that produces a genuine sense of obligation for the IFC and its clients.

Finally, the *Convention on Combating Bribery of Foreign Public Officials in International Business Transactions* (*OECD Anti-Bribery Convention*)[8] and the *Recommendation of the Council for Further Combating Bribery of Foreign Public Officials in International Business Transactions* (*OECD 2009 Recommendation*)[9] adopted by the OECD are two international legal norms that relate to the codification of foreign investors' responsibilities. Since an initial push from the United States and powerful private actors to elaborate an international agreement establishing the liability of legal persons for the bribery of foreign public officials, it is plain that these two instruments are embedded in solid shared understandings with respect to their legal character. Despite some contradictions related to the *OECD Anti-Bribery Convention* with respect to small facilitation payments that are mitigated by the *OECD 2009 Recommendation*, these two instruments meet all the criteria of legality included in the interactional theory of international law. The implementation of these instruments revolving around a system of peer review also ensures a practice according to which compliance with the *OECD Anti-Bribery Convention* and the *OECD 2009 Recommendation* is considered as compulsory by member states.

7 *International Finance Corporation's Performance Standards on Environmental and Social Sustainability*, 1 January 2012, online: IFC www.ifc.org/wps/wcm/connect/Topics_Ext_Content/IFC_External_Corporate_Site/IFC+Sustainability/Our+Approach/Risk+Management/Performance+Standards/ (accessed 26 March 2018).

8 *Convention on Combating Bribery of Foreign Public Officials in International Business Transactions*, 17 December 1997, 37 ILM 1 (entered into force 15 February 1999).

9 *Recommendation of the Council for Further Combating Bribery of Foreign Public Officials in International Business Transactions*, 26 November 2009, Doc No C(2009)159/REV1/FINAL (amended on 18 February 2010, Doc No C(2010)19).

Most importantly, the application of the interactional theory of international law allows a fuller account of the sense of obligation (or lack thereof) emanating from international instruments that reaches beyond their informal or formal character under international law. When considering their content and interactions between international actors, informal international instruments such as the *IFC Performance Standards* and the *OECD 2009 Recommendation* produce a stronger sense of obligation than the *UNCAC*. Positioning the instruments on a continuum that varies from social norms to legal norms allows a refined understanding of the evolving codification of foreign investors' responsibilities by intergovernmental organizations that cannot be fully captured by a strict legal positivist approach.

This analysis of the codification of foreign investors' responsibilities by intergovernmental organizations within a broader context of neoliberal globalization becomes particularly relevant in light of the recent efforts to elaborate a formal international treaty on business and human rights at the UN. In June 2014, the Human Rights Council decided to establish an open-ended intergovernmental working group "to elaborate an international legally binding instrument to regulate, in international human rights law, the activities of transnational corporations and other business enterprises."[10] At the time of writing this book, the Open-Ended Intergovernmental Working Group on Transnational Corporations and Other Business Enterprises with Respect to Human Rights had held three sessions and the Chair-Rapporteur had recommended to present a "draft legally binding instrument" before its fourth session.[11] However, the mere adoption of the resolution by the Human Rights Council and the working group sessions have shed light on diverging views with respect to the negotiation of such a treaty.[12]

Given that a concrete text of this initiative was not ready at the time of writing this book, a proper account of this initiative relying on the interactional theory of international law was premature. However, the analysis of other instruments elaborated and implemented by intergovernmental organizations brings important lessons regarding the elaboration of a formal international treaty in this regard. Even if a formal agreement could be reached, the strong opposition from powerful actors seriously threatens the emergence of shared understandings regarding its normative character, the elaboration of a treaty that meets the criteria of legality and the consolidation of a practice that reinforces its legal character amidst the members of a community of practice. While a formal business and human rights treaty would represent an

10 *Elaboration of an International Legally Binding Instrument on Transnational Corporations and other Business Enterprises with Respect to Human Rights*, HRC Res 26/9, 2014, UN Doc A/HRC/RES/26/9, para 1.

11 See *Report on the Third Session of the Open-Ended Intergovernmental Working Group on Transnational Corporations and other Business Enterprises with respect to Human Rights*, 2018, UN Doc A/HRC/37/67, para 127.

12 See e.g. Carlos Lopez & Ben Shea, "Negotiating a Treaty on Business and Human Rights: A Review of the First Intergovernmental Session" (2016) 1 Bus & Hum Rights J 111; Justine Nolan, "A Business and Human Rights Treaty" in Dorothée Baumann-Pauly & Justine Nolan, eds, *Business and Human Rights: From Principles to Practice* (London: Routledge, 2016) 70.

interesting innovation with respect to the codification of foreign investors' responsibilities by intergovernmental organizations, an interactional account of previous initiatives demonstrates that a genuine sense of obligation is not guaranteed by the adoption of a formal instrument under international law.

Overall, while instruments codifying foreign investors' responsibilities evidence a double movement in international investment law where "society protect[s] itself against the perils inherent in a self-regulating market system,"[13] this movement remains largely unfinished. Of course, the analysis provided in the previous chapters suggests that a deeper normative integration of foreign investors' responsibilities in international investment law and the elaboration of instruments whose observance is perceived as being mandatory has been achieved in some instances. However, in a context of neoliberal globalization, the strongest impediment to fostering the imposition of obligations to foreign investors through legal norms remains the interests of the most powerful actors. This book demonstrates that advancing this double movement can only be possible if the most powerful actors of the international investment lawmaking process are convinced that these obligations can level the playing field and avoid undue advantages to actors that negatively impact the environment and the communities in which they operate. Identifying promising normative avenues and acknowledging the necessity of overcoming the opposition from powerful actors are the first steps toward increasing the accountability of foreign investors under international law.

13 Karl Polanyi, *The Great Transformation: The Political and Economic Origins of Our Time*, 2nd ed (Boston, MA: Beacon Press, 2001 [1944]) at 80.

Bibliography

International Materials

International Agreements

Accord entre la Confédération suisse et la République du Kosovo concernant la promotion et la protection réciproque des investissements, 27 October 2011, online: Confédération suisse www.admin.ch/opc/fr/official-compilation/2012/3733.pdf (accessed 26 March 2018) (entered into force 13 June 2012).

Agreement between Canada and the Republic of Serbia for the Promotion and Protection of Investments, 1 September 2014, Can TS 2015 No 6 (entered into force 7 April 2015).

Agreement between the Government of Canada and the Government of Burkina Faso for the Promotion and Protection of Investments, 20 April 2015, online: Global Affairs Canada http://international.gc.ca/trade-commerce/trade-agreements-accords-commerciaux/agr-acc/burkina_faso/fipa-apie/index.aspx?lang=eng (accessed 26 March 2018) (entered into force 11 October 2017).

Agreement between the Government of Canada and the Government of the Republic of Benin on the Promotion and Reciprocal Protection of Investments, 8 January 2013, Can TS 2014 No 13 (entered into force 12 May 2014).

Agreement between the Government of the Republic of Kosovo and the Government of the Republic of Austria on Promotion and Protection of Investments, 22 January 2010, online: Ministry of Foreign Affairs www.mfa-ks.net/repository/docs/Marrveshja_Ks-Aus_(anglisht).pdf (accessed 26 March 2018).

Agreement between Japan and the Sultanate of Oman for the Reciprocal Promotion and Protection of Investment, 19 June 2015, online: Investment Policy Hub http://investmentpolicyhub.unctad.org/Download/TreatyFile/3481 (accessed 26 March 2018) (entered into force 21 July 2017).

Agreement between the Slovak Republic and the Islamic Republic of Iran, 19 January 2016, online: Investment Policy Hub http://investmentpolicyhub.unctad.org/Download/TreatyFile/3601 (accessed 26 March 2018) (entered into force 30 August 2017).

Agreement Establishing an Association between the European Community and its Member States, of the one Part, and the Republic of Chile, of the other Part, 30 December 2002, OJ, L/352 (entered into force 1 February 2003).

Agreement for the Promotion and Protection of Investment between the Republic of Austria and the Republic of Tajikistan, 15 December 2010, online: Investment Policy Hub http://investmentpolicyhub.unctad.org/Download/TreatyFile/3308 (accessed 26 March 2018) (entered into force 21 December 2012).

Agreement on Encouragement and Reciprocal Protection of Investments between the Kingdom of the Netherlands and the United Arab Emirates, 26 November 2013, online: Investment Policy Hub http://investmentpolicyhub.unctad.org/Download/TreatyFile/4774 (accessed 26 March 2018).

Agreement on Promotion, Protection and Guarantee of Investments Among Member States of the Organisation of the Islamic Conference, 5 June 1981, online: Investment Policy Hub: http://investmentpolicyhub.unctad.org/Download/TreatyFile/2399 (accessed 26 March 2018) (entered into force 23 September 1986).

Association Agreement between the European Union and the European Atomic Energy Community and that Member States, of the one part, and Georgia, of the other part, 27 June 2014, OJ, L/261 (entered into force 1 July 2016).

Charter of the United Nations, 26 June 1945, Can TS 1945 No 7 (entered into force 24 October 1945).

Comprehensive and Progressive Agreement for the Trans-Pacific Partnership, 8 March 2018, online: New Zealand Foreign Affairs and Trade www.mfat.govt.nz/en/trade/free-trade-agreements/free-trade-agreements-concluded-but-not-in-force/cptpp/comprehensive-and-progressive-agreement-for-trans-pacific-partnership-text/#chapters (accessed 26 March 2018).

Comprehensive Economic and Trade Agreement (CETA) between Canada, of the one Part, and the European Union, of the other Part, 29 February 2016, online: European Commission's Directorate General for Trade http://trade.ec.europa.eu/doclib/docs/2016/february/tradoc_154329.pdf (accessed 26 March 2018) (entered into force 21 September 2017).

Constitution of the International Labour Organization, 1 April 1919, 15 UNTS 40 (entered into force 28 June 1919).

Convention on Combating Bribery of Foreign Public Officials in International Business Transactions, 17 December 1997, 37 ILM 1 (entered into force 15 February 1999).

Convention on the Organisation for Economic Co-operation and Development, 14 December 1960, Can TS 1961 No 18 (entered into force 30 September 1961).

Convention on the Settlement of Disputes between States and Nationals of Other States, 18 March 1965, 575 UNTS 159 (entered into force 14 October 1966).

Criminal Law Convention on Corruption, 27 January 1999, 2216 UNTS 225, STE 173 (entered into force 1 July 2002).

Economic Partnership Agreement between the CARIFORUM States, of the one part, and the European Community and its Members, of the other part, 15 October 2008, 289 OJ 3.

Free Trade Agreement between Canada and the Republic of Colombia, 21 November 2008, Can TS 2011 No 11 (entered into force 15 August 2011).

Free Trade Agreement between Canada and the Republic of Korea, 11 March 2014, Can TS 2015 No 3 (entered into force 1 January 2015).

Free Trade Agreement between Canada and the Republic of Peru, 29 May 2008, Can TS 2009 No 15 (entered into force 1 August 2009).

Free Trade Agreement between the EFTA States and Georgia, 27 June 2016, online: EFTA www.efta.int/sites/default/files/documents/legal-texts/free-trade-relations/georgia/EFTA-Georgia-FTA-Main-Agreement.PDF (accessed 26 March 2018) (entered into force 1 September 2017).

Free Trade Agreement between the European Union and its Members, of the one Part, and the Republic of Korea, of the other Part, 6 October 2010, 127 OJ 6 (entered into force July 2011).

Free Trade Agreement between the Republic of Colombia and the EFTA States, 25 November 2008, online: EFTA www.efta.int/media/documents/legal-texts/free-trade-relations/

colombia/EFTA-Colombia%20Free%20Trade%20Agreement%20EN.pdf (accessed 26 March 2018) (entered into force 1 July 2011).

Investment Agreement for the COMESA Common Investment Area, 2007, online: Investment Policy Hub http://investmentpolicyhub.unctad.org/Download/TreatyFile/3092 (accessed 26 March 2018).

Statute of the International Court of Justice, 26 June 1945, 59 US Stat 1031 (entered into force 24 October 1945).

Trans-Pacific Partnership, 4 February 2016, online: New Zealand Foreign Affairs and Trade www.mfat.govt.nz/en/about-us/who-we-are/treaty-making-process/trans-pacific-partnership-tpp/text-of-the-trans-pacific-partnership/ (accessed 26 March 2018).

United Nations Convention Against Corruption, 31 October 2003, 2349 UNTS 41 (entered into force 14 December 2005).

United Nations Convention Against Transnational Organized Crime, 15 November 2000, 2225 UNTS 209 (entered into force 29 September 2003).

United States–Chile Free Trade Agreement, 6 June 2003, 42 ILM 1026 (entered into force 1 January 2004).

United States–Singapore Free Trade Agreement, 6 May 2003, 42 ILM 1026 (entered into force 1 January 2004).

International Arbitration Cases

Apotex Holdings Inc. and Apotex Inc. v United States of America (2014), Award, online: italaw www.italaw.com/sites/default/files/case-documents/italaw3324.pdf (accessed 26 March 2018) (ICSID).

Azpetrol International Holdings B.V., Azpetrol Group B.V. and Azpetrol Oil Services Group B.V. v Republic of Azberijan (2009), Award, online: italaw www.italaw.com/sites/default/files/case-documents/ita0059.pdf (accessed 26 March 2018) (ICSID).

Azurix Corp v Republic of Argentina (2006), Award, online: italaw www.italaw.com/sites/default/files/case-documents/ita0061.pdf (accessed 26 March 2018) (ICSID).

Bear Creek Mining Corporation v Republic of Peru (2017), Award, online: italaw www.italaw.com/sites/default/files/case-documents/italaw9381.pdf (accessed 26 March 2018) (ICSID).

Bernhard Von Pezold and others v Republic of Zimbabwe and Border Timbers Limited, Border Timbers International (Private) Limited, and Hangani Development Co. (Private) Limited v Republic of Zimbabwe (2012), Procedural Order No 2, online: italaw www.italaw.com/sites/default/files/case-documents/ita1043.pdf (accessed 26 March 2018) (ICSID).

Bernhard Friedrich Arnd Rüdiger Von Pezold and others v Republic of Zimbabwe (2015), Award, online: italaw www.italaw.com/sites/default/files/case-documents/italaw7095_0.pdf (accessed 26 March 2018) (ICSID).

Burlington Resources Inc. v Republic of Ecuador (2012), Decision on Liability, online: italaw www.italaw.com/sites/default/files/case-documents/italaw1094_0.pdf (accessed 26 March 2018) (ICSID).

Burlington Resources Inc. v Republic of Ecuador (2017), Decision on Counterclaims, online: italaw www.italaw.com/sites/default/files/case-documents/italaw8206.pdf (accessed 26 March 2018) (ICSID).

Chemtura Corporation v Canada (2010), Award, online: italaw www.italaw.com/sites/default/files/case-documents/ita0149_0.pdf (accessed 26 March 2018) (UNCITRAL).

Compañía del Desarrollo de Santa Elena, S.A. v Republic of Costa Rica (2000), Award, 39 ILM 1317 (ICSID).

Copper Mesa Mining Corporation v Republic of Ecuador (2015), Award, online: italaw www.italaw.com/sites/default/files/case-documents/italaw7443.pdf (accessed 26 March 2018) (UNCITRAL).

Crystallex International Corporation v Bolivarian Republic of Venezuela (2016), Award, online: italaw www.italaw.com/sites/default/files/case-documents/italaw7194.pdf (accessed 26 March 2018) (ICSID Additional Facility).

Emilio Agustin Maffezini v Kingdom of Spain (2000), Award, 5 ICSID Rep 419 (ICSID).

Empresas Lucchetti, S.A. and Lucchetti Peru S.A. v Republic of Peru (2005), Award, online: italaw www.italaw.com/sites/default/files/case-documents/ita0275.pdf (accessed 26 March 2018) (ICSID).

Fraport AG Frankfurt Airport Services Worldwide (2007), Dissenting Opinion of Mr. Bernardo M. Cremades, online: italaw www.italaw.com/sites/default/files/case-documents/ita0340.pdf (accessed 26 March 2018) (ICSID).

Fraport AG Frankfurt Airport Services Worldwide v Republic of the Philippines (2014), Award, online: italaw www.italaw.com/sites/default/files/case-documents/italaw4114.pdf (accessed 26 March 2018) (ICSID).

Glamis Gold, Ltd v United States of America (2006), Quechan Indian Nation Supplemental Non-Disputing Party Submission, online: USTR www.state.gov/documents/organization/75016.pdf (accessed 26 March 2018) (UNCITRAL).

Glamis Gold, Ltd v United States of America (2006), Sierra Club and Earthworks Non-Disputing Party Submission, online: USTR www.state.gov/documents/organization/74832.pdf (accessed 26 March 2018) (UNCITRAL).

Glamis Gold, Ltd v United States of America (2009), Award, 48 ILM 1039 (UNCITRAL).

Gold Reserve Inc. v Bolivarian Republic of Venezuela (2014), Award, online: italaw www.italaw.com/sites/default/files/case-documents/italaw4009.pdf (accessed 26 March 2018) (ICSID Additional Facility).

Gustav F W Hamester GmbH& Co KG v Republic of Ghana (2010), Award, online: italaw www.italaw.com/sites/default/files/case-documents/ita0396.pdf (accessed 26 March 2018) (ICSID).

Hesham Talaat M. Al-Warraq v Republic of Indonesia (2012), Award on Respondent's Preliminary Objections to Jurisdiction and Admissibility, online: italaw www.italaw.com/sites/default/files/case-documents/italaw3174_0.pdf (accessed 26 March 2018) (UNCITRAL).

Hesham Talaat M. Al-Warraq v Republic of Indonesia (2014), Final Award, online: italaw www.italaw.com/sites/default/files/case-documents/italaw4164.pdf (accessed 26 March 2018) (UNCITRAL).

Impregilo S.p.A. v Argentine Republic (2011), Award, online: italaw www.italaw.com/sites/default/files/case-documents/ita0418.pdf (accessed 26 March 2018) (ICSID).

International Thunderbird Gaming Corporation v United Mexican States (2005), Separate Opinion, online: italaw www.italaw.com/sites/default/files/case-documents/ita0432.pdf (accessed 26 March 2018) (UNCITRAL).

Marion Unglaube and Reinhard v Republic of Costa Rica (2012), Award, online: italaw www.italaw.com/sites/default/files/case-documents/ita1052.pdf (accessed 26 March 2018) (ICSID).

Metalclad Corporation v Mexico (2001), Award, 40 ILM 36 (ICSID Additional Facility).

Metal-Tech Ltd v Republic of Uzbekistan (2013), Award, online: italaw www.italaw.com/sites/default/files/case-documents/italaw3012.pdf (accessed 26 March 2018) (ICSID).

Niko Resources (Bangladesh) Ltd v People's Republic of Bangladesh et al (2013), Decision on Jurisdiction, online: italaw www.italaw.com/sites/default/files/archive/italaw1561_0.pdf (accessed 26 March 2018) (ICSID).

Parkerings-Companiet AS v Republic of Lithuania (2007), Award, online: italaw www.italaw.com/sites/default/files/case-documents/ita0619.pdf (accessed 26 March 2018) (ICSID).

Perenco Ecuador Limited v Republic of Ecuador (2015), Interim Decision on the Environmental Counterclaim, online: italaw www.italaw.com/sites/default/files/case-documents/italaw6315.pdf (accessed 26 March 2018) (ICSID).

Philip Morris Brands SÀRL, Philip Morris Products S.A. and Abal Hermanos S.A. v Oriental Republic of Uruguay (2016), Award, online: italaw www.italaw.com/sites/default/files/case-documents/italaw7417.pdf (accessed 26 March 2018) (ICSID).

Siemens A.G. v Argentine Republic (2007), Award, 14 ICSID Reports 518 (ICSID).

Southern Pacific Properties (Middle East) Limited v Arab Republic of Egypt (1992), Award, 8 ICSID Review 328 (ICSID).

Southern Pacific Properties (Middle East) Limited v Arab Republic of Egypt (1992), Dissenting Opinion, 8 ICSID Review 400 (ICSID).

Spyridon Roussalis v Romania (2011), Award, online: italaw www.italaw.com/sites/default/files/case-documents/ita0723.pdf (accessed 26 March 2018) (ICSID).

Suez, Sociedad General de Aguas de Barcelona S.A. and Vivendi Universal S.A. v Argentine Republic and *AWG Group v Argentine Republic* (2010), Decision on Liability, online: italaw www.italaw.com/sites/default/files/case-documents/ita0826.pdf (accessed 26 March 2018) (ICSID).

Técnicas Medioambientales Tecmed S.A. v Mexico (2004), Award, 43 ILM 133 (ICSID Additional Facility).

Urbaser S.A. and Consorcio de Aguas Bilbao Bizkaia Ur Partzuergoa v Argentine Republic (2016), Award, online: italaw www.italaw.com/sites/default/files/case-documents/italaw8136_1.pdf (accessed 26 March 2018) (ICSID).

Wena Hotels Ltd v Arab Republic of Egypt (2000), Award, 41 ILM 896 (ICSID).

William Ralph Clayton, William Richard Clayton, Douglas Clayton, Daniel Clayton and Bilcon of Delaware v Government of Canada (2015), Award on Jurisdiction and Liability, online: italaw www.italaw.com/sites/default/files/case-documents/italaw4212.pdf (accessed 26 March 2018) (UNCITRAL).

William Ralph Clayton, William Richard Clayton, Douglas Clayton, Daniel Clayton and Bilcon of Delaware v Government of Canada (2015), Dissenting Opinion of Professor Donald McRae, online: italaw www.italaw.com/sites/default/files/case-documents/italaw4213.pdf (accessed 26 March 2018) (UNCITRAL).

World Duty Free Company Limited v Republic of Kenya (2006), Award, 46 ILM 339 (ICSID).

Organisation for Economic Co-Operation and Development Documents

Commentaries on the Convention on Combating Bribery of Foreign Public Officials in International Business Transactions, 21 November 1997 (Paris: OECD, 2011).

Decision of the Council on the OECD Guidelines for Multinational Enterprises, 27 June 2000, Doc No (2000)96/FINAL.

Decision of the Council on the OECD Guidelines for Multinational Enterprises, 25 May 2011, Doc No C/MIN(2011)11/FINAL (2011).

Declaration on International Investment and Multinational Enterprises, 21 June 1976, Doc No C(76)99/FINAL (1976).

Declaration on International Investment and Multinational Enterprises, 13 June 1979, Doc No C(79)102/FINAL (1979).

Declaration on International Investment and Multinational Enterprises, 17 May 1984, Doc No C/MIN(84)6(FINAL) (1984).

Declaration on International Investment and Multinational Enterprises, 5 June 1991, Doc No C/MIN(91)7 (1991).

Declaration on International Investment and Multinational Enterprises, 27 June 2000, Doc No C(2000)96/REV1 (2000).

Declaration on International Investment and Multinational Enterprises, 25 May 2011, Doc No C/MIN(2011)11/FINAL (2011).

OECD, *Annual Report on the OECD Guidelines for Multinational Enterprises 2002: Focus on Responsible Supply Chain Management* (Paris, OECD: 2002).

OECD, *Annual Report on the OECD Guidelines for Multinational Enterprises 2003: Enhancing the Role of Business in the Fight Against Corruption* (Paris, OECD: 2003).

OECD, *Annual Report on the OECD Guidelines for Multinational Enterprises 2005: Corporate Responsibility in the Developing World* (Paris, OECD: 2005).

OECD, *Annual Report on the OECD Guidelines for Multinational Enterprises 2007: Corporate Responsibility in the Financial Sector* (Paris, OECD: 2007).

OECD, *Annual Report on the OECD Guidelines for Multinational Enterprises 2008: Employment and Industrial Relations* (Paris: OECD, 2008).

OECD, *Annual Report on the OECD Guidelines for Multinational Enterprises 2009: Consumer Empowerment* (Paris: OECD, 2009).

OECD, *Annual Report on the OECD Guidelines for Multinational Enterprises 2011: A New Agenda for the Future* (Paris, OECD: 2011).

OECD, *Annual Report on the OECD Guidelines for Multinational Enterprises 2012: Mediation and Consensus Building* (Paris: OECD, 2012).

OECD, *Annual Report on the OECD Guidelines for Multinational Enterprises 2013: Responsible Business Conduct in Action* (Paris, OECD: 2013).

OECD, *Annual Report on the OECD Guidelines for Multinational Enterprises 2014: Responsible Business Conduct by Sector* (Paris: OECD, 2014).

OECD, *Annual Report on the OECD Guidelines for Multinational Enterprises 2016* (Paris: OECD, 2016).

OECD, Committee on International Investment and Multinational Enterprises, *Conference on the OECD Guidelines for Multinational Enterprises: Summary of Proceedings*, Doc No DAFFE/IME(98)18 (1998).

OECD, *Database of Specific Instances*, online: OECD http://mneguidelines.oecd.org/database/ (accessed 26 March 2018).

OECD, Directorate for Financial, Fiscal and Enterprise Affairs, *OECD Guidelines for Multinational Enterprises: Statements Made on the Adoption of the Review 2000* (Paris: OECD, 2000).

OECD, Directorate for Financial, Fiscal and Enterprise Affairs, *Mid-Term Study of Phase 2 Reports: Application of the Convention on Combating Bribery of Foreign Public Officials in International Business Transactions and the 1997 Recommendation on Combating Bribery in International Business Transactions* (Paris: OECD, 2006).

OECD, Investment Division, *Terms of Reference for an Update of the OECD Guidelines for Multinational Enterprises* (Paris: OECD, 2010).

OECD, *Japanese NCP: Peer Learning and Review* (Paris: OECD, 2012).

OECD, *NCP Peer Reviews*, online: OECD https://mneguidelines.oecd.org/ncppeerreviews.htm (accessed 26 March 2018).

OECD, *OECD Due Diligence Guidance for Responsible Supply Chain of Minerals from Conflict-Affected and High-Risk Areas* (Paris: OCDE, 2013).

OECD, *OECD Guidelines for Multinational Enterprises, 2011 Edition* (Paris: OECD, 2011).

OECD, *Review of the OECD Anti-Bribery Instruments: Compilation of Responses to Consultation Papers* (Paris: OECD, 2008).

OECD, *Shared Commitment to Fight Against Foreign Bribery* (Paris: OECD, 2007).

OECD, *The OECD Guidelines for Multinational Enterprises*, Doc No OECD/GD(97)40 (1997).

OECD, Working Group on Bribery, *Annual Report 2007* (Paris: OECD, 2007).

OECD, Working Group on Bribery, *Annual Report 2010* (Paris: OECD, 2010).

OECD, Working Group on Bribery, *Annual Report 2011* (Paris: OECD, 2011).

OECD, Working Group on Bribery, *Annual Report 2013* (Paris: OECD, 2013).

OECD, Working Group on Bribery, *Annual Report 2014* (Paris: OECD, 2014).

OECD, Working Group on Bribery in International Business Transactions, *Consultation Paper: Review of the OECD Instruments on Combating Bribery of Foreign Public Officials in International Business Transactions Ten Years After Adoption* (Paris: OECD, 2008).

OECD, Working Group on Bribery in International Business Transactions, *Policy Statement on Bribery in International Business Transactions* (Paris: OECD, 2009).

OECD StatExtract, *Foreign Direct Investment FDI Series of BOP and IIP Aggregates*, online: OECD http://stats.oecd.org/Index.aspx?DataSetCode=FDI_BOP_IIP# (accessed 26 March 2018).

Recommendation of the Council for Further Combating Bribery of Foreign Public Officials in International Business Transactions, 26 November 2009, Doc No C(2009)159/REV1/FINAL (amended on 18 February 2010, Doc No C(2010)19).

Recommendation of the Council on Bribery and Officially Supported Export Credits, 14 December 2006, Doc No C(2006)163 (2006).

Recommendation of the Council on Bribery in International Business Transactions, 27 May 1994, Doc No C(94)75/FINAL (1994).

Recommendation of the Council on Due Diligence Guidance for Responsible Supply Chains of Minerals from Conflict-Affected and High-Risk Areas, 17 July 2012, Doc No C(2012)93 (2012).

Recommendation of the Council on Tax Measures for Further Combating Bribery of Foreign Public Officials in International Business Transactions, 25 May 2009, Doc No C(2009)64 (2009).

Revised Recommendation of the Council on Combating Bribery in International Business Transactions, 23 May 1997, Doc No C(97)123/FINAL (1997).

Risk Awareness Tool for Multinational Enterprises in Weak Governance Zones, 8 June 2006, online: OECD www.oecd.org/daf/inv/corporateresponsibility/36885821.pdf (accessed 26 March 2018).

Second Revised Decision of the Council on Inter-Governmental Consultation Procedures on the Guidelines for Multinational Enterprises, June 1984, Doc No C(84)90 (1984).

United States Proposal on the Issue of Illicit Payments, 23 March 1989, Doc No C(89)49 (1989).

International Labour Organization Documents

ILO, *Follow-up on the Symposium on the Tripartite Declaration of Principles concerning Multinational Enterprises and Social Policy and related Multilateral Initiatives*, 291th Sess, GB.291/MNE/1 (2004).

ILO, *ILO Collaboration with Other Intergovernmental and International Organizations in Promoting the Principles of the Tripartite Declaration of Principles concerning Multinational Enterprises and Social Policy*, 322th Sess, GB.322/POL/8 (2014).

ILO, *ILO Declarations*, online: ILO www.ilo.org/global/about-the-ilo/how-the-ilo-works/departments-and-offices/jur/legal-instruments/WCMS_428589/lang--en/index.htm (accessed 26 March 2018).

ILO, *Multinational Enterprises, Development and Decent Work: Report on the Promotion and the Application of the Tripartite Declaration of Principles concerning Multinational Enterprises and Social Policy in the Americas* (Geneva: ILO, 2014).

ILO, *Procedure for the Examination of Disputes concerning the Application of the Tripartite Declaration*, 233th Sess, Official Bulletin, Vol LXIX, Series A, No 3 (1986).

ILO, *Progress of ILO Activities on Multinational Enterprises*, 198th Sess, GB.198/5/6 (1975).

ILO, *Proposal for Evaluating the Effect Given to the Tripartite Declaration of Principles concerning Multinational Enterprises and Social Policy*, 301th Sess, GB.301/MNE/4 (2008).

ILO, *Report of the Committee on Multinational Enterprises*, 229th Sess, Official Bulletin, Vol LXVIII, Series A, No 3 (1985).

ILO, *Report of the Committee on Multinational Enterprises*, 239th Sess, Official Bulletin, Vol LXXI, Series A, No 3 (1988).

ILO, *Report on the Subcommittee on Multinational Enterprises*, 272th Sess, Official Bulletin, Vol LXXXI, Series A, No 2 (1998).

ILO, *Seventh Survey on the Effect Given to the Tripartite Declaration of Principles concerning Multinational Enterprises and Social Policy: Summary of Reports Submitted by Governments and by Employers' and Workers' Organizations*, 280th Sess, GB.280/MNE/1/2 (2001).

ILO, *Summary of Fourth Government Reports on the Effect Given to the Tripartite Declaration of Principles concerning Multinational Enterprises and Social Policy Submitted to the Committee on Multinational Enterprises*, 244th Sess, GB.244/MNE/1/1/D.1 (1989).

ILO, *Summary of Reports Submitted by Governments and by Employers' and Workers' Organisations for the Fifth Survey on the Effect Given to the Tripartite Declaration of Principles concerning Multinational Enterprises and Social Policy Submitted to the Committee on Multinational Enterprises*, 1992, TDME/REP 5 (Rev.).

ILO, *Summary of Reports Submitted by Governments and by Employers' and Workers' Organisations for the Sixth Survey on the Effect Given to the Tripartite Declaration of Principles concerning Multinational Enterprises and Social Policy*, 268th Sess, GB.268/MNE/1/1B (1997).

ILO, *Summary of Second Government Reports on the Effect Given to the Tripartite Declaration of Principles concerning Multinational Enterprises and Social Policy Submitted to the Committee on Multinational Enterprises*, 224th Sess, GB.224/MNE/1/1/D.1 (1983).

ILO, *Summary of the Reports on the Effect Given to the Tripartite Declaration of Principles concerning Multinational Enterprises and Social Policy*, 1980, GB/MNE/1980/D.1.

ILO, *Tripartite Advisory Meeting on the Relationship of Multinational Enterprises and Social Policy – Report of the Meeting*, 1976, MNE/1976/D.12.

ILO, *Tripartite Declaration of Principles concerning Multinational Enterprises and Social Policy: Possibilities of a Follow-up Procedure*, 205th Sess, GB.205/10/2 (1978).

ILO, *Tripartite Forum on Promoting the Tripartite Declaration of Principles concerning Multinational Enterprises and Social Policy: Summary of Proceedings*, 2002, TFTDME/2002/1.

ILO, *Reconvened Tripartite Advisory Meeting on the Relationship of Multinational Enterprises and Social Policy*, 1977, MNE/1977/D.8.

ILO, *Report of the Subcommittee on Multinational Enterprises*, 264th Sess, GB.264/13 (1995).
ILO, *Update on the Implementation of the Promotional Framework and Follow-up to the Tripartite Declaration of Principles concerning Multinational Enterprises and Social Policy, Including ILO Collaboration with other Intergovernmental and International Organizations*, 325th Sess, GB.325/POL/9 (2015).
Tripartite Declaration of Principles concerning Multinational Enterprises and Social Policy, November 1977, 17 ILM 422.
Tripartite Declaration of Principles concerning Multinational Enterprises and Social Policy, November 2000, 41 ILM 186.
Tripartite Declaration of Principles concerning Multinational Enterprises and Social Policy, March 2006, online: ILO www.ilo.org/empent/Publications/WCMS_211136/lang--en/index.htm (accessed 26 March 2018).
Tripartite Declaration of Principles concerning Multinational Enterprises and Social Policy, March 2017, online: ILO www.ilo.org/empent/Publications/WCMS_094386/lang--en/index.htm (accessed 26 March 2018).

United Nations Documents

Action against Corruption, GA Res 54/128, UNGAOR, 54th Sess, Supp No 49, UN Doc A/RES/54/128, (2000).
An Effective Legal Instrument Against Corruption, GA Res 55/61, UNGAOR, 55th Sess, Supp No 49, UN Doc A/RES/55/61, (2001).
Business and Human Rights: Mandate of the Working Group on the Issue of Human Rights and Transnational Corporations and other Business Enterprises, HRC Res 35/7, 2017, UN Doc A/HRC/RES/35/7.
Charter of Economic Rights and Duties of States, GA Res 3281(XXIX), UNGAOR, 29th Sess, Supp No 31, UN Doc A/9631, (1974) 50.
Civil Society and Private Sector Forum, Forum for Anti-Corruption Activities and Forum for Parliamentarians: Side Events Held on the Occasion of the First Session of the Conference of the State Parties to the United Nations Convention against Corruption, 2006, UN Doc CAC/COSP/2006/CRP.6.
Code of Conduct on Transnational Corporations (Draft), 1990, UN Doc E/1990/94.
Commentary on the Norms on the Responsibilities of Transnational Corporations and other Business Enterprises with regard to Human Rights, 2003, UN Doc E/CN.4/Sub.2/2003/38/Rev.2.
Committee on World Food Security, *Principles for Responsible Investment in Agriculture and Food Systems*, 2014, CFS 2014/41/4/Rev.1 at para 19(A)(v).
Declaration on the Establishment of a New International Economic Order, GA Res 3201(S-VI), UNGAOR, 6th Ext Sess, Supp No 1, UN Doc A/9559, (1974) 3.
Department of Economic and Social Affairs, *Multinational Corporations in World Development* (New York: United Nations, 1973).
Elaboration of an International Legally Binding Instrument on Transnational Corporations and other Business Enterprises with Respect to Human Rights, HRC Res 26/9, 2014, UN Doc A/HRC/RES/26/9.
Final Report of the Panel of Experts on the Illegal Exploitation of Natural Resources and other Forms of Wealth of the Democratic Republic of the Congo, 2002, UN Doc S/2002/1146.
Human Rights and Transnational Corporations and other Business Enterprises, CHR Res 2005/69, UNESCOR, 2005, Supp No 3, UN Doc E/2005/23, 268.

Human Rights and Transnational Corporations and other Business Enterprises, HRC Res 17/4, 2011, UN Doc A/HRC/RES/17/4.

Human Rights and Transnational Corporations and other Business Enterprises, HRC Res 26/22, 2014, UN Doc A/HRC/RES/26/22.

Human Rights Council, GA Res 60/251, UNGAOR, 60th Sess, Supp No 49, UN Doc A/RES/60/251 (2006).

Joint Written Statement Submitted by Europe-Third World Centre, a Non-Governmental Organization in General Consultative Status, and American Association of Jurists a Non-Governmental Organization in Special Consultative Status, 2003, UN Doc E/CN.4/Sub.2/2003/NGO/37.

Joint Written Statement Submitted by the International Chamber of Commerce and the International Organization of Employers, Non-Governmental Organizations in General Consultative Status, 2003, UN Doc E/CN.4/Sub.2/2003/NGO/44.

Mandate of the Special Representative of the Secretary-General on the Issue of Human Rights and Transnational Corporations and other Business Enterprises, HRC Res 8/7, 2008, UN Doc A/HRC/8/52, 30.

Mechanism for the Review of Implementation of the United Nations Convention against Corruption, CAC Res 4/1, 2011, UN Doc CAC/COSP/2011/14.

Non-Governmental Organizations and the Mechanism for the Review of Implementation of the United Nations Convention against Corruption, CAC Res 4/6, 2011, UN Doc CAC/COSP/2011/14.

Norms on the Responsibilities of Transnational Corporations and other Business Enterprises with Regard to Human Rights, 2003, UN Doc E/CN.4/Sub.2/2003/12/Rev.2.

OHCHR, *The Corporate Responsibility to Respect Human Rights: An Interpretative Guide* (Geneva: United Nations, 2012).

Report of the Ad Hoc Committee for the Negotiation of a Convention against Corruption on its First Session, Held in Vienna from 21 January to 1 February 2002, 2002, UN Doc A/AC.261/4.

Report of the Ad Hoc Committee for the Negotiation of a Convention against Corruption on its Third Session, Held in Vienna from 30 September to 11 October 2002, 2002, UN Doc A/AC.261/9.

Report of the Ad Hoc Committee for the Negotiation of a Convention against Corruption on its Fifth Session, Held in Vienna from 10 to 21 March 2003, 2003, UN Doc A/AC.261/16.

Report of the Ad Hoc Committee for the Negotiation of a Convention against Corruption on its Sixth Session, Held in Vienna from 21 July to 8 August 2003, 2003, UN Doc A/AC.261/22.

Report of the Ad Hoc Committee for the Negotiation of a Convention against Corruption on its Seventh Session, Held in Vienna from 29 September to 1 October 2003, 2003, UN Doc A/AC.261/25.

Report of the Ad Hoc Committee for the Negotiation of a Convention against Corruption on the Work of its First to Seventh Sessions, 2003, UN Doc A/58/422.

Report of the Conference of the State Parties to the United Nations Convention against Corruption on its First Session, Held in Amman from 10 to 14 December 2006, 2006, UN Doc CAC/COSP/2006/12.

Report of the Conference of the State Parties to the United Nations Convention against Corruption on its Second Session, Held in Nusa Dua, Indonesia, from 28 January to 1 February 2008, 2008, UN Doc CAC/COSP/2008/15.

Report of the Conference of the State Parties to the United Nations Convention against Corruption on its Fourth Session, Held in Marrakech, Morocco, from 24 to 28 October 2011, 2011, UN Doc CAC/COSP/2011/14.

Report of the Conference of the State Parties to the United Nations Convention against Corruption on its Fifth Session, Held in Panama City from 25 to 29 November 2013, 2014, UN Doc CAC/COSP/2013/18.

Report of the Conference of the State Parties to the United Nations Convention against Corruption on its Sixth Session Held in St. Petersburg, Russian Federation, from 2 to 6 November 2015, 2015, UN Doc CAC/COSP/2015/10.

Report of the Implementation Review Group on its First Session, Held in Vienna from 28 June to 2 July 2010, 2010, UN Doc CAC/COSP/IRG/2010/7.

Report of the Implementation Review Group on its Second Session, Held in Vienna from 30 May to 2 June 2011, 2011, UN Doc CAC/COSP/IRG/2011/4.

Report of the Implementation Review Group on its Third Session, Held in Vienna from 18 to 22 June 2012, 2012, UN Doc CAC/COSP/IRG/2012/6.

Report of the Implementation Review Group on its Resumed Third Session, Held in Vienna from 14 to 16 November 2012, 2012, UN Doc CAC/COSP/IRG/2012/6/Add.1.

Report of the Implementation Review Group on its Fifth Session, Held in Vienna from 13 to 15 October 2014, 2014, UN Doc CAC/COSP/IRG/2014/11/Add.1.

Report of the Implementation Review Group on its Resumed Fifth Session, Held in Vienna from 13 to 15 October 2014, 2014, UN Doc CAC/COSP/IRG/2014/11/Add.1.

Report of the Implementation Review Group on its Sixth Session, Held in Vienna from 1 to 5 June 2015, 2015, UN Doc CAC/COSP/IRG/2015/5.

Report of the Implementation Review Group on its Resumed Sixth Session, Held in St. Petersburg, Russian Federation, on 3 and 4 November 2015, 2015, UN Doc CAC/COSP/IRG/2015/5/Add.1.

Report of the Informal Preparatory Meeting of the Ad Hoc Committee for the Negotiation of a Convention Against Corruption, Held in Buenos Aires from 4 to 7 December 2001, 2001, UN Doc A/AC.261/2.

Report of the Meeting of the Intergovernmental Open-Ended Expert Group to Prepare Draft Terms of Reference for the Negotiation of an International Legal Instrument against Corruption, 2001, UN Doc A/AC.260/2.

Report of the Sessional Working Group on the Working Methods and Activities of Transnational Corporations on its First Session, 1999, UN Doc E/CN.4/Sub.2/1999/9.

Report of the Sessional Working Group on the Working Methods and Activities of Transnational Corporations on its Second Session, 2000, UN Doc E/CN.4/Sub.2/2000/12.

Report of the Sessional Working Group on the Working Methods and Activities of Transnational Corporations on its Third Session, 2001, UN Doc E/CN.4/Sub.2/2001/9.

Report of the Sessional Working Group on the Working Methods and Activities of Transnational Corporations on its Fourth Session, 2002, UN Doc E/CN.4/Sub.2/2002/13.

Report of the Working Group on the Issue of Human Rights and Transnational Corporations and other Business Enterprises, 2012, UN Doc A/HRC/20/29.

Report of the Working Group on the Issue of Human Rights and Transnational Corporations and other Business Enterprises, 2013, UN Doc A/HRC/23/32.

Report of the Working Group on the Issue of Human Rights and Transnational Corporations and other Business Enterprises, 2014, UN Doc A/HRC/26/25.

Report of the Working Group on the Issue of Human Rights and Transnational Corporations and other Business Enterprises, 2015, UN Doc A/70/216.

Report on the Meeting of the Open-Ended Intergovernmental Working Group on Review of the Implementation of the United Nations Convention against Corruption Held in Vienna from 15 to 17 December 2008, 2008, UN Doc CAC/COSP/WG.1/2008/8.

Report on the Meeting of the Open-Ended Intergovernmental Working Group on Review of the Implementation of the United Nations Convention against Corruption Held in Vienna from 11 to 13 May 2009, 2009, UN Doc CAC/COSP/WG.1/2009/3.

Report on the Third Session of the Open-Ended Intergovernmental Working Group on Transnational Corporations and other Business Enterprises with respect to Human Rights, 2018, UN Doc A/HRC/37/67.

Responsibility of Transnational Corporations and other Business Enterprises with regard to Human Rights, CHR Res 2003/16, 2003, UN Doc E/CN.4/Sub.2/2003/L.11, 52.

Responsibilities of Transnational Corporations and related Business Enterprises with regard to Human Rights, ESC Dec 2004/116, UNESCOR, 2004, Supp No 3, UN Doc E/CN.4/2004/127, 332 at 333.

Review Mechanism, CAC Res 3/1, 2009, UN Doc CAC/COSP/2009/15.

Review of Implementation, CAC Res 1/1, 2006, UN Doc CAC/COSP/2006/12.

Review of Implementation, CAC Res 2/1, 2008, UN Doc CAC/COSP/2008/15.

Secretary-General, *Cooperation between the United Nations and All Relevant Partners, in Particular the Private Sector*, 2001, UN Doc A/56/323.

Special Representative of the Secretary-General on the Issue of Human Rights and Transnational Corporations and Other Business Enterprises, *Business and Human Rights: Further Steps Toward the Operationalization of the 'Protect, Respect and Remedy' Framework*, 2010, UN Doc A/HRC/14/27.

Special Representative of the Secretary-General on the issue of human rights and transnational corporations and other business enterprises, *Guiding Principles on Business and Human Rights: Implementing the United Nations 'Protect, Respect and Remedy' Framework*, 2011, UN Doc A/HRC/17/31.

Special Representative of the Secretary-General on the Issue of Human Rights and Transnational Corporations and Other Business Enterprises, *Interim Report of the Special Representative of the Secretary-General on the Issue of Human Rights and Transnational Corporations and other Business Enterprises*, 2006, UN Doc E/CN.4/2006/97.

Special Representative of the Secretary-General on the Issue of Human Rights and Transnational Corporations and Other Business Enterprises, *Promotion and Protection of All Human Rights, Civil, Political, Economic, Social and Cultural Rights, Including the Right to Development – Protect, Respect and Remedy: A Framework for Business and Human Rights*, 2008, UN Doc A/HRC/8/5.

Special Representative of the Secretary-General on the Issue of Human Rights and Transnational Corporations and Other Business Enterprises, *Report of the Special Representative of the Secretary-General on the Issue of Human Rights and Transnational Corporations and other Business Enterprises – Addendum – Summary of Five Multi-Stakeholder Consultations*, 2008, UN Doc A/HRC/8/5/Add.1.

Statement Submitted by Transparency International, a Non-Governmental Organization in Consultative Status with the Economic and Social Council, 2013, UN Doc CAC/COSP/IRG/2013/NGO/3.

Statement Submitted by Transparency International, a Non-Governmental Organization in Consultative Status with the Economic and Social Council, and by the Transparency and Accountability Network, a Non-Governmental Organization not in Consultative Status with the Economic and Social Council, 2013, UN Doc CAC/COSP/IRG/2013/NGO/1.

Sub-commission on the Promotion and Protection of Human Rights, *Report of the United Nations High Commissioner on Human Rights on the Responsibilities of Transnational Corporations and related Business Enterprises with regard to Human Rights*, 2005, UN Doc E/CN.4/2005/91.

The Effects of the Working Methods and Activities of Transnational Corporations on the Enjoyment of Human Rights, CHR Res 2001/3, 2001, UN Doc E/CN.4/SUB.2/2001/40, 17.

The Impact of Transnational Corporations on the Development Process and on International Relations, ESC Res 1908(LVII), UNESCOR, 1974, UN Doc E/5570, 13.

The Impact of Transnational Corporations on the Development Process and on International Relations, ESC Res 1913(LVII), UNESCOR, 1974, Supp No 1A, UN Doc E/5570/Add.1, 3.

The Impact of Transnational Corporations on the Development Process and on International Relations: Report of the Group of Eminent Persons to Study the Role of Multinational Enterprises on Development and on International Relations, 1974, UN Doc E/5500/Add.1.

The Relationship between the Enjoyment of Economic, Social and Cultural Rights and the Right to Development, and the Working Methods and Activities of Transnational Corporations, CHR Res 1998/8, 1998, UN Doc E/CN.4/SUB.2/1998/45, 30.

The Relationship between the Enjoyment of Economic, Social and Cultural Rights and the Right to Development, and the Working Methods and Activities of Transnational Corporations, CHR Res 2002/8, 2002, UN Doc E/CN.4/SUB.2/2002/46, 24.

Terms of Reference for the Negotiation of an International Legal Instrument Against Corruption, GA Res 56/260, UNGAOR, 56th Sess, Supp No 49, UN Doc A/RES/56/260, (2002).

Towards Global Partnership – 37th Plenary Meeting, 2001, UN Doc A/56/PV.37.

Towards Global Partnerships, GA Res 56/76, UNGAOR, 56th Sess, Supp No 49, UN Doc A/RES/56/76, (2002).

Towards Global Partnerships, GA Res 64/223, UNGAOR, 64th Sess, Supp No 49, UN Doc A/RES/64/223, (2010).

Towards Global Partnerships: A Principle-Based Approach to Enhanced Cooperation between the United Nations and All Relevant Partners, GA Res 70/224, UNGAOR, 70th Sess, Supp No 49, UN Doc A/RES/70/224, (2016).

UNCTAD, *Investment Policy Framework for Sustainable Development* (New York and Geneva: United Nations, 2015).

UNCTAD, *World Investment Report 2015: Reforming International Investment Governance* (New York and Geneva: United Nations, 2015).

UNHCHR, *Stakeholder Submissions to the Report of the High Commissioner for Human Rights on the Responsibilities of Transnational Corporations and related Business Enterprises with regard to Human Rights*, online: OHCHR https://web.archive.org/web/20140520213840/http://www2.ohchr.org/english/issues/globalization/business/contributions.htm (accessed 26 March 2018).

United Nations, Press Release, SG/SM/6881, "Secretary-General Proposes Global Compact on Human Rights, Labour, Environment, in Address to World Economic Forum in Davos" (1 February 1999) online: United Nations www.un.org/press/en/1999/19990201.sgsm6881.html (accessed 26 March 2018).

United Nations, Press release, SG/SM/7495, "Secretary-General Welcomes International Corporate Leaders to Global Compact Meeting" (26 July 2000) online: United Nations www.un.org/press/en/2000/20000726.sgsm7495.doc.html (accessed 26 March 2018).

United Nations, Press Release, SG/SM/8212-ECO/24, "United Nations Joint Statement on Global Compact by Secretary-General and President of International Organization of Employers (IOE)" (26 April 2002) online: United Nations www.un.org/press/en/2002/sgsm8212.doc.htm (accessed 26 March 2018).

United Nations, *Global Compact Summit: China – Building Alliances for a Sustainable Global Economy: Final Report* (New York: United Nations Global Compact Office, 2006).

United Nations, *Global Corporate Sustainability Report 2013* (New York: United Nations Global Compact Office, 2013.

United Nations, *The Global Compact Leaders Summit 2004: Final Report* (New York: United Nations Global Compact Office, 2004).

United Nations, *The Global Compact Leaders Summit 2007 – Facing Realities: Getting Down to Business* (New York: United Nations Global Compact Office, 2007).

United Nations, *The United Nations Today* (New York: United Nations, 2008).

United Nations, *United Nations Global Compact Activity Report 2013* (New York: United Nations Global Compact Office, 2014).

United Nations, *UN Global Compact Annual Review – 2007 Leaders Summit* (New York: United Nations Global Compact Office, 2007).

United Nations, *United Nations Global Compact: Annual Review 2008* (New York: United Nations Global Compact Office, 2009).

United Nations, *United Nations Global Compact Annual Review: Anniversary Edition* (New York: United Nations Global Compact Office, 2010).

United Nations, *United Nations Global Compact: Annual Review 2010* (New York: United Nations Global Compact Office, 2011).

United Nations Global Compact, online: United Nations Global Compact www.unglobalcompact.org/what-is-gc/mission/principles (accessed 26 March 2018).

United Nations Global Compact, *Integrity Measures* (June 2016), online: United Nations Global Compact www.unglobalcompact.org/docs/about_the_gc/Integrity_measures/Integrity_Measures_Note_EN.pdf (accessed 26 March 2018).

United Nations Global Compact, *Our Participants*, online: United Nations Global Compact www.unglobalcompact.org/what-is-gc/participants (accessed 16 April 2018).

United Nations Office on Drugs and Crime, *Legislative Guide for the Implementation of the United Nations Convention Against Corruption* (New York: United Nations, 2006).

United Nations Office on Drugs and Crime, *Travaux Préparatoires of the Negotiations for the Elaboration of the United Nations Convention Against Corruption* (New York: United Nations, 2010).

United Nations Treaty Collection: online United Nations https://treaties.un.org/Pages/ViewDetails.aspx?src=TREATY&mtdsg_no=XVIII-14&chapter=18&clang=_en (accessed 26 March 2018).

United Nations Convention Against Corruption, GA Res 58/4, UNGAOR, 58th Sess, Supp No 49, UN Doc A/RES/58/4, (2003).

United Nations Convention against Corruption: Status of Ratifications as at 18 October 2017, 2017, UN Doc CAC/COSP/2017/CRP.2.

United Nations Declaration against Corruption and Bribery International Commercial Transaction, GA Res 51/191, UNGAOR, 51st Sess, Supp No 49, UN Doc A/RES/51/191, (1997).

Working Group on Business and Human Rights, *Guidance on National Action Plans on Business and Human Rights* (November 2016), online: OHCHR www.ohchr.org/Documents/Issues/Business/UNWG_NAPGuidance.pdf (accessed 26 March 2018).

Written Statement Submitted by Human Rights Advocates, a Non-Governmental Organization in Special Consultative Status, 2003, UN Doc E/CN.4/Sub.2/2003/NGO/13.

Written Statement Submitted by Human Rights Advocates Inc., a Non-Governmental Organization in Special Consultative Status, 2011, UN Doc A/HR/17/NGO/3.

World Bank Group Documents

CAO Operational Guidelines, March 2013, online: CAO www.cao-ombudsman.org/documents/CAOOperationalGuidelines_2013.pdf (accessed 26 March 2018).

CAO, *2006–07 Annual Report* (Washington: CAO, 2007).

CAO, *2008–09 Annual Report* (Washington: CAO, 2009).

CAO, *A Review of IFC's Safeguard Policies – Core Business: Achieving Consistent and Excellent Environmental and Social Outcomes* (Washington: World Bank, 2003).

CAO, *Advisory Note: IFC's Policy and Performance Standards on Social and Environmental Sustainability and Disclosure Policy – Commentary on IFC's Progress Report on the First 18 Months of Application* (17 December 2007), online: CAO www.cao-ombudsman.org/howwework/advisor/documents/CAOpublicstatementIFCperformancestandards121707.pdf (accessed 26 March 2018).

CAO, *Annual Report 2011* (Washington: CAO, 2011).

CAO, *IFC's Review of Safeguard Policies & Policy on Disclosure of Information*, online: CAO www.cao-ombudsman.org/howwework/advisor/documents/CAOcommentsonthefinalPPSdraftsFINAL-February22006.pdf (accessed 26 March 2018).

CAO, *Safeguard Policy Review Revisited: Has IFC Addressed the Recommendations of the CAO Safeguard Policy Review?*, online: CAO www.cao-ombudsman.org/howwework/advisor/documents/FINALCAOSafeguardPolicyReviewRevisited-Aug19.pdf (accessed 26 March 2018).

CAO, *The CAO at 10: Annual Report FY2010 and Review FY2000–10* (Washington: CAO, 2010).

Environmental and Social Review Procedures Manual, October 2016, online: IFC www.ifc.org/wps/wcm/connect/d0db8c41-cfb0-45e9-b66a-522c88f270a5/ESRP_Oct2016.pdf?MOD=AJPERES (accessed 26 March 2018).

Environmental, Health, and Safety General Guidelines, 30 April 2007, online: IFC www.ifc.org/wps/wcm/connect/554e8d80488658e4b76af76a6515bb18/Final%2B-%2BGeneral%2BEHS%2BGuidelines.pdf?MOD=AJPERES (accessed 26 March 2018).

IFC, *Environmental and Social Performance Standards and Guidance Notes*, online: IFC www.ifc.org/wps/wcm/connect/topics_ext_content/ifc_external_corporate_site/ifc+sustainability/our+approach/risk+management/performance+standards/environmental+and+social+performance+standards+and+guidance+notes (accessed 26 March 2018).

IFC, *IFC's Policy and Performance Standards on Social and Environmental Sustainability and Policy on Disclosure of Information: Report on the First Three Years of Application* (29 July 2009), online: IFC www.ifc.org/wps/wcm/connect/90f2d88046b63bdaa9f7abb254bfb7d4/IFC_Third_Year_Report_PS_DP_.pdf?MOD=AJPERES (accessed 26 March 2018).

IFC, *IFC Policy and Performance Standards on Social and Environmental Sustainability: Review and Update* (26 August 2009), online: IFC www.ifc.org/wps/wcm/connect/d9f9008049800946a606f6336b93d75f/PPS%2BOverview%2Bof%2BConsultation%2Band%2BEngagement_English.pdf?MOD=AJPERES (accessed 26 March 2018).

IFC, *IFC Sustainability Framework* (Washington: IFC, 2012).

IFC, *Progress Report on IFC's Policy and Performance Standards on Social and Environmental Sustainability, and Policy on Disclosure of Information* (14 April 2010), online: IFC www.ifc.org/wps/wcm/connect/d29bff0049800841a2a0f-2336b93d75f/Compounded%2BCODE_Progress%2BReport%2Bon%2BIFC%2527s%2BSustainability%2BFramework_Review%2Band%2BUpdate.pdf?MOD=AJPERES (accessed 26 March 2018).

IFC, *Review and Update of the Policy and Performance Standards on Social and Environmental Sustainability and Policy on Disclosure of Information* (9 July 2010), online: IFC www.ifc.org/wps/wcm/connect/15cd8200498007f0a1cff3336b93d75f/Moscow%2BOpen%2BHouse%2BSummary.pdf?MOD=AJPERES (accessed 26 March 2018).

IFC, *Review and Update of the Policy and Performance Standards on Social and Environmental Sustainability and Policy on Disclosure of Information: Consultations' Report – Istanbul, Turkey* (22 June 2010), online: IFC www.ifc.org/wps/wcm/connect/8138608049800964a676f6336b93d75f/PS_Consultations_Istanbul.pdf?MOD=AJPERES (accessed 26 March 2018).

IFC, *Safeguard Policies*, online: IFC www.ifc.org/wps/wcm/connect/Topics_Ext_Content/IFC_External_Corporate_Site/IFC+Sustainability/Our+Approach/Risk+Management/Performance+Standards/#pre2006 (accessed 26 March 2018).

IFC, *Subscriptions and Voting Power of Member Countries* (10 April 2018), online: The World Bank http://siteresources.worldbank.org/BODINT/Resources/278027-1215524804501/IFCCountryVotingTable.pdf (accessed 11 April 2018).

IFC, *Understanding the IFC's Environmental and Social Due Diligence Process*, online: IFC www.ifc.org/wps/wcm/connect/b58ead804942ee5da7a5ff4f5ddda76e/IFC+Process.pdf?MOD=AJPERES (accessed 26 March 2018).

IFC, *Update of IFC's Policy and Performance Standards on Environmental and Social Sustainability, and Access to Information Policy* (14 April 2011), online: IFC www.ifc.org/wps/wcm/connect/fca42a0049800aaaaba2fb336b93d75f/Board-Paper-IFC_SustainabilityFramework-2012.pdf?MOD=AJPERES (accessed 26 March 2018).

International Finance Corporation Access to Information Policy, 1 January 2012, online: IFC www.ifc.org/wps/wcm/connect/98d8ae004997936f9b7bffb2b4b33c15/IFCPolicyDisclosureInformation.pdf?MOD=AJPERES (accessed 26 March 2018).

International Finance Corporation Articles of Agreement, 27 June 2012, online: IFC www.ifc.org/wps/wcm/connect/1c95b500484cb68d9f3dbf5f4fc3f18b/IFC_Articles_of_Agreement.pdf?MOD=AJPERES (accessed 26 March 2018).

International Finance Corporation's Guidance Note: Performance Standards on Environmental and Social Sustainability, 1 January 2012, online: IFC www.ifc.org/wps/wcm/connect/e280ef804a0256609709ffd1a5d13d27/GN_English_2012_Full-Document.pdf?MOD=AJPERES (accessed 26 March 2018).

International Finance Corporation's Performance Standards on Social & Environmental Sustainability, 30 April 2006, online: IFC www.ifc.org/wps/wcm/connect/Topics_Ext_Content/IFC_External_Corporate_Site/IFC+Sustainability/Our+Approach/Risk+Management/Performance+Standards/ (accessed 26 March 2018).

International Finance Corporation's Performance Standards on Environmental and Social Sustainability, 1 January 2012, online: IFC www.ifc.org/wps/wcm/connect/Topics_Ext_Content/IFC_External_Corporate_Site/IFC+Sustainability/Our+Approach/Risk+Management/Performance+Standards/ (accessed 26 March 2018).

International Finance Corporation's Policy on Environmental and Social Sustainability, 1 January 2012, online: IFC www.ifc.org/wps/wcm/connect/7540778049a792dcb87efaa8c6a8312a/SP_English_2012.pdf?MOD=AJPERES (accessed 26 March 2018).

Multilateral Investment Guarantee Agency's Performance Standards on Social & Environmental Sustainability, 1 October 2007, online: MIGA www.miga.org/documents/performance_standards_social_and_env_sustainability.pdf (accessed 26 March 2018).

Multilateral Investment Guarantee Agency Performance Standards on Environmental and Social Sustainability, 1 October 2013, online: MIGA www.miga.org/documents/performance_standards_env_and_social_sustainability.pdf (accessed 26 March 2018).

Operational Policy 4.03 – Performance Standards for Private Sector Activities, May 2013, online: World Bank https://policies.worldbank.org/sites/ppf3/PPFDocuments/Forms/DispPage.aspx?docid=1566 (accessed 26 March 2018).

World Bank, *A Guide to the World Bank*, 3rd ed (Washington: The World Bank, 2011).

World Bank, *Annual Report 2017: End Extreme Poverty, Boost Shared Prosperity* (Washington: The World Bank, 2017).

European Union Documents

EC, Commission, *A Renewed EU Strategy 2011–14 for Corporate Social Responsibility* (Brussels: EC, 2011).

EC, *Council Framework Decision 2003/568/JHA of 22 July 2003 on Combating Corruption in the Private Sector*, [2003] OJ, L 192/54.

European Parliament, *Report Containing the European Parliament's Recommendations to the European Commission on the Negotiations for the Transatlantic Trade and Investment Partnership* (1 June 2015), online: European Parliament www.europarl.europa.eu/sides/getDoc.do?pubRef=-//EP//NONSGML+REPORT+A8-2015-0175+0+DOC+PDF+V0//EN (accessed 26 March 2018).

European Parliament, *Resolution of 6 April 2011 on the Future European International Investment Policy*, online: European Parliament www.europarl.europa.eu/sides/getDoc.do?pubRef=-//EP//TEXT+TA+P7-TA-2011-0141+0+DOC+XML+V0//EN (accessed 26 March 2018).

European Parliament, *Resolution of 9 October 2013 on the EU–China Negotiations for a Bilateral Investment Agreement*, online: European Parliament www.europarl.europa.eu/sides/getDoc.do?type=TA&language=EN&reference=P7-TA-2013-411 (accessed 26 March 2018).

Other International Documents

Amnesty International, Press Release, "The 2010–2011 Update of the OECD Guidelines for Multinational Enterprises Has Come to an End: The OECD Must Now Turn Into Effective Implementation" (23 May 2011), online: Amnesty International www.amnesty.org/en/documents/IOR30/001/2011/en/ (accessed 26 March 2018).

Amnesty International, *Letter from Seema Joshi to the Working Group on Human and Transnational Corporations and other Business Enterprises* (8 December 2011), online: OHCHR www.ohchr.org/EN/Issues/Business/Pages/Submissions.aspx (accessed 26 March 2018).

Amnesty International et al, *Joint Civil Society Statement on the Draft Guiding Principles on Business and Human Rights* (14 January 2011), online: Business and Human Rights Resource Centre http://business-humanrights.org/en/un-secretary-generals-special-representative-on-business-human-rights/un-protect-respect-and-remedy-framework/guiding-principles/submissions-to-consultation-on-draft-guiding (accessed 26 March 2018).

Australian Human Rights Centre, *Submission concerning the United Nations Norms on the Responsibilities of Transnational Corporations and Other Business Enterprises with regard to Human Rights* (29 September 2004), online: OHCHR https://web.archive.org/web/20140520213840/http://www2.ohchr.org/english/issues/globalization/business/contributions.htm (accessed 26 March 2018).

BASF, *Comments on the UN Draft Norms*, online: OHCHR https://web.archive.org/web/20140520213840/http://www2.ohchr.org/english/issues/globalization/business/contributions.htm (accessed 26 March 2018).

BIAC, *BIAC Statement on the Adoption of the Update of the OECD Guidelines for Multinational Enterprises at the OECD Ministerial Council Meeting on 25–26 May 2011* (May 2011), online: BIAC http://biac.org/wp-content/uploads/2017/07/FIN-11-05-19-Final-BIAC-statement-on-updated-Guidelines-for-MCM-2011.pdf (accessed 26 March 2018).

BP, *Responsibilities of Transnational Corporations and related Business Enterprises with regard to Human Rights* (1 October 2004), online: OHCHR https://web.archive.org/web/20140520213840/http://www2.ohchr.org/english/issues/globalization/business/contributions.htm (accessed 26 March 2018).

Business and Human Rights Resource Centre, "Business Leaders Initiative on Human Rights", online: Business and Human Rights Resource Centre http://business-humanrights.org/company-policysteps/other/business-leaders-initiative-on-human-rights-blihr (accessed 26 March 2018).

Business Leaders Initiative on Human Rights, *Submission to the Office of the UN High Commissioner for Human Rights relating to the 'Responsibilities of Transnational Corporations and related Business enterprises with regard to Human Rights'* (28 September 2004), online: OHCHR https://web.archive.org/web/20140520213840/http://www2.ohchr.org/english/issues/globalization/business/contributions.htm (accessed 26 March 2018).

Canada, *Agreement between Canada and ____ for the Promotion and Protection of Investments* (25 August 2014) (on file with the author).

Canada, *Submission of Canada to the High Commissioner of Human Rights on the Responsibilities of Business Enterprises with regard to Human Rights*, online: OHCHR https://web.archive.org/web/20140520213840/http://www2.ohchr.org/english/issues/globalization/business/contributions.htm (accessed 26 March 2018).

Center for International Environmental Law, *Submission by Civil Society Organizations to the International Finance Corporation: Commenting on the Social and Environmental Sustainability Policy, Performance Standards and Disclosure* (11 March 2010), online: Halifax Initiative www.halifaxinitiative.org/sites/halifaxinitiative.org/files/Civil%20Society%20Submission%20to%20IFC%2011Mar10.pdf (accessed 26 March 2018).

Christian Aid, *Behind the Mask: The Real Face of CSR*, online: OHCHR https://web.archive.org/web/20140520213840/http://www2.ohchr.org/english/issues/globalization/business/contributions.htm (accessed 26 March 2018).

Denmark, *Danish National Action Plan – Implementation of the UN Guiding Principles on Business and Human Rights* (April 2014), online: OHCHR www.ohchr.org/EN/Issues/Business/Pages/NationalActionPlans.aspx (accessed 26 March 2018).

EarthRights International, *Joint Civil Society Statement on the Global Compact and Corporate Accountability* (23 June 2004), online: EarthRights International https://web.archive.org/web/20101223032244/https://www.earthrights.org/campaigns/joint-civil-society-statement-global-compact-and-corporate-accountability (accessed 26 March 2018).

EarthRights International, News Release, "OECD Guidelines Update: Substantive Improvements, Procedural Disappointments" (25 May 2011), online: EarthRights

International https://web.archive.org/web/20120418015506/https://www.earthrights.org/campaigns/oecd-guidelines-update-substantive-improvements-procedural-disappointments (accessed 26 March 2018).

Equator Principles, 4 June 2013, online: Equator Principles http://equator-principles.com/wp-content/uploads/2017/03/equator_principles_III.pdf (accessed 26 March 2018).

European Union, *Contribution of the European Union before the First Session of the UN Working Group on Human Rights and Transnational Corporations and other Business Enterprises* (6 January 2012), online: OHCHR www.ohchr.org/EN/Issues/Business/Pages/Submissions.aspx (accessed 26 March 2018).

European Union, *EU Comments on the Draft Guiding Principles for the Implementation of the UN 'Protect, Respect and Remedy' Framework* (31 January 2011), online: Business and Human Rights Resource Centre http://business-humanrights.org/en/un-secretary-generals-special-representative-on-business-human-rights/un-protect-respect-and-remedy-framework/guiding-principles/submissions-to-consultation-on-draft-guiding (accessed 26 March 2018).

Extractive Industry Transparency Initiative, online: EITI https://eiti.org (accessed 26 March 2018).

Fédération internationale des ligues des droits de l'homme, *Statement of Support for the UN Human Rights Norms for Business* (18 March 2004), online: FIDH www.fidh.org/en/issues/globalisation-human-rights/business-and-human-rights/Statement-of-Support-for-the-UN (accessed 26 March 2018).

Fédération internationale des ligues des droits de l'Homme, *Contribution of the FIDH to the Consultation of the OHCHR on the Human Rights Responsibilities of Business* (September 2004), online: OHCHR https://web.archive.org/web/20140520213840/http://www2.ohchr.org/english/issues/globalization/business/contributions.htm (accessed 26 March 2018).

Finland, *National Action Plan for the Implementation of the UN Guiding Principles on Business and Human Rights* (October 2014), online: OHCHR www.ohchr.org/EN/Issues/Business/Pages/NationalActionPlans.aspx (accessed 26 March 2018).

Friends of the Earth Japan et al, *Comments on the IFC's Draft Policy on and Performance Standards on Social & Environmental Sustainability and the Draft Policy on Disclosure of Information* (25 November 2005), online: JACSES.org www.jacses.org/sdap/mof/gijiroku/CommentsonIFCSafeguard&Disclosure.pdf (accessed 26 March 2018).

GAP, *Letter from Wilma Walace* (28 September 2004), online: OHCHR https://web.archive.org/web/20140520213840/http://www2.ohchr.org/english/issues/globalization/business/contributions.htm (accessed 26 March 2018).

Greenpeace, *Responsibilities of Transnational Corporations and related Business Enterprises with regard to Human Rights* (30 September 2004), online: OHCHR https://web.archive.org/web/20140520213840/http://www2.ohchr.org/english/issues/globalization/business/contributions.htm (accessed 26 March 2018).

Human Rights Watch, *Statement on the United Nations Norms on the Responsibilities of Transnational Corporations and other Business Enterprises with regard to Human Rights to the Office of the United Nations High Commissioner for Human Rights* (30 September 2004), online: OHCHR https://web.archive.org/web/20140520213840/http://www2.ohchr.org/english/issues/globalization/business/contributions.htm (accessed 26 March 2018).

Human Rights Watch, *'Moving from Guidance to Compliance': Human Rights Watch Recommendations to the UN Expert Body on Business and Human Rights* (December 2011), online: OHCHR www.ohchr.org/EN/Issues/Business/Pages/Submissions.aspx (accessed 26 March 2018).

India, *Bilateral Investment Treaty between the Government of the Republic of India and ______* (28 December 2015), online: Investment Policy Hub http://investmentpolicyhub.unctad.org/Download/TreatyFile/3560 (accessed 26 March 2018).

International Business Leaders Forum et al., *Guide to Human Rights Impact Assessment and Management* (2010), online: Global Compact www.unglobalcompact.org/docs/issues_doc/human_rights/GuidetoHRIAM.pdf (accessed on 26 March 2018).

International Chamber of Commerce, *Request for Input on Report concerning the 'Responsibilities of Transnational Corporations and related Enterprises with regard to Human Rights* (7 September 2004), online: OHCHR https://web.archive.org/web/20140520213840/http://www2.ohchr.org/english/issues/globalization/business/contributions.htm (accessed 26 March 2018).

International Commission of Jurists, *Submission to the United Nations Office if the High Commissioner for Human Rights on Business and Human Rights* (26 October 2004), online: OHCHR https://web.archive.org/web/20140520213840/http://www2.ohchr.org/english/issues/globalization/business/contributions.htm (accessed 26 March 2018).

International Co-ordinating Committee of National Institutions for the Promotion and Protection of Human Rights, Kenya National Commission on Human Rights, *UN Representative on Business and Human Rights' Draft Guiding Principles for the Implementation of the UN 'Protect, Respect, and Remedy' Framework'* (January 2011), online: Business and Human Rights Resource Centre http://business-humanrights.org/en/un-secretary-generals-special-representative-on-business-human-rights/un-protect-respect-and-remedy-framework/guiding-principles/submissions-to-consultation-on-draft-guiding (accessed 26 March 2018).

International Co-ordinating Committee of National Institutions for the Promotion and Protection of Human Rights, Nicaragua, *Submissions to the United Nations Working Group on Transnational Corporations and other Business Enterprises* (December 2011), online: OHCHR www.ohchr.org/EN/Issues/Business/Pages/Submissions.aspx (accessed 26 March 2018).

International Co-ordinating Committee of National Institutions for the Promotion and Protection of Human Rights, Scottish Human Rights Commission, *UN Representative on Business and Human Rights' Draft Guiding Principles for the Implementation of the UN 'Protect, Respect, and Remedy' Framework'* (January 2011), online: Business and Human Rights Resource Centre http://business-humanrights.org/en/un-secretary-generals-special-representative-on-business-human-rights/un-protect-respect-and-remedy-framework/guiding-principles/submissions-to-consultation-on-draft-guiding (accessed 26 March 2018).

International Federation of Human Rights et al, *Joint Civil Society Statement on Business and Human Rights to the 17th Session of the UN Human Rights Council* (15 June 2011), online: Business and Human Rights Resource Centre http://business-humanrights.org/en/un-secretary-generals-special-representative-on-business-human-rights/reports-to-un-human-rights-council/2011 (accessed 26 March 2018).

International Labour Office, *Letter from Mr. Zdzislaw Kedzia* (2 August 2004), online: OHCHR https://web.archive.org/web/20140520213840/http://www2.ohchr.org/english/issues/globalization/business/contributions.htm (accessed 26 March 2018).

International Organisation of Employers et al, *Joint IOE-ICC-BIAC Comments on the Draft Guiding Principles on Business and Human Rights* (26 January 2011), online: Business and Human Rights Resource Centre http://business-humanrights.org/en/un-secretary-generals-special-representative-on-business-human-rights/un-protect-respect-and-remedy-framework/guiding-principles/submissions-to-consultation-on-draft-guiding (accessed 26 March 2018).

International Organisation of Employers et al, *Joint Recommendation to the United Nations Working Group on Business and Human Rights* (8 December 2011), online: OHCHR www.ohchr.org/EN/Issues/Business/Pages/Submissions.aspx (accessed 26 March 2018).

Lithuania, *Lithuania's National Action Plan on the Implementation of the United Nations Guiding Principles on Business and Human Rights* (February 2015), online: OHCHR www.ohchr.org/EN/Issues/Business/Pages/NationalActionPlans.aspx (accessed 26 March 2018).

LSE Investment and Human Rights Project & Laboratory for Advanced Research on the Global Economy, *Guide to implementing the UN Guiding Principles on Business and Human Rights in Investment Policymaking* (March 2016), online: LSE http://blogs.lse.ac.uk/investment-and-human-rights/files/2016/02/3689_LSE_UNGPs_Guide_En_FIN_NEW_Web.pdf (accessed 26 March 2018).

MISEREOR et al, *The Responsibilities of Transnational Corporations and related Business Enterprises with regard to Human Rights* (30 September 2004), online: OHCHR https://web.archive.org/web/20140520213840/http://www2.ohchr.org/english/issues/globalization/business/contributions.htm (accessed 26 March 2018).

Netherlands, *Reply of the Netherlands to the OHCHR Questionnaire on Responsibilities of Transnational Corporations and related Business Enterprises with regard to Human Rights* (29 September 2004), online: OHCHR https://web.archive.org/web/20140520213840/http://www2.ohchr.org/english/issues/globalization/business/contributions.htm (accessed 26 March 2018).

Netherlands, *National Action Plan on Business and Human Rights* (December 2013), online: OHCHR www.ohchr.org/EN/Issues/Business/Pages/NationalActionPlans.aspx (accessed 26 March 2018).

Norway, *Agreement between the Kingdom of Norway and ____ for the Promotion and the Protection of Investment* (13 May 2015), online: Government of Norway www.regjeringen.no/contentassets/e47326b61f424d4c9c3d470896492623/draft-model-agreement-english.pdf (accessed 26 March 2018).

Norway, *Decision 2004/116 – Responsibilities of Transnational Corporations and related Business Enterprises with regard to Human Rights* (4 November 2004), online: OHCHR https://web.archive.org/web/20140520213840/http://www2.ohchr.org/english/issues/globalization/business/contributions.htm (accessed 26 March 2018).

OECD Watch, *OECD Watch Statement on the Update of the OECD Guidelines for MNEs: Improved Content and Scope, but Procedural Shortcomings Remain* (25 May 2011), online: OECD Watch http://oecdwatch.org/publications-en/Publication_3675 (accessed 26 March 2018).

Oxfam, *Submission by Oxfam International under Decision 2004/116 on the 'Responsibilities of Transnational Corporations and related Business Enterprises with regards to Human Rights'* (17 November 2004), online: OHCHR https://web.archive.org/web/20140520213840/http://www2.ohchr.org/english/issues/globalization/business/contributions.htm (accessed 26 March 2018).

Oxfam International, *Oxfam International's Perspective on the Draft Guiding Principles for the Implementation of the United Nations 'Protect, Respect and Remedy' Framework* (31 January 2011), online: Business and Human Rights Resource Centre http://business-humanrights.org/en/un-secretary-generals-special-representative-on-business-human-rights/un-protect-respect-and-remedy-framework/guiding-principles/submissions-to-consultation-on-draft-guiding (accessed 26 March 2018).

Shell, *Request from the Office of the UN High Commissioner for Human Rights* (24 September 2004), online: OHCHR https://web.archive.org/web/20140520213840/http://www2.ohchr.org/english/issues/globalization/business/contributions.htm (accessed 26 March 2018).

Southern African Development Community, *SADC Model Bilateral Investment Treaty Template* (July 2012), online: International Institute for Sustainable Development www.iisd.org/itn/wp-content/uploads/2012/10/sadc-model-bit-template-final.pdf (accessed 26 March 2018).

Sweden, *Action Plan for Business and Human Rights* (August 2015), online: OHCHR www.ohchr.org/EN/Issues/Business/Pages/NationalActionPlans.aspx (accessed 26 March 2018).

United Kingdom, *Good Business: Implementing the UN Guiding Principles on Business and Human Rights* (September 2013), online: OHCHR www.ohchr.org/EN/Issues/Business/Pages/NationalActionPlans.aspx (accessed 26 March 2018).

United Kingdom, *UK Government Comments on the Draft UN Guiding Principles for the Implementation of the 'Protect, Respect and Remedy' Framework* (January 2011), online: Business and Human Rights Resource Centre http://business-humanrights.org/en/un-secretary-generals-special-representative-on-business-human-rights/un-protect-respect-and-remedy-framework/guiding-principles/submissions-to-consultation-on-draft-guiding (accessed 26 March 2018).

United Nations Global Compact, *Statement by the UN Global Compact Human Rights Working Group to the Special-Representative of the Secretary-General on Business and Human Rights* (January 2011), online: Business and Human Rights Resource Centre http://business-humanrights.org/en/un-secretary-generals-special-representative-on-business-human-rights/un-protect-respect-and-remedy-framework/guiding-principles/submissions-to-consultation-on-draft-guiding (accessed 26 March 2018).

United States Chamber of Commerce, *Comments of the United States Chamber of Commerce on the Draft Guiding Principles on Business and Human Rights* (31 January 2011), online: Business and Human Rights Resource Centre http://business-humanrights.org/en/un-secretary-generals-special-representative-on-business-human-rights/un-protect-respect-and-remedy-framework/guiding-principles/submissions-to-consultation-on-draft-guiding (accessed 26 March 2018).

United States Council for International Business, *Submission to the High Commissioner for Human Rights for the Report on the 'Responsibilities of Transnational Corporations and related Business Enterprises with regard to Human Rights'*, online: OHCHR https://web.archive.org/web/20140520213840/http://www2.ohchr.org/english/issues/globalization/business/contributions.htm (accessed 26 March 2018).

United States of America, *Re: Note Verbale from the OHCHR of August 3, 2004 (GVA2537)* (30 September 2004), online: OHCHR https://web.archive.org/web/20140520213840/http://www2.ohchr.org/english/issues/globalization/business/contributions.htm (accessed 26 March 2018).

United States of America, *US Comments on IFC Policy and Performance Standards on Social and Environmental Sustainability and Policy on Disclosure of Information* (January 2010), online: US Department of the Treasury www.treasury.gov/resource-center/international/development-banks/Documents/jan2010_policy.pdf (accessed 26 March 2018).

United States of America, Department of State, *Foreign Relations of the United States, 1977–1980*, Vol III (Washington, DC: Department of State, 2013).

UN Guiding Principles Reporting Framework (February 2015), online: UN Guiding Principles Reporting Framework www.ungpreporting.org/reporting-framework/ (accessed 26 March 2018).

Voluntary Principles on Security and Human Rights, online: Voluntary Principles www.voluntaryprinciples.org (accessed 26 March 2018).

Foreign Legislation

Foreign Corrupt Practices Act, 15 USC § 78 (1977).

Secondary Sources

Books

Alvarez, José E. *International Organizations as Law-Makers* (Oxford: Oxford University Press, 2005).

Arnone, Marco & Leonardo S Borlini. *Corruption: Economic Analysis and International Law* (Northampton: Edward Elgar, 2014).

Braithwaite, John & Peter Drahos. *Global Business Regulation* (Cambridge: Cambridge University Press, 2000).

Brunnée, Jutta & Stephen J Toope. *Legitimacy and Legality in International Law: An Interactional Account* (Cambridge: Cambridge University Press, 2010).

Bryman, Alan. *Social Research Methods* (Oxford: Oxford University Press, 2001).

Clapham, Andrew. *Human Rights Obligations of Non-state Actors* (Oxford: Oxford University Press, 2006).

De Jonge, Alice. *Transnational Corporations and International Law: Accountability in the Global Business Environment* (Northampton, UK: Edward Elgar, 2011).

Deva, Surya. *Regulating Corporate Human Rights Violations: Humanizing Business* (London: Routledge, 2012).

Finnemore, Martha. *National Interests in International Society* (Ithaca, NY: Cornell University Press, 1996).

Hamdani, Khalil & Lorraine Ruffing. *United Nations Centre on Transnational Corporations: Corporate Conduct and the Public Interest* (London: Routledge, 2015).

Hathaway, Oona Anne & Harold Hongju Koh. *Foundations of International Law and Politics* (New York: Foundation Press, 2005).

Held, David et al. *Global Transformations: Politics, Economics and Culture* (Cambridge: Polity Press, 1999).

Karavias, Markos. *Corporate Obligations under International Law* (Oxford: Oxford University Press, 2013).

Klabbers, Jan. *An Introduction to International Organizations Law*, 3rd ed (Cambridge: Cambridge University Press, 2015).

Kratochwil, Friedrich V. *Rules, Norms, and Decisions: On the Conditions of Practical and Legal Reasoning in International Relations and Domestic Affairs* (Cambridge: Cambridge University Press, 1991).

Kulick, Andreas. *Global Public Interest in International Investment Law* (Cambridge: Cambridge University Press, 2012).

Malanczuk, Peter. *Akehurst's Modern Introduction to International Law*, 7th rev ed (London: Routledge, 1997).

Maupain, Francis. *The Future of the International Labour Organization in the Global Economy* (Oxford: Hart Publishing, 2013).

Miles, Kate. *The Origins of International Investment Law: Empire, Environment and the Safeguarding of Capital* (Cambridge: Cambridge University Press, 2013).

Muchlinski, Peter T. *Multinational Enterprises and the Law*, 2nd ed (Oxford: Oxford University Press, 2007).

Newcombe, Andrew & Lluís Paradell. *Law and Practice of Investment Treaties: Standards of Treatment* (Alphen aan den Rijn: Kluwer Law International, 2009).

Polanyi, Karl. *The Great Transformation: The Political and Economic Origins of Our Time*, 2nd ed (Boston, MA: Beacon Press, 2001).

Rose, Cecily. *International Anti-Corruption Norms: Their Creation and Influence on Domestic Legal Systems* (Oxford: Oxford University Press, 2015).

Ruggie, John Gerard. *Just Business: Multinational Corporations and Human Rights* (New York: W. W. Norton & Company, 2013).

Schneiderman, David. *Constitutionalizing Economic Globalization: Investment Rules and Democracy's Promise* (Cambridge: Cambridge University Press, 2008).

———. *Resisting Economic Globalization: Critical Theory and International Investment Law* (New York: Palgrave Macmillan, 2013).

Schultz, Thomas. *Transnational Legality: Stateless Law and International Arbitration* (Oxford: Oxford University Press, 2014).

Simons, Penelope & Audrey Macklin. *The Governance Gap: Extractive Industries, Human Rights, and the Home State Advantage* (New York: Routledge, 2014).

Sinclair, Adriana. *International Relations Theory and International Law: A Critical Approach* (Cambridge: Cambridge University Press, 2010).

Sornarajah, Muthucumaraswamy. *The International Law on Foreign Investment*, 3rd ed (Cambridge: Cambridge University Press, 2010).

———. *Resistance and Change in the International Law on Foreign Investment* (Cambridge: Cambridge University Press, 2015).

Steger, Manfred B & Ravi K Roy. *Neoliberalism: A Very Short Introduction* (Oxford: Oxford University Press, 2010).

Strange, Susan. *The Retreat of the State: The Diffusion of Power in the World Economy* (Cambridge: Cambridge University Press, 1996).

Turner, Rachel S. *Neo-liberal Ideology: History, Concepts and Policies* (Edinburgh: Edinburgh University Press, 2008).

Wendt, Alexander. *Social Theory of International Politics* (Cambridge: Cambridge University Press, 1999).

Wilks, Stephen. *The Political Power of the Business Corporation* (Cheltenham: Edward Elgar, 2013).

Zerk, Jennifer A. *Multinationals and Corporate Social Responsibility: Limitations and Opportunities in International Law* (Cambridge: Cambridge University Press, 2006).

Collections of Essays

Adler, Emanuel. "Constructivism in International Relations: Sources, Contributions and Debates" in Walter Carlsnaes, Thomas Risse & Beth A Simmons, eds, *Handbook of International Relations*, 2nd ed (London: Sage Publications, 2013) 112.

Ascensio, Hervé. "Les normes produites à l'OCDE et les formes de normativité" in Hervé Ascensio & Nicola Bonucci, eds, *Le pouvoir normatif de l'OCDE* (Paris: Éditions A. Pedone, 2014) 7.

Bilchitz, David. "A Chasm Between 'Is' and 'Ought'? A Critique of the Normative Foundations of the SRGS's Framework and the Guiding Principles" in Surya Deva & David Bilchitz, eds, *Human Rights Obligations of Business: Beyond the Corporate Responsibility to Protect?* (Cambridge: Cambridge University Press, 2013) 107.

Bilchitz, David & Surya Deva. "The Human Rights Obligations of Business: A Critical Framework for the Future" in Surya Deva & David Bilchitz, eds, *Human Rights Obligations of Business: Beyond the Corporate Responsibility to Protect?* (Cambridge: Cambridge University Press, 2013) 1.

Bjorklund, Andrea K. "Improving the International Investment Law and Policy System, Report of the Rapporteur – Second Columbia International Investment Conference: What's Next in International Investment Law and Policy?" in José E Alvarez et al, eds, *The Evolving International Investment Regime: Expectations, Realities, Options* (Oxford: Oxford University Press, 2011) 213.

Böhmer, Alexander. "Organisation for Economic Co-operation and Development" in Christian Tietje & Alan Brouder, eds, *Handbook of Transnational Economic Governance Regimes* (Leiden: Martinus Nijhoff Publishers, 2009) 227.

Buhmann, Karin. "The Development of the 'UN Framework': A Pragmatic Process Towards a Pragmatic Output" in Radu Mares, ed, *The UN Guiding Principles on Business and Human Rights: Foundations and Implementation* (Leiden: Martinus Nijhoff Publishers, 2012) 85.

———. "Navigating from 'Train Wreck' to being 'Welcomed': Negotiation Strategies and Argumentative Patterns in the Development of the UN Framework" in Surya Deva & David Bilchitz, eds, *Human Rights Obligations of Business: Beyond the Corporate Responsibility to Protect?* (Cambridge: Cambridge University Press, 2013) 29.

Chouliaraki, Lilie & Norman Fairclough. "The Critical Analysis of Discourse" in William K Carroll, ed, *Critical Strategies for Social Research* (Toronto: Canadian Scholars' Press Inc., 2004) 262.

Cutler, A Claire. "Transnational Business Civilization, Corporations, and the Privatization of Global Governance" in Christopher May, ed, *Global Corporate Power* (Boulder, CO: Lynne Rienner Publishers, 2006) 199.

———. "The Privatization of Authority in the Global Political Economy" in Gary Teeple & Stephen McBride, eds, *Relations of Global Power: Neoliberal Order and Disorder* (Toronto: University of Toronto Press, 2011) 41.

De Schutter, Olivier. "The Challenge of Imposing Human Rights Norms on Corporate Actors" in Olivier De Schutter, ed, *Transnational Corporations and Human Rights* (Portland, OR: Hart Publishing, 2006) 1.

Deva, Surya. "Treating Human Rights Lightly: A Critique of the Consensus Rhetoric and the Language Employed by the Guiding Principles" in Surya Deva & David Bilchitz, eds, *Human Rights Obligations of Business: Beyond the Corporate Responsibility to Protect?* (Cambridge: Cambridge University Press, 2013) 78.

Dumberry, Patrick. "Corporate Investors' International Legal Personality and their Accountability for Human Rights Violations under IIAs" in Armand de Mestral & Céline Lévesque, eds, *Improving International Investment Agreements* (New York: Routledge, 2013) 179.

Dumberry, Patrick & Gabrielle Dumas-Aubin. "How to Impose Human Rights Obligations on Corporations under Investment Treaties? Pragmatic Guidelines for the Amendment of BITs" in Karl P. Sauvant, ed, *Yearbook on International Investment Law & Policy 2011–2012* (Oxford: Oxford University Press, 2013) 569.

Dumberry, Patrick & Érik Labelle-Easthaugh. "Non-State Actors in International Investment Law: The Legal Personality of Corporations and NGOs in the Context of Investor-State Arbitration" in Jean d'Aspremont, ed, *Participants in the International Legal System: Multiple Perspectives on Non-State Actors in International Law* (New York: Routledge, 2011) 360.

Dunoff, Jeffrey L & Mark A Pollack. "International Law and International Relations: Introducing an Interdisciplinary Dialogue" in Jeffrey L Dunoff & Mark A Pollack, eds, *Interdisciplinary Perspectives on International Law and International Relations: The State of the Art* (Cambridge: Cambridge University Press, 2013) 3.

Dupuy, Pierre-Marie. "Unification Rather than Fragmentation of International Law? The Case of International Investment Law and Human Rights Law" in Pierre-Marie Dupuy, Francesco Francioni & Ernst-Ulrich Petersmann, eds, *Human Rights in International Investment Law and Arbitration* (Oxford: Oxford University Press, 2009) 45.

Günter, Hans. "The Tripartite Declaration of Principles (ILO): Standards and Follow-Up" in *Legal Problems of Codes of Conduct for Multinational Enterprises* (Hingham, MA: Kluwer Law and Taxation, 1980) 155.

Harrison, James. "Human Rights Arguments in Amicus Curiae Submissions: Promoting Social Justice?" in Pierre-Marie Dupuy, Francesco Francioni & Ernst-Ulrich Petersmann, eds, *Human Rights in International Investment Law and Arbitration* (Oxford: Oxford University Press, 2009) 396.

Helfand, Michael A. "Introduction" in Michael A Helfand, ed, *Negotiating State and Non-State Law: The Challenge of Global and Local Legal Pluralism* (Cambridge: Cambridge University Press, 2015) 1.

Hepburn, Jarrod & Vuyelwa Kuuya. "Corporate Social Responsibility and Investment Treaties" in Marie-Claire Cordonier Segger, Markus W Gehring & Andrew Newcombe, eds, *Sustainable Development in World Investment Law* (Alphen aan den Rijn: Kluwer Law International, 2011) 589.

Hirsch, Moshe. "Investment Tribunals and Human Rights: Divergent Paths" in Pierre-Marie Dupuy, Francesco Francioni & Ernst-Ulrich Petersmann, eds, *Human Rights in International Investment Law and Arbitration* (Oxford: Oxford University Press, 2009) 97.

Johnstone, Ian. "Law-Making in International Organizations: Perspectives from IL/IR Theory" in Jeffrey L Dunoff & Mark A Pollack, eds, *Interdisciplinary Perspectives on International Law and International Relations: The State of the Art* (Cambridge: Cambridge University Press, 2013) 266.

Kammerhofer, Jörg. "The Theory of Norm Conflict Solutions in International Investment Law" in Marie-Claire Cordonier Segger, Markus W Gehring & Andrew Newcombe, eds, *Sustainable Development in World Investment Law* (Alphen aan den Rijn: Kluwer Law International, 2011) 83.

Kott, Sandrine & Joëlle Droux. "Introduction: A Global History Written from the ILO" in Sandrine Kott & Joëlle Droux, eds, *Globalizing Social Rights: The International Labour Organization and Beyond* (New York: Palgrave Macmillan, 2013) 1.

Kreindler, Richard. "Legal Consequences of Corruption in International Investment Arbitration: An Old Challenge with New Answers" in Laurent Lévy & Yves Derains, eds, *Liber Amicorum en l'honneur de Serge Lazareff* (Paris: Editions Pedone, 2011) 383.

Lee, Simon & Stephen McBride. "Introduction: Neo-Liberalism, State Power and Global Governance in the Twenty-First Century" in Simon Lee & Stephen McBride, eds, *Neo-Liberalism, State Power and Global Governance* (Dordrecht: Springer, 2007) 1.

Mayrand, Hélène. "L'apport mutuel entre constructivism et théories critiques" in Rémi Bachand, ed, *Théories critiques et droit international* (Brussels: Bruylant, 2013) 147.

Michalowski, Sabine. "Due Diligence and Complicity: A Relationship in Need of Clarification" in Surya Deva & David Bilchitz, eds, *Human Rights Obligations of Business: Beyond the Corporate Responsibility to Protect?* (Cambridge: Cambridge University Press, 2013) 218.

Morgera, Elisa. "From Corporate Social Responsibility to Accountability Mechanisms" in Pierre-Marie Dupuy & Jorge E Viñuales, eds, *Harnessing Foreign Investment to Promote Environmental Protection: Incentives and Safeguards* (Cambridge: Cambridge University Press, 2013) 321.

Muchlinski, Peter. "Corporate Social Responsibility" in Peter Muchlinski, Frederico Ortino & Christoph Schreuer, eds, *The Oxford Handbook of International Investment Law* (Oxford: Oxford University Press, 2008) 637.

———. "Policy Issues" in Peter Muchlinski, Frederico Ortino & Christoph Schreuer, eds, *The Oxford Handbook of International Investment Law* (Oxford: Oxford University Press, 2008) 3.

———. "Multinational Enterprises as Actors in International Law: Creating 'Soft Law' Obligations and 'Hard Law' Rights" in Math Noortmann & Cedric Ryngaert, eds, *Non-State Actors Dynamics in International Law: From Law-Takers to Law-Makers* (Farnham: Ashgate Publishing, 2010) 9.

———. "Regulating Multinationals: Foreign Investment, Development, and the Balance of Corporate and Home Country Rights and Responsibilities in a Globalizing World" in José E Alvarez et al, eds, *The Evolving International Investment Regime: Expectations, Realities, Options* (Oxford: Oxford University Press, 2011) 30.

Newcombe, Andrew. "Investor Misconduct: Jurisdiction, Admissibility or Merits?" in Chester Brown & Kate Miles, eds, *Evolution in Investment Treaty Law and Arbitration* (Cambridge: Cambridge University Press, 2011) 187.

———. "Investor Misconduct" in Armand de Mestral & Céline Lévesque, eds, *Improving International Investment Agreements* (New York: Routledge, 2013) 195.

Nolan, Justine. "A Business and Human Rights Treaty" in Dorothée Baumann-Pauly & Justine Nolan, eds, *Business and Human Rights: From Principles to Practice* (London: Routledge, 2016) 70.

O'Brien, Robert. "NGOs, Global Civil Society and Global Economic Regulation" in Sol Picciotto & Ruth Mayne, eds, *Regulating International Business: Beyond Liberalization* (New York: St. Martin's Press, 1999) 257.

Pavoni, Riccardo. "Environmental Rights, Sustainable Development, and Investor-State Case Law: A Critical Appraisal" in Pierre-Marie Dupuy, Francesco Francioni & Ernst-Ulrich Petersmann, eds, *Human Rights in International Investment Law and Arbitration* (Oxford: Oxford University Press, 2009) 525.

Porter, Tony & Michael Webb. "Role of the OECD in the Orchestration of Global Knowledge Networks" in Rianne Mahon & Stephen McBride, eds, *The OECD and Transnational Governance* (Vancouver: UBC Press, 2008) 43.

Ramasastry, Anita. "Closing the Governance Gap in the Business and Human Rights Arena: Lessons from the Anti-Corruption Movement" in Surya Deva & David Bilchitz, eds, *Human Rights Obligations of Business: Beyond the Corporate Responsibility to Protect?* (Cambridge: Cambridge University Press, 2013) 162.

Reiner, Clara & Christoph Schreuer. "Human Rights and International Investment Arbitration" in Pierre-Marie Dupuy, Francesco Francioni & Ernst-Ulrich Petersmann, eds, *Human Rights in International Investment Law and Arbitration* (Oxford: Oxford University Press, 2009) 82.

Risse, Thomas. "Transnational Actors and World Politics" in Walter Carlsnaes, Thomas Risse & Beth A Simmons, eds, *Handbook of International Relations*, 2nd ed (London: Sage Publications, 2013) 426.

Robé, Jean-Philippe. "Multinational Enterprises: The Constitution of a Pluralistic Legal Order" in Gunther Teubner, ed, *Global Law Without a State* (Aldershot, UK: Dartmouth, 1997) 45.

Schneiderman, David. "Power and Production in Global Legal Pluralism: An International Political Economy Approach" in Amanda Perry-Kessaris, ed, *Socio-Legal Approaches to International Economic Law: Text, Context, Subtext* (New York: Routledge, 2013) 98.

Sims, Emily. "The ILO Declaration of Principles Concerning Multinational Enterprises and Social Policy: Strengths & Provisions" in Roger Blanpain & Michele Colucci, eds, *International Encyclopedia for Labour Law and Industrial Relations* (Alphen aan den Rijn: Kluwer Law International, 2013) 1.

Taillant, Jorge Daniel & Jonathan Bonnitcha. "International Investment Law and Human Rights" in Marie-Claire Cordonier Segger, Markus W Gehring & Andrew Newcombe, eds, *Sustainable Development in World Investment Law* (Alphen aan den Rijn: Kluwer Law International, 2011) 59.

Tan, Celine. "Navigating New Landscapes: Socio-Legal Mapping of Plurality and Power in International Economic Law" in Amanda Perry-Kessaris, ed, *Socio-Legal Approaches to International Economic Law: Text, Context, Subtext* (New York: Routledge, 2013) 19.

Van Dijk, Teun A. "Critical Discourse Analysis" in Deborah Schiffrin, Deborah Tannen & Heidi H Hamilton, eds, *The Handbook of Discourse Analysis* (Malden, MA: Blackwell Publishing, 2001) 352.

Vogelaar, Theo W. "The OECD Guidelines: Their Philosophy, History, Negotiation, Form, Legal Nature, Follow-up Procedures and Review" in Norbert Horn, ed, *Legal Problems of Codes of Conduct for Multinational Enterprises* (Hingham, MA: Kluwer Law & Taxation, 1980) 127.

Weiss, Gilbert & Ruth Wodak. "Theory, Interdisciplinarity and Critical Discourse Analysis" in Gilbert Weiss & Ruth Wodak, eds, *Critical Discourse Analysis: Theory and Interdisciplinarity* (New York: Palgrave Macmillan, 2003) 1.

Wettstein, Florian. "From Side Show to Main Act: Can Business and Human Rights save Corporate Responsibility?" in Dorothée Baumann-Pauly & Justine Nolan, eds, *Business and Human Rights: From Principles to Practice* (London: Routledge, 2016) 78.

Williams, Russell Alan. "The OECD and Foreign Investment Rules: The Global Promotion of Liberalization" in Rianne Mahon & Stephen McBride, eds, *The OECD and Transnational Governance* (Vancouver: UBC Press, 2008) 117.

Wodak, Ruth & Michael Meyer. "Critical Discourse Analysis: History, Agenda, Theory, and Methodology" in Ruth Wodak & Michael Meyer, eds, *Methods in Critical Discourse Analysis* (Thousand Oaks, CA: Sage Publications, 2009) 1.

Periodicals

Abbott, Kenneth W. "Modern International Relations Theory: A Prospectus for International Lawyers" (1989) 14 Yale J Int'l L 335.

Abbott, Kenneth W & Duncan Snidal. "Values and Interests: International Legalization in the Fight against Corruption" (2002) 31:S1 J Legal Stud S141.

Addo, Michael K. "The Reality of the United Nations Guiding Principles on Business and Human Rights" (2014) 14 Hum Rts L Rev 133.
Adeyemi, Adebola. "Changing the Face of Sustainable Development in Developing Countries: The Role of the International Finance Corporation" (2014) 16 Envtl L Rev 91.
Alvarez, José E. "Critical Theory and the North American Free Trade Agreement's Chapter Eleven" (1996) 28 U of Miami Inter-Am L Rev 303.
———. "The Public International Law Regime Governing International Investment" (2009) 344 Rec des Cours 193.
Arato, Julian. "Corporations as Lawmakers" (2015) 56 Harv Int'l L J 229.
Augenstein, Daniel & David Kinley. "Beyond the 100 Acre Wood: In which International Human Rights Law Finds New Ways to Tame Global Corporate Power" (2015) 19 Int'l J Hum Rights 828.
Backer, Larry Cata. "Multinational Corporations, Transnational Law: The United Nations' Norms on the Responsibilities of Transnational Corporations as a Harbinger of Corporate Social Responsibility in International Law" (2006) 37 Colum Hum Rts L Rev 287.
Barnett, Michael N & Martha Finnemore. "The Politics, Power, and Pathologies of International Organizations" (1999) 53 Int'l Organization 699.
Berman, Paul Schiff. "Global Legal Pluralism" (2007) 80 S Cal L Rev 1155.
Blanpain, Roger. "The OECD Guidelines for Multinational Enterprises – The Badger Case" (1978) 126 J Royal Soc'y Arts 326.
Catá Backer, Larry. "Multinational Corporations, Transnational Law: The United Nations' Norms on the Responsibilities of Transnational Corporations as a Harbinger of Corporate Social Responsibility in International Law" (2006) 37 Colum Hum Rts L Rev 287.
Černič, Jernej Letnar. "Corporate Responsibility for Human Rights: Analyzing the ILO Tripartite Declaration of Principles concerning Multinational Enterprises and Social Policy" (2009) 6 Miskolc J Int'l L 24.
Charney, Jonathan I. "Transnational Corporations and Developing Public International Law" (1983) 1983:4 Duke LJ 748.
Cutler, A Claire. "Constituting Capitalism: Corporations, Law, and Private Transnational Governance" (2009) 5 STAIR 99.
———. "Legal Pluralism as the 'Common Sense' of Transnational Capitalism" (2013) 3:4 Oñati S-L Series 719.
Dashwood, Hevina S. "Canadian Mining Companies and Corporate Social Responsibility: Weighing the Impact of Global Norms" (2007) 40:1 Can J Pol Sc 129.
Davarnejad, Leyla. "In the Shadow of Soft Law: The Handling of Corporate Social Responsibility Disputes under the OECD Guidelines for Multinational Enterprises" (2011) 2011 J Disp Resol 351.
Deva, Surya. "UN's Human Rights Norms for Transnational Corporations and Other Business Enterprises: An Imperfect Step in the Right Direction" (2004) 10 ILSA J Int'l & Comp L 493.
———. "Global Compact: A Critique of the U.N.'s Public-Private Partnership for Promoting Corporate Citizenship" (2006) 34 Syracuse J Int'l L & Com 107.
Dumberry, Patrick & Gabrielle Dumas-Aubin. "When and How Allegations of Human Rights Violations can be Raised in Investor-State Arbitration" (2012) 13:3 J World Invest & Trade 349.
Finnemore, Martha. "Are Legal Norms Distinctive?" (2000) 32 NYU J Int'l L & Pol 699.
Finnemore, Martha & Kathryn Sikkink. "International Norm Dynamics and Political Change" (1998) 52 Int'l Organization 887.

———. "Taking Stock: The Constructivist Research Program in International Relations and Comparative Politics" (2001) 4:1 Ann Rev Pol Science 391.

Fischer-Lescano, Andreas & Gunther Teubner. "Regime-Collisions: The Vain Search for Legal Unity in the Fragmentation of Global Law" (2004) 25 Mich J Int'l L 999.

Goldstein, Judith et al. "Introduction: Legalization and World Politics" (2000) 54 Int'l Organization 385.

Hepburn, Jarrod. "In Accordance with Which Host State Laws? Restoring the 'Defence' of Investor Illegality in Investment Arbitration" (2014) 5 J Int'l Disp Settlement 531.

Hunter, David B. "Civil Society Networks and the Development of Environmental Standards at International Financial Institutions" (2008) 8 Chi J Int'l L 437.

Jensen, Nathan M. "Democratic Governance and Multinational Corporations: Political Regimes and Inflows of Foreign Direct Investment" (2003) 57 Int'l Organization 587.

Joseph, Sarah. "Taming the Leviathans: Multinational Enterprises and Human Rights" (1999) 46 Nethl Int'l L Rev 171.

Kendra, Thomas & Anna Bonini. "Dealing with Corruption Allegations in International Investment Arbitration: Reaching a Procedural Consensus?" (2014) 31 J Int'l Arb 439.

Lalive, Pierre. "Ordre public transnational (ou réellement international) et arbitrage international" (1986) 3 Rev arb 329.

Lamm, Carolyn B, Brody K Greenwald & Kristen M Young. "From World Duty Free to Metal-Tech: A Review of International Investment Treaty Arbitration Cases Involving Allegations of Corruption" (2014) 29 ICSID Rev 328.

Llamzon, Aloysius. "State Responsibility for Corruption: The Attribution Asymmetry in International Investment Arbitration" (2013) 10:3 TDM 1.

Lopez, Carlos & Ben Shea. "Negotiating a Treaty on Business and Human Rights: A Review of the First Intergovernmental Session" (2016) 1 Bus & Hum Rights J 111.

Lowe, Vaughan. "Corporations as International Actors and International Law Makers" (2004) 14 Italian YB Int'l L 23.

Mares, Radu. "Global Corporate Social Responsibility, Human Rights and Law: An Interactive Regulatory Perspective on the Voluntary-Mandatory Dichotomy" (2010) 1 Transn'l Legal Theory 221.

McCorquodale, Robert. "Corporate Social Responsibility and International Human Rights Law" (2009) 87 J Bus Ethics 385.

Meshel, Tamar. "The Use and Misuse of the Corruption Defence in International Investment Arbitration" (2013) 30:3 J Int'l Arb 267.

———. "Human Rights in Investor-State Arbitration: The Human Right to Water and Beyond" (2015) 6 J Int Disp Settlement 277.

Metcalfe, David. "The OCED Agreement to Criminalize Bribery: A Negotiation Analytic Perspective" (2000) 5 Int'l Negotiation 129.

Miles, Cameron A. "Corruption, Jurisdiction and Admissibility in International Investment Claims" (2012) 3:2 J Int'l Disp Settlement 329.

Muchlinski, Peter. "Human Rights, Social Responsibility and the Regulation of International Business: The Development of International Standards by Intergovernmental Organisations" (2003) 3 Non-St Actors & Int'l L 123.

———. "'Caveat Investor'? The Relevance of the Conduct of the Investor under the Fair and Equitable Treatment Standard" (2006) 55:3 ICQL 527.

———. "The Changing Face of Transnational Business Governance: Private Corporate Law Liability and Accountability of Transnational Groups in a Post-Financial Crisis World" (2011) 18 Ind J Global Legal Stud 665.

Nowrot, Karsten. "How to Include Environmental Protection, Human Rights and Sustainability in International Investment Law?" (2014) 15 J World Invest & Trade 612.
Oshionebo, Evaristus. "The U.N. Global Compact and Accountability of Transnational Corporations: Separating Myth from Realities" (2007) 19 Fla J Int'l L 1.
Park, Susan. "Norm Diffusion within International Organizations: A Case Study of the World Bank" (2005) 8 J Int'l Rel & Dev 111.
———. "How Transnational Environmental Advocacy Networks Socialize International Financial Institutions: A Case Study of the International Finance Corporation" (2005) 5 Global Envtl Politics 95.
———. "The World Bank Group: Championing Sustainable Development Norms?" (2007) 13 Global Governance 535.
Ratner, Steven R. "Corporations and Human Rights: A Theory of Legal Responsibility" (2001) 111:3 Yale LJ 443.
Rose, Cecily. "Circumstantial Evidence, Adverse Influences, and Findings of Corruption: Metal-Tech Ltd. v. The Republic of Uzbekistan" (2014) 15 J World Invest & Trade 747.
Ruggie, John Gerard & John F Sherman III. "Adding Human Rights Punch to the New Lex Mercatoria : The Impact of the UN Guiding Principles on Business and Human Rights on Commercial Legal Practice" (2015) 6 J Int'l Disp Settlement 455.
Sacerdoti, Giorgio. "The 1997 OECD Convention on Combating Bribery of Foreign Public Officials in International Business Transactions: An Example of Piece-Meal Regulation of Globalisation" (1999) 9 Italian YB Int'l L 26.
———. "Corruption in Investment Transactions: Policy Initiatives, Legal Principles and Arbitral Practice" (2009) 24:2 ICSID Rev 565.
Salacuse, Jeswald W. "The Treatification of International Investment Law" (2007) 13 Law & Bus Rev Am 155.
Sauvant, Karl P. "The Negotiations of the United Nations Code of Conduct on Transnational Corporations: Experience and Lessons Learned" (2015) 16 J World Invest & Trade 11.
Schwamm, Henri. "The OECD Guidelines for Multinational Enterprises" (1978) 12 J World Trade L 342.
Shawcross, Hartley W. "The Problems of Foreign Investment in International Law" (1961) 102 Rec des Cours 335.
Simons, Penelope. "International Law's Invisible Hand and the Future of Corporate Accountability for Violations of Human Rights" (2012) 3:1 J Hum R and Env't 5.
Tamanaha, Brian Z. "Understanding Legal Pluralism: Past to Present, Local to Global" (2008) 30 Sydney L Rev 375.
Tirado, Joe, Matthew Page & Daniel Meagher. "Corruption Investigations by Governmental Authorities and Investment Arbitration: An Uneasy Relationship" (2014) 29 ICSID Rev 493.
Tronnes, Robert D. "Ensuring Uniformity in the Implementation of the 1997 OECD Convention on Combating Bribery of Foreign Public Officials in International Business Transactions" (2000) 33 Geo Wash J Int'l L & Ecn 97.
Viñuales, Jorge E. "Foreign Investment and the Environment in International Law: An Ambiguous Relationship" (2010) 80:1 BYIL 244.
Wallace, Rebecca M M & Olga Martin-Ortega. "The UN Norms: A First Step to Universal Regulation of Transnational Corporations' Responsibilities for Human Rights?" (2004) 26 Dublin U L J 304.

Webb, Michael. "Defining the Boundaries of Legitimate State Practice: Norms, Transnational Actors and the OECD's Project on Harmful Tax Competition" (2004) 11 Rev Int'l Pol Ecn 787.

Webb, Philippa. "The United Nations Convention Against Corruption: Global Achievement or Missed Opportunity?" (2005) 8 J Int'l Ecn L 191.

Weissbrodt, David & Muria Kruger. "Norms on the Responsibilities of Transnational Corporations and Other Business Enterprises with Regard to Human Rights" (2003) 97:4 Am J Int'l L 901.

Yackee, Jason Webb. "Investment Treaties and Investor Corruption: An Emerging Defense for Host States" (2012) 52 Va J Int'l L 723.

Working Papers

d'Aspremont, Jean. *Bindingness*, ACIL Research Paper 19 (Amsterdam, 2015).

Gordon, Kathryn & Joachim Pohl. *Environmental Concerns in International Investment Agreements: A Survey*, OECD Working Paper on International Investment No 2011/1 (Paris, 2011).

Gordon, Kathryn, Joachim Pohl & Marie Bouchard. *Investment Treaty Law, Sustainable Development and Responsible Business Conduct: A Fact Finding Survey*, OECD Working Paper on International Investment No 2014/1 (Paris, 2014).

Günter, Hans. *The Tripartite Declaration of Principles concerning the Multinational Enterprises and Social Policy (History, Contents, Follow-up and Relationship with Relevant Instruments of Other Organizations)*, Multinational Enterprises Programme Working Paper 18 (Geneva, 1981).

Index

For Product Safety Concerns and Information please contact our EU representative GPSR@taylorandfrancis.com
Taylor & Francis Verlag GmbH, Kaufingerstraße 24, 80331 München, Germany

www.ingramcontent.com/pod-product-compliance
Ingram Content Group UK Ltd.
Pitfield, Milton Keynes, MK11 3LW, UK
UKHW010958180926
475701UK00004B/433
9780367586843